D0438450

AMERICA ON FILM

Of Related Interest from Continuum

Africa on Film: Beyond Black and White, Kenneth M. Cameron
The Art of AIDS: From Stigma to Conscience, Rob Baker
The Book of Westerns, Ian Cameron and Douglas Pye, editors.
The Cinema of Martin Scorsese, Lawrence S. Friedman
The Cinema of Oliver Stone, Norman Kagan
Dictionary of Teleliteracy: Television's 500 Biggest Hits, Misses, and Events, David Bionculli
Clint Eastwood: Filmmaker and Star, Edward Gallafent
Hitchcock in Hollywood, Joel W. Finler
Italian Cinema: From Neorealism to the Present, New Expanded Edition, Peter Bondanella
Katharine Hepburn: Star as Feminist, Andrew Britton
A Project for the Theatre, Ingmar Bergman
Robert Altman: Hollywood Survivor, Daniel O'Brien
Steven Spielberg: The Man, His Movies, and Their Meaning, New Expanded Edition, Philip M. Taylor
Teleliteracy: Taking Television Seriously, David Bianculli
Television's Second Golden Age, Robert J. Thompson
Toms, Coons, Mulattoes, Mammies, and Bucks: An Interpretive History of Blacks in American Films, New Third Edition, Donald Bogle

For more information on these and other titles on the arts, write to:

Continuum
370 Lexington Avenue
New York, NY 10017

NATIONAL UNIVERSITY
LIBRARY SACRAMENTO

AMERICA ON FILM

Hollywood and American History

Kenneth M. Cameron

CONTINUUM • NEW YORK

1997
The Continuum Publishing Company
370 Lexington Avenue
New York, NY 10017

Copyright © 1997 by Kenneth M. Cameron

All rights reserved. No part of this book may be reproduced, stored in a retrieval
system, or transmitted, in any form or by any means, electronic, mechanical,
photocopying, recording, or otherwise, without the written permission of
The Continuum Publishing Company.

Printed in the United States of America

Library of Congress Cataloging-in-Publication Data

Cameron, Kenneth M., 1931–
    America on film : Hollywood and American history / Kenneth M.
Cameron.
        p.   cm.
    Filmography: p.
    Includes bibliographical references and index.
    ISBN 0-8264-1033-2 (hardcover : alk. paper)
    1. Historical films—United States—History and criticism.
2. United States in motion pictures. 3. Motion pictures and
history.   I. Title.
PN1995.9.H5C36 1997
791.43'658—dc21   97-15246
                                                              CIP

CONTENTS

(Photographs may be found between pages 76–77 and 142–143)

For
George Bryan
1938–96

"What's this one for?" he asked.
"Which one?"
"The overcoat—if I might make bold to enquire."
"Just the war."
"Ah," he said attentively. "*The War* . . . ."

Anthony Powell, *The Soldier's Art*

PREFACE

The director holds up a cautionary hand. "Movie audiences are made up mostly of people between fifteen and twenty-two," he says. "They want to see three things: people defying authority, people destroying property, and people taking their clothes off."

He is making a movie about the American Revolution. When the facts of history conflict with the audience's demands, he tells us, the audience wins. Put movies in one pan of the scale and history in the other, and history turns out to be made of feathers.

Can this be true? Are history and film naturally unsympathetic?

The picture in which the director lays down this rule is Alan Alda's *Sweet Liberty* (1986); Alda plays a historian whose book is being filmed. *Sweet Liberty* is a pleasant comedy, not an essay on historiography, yet it raises interesting questions. Along with the one about the kind of history that gets into movies is the question, What is history, anyway (truth, propaganda, journalism, celebration, memory)? There is the question of what professionals mean by "history" and what the rest of us mean; there is a question about words like "truth" and "fact" and whether they change over time (Was historical truth more truthful than it is now?). And there is, for movies, the question of the relationship between a good movie and good history.

This book attempts to deal with some of these questions.

I would like there to be a relationship between the idea of history and time ("the past"), but I cannot put a temporal criterion on history that will work for film. Therefore, in this book, "the past" started a nanosecond ago. In terms of time, journalism and history sleep in the same bed.

I would like there to be a relationship between history and fact, and I reject the notion that fact is unprovable or nonexistent; therefore, in this book, some correspondence between fact and film is required. I have relied on G. Kitson Clark's elegant term, "the framework of fact," which expresses both history's fundamental need for fact and its essential operating upon fact with processes that become the flesh of history and hide the framework. Fact is skeleton, armature; history is body: the historian is related to God in the ability, occasionally, to take a rib and create life.

Historical films, then, must have some relation to a framework of fact. To appear in this book's filmography and to figure in its studies, films must have enough framework of fact to meet a simple requirement: they must each include a real person and some version of a real and specific event (e.g., not the Civil War, but the raid on St. Alban's, Vermont), although "real event" has somewhat elastic limits, especially in comedy. Obviously, these criteria will include biography. Because I am interested here only in American history and American films, however, only American films that include American framework of fact qualify ("American" having some latitude—e.g., Columbus). The criteria have caused me to reject films one might expect to find: *Christopher Columbus* (1949) with Frederic March (American events, but British production); *Old Gringo* (1989) (one real person, but invented events); *The Birth of a Nation* (1915) (insufficient real persons). I have added a short list of marginal films to the filmography; these fall along the edges of the criteria, are not included in any of the figures, and are only occasionally discussed (e.g., *San Francisco* [1936], which has a real event, no real persons, but persuasive cultural history).

"Events" and "people" are inclusive terms here. I have moments of wishing that history, as it used to, dealt only with great men and big events (it would be so much easier), but this cannot be; therefore, in this book neither people nor events need be categorical: subjects covered are not only male or political or warlike or powerful or white. As a result, there are no criteria of magnitude or kind: "history" here deals with politics and showbusiness, war and sports, business and labor, crime and country music, color and whiteness, maleness and femaleness.

This inclusiveness has caused there to be more than five hundred films in the filmography and another forty or so in the marginal list. Many of the early films are lost; many others exist in nonviewing copies; a few exist in viewing copies but seemed not worth the considerable effort of getting to them. Even so, I have studied more than three hundred in the main filmography, many of the marginals (to determine that they were in fact marginal), and quite a few others (to be sure that they should be excluded). I cannot do justice to more than three hundred films in a book of this length: it would take at least twice the pages. I rejected the idea of doing a short paragraph for every film I studied, although I have had to do so more often than I like. Still, whenever possible, I have left out entirely films that were redundant with a film discussed at length, but inferior or less revealing. Such films abound among musical biographies and Westerns, indeed, wherever a genre has evolved. I have tried to include everything I thought important, and I confess to preferring films I love where there had to be a choice. Nonetheless, I know that many people will not find here one film they believe should have been included. I apologize for those I am wrong about, and I sympathize with the loss of all the others. For various reasons, the omissions are bound to include films somebody will expect to see: *Gone with the Wind* (fiction), *Gettysburg* (televsion documentary), *Gable and Lombard* (drivel), *The Rough Riders* (lost), and a host of others. Those films that are discussed are grouped by types, and within the group are discussed in the chronological order of their events, not their release.

The problem of periodizing these films has been resolved, not solved, and in the blandest way. I rejected most schemes because each carries its own assumptions (e.g., periodization by political events). I decided, instead, on decades, as being at least more or less meaningless. The decades begin with years ending in zero: this is not usual, I know, but it allows me to mean by the 1920s all years starting with 192-.

NINTEENTH-CENTURY HISTORY had had one foot in patriotism: concerned with great men and great (political and military) events, it implied that its subjects were exemplars, and it presented its heroes in exemplary narratives. Since then, history has moved toward specialization—economic history, social history, military history, diplomatic history, cultural history, psycho-history. It has also suffered a bad case of relativism, and history has been Balkanized by "isms": now there are Marxist, feminist, black, structuralist, lesbian, total, womanist, and many other kinds of history. The nineteenth-century historian Francis Parkman, firm in the conviction that being white, male, and well-off made him representatively human, seems quaint. History-writing is now a contentious discipline; ideas of proof that would have satisfied in 1850 would now be laughable; hypotheses are advanced, defended, and attacked: and a format of citations, notes, and bibliography tries to assure rigor, if not enjoyable reading.

Film was born as scientific history was taking hold, but the people who made early films had been raised on narrative history. They were also engaged in a primarily narrative enterprise, if only because of the example of stage drama. Filmed history, therefore, was under pressures to be narrative history, whatever was happening among historians. As well, there were pressures having more to do with film itself: dramatic films suffered constraints that determined their form—the depiction of human beings in action; the reliance on narrative; conventions of length; technological qualities (e.g., lack of sound until 1927; rarity of color until the mid-1930s). As the director in *Sweet Liberty* makes clear, films also suffer commercial constraints that affect both content and form: they must have wide appeal; they must meet ethical or moral standards (usually the most conservative rather than the least); they must be made within certain industrial structures (e.g., the studio system); they typically must use and flatter a star or stars; and so on.

Therefore, other questions arise about American film and American history:
• Can narrative film write history? Film does not normally show the apparatus that the historical article or book shows (sources, evidence, endnotes, appendices, statistics), and film cannot either argue or respond to critique as the historical article or book does. Given these constraints, how well can film write history?
• Can a film be both good film and good history?
• Do American historical films show changes over time? If so, are these changes in the periods that are shown? In the subjects? In the kinds of historical figure?
• If there are changes over time in the films, can causes be assigned? If they can, are they causes that come from the world of film or from outside film?

- Do changes in historical theory show in historical film? Is there anything about film—its commercial nature, its industrial structure, its idea of art—that either impedes or enhances the effect of such changes?
- Is there any necessary relationship between history and style? The dominant style of commercial film has been realism. To a naive audience, realism "normalizes"; that is, the style makes the image "true." Does this affect film's ability to deal with contested evidence? Have there been stylistic alternatives to realism?
- Can American history be told with American historical film?

I AM INDEBTED to a number of people and institutions: above all, to Patti P. Gillespie, for constant advice and encouragement, and the patience to listen to endless maundering; to Madeline Matz and Rosemary Hanes of the Motion Picture Division of the Library of Congress, for their unfailing help and their many suggestions of titles I should otherwise have missed; and to the staffs and collections of the Museum of Modern Art, the George Eastman House International Museum of Photography, and the British Film Institute. In addition, I want to thank Sharon Ahmen for sharing her research on "coon singing"; and Patricia Gallahan for technical help.

PART I

Celebrating the Past

CHAPTER ONE

1900–1919: HISTORY ACCORDING TO LONGFELLOW

The film is only thirty-one seconds long. It has no plot. It has no story. It has no characters. Yet it is clearly a historical film.

Three men come into the frame from the viewer's left, to march in place in front of a painted backdrop. Smoke or steam rises behind and to the viewer's right of them. A broken wheel lies in front of them and to the viewer's left. Two of the men play drums, the one in the center a fife. They do not wear the clothes of the year of the film's making, 1905; rather, they wear knee breeches and long waistcoats and open shirts with full sleeves.

They march in place; the drummers drum and the fifer seems to play, but we hear nothing because the film is silent. After nearly twenty seconds, they wheel and march out of the frame to the viewer's right. A larger puff of smoke rises, as if from a small explosion. The three men march back into the frame from the right and take their same positions and continue to play.

The film is called *The Spirit of 76*.

If you asked the film's audience of 1905 what the film was about, you would get many answers: it is about America; it is about the Revolution; it is about a painting; it is about courage; it is about democracy; it is about independence.

It is about history.

HISTORY MARCHED, STRODE, slithered, rode, and paddled into film almost with its beginnings. It wore buckskin fringe, tricorn hats, hoop skirts, feathers, and red coats; it carried muskets, bows, fans, and six-guns. From the very beginning, such films were recognizable as "history." Despite the crudeness of early film technology, despite the extreme shortness of the films themselves, despite a naiveté that severely limited the amount of data contained in most frames, films were made to seem accurate as portrayals of times long gone and of people long dead.

Even the earliest of them, however, raises questions about how the idea of history was communicated and what forces had prepared the audience for history on film, even while providing information with which to answer those questions.

KIT CARSON FIRST appeared in commercial films in 1903. AM & B's *Kit Carson* was primitive, some of its sequences almost comatose, its camera static: in eleven short sequences, it fixed the camera and stared at an action so simple that a viewer of the 1990s looks for a significance that was not intended. What was seen was what there was: the seeing was all.

The film shows Carson in a fur hat and a fringed jacket. In the first sequence, in camp, he waits for a companion to wake, lights a remarkably smoky campfire, drinks and washes at a stream, and picks up his (clearly empty) pack basket. And the two men walk out of the frame. There has been no dialogue, no exposition, no preparation. It is enough that this moving figure, this "great," is shown, identified by the title as a hero from America's past. (Other titles may be missing from the extant copy.)

A change of camera angle signals, as it always will in this film, a new event. "Indians," unidentifiable as to tribe but identifiably "Indians" because each has a single feather worn on the head, sneak into the campsite and swarm over it, indicating "searching"—they sniff and put their heads to the ground; they peer.

Another camera change presents Carson and his companion walking in the woods, their guns carried on their shoulders, like soldiers. They set up another camp and build another tremendously smoky fire. They eat. They point. They go to sleep. No environmental change has suggested passage of time.

In a new sequence, the Indians find the camp and attack. Carson is captured; his companion is killed, then scalped by an Indian who goes off waving the scalp (clearly a hairpiece) like a feather boa.

A new camera position shows woods, water, and a log bleeding off the audience-left side of the frame. There is no visual connection to the previous sequence. Now, the Indians, who exited the previous sequence from left to right, enter from right toward the camera, then turn left along the log. Carson, a prisoner, comes next to last; when on the log, he pushes the Indian behind him into the water and runs away. Belatedly, the other Indians run after him. This pursuit leads to a canoe chase in a new sequence.

A new camera position shows different Indians (signaled by different dress) setting an ambush; they attack Carson's canoe and capture him.

Another camera position, this time from a slightly elevated position, looks at two tepees and a tree, with Indian women (skirts). Male Indians bring Carson in and tie him to the tree, then throw tomahawks at him, the actors indicating savage glee. One thrusts a flaming branch in his face. The males drift away or go to sleep. A woman creeps up and unties Carson and he escapes.

A final setup shows a log cabin and a man chopping wood. Carson appears. A woman and children come from the cabin and gather around him, and the film ends.

This (1903) is early days for motion pictures. The visual simplicity is hardly surprising; the narrative complexity is—two captures, two sets of Indians, a death, a release from captivity, a reunion. However, the narrative devices are utterly basic, without parallel action or preparation, except for the single instance of the Indians' setting of the ambush. There is no "meanwhile." Nor is there reliance on any known Kit Carson event or legend. And what we might assume would be required for an "authentic" Kit Carson is missing—known facts of place (he was active in the Southwest and California, but the film seems to take place in the North woods), precision of date, facts or tradition of character.

This small film seems to have felt no need of such authentication. It is content with the character's name, the simple signals of fur hat, fringe, feather, and gun, and events that show him in motion. It distinguishes two kinds of male character, white and Indian; the first is comfortable in the woods and is resourceful (the escape on the log); the second is bestial (the sniffing), less intelligent (again, the escape on the log), and brutal (the scalping, the torture). Female character, although unexplained, seems to be compassionate (the Indian woman who frees Carson, the woman at the cabin).

What is significant about *Kit Carson* is its reliance on its audience's recognition of simple signs (costume, weapons, acts like scalping) and on its audience's ability to fill narrative gaps, mostly of motivation—who Carson was, why he was in the woods, what the relationship between whites and Indians was, why an Indian woman would free a white captive. Acting consisted mostly of performing activities (lighting a fire, walking, paddling a canoe) and sometimes of doing what actors now call "indicating," over-doing a simple act so the audience will perceive it as a message about itself (the sniffing, the glee shown during the torture). There appears to have been no manipulation of pace to control narrative suspense.

A related but more sophisticated film was D. W. Griffith's *Leather Stocking* (1909). Again, whites and Native Americans are enemies; again, the title provides a field of information about action and period, specifically recalling James Fenimore Cooper's *Leatherstocking Tales*. It is not a literal rendering of *The Last of the Mohicans*, but in its overcompressed way recalls it: an "Indian" leads a British officer, two women, and a servant into the woods; they meet with a white man in a coonskin cap and fringed trousers and, shortly after, are ambushed; the man in the coonskin leads them to a stockade, then disguises himself in a bearskin and goes for help; the "Indians" attack the stockade and break in but are defeated when the man in the coonskin hat (identified in a title as Hawkeye) returns with help.

As in *Kit Carson*, the signs are simple: costume—generic eighteenth-century uniforms for military men, long skirts and caps for women—and weapons (recognizable flintlocks). No real authenticity is offered in either; rather, a known "look" seems to be sufficient: e.g., in the uniforms, the swept-back skirts of Revolutionary War coats, the tricorn hat, breeches. The coats in particular are actually wrong for the French and Indian War of Cooper's novels, but they suffice to communicate "eighteenth-century."*

The signs for "Indian" are more complex than those in *Kit Carson*: white actors now wear rubber baldpates to which hair and feathers have been attached (accounting for the still-used term "rubberhead" for a white portraying a Native American). They wear historically and ethnologically inaccurate furs, probably intended to communicate savagery, as Griffith had used furs on Africans in *The Zulu's Heart* the year before.[1]

Hawkeye's signs are also variably authentic—a flintlock musket, coonskin hat, and fringed clothing, apparently leather. However, occasional frames show that the lower garment, at least, is a pair of cloth trousers with fringe sewn down the outer seams. What of the "leather stocking" of the title? Cooper makes it quite clear in *The Last of the Mohicans* that "leather stockings" are leggings, not pants, and he makes no mention of fringe. Such leggings are common in eighteenth-century illustrations of Native Americans and of whites wearing Native American dress (e.g., Benjamin West's portrait of Guy Johnson). Cooper also describes Natty Bumppo as wearing a green cloth "hunting frock" with faded yellow fringe, and he correctly says that this was a common garment in the eighteenth century (the "rifleman's shirt," usually white). But Cooper's fringe was picked-out linen, not slashed leather, and Cooper's hero wears a leather cap, not a coonskin. Thus, the Hawkeye of *Leather Stocking* has more in common visually with the hero of *Kit Carson* than with his own original in Cooper. It appears that in both films a few signs—gun, coonskin, fringed leather—communicated both period and character, and that these, with the films' names, aroused audience recognition and interest, just as the breeches and waistcoats and the title provided adequate information in *The Spirit of 76*.

The films' very simplicity, their visual skimpiness, however, raise a basic issue: Where did these signs, which served as a kind of visual shorthand, allowing such economy, come from?

IN 1947, A. Nicholas Vardac asked a brilliant, if tortuous question: "Can the motion picture . . . be considered as the ultimate aesthetic expression of a cycle of realistic-pictorial theatrical production which had been a part of the rebirth of the objective spirit in the middle of the eighteenth century and

---

* The Duke of Saxe-Meiningen, one of the pioneers of realistic staging in the last third of the nineteenth century, tried to get his costumes accurate within a third of a century. Griffith pretty much hit that mark, perhaps by accident.

which was to mature through the nineteenth-century age of invention?"[2] In other words, was the motion picture a necessary outgrowth of the theater?

Certainly, the debt of the American motion picture industry to the American theatrical industry should not be minimized. By early in the twentieth century, stage actors and stage plays were filtering into movies; so were stage directors (then a fairly recent phenomenon in themselves) and scenic artists.

D. W. Griffith was the most significant figure to make this transition. A journeyman stage actor, he came to film directing after a theatrical career of no distinction whatever. Yet, he clearly brought with him the visual tradition of the stage (pictorialism—telling stories with stage pictures); the production style (neoromantic realism); and the dominant genre (melodrama). He used the camera and edited in ways that marked the birth of a new art; yet, the visual tradition, the style, and the genre of the stage remained, leading one historian to remark that he "remained firmly under the spell of late Victorian dramatic conventions."[3] He became the embodiment of Vardac's perception that when theatrical scenery reached the limit of its technology—when, that is, variable focus, parallel lines of action, and what we now call editing were a logical but technically impossible next step for the theater—the art of film was needed.

Vardac thus saw to the heart of a relationship between American theater and early American film. The theater of the late eighteenth and the nineteenth centuries, with its spectacle, its movement, its melodramatic realism, was pre-film—what Vardac called an "audience need" for film.[4] By 1890, theater was waiting for Griffith the film director, not Griffith the stage actor.

In looking at historical motion pictures, therefore, we have to remember that historical plays were an important part of the pre-film theater. As early as 1790, *The Battle of Eutaw Springs* was being staged in Charleston; the Boston theater had John Daly Burk's *Bunker-Hill* in 1797; New York had "a new national pantomime," *The Independence of America*, in 1796, Burk's *Bunker-Hill* the year after; Philadelphia had *Columbus, or A World Discover'd* and a "historical pantomime," *The American Heroine*, in 1797. In 1798, William Dunlap wrote his tragedy *Andre*; it didn't go, but he turned it into one of the most enduring of plays in 1803 as *The Glory of Columbia, Her Yeomanry!*, which included a nasty Benedict Arnold and three militiamen who arrested Andre and saved the Revolution. Thereafter, historical plays and spectacle about the nation's founding were regulars until at least the Civil War, the Burk and Dunlap plays in particular being trotted out every Fourth of July and Evacuation Day. History and commercial performance were bedfellows.

History was often noble words on the stage, but it was also vigorous pantomime and wordless spectacle. The battle scene in Burk's *Bunker-Hill*, for example, has only a brief stage direction—"Bunker Hill fortified—Distant view of sea and ships. English reinforced, march towards the Hill. The cannons play at intervals. . . . Three times the English make the assault and three times they are beat back." The scene, however, was described by Burk himself as lasting, in the Boston production, "twelve or fifteen minutes." Silent film would do it even better.

It is hardly surprising to find dozens of historical and patriotic titles among the pictures made in film's first decades. Most are now forgotten, even lost. Usually short, they have schoolbook titles—*Benedict Arnold* (1909), *Betsy Ross* (1917), *The Boston Tea Party* (1908), *The Birth of the Star-Spangled Banner* (1914), *The Death of Nathan Hale* (1911), *How Washington Crossed the Delaware* (1912), *Old Glory* (1910), *George Washington Under the American Flag* (1909). Indeed, at least twenty-four films about the Revolution were made before 1920; five more were concerned with the flag; two others with the French and Indian War (e.g., *Wolfe or the Conquest of Quebec*). This is history as a collection of Greatest Hits, moments that have come into the culture and the language and are so embedded in patriotism that they have become myths.

To say that the only antecedents of these films were theatrical plays would be ridiculous. On the other hand, to ignore the theater as a conduit for these subjects and their meanings between history and film would be blind.

To a considerable extent, theater was also the conduit for the visual counterpart of what Sorlin called "historical capital"—history "known to all members of [the] community."[5] The theater that immediately preceded film had been intensely pictorial and antiquarian, and increasingly dominated by men like David Belasco, who used historical accuracy of costumes and properties as an audience come-on. In turn, both pictorialism and antiquarianism were directly related to the trove of historical paintings that by 1876 "were already among the popular national icons reproduced in magazines and school history texts."[6] It is not accidental that both the title and the imagery of one of the earliest historical films, *The Spirit of 76*, refer to a painting.

To the question, then, "How did the audience know the men in *The Spirit of 76* were supposed to be in the eighteenth century?" the answer is partly that they knew the painting to which the title referred. To such a question as, "How did the audience know the officer in *Leather Stocking* wore an eighteenth-century uniform?" the answer is that the line of the coat, the breeches, and the hat had been locked into an idea of "eighteenth century" by repetition in painting, schoolbook, magazine, dime novel, civic pageant, theatrical play, and, probably, such activities as children's dress-ups and parlor games. On the other hand, to such a question as "Why did the audience believe that Hawkeye wore a coonskin cap and fringed leather clothes, when Cooper describes him differently?" the answer is more complex, because it requires showing how an inauthentic sign came to be accepted as an authentic one.

Fringed leather clothing is perhaps the first and most durable of historical errors in American illustration. At issue is the use of fringed buckskin (sometimes elkskin), especially a suit of fringed buckskin, to clothe, and more importantly to identify—to comprise a sign for—the American frontiersman.

(The coonskin hat is a separate sign and derives, it is generally agreed, from the political symbolism of the 1830s.) The trousers are rather tight, seamed down the sides, with fringe along the seams. The top is fringed down the sleeves and usually along a yoke, front and back, and at the bottom; sometimes the shirt is shown belted, increasingly so after about 1880.

By "the moment of film," the buckskin suit was a long-established sign that said "frontier," not merely for its proper period (1820–50) but for all periods. In actuality, it is difficult to prove that whites on the frontier wore fringed leather before the 1820s, arguably even later than that. As we have already seen, linen "hunting frocks" were worn in the eighteenth century. Daniel Morgan, for example, is shown wearing such a linen frock in Trumbull's painting of Burgoyne's surrender; less flattering paintings from the Revolution—several German watercolors of American soldiers, for example—make the linen frock look like an unraveling sweater.

Indians of the Northeast had worn leather before Europeans appeared, but not fringed and not in suits. Like other Stone Age people, they preferred cloth as soon as they got it: cloth was colorful, warm, and easy to sew. Leather, by contrast, is hard to acquire (one suit can take five deerskins), hard to tan and sew, and often uncomfortable to wear—hot in summer, cold and slimy in the wet. As anyone who has worn "skins" will attest, wearing deerskin in a downpour is like putting on a squid.

However, whites adopted one aspect of the Northeastern Indian leather costume—the legging. Unfringed, seamed in the back, it was good protection in the woods. This is Cooper's "leather stocking." By the Revolution, however, it was mostly replaced with wool, even among British-sponsored Indians.

Paintings and engravings of the colonial period do not show fringed buckskin on whites. One searches eighteenth-century pictures in vain for frontiersmen wearing it.[7] Portraits of men like Daniel Boone do not show it. However, it does begin to appear in pictures of Lewis and Clark (1805), in engravings of c. 1830 of actors playing Indians (e.g., Edwin Forrest as Metamora), and in Alfred Miller's paintings of the mountain men (c. 1830). David Hackett Fischer argues that it was taken west of the Alleghenies by "backcountry-borderer" immigrants, but he cites only a reminiscence of 1833 for "a few [shirts] of dressed buckskins."[8] Apparently, the fashion came East from contact with the Indians of the far Plains and Rockies. By 1870, it was universal: an actor playing Davy Crockett in 1873 wore *cap-a-pie* leather and coonskin:[9] the type had consumed the individual, and the icon had consumed the fact.

Thus, fringed buckskin clothing had become a sign for wildness, frontier, real America, by perhaps the 1850s. After that, it seems to have fed backward into the understanding of the past (e.g., George Caleb Bingham's 1851 painting of Daniel Boone in the 1760s)[10] and been popularized by paintings, books, and so on. As a stage and film costume, and as a sign for manliness, its cut had the added virtue of a "heavy stress on masculinity."[11]

Between Griffith in 1910 and Cooper's description of Hawkeye in 1826 lay generations of symbolism. Griffith inherited, not a costume, but a myth; not a historical fact, but a meaning.

History thus came to film with much of its visual language already decided. Film was able to take it over more or less whole and use it to communicate quickly and directly, often augmenting its own language in the process. At the same time, film risked becoming the prisoner of its own signs, transmitting received error along with received truth.

ONE INDICATION OF the use of received language is approval by authority. Selig's *The Coming of Columbus* (1912) got such approval in the form of an award from the Vatican,[12] probably for its intense piety in both action and signs: a cross or a monk is present in most frames; Columbus kisses the cross often. A puff piece called it "the greatest achievement yet wrought by cinematography."[13]

The Coming of Columbus was an elaborate production that used replicas of Columbus's ships, which were made for the Chicago Exposition and in 1912 anchored along Chicago's waterfront. The costumes were typical antiquarian versions of the high Renaissance. Most of the settings were painted, sometimes with false perspective; the model was late-nineteenth-century stage decor.[14] Spectacle was a goal—processions, courts, a royal tent on a battlefield; these typically corresponded with a ceremony (receptions, blessings, pleas), so that the action moved from ceremony to ceremony, suggesting a world of hierarchical order. The camera was mostly static.

Columbus's story here is the story from the schoolbook—Isabella, the ships, near-mutiny, discovery, with little conflict. The natives of Hispaniola are gentle generic savages; their love of Columbus is instantaneous, and there is no hint that Columbus or his men brought them anything but benefit. When Columbus is arrested and taken back to Spain in chains, no judgment is made: "So Passes the Glory of Man," a title tells us. Historical film, if *The Coming of Columbus* is an example, is a procession of tableaux vivants meant to recall nineteenth-century academic painting, with no questions asked about causes or consequences.

George Washington Under the British Flag (1909) was far less ceremonial. It tried to show Washington from his first command to his marriage with Martha Custis. It was careless about material culture (a Victorian print and a twentieth-century mirror appear in one scene) but less awe-struck by Washington than later films would be. The costume signs are the same as in *Leather Stocking* for Native Americans, military men, and frontiersmen (e.g., one Virginian wears a fur hat). The centerpiece is Braddock's defeat, with particular emphasis on Washington's warning Braddock against the Indians, Braddock's ignoring him and being "slaughtered." As usual, there is no context, hardly any sense of motivation: like Columbus, Washington *is*, even as a young man. Greatness is character.

Most early films about the Revolution (including, apparently, the companion film to *Washington Under the British Flag*, *Washington Under the American Flag*) are now lost. The survivors include *The Midnight Ride of Paul Revere* (1917), a literal rendition of Longfellow, as a title says: "From the poem by Henry Wadsworth Longfellow." Lines from the poem comprise other titles, so that Longfellow gives the film authority, even while it claims authenticity by showing actual locations "photographed at Historic Locations in Concord and Lexington." Precision in dating ("18 April 1775") suggests historical accuracy. The film aims to be an exciting story of Revere and the beginning of the Revolution. A need to authenticate, however, is so strong that a modern plaque identifying Old North Church is shown when the incident of the lanterns is reached; it is an anachronism to the narrative but a seal of approval to the history—an apparently acceptable contradiction.

As with other films, character is largely external to the work; the audience is to fill in Paul Revere as it filled in Kit Carson or Columbus. Activity, on the other hand, is sometimes frenetic—Revere rides and rides and rides, hectoring what seems to be half of New England, single-handedly alerting the colony to its danger. The army that Revere turns out is democratic and diverse—a woman joins an old codger and a generic Minuteman—and the conclusion is inescapable (because no other is made visually possible) that the entire populace turned out to start the Revolution.

Again, *Paul Revere* plays to prior audience knowledge. Lacking is any sense of what really went on that eighteenth of April in seventy-five, because there is nothing within the film to cause, or even allow, question. There is a failure both of context—whether conceived as politics, economics, or culture—and of fact, or at least of probability: Revere cannot possibly have ridden to every hamlet and farm; he cannot personally have waked all the Minutemen. As David Hackett Fisher has shown, Revere was a dynamic man, "consumed with restless energy and much attracted to risk," but hardly the only begetter of the news that the British were coming.[15] The populace did not turn out because he shouted under their windows; the trained militias did, because riders made ready by him spread a call for action. Revere was captured (not mentioned in the film); he had a companion (not seen in the film); he was last seen hustling Hancock's papers into hiding (not part of the film).

Fisher argues that Longfellow's agenda in writing the poem was "a call to arms" at the beginning of the Civil War, for which a "solitary actor against the world" was wanted; the resulting distortions led to a poem that "was grossly, systematically, and deliberately inaccurate."[16] Inevitably, so is the film a prisoner of widely accepted and beloved error.

The Boston Tea Party (1917) was mostly fiction, set against real events and involving its fictional lovers in them. The signs are the same, even to the "Indian" signs that the conspirators put on to throw the tea into Boston harbor. Several sequences show the Sons of Liberty; despite titles and even a process shot showing "The Glorious Future" as a symbolic tableau, however, little is communicated of ideas of liberty, taxation, or representation. Much more is made of simplistic visuals, reinforced by titles: "The Bible in the homes of the colonists is in sharp contrast to the gaiety at the [British] ball." The same contrast is underscored in male costume—overdecorated British officers, simple Americans.

Another film entitled *The Spirit of 76* (made in 1917) is, alas, no longer with us. Notorious because its writer-producer, Robert Goldstein, was jailed for more than a year and the film was seized for its anti-British slant, it would now be worth seeing as the film that caused a federal judge to rule that "a truthful representation of an historical fact" was censorable because it might foment "disloyalty or insubordination" among the military.[17]

On the basis of the lengthy treatment submitted for copyright,[18] there seems to have been little danger of truthful representation of anything. *The Spirit of 76* appears to have been a lurid war drama that cast the British as deep-dyed villains in a moral battle. They shoot civilians, skewer babies on bayonets, and drag women about by the hair. Worst of all is Walter Butler, that hapless historical figure whose name is wrongly connected with every attack on the Mohawk Valley between 1775 and 1783. Goldstein's most remarkable imagery, in the written treatment, however, is devoted to Native Americans, particularly the Iroquois, whose Long House is decorated with skulls, whose "maidens" stage orgies after inhaling drugged incense, and whose "frenzies" are regularly whipped up by a grotesque witch, the Toad Woman.

The stated purpose of *The Spirit of 76* was to show the triumph of democracy over monarchy. To that end, it began with a parade of "allegorical scenes" on the Rule of Might (cave people); the Rule of Avarice (the Romans); the Rule of Intrigue (Antony and Cleopatra); the Rule of Fear (Venice and the Inquisition); and the Rule of Arrogance (William Tell). In the main narrative, George III marries a "Quaker maiden," Catherine Montour, "in a large Cathedral" at night "by the left hand" (that is, morganatically); the Iroquois Joseph Brant—"educated at a university . . . a polished gentleman [who] later degenerates into an Indian"—appears, casting a "weird, menacing" shadow on the wall. When, however, Lord Chatham tells George III that he must give Catherine up and marry a princess, "intense disappointment [changes] her character" and "the excitement works the king up to madness . . . ," causing the American Revolution.

Having been denied her chance to be queen of England, Catherine sails to America and becomes queen of the Iroquois. British soldiers are shown racing horses in the streets of Boston, and "they ride down an old man and a little girl." Walter Butler causes the Boston Massacre by ordering soldiers to fire on a mob. Paul Revere rides; "Pitcairn in a rage orders the soldiers to shoot" at the militia on Lexington Green, and shortly we see the Battle of Bunker Hill. Several subsidiary love plots follow. One pair of lovers ride through the woods "dressed in leather ranger's costume, with coonskin hats."

After "a reproduction of the famous French painting" of the Declaration of Independence, "the Toad Woman [runs] through the forest . . . always a sign of the meeting of the [Iroquois] Council" in a structure that is "very weird," with a post in the center "decorated with skulls, Indian carvings, and so forth." An orgy takes place. The action shifts to Washington at Trenton, then to "Charlestown, South Carolina," with "Indians, nigger-slaves, mixed with Southern planters," and then Catherine races back to London to hex Chatham to his death in the House of Commons, "an exact reproduction."

Howe's farewell gala in Philadelphia sees a returned Catherine persuading Peggy Shippen to cause her husband, Benedict Arnold, to turn traitor. After some more Revolutionary events, Lieutenant Boyd (one of the juveniles) is to be tortured in the Long House, but he gives a Masonic sign to Brant and is spared, at least until Butler comes in and stabs him "from behind." Butler is then pursued by Tim Murphy, who shoots him. After Yorktown, Catherine, now "old and gray" and "in rags" creeps into George III's room in London. "He has grown old and raves." He strangles her. Benedict Arnold, seen earlier plotting with Major Andre, is living in a London garret; he kisses the American flag and dies.

The film ends with a "close-up of a white marble bust of Washington. . . . "[19]

Somewhere between a nightmare and a particularly stupid final exam answer, *The Spirit of 76* was made worse by horrendous anachronisms; one reviewer expressed "mental derision" at sight of a modern corset, a concrete sidewalk, and mill-planed lumber.[20] The howlers of historical fact are even more remarkable: there was a real Walter Butler, to be sure, but he was not a monster; there was a Lieutenant Boyd who was tortured horribly by the Iroquois in 1779, and he did meet Brant and supposedly gave him a Masonic sign to seek his protection, but it did not happen in "the Long House," but in the woods near the Genesee River; there was a Tim Murphy, but he certainly was nowhere near Walter Butler when he was shot. There was even a Catherine Montour, but she was hardly a Quaker, never lived in London, and wasn't queen even for a day.

It is, in fact, for its very historical excesses that *The Spirit of 76* would be worth seeing. Its shot list is a clue to the historical capital of 1917, and to prejudices the producer expected the audience to share: against Native Americans, here always associated with witchcraft and signs of death; against the British, above all against the English king and the English aristocracy; for democracy, or at least white populism.

Another film, *The Beautiful Mrs. Reynolds* (1918), began in the Revolution and ended with the shooting of Alexander Hamilton (Carlyle Blackwood) by Aaron Burr (Arthur Ashley). It included George and Martha Washington, Israel Putnam, Thomas Jefferson, and of course Mrs. Reynolds, the woman with whom Hamilton was supposed to be having an affair. Its complex plot included Burr's jealousy of Hamilton, Burr's attempt to blackmail Hamilton with Mrs. Reynolds's letters, and of course the duel; the original dueling pistols were supposedly used, a nice Belasco-style touch.[21] Advertising stressed "the most powerful love story of American history" and "history made human. Based upon facts, but exceeding fiction."[22] Based upon facts it was, but the emphasis was clearly on romantic melodrama, which appears to be what was meant by "human."

THE REVOLUTIONARY FILMS were outnumbered by Civil War films, again mostly short and many now lost. Again, there was precedent in the theater in such plays as *Shenandoah*, Belasco's *The Heart of Maryland*, W. C. DeMille's (Cecil B.'s father's) *The Warrens of Virginia*, and William Gillette's durable *Secret Service*. Again, the principal signs were uniforms and weapons: surplus Civil War and militia gear were abundant.

Of nearly thirty Civil War films, sixteen dealt with battles or battle-related incidents (e.g., *The Battle of Bull Run* (1913), *The Battle of Shiloh* (1913), *With Longstreet at Seven Pines* (1911); seven dealt with Lincoln; and the remainder varied from *The Battle Hymn of the Republic* to *Escape from Andersonville*. Almost all were early (twenty-nine before 1913). Most other Civil War titles between 1913 and 1920 were fictional (e.g., *The Birth of a Nation*); several had begun as plays (*Heart of Maryland*, *The Warrens of Virginia*.)

The great bulk of these pre-1920 Civil war films were early and short. Many appear to have been in the actuality tradition, probably little more than smoke and titles. Most relied on recognizability in their names—Lincoln, Lee, Sherman, Sheridan, Grant, among persons; Shiloh, Gettysburg, Vicksburg, Andersonville among places. Most assumed knowledge of the events.

Some, on the other hand, set fictional plots against great events and great names. Such a film is *With Lee in Virginia* (c. 1913), whose love plot is woven clumsily with Lee's assumption of command in Virginia, after which the love plot takes over the film and Lee becomes only a deus ex machina. Early on, its principal focus is the prewar Lee, his agonizing over being offered command of federal troops by Lincoln, and his decision (after prayer) to resign so as to command in Virginia. This segment, titled "The Mental Struggle," gives way to a brief sequence of Lincoln and his cabinet. The actor is recognizably "Lincoln," although already old and infirm; reading Lee's resignation, he is stricken and sinks into a chair. This, however, is about the end of factual history in the film, except for one more shot of Lee, now with the familiar white beard and hair.

The love plot is exceptional only in its making its villain's (Horton's) enlistment in the Union army the result of "bitterness" because of rejected love, and in its making two aging blacks (played by whites in blackface) the center of the film's pathos. The black man makes, as a title has it, "The Final Sacrifice"—being shot by a firing squad to protect the white heroine. The black woman, in Aunt Jemima kerchief and apron, is seen lamenting at a gravestone, and the film ends with an extended shot of her alone on the porch of a cabin, weeping.

With Lee in Virgina is a film of very mixed signals. Its overall sympathy is Southern, although its image of Lincoln is that of the tragic martyr. Its villain is a Union officer. Slavery is never mentioned. Blacks support the Southern cause and bear the greatest suffering.

Other films of the Civil War cluster dealt with minor events. *The Rail-road Raiders of 62* (1911) lacked the recognizability of Shiloh but was the first of three films about this minor incident (*The General,* 1927; *The Great Loco-motive Chase,* 1956). It relied not on "greats" but on a unique incident and the courage it revealed on both sides—one locomotive chasing another as Union saboteurs tried to destroy part of the Confederate rail system. For its day, it was interestingly filmed, with angled shots that emphasized the rush of the locomotives and the uncoupling of the cars as the trains moved. The intricacy of real events could not be shown in so short a film, however; like others, it used its brief footage to show action, relying on titles for context. They suggest respect for both sides: "The Undaunted 'Rebs'"; "No Quarter: The Tragedy of War," as Confederate troops set fire to the building where the last of the Union saboteurs have hidden.

Indeed, this apparent tolerance toward both sides extends to the whole Civil War group, whose inclusion of films about both sides suggests a moral equivalency, in striking contrast to the Revolutionary films. Reconciliation was a popular theme (e.g., *Shenandoah*); the bitterness aroused by abolition and slavery was not. The fictional *The Crisis* (1916) appears to have been unusual in having dealt with slavery as an evil, its opening title pronouncing, "The South Wind bore to the ears of the world the wail of the slave," followed by a slave-auction sequence.

On the whole, the Civil War films seem apolitical, perhaps amoral, emphasizing battles and military events. Certain names and at least one face—Lincoln's—were assumed to be instantly recognizable; a number of generals were evidently represented by a beard, a uniform, and a horse. As before, character was external to the film, brought to it by the audience.

By implication, "history" in the early Civil War films did not mean questioning or analysis. It meant passive observation. As with *The Coming of Columbus* and *The Midnight Ride of Paul Revere,* the audience for the historical film appears to have been thought of as analogous to children in a schoolroom. History was handed down from above, "projected," and its tone was didactic or celebratory. Its themes were mostly military, its heroes male, mature, white. The sufferings of blacks were shown, but they were promised no relief, having no place in neoromantic plot; they were victims who did not partake of the poetic justice that rewarded the good whites.

NATIVE AMERICANS IN *Kit Carson* and *Leather Stocking* were the enemy. Indeed, they were the visible obstacle to white domination of the continent, as if terrain, weather, happenstance, logistics, had all been bundled into the one menace. Their signs communicated savagery (feathers, skins) and their actions suggested subhumanity.

Not all films about Native Americans were negative, however. Some early films extended an ambivalence implicit in Squanto and Pocohontas and seen in Cooper's novels and in plays as early as *Metamora* (1829). *Hiawatha* (1913) took its authority from Longfellow. It had Native American actors—a rarity—authentic dress, and a positive attack. Longfellow's poem was a Romantic version of an Indian myth, a mixture of the authentic and the benignly fake; the film has the added strength of visual authentication. *Hiawatha* opens with a mystery: a face is seen in a circle of light supposedly emanating from a rock, although technical naiveté makes it clear that the circle is a projection. The face is an appearance of divinity, there to demand why humans fight with each other. Succeeding sequences are now most interesting for their ethnological detail, particularly of Woodland Indian clothing of the turn of the century, no attempt having been made to imitate precontact material culture. Some of the photography is handsome, some of it intriguing, including double images to show famine and fever as white-robed skeletons invading the lodges, as well as multiple camera angles, and takes of varying lengths. The acting is uniformly bad, and the plot, such as it is—the Minniehaha romance, conflict with an evil man, the coming of a Jesuit—seems arbitrary. Nonetheless, *Hiawatha* is a very early example of a positive film about Native Americans (as imagined by whites, to be sure) that acknowledges their historical priority and sees them as moral and emotional beings.

When filmed history moved to the winning of the West, however, Native Americans again became the enemy. *The Fall of Black Hawk* (1912), was based on a brief "war" of the 1830s (called by Samuel Eliot Morison "a disgraceful frontier frolic").[23] Visually weak, it had generic Indians, and white soldiers in Civil War costumes.

A far better film was Thomas Ince's *Custer's Last Fight* (1912), one of at least three from this period about the Indian Wars (the first in 1909). Here, of course, the Indians are the victors, although—despite the subsequent fame of Crazy Horse and Sitting Bull—the incident at the Little Big Horn is, for whites, inevitably Custer's. The event was only thirty-eight years past when the film was made; many in its audience must have remembered when the news came over the telegraph. Others had probably encountered prints and paintings of it, the best known that produced by a beer company, or the doggerel poetry about it, or some example of the tireless memorializing carried on by Custer's widow. And if they had missed those, they could barely have managed to be unaware of the theatrical versions retailed by William Cody and the Wild West Show.[24]

Custer's "last stand" was thus part of the national mythos when Ince made his film. *Custer's Last Fight* seems, in fact, to have been intended to give the myth visual authentication. Its titles proclaimed it "an actual reproduction of . . . the reddest chapter in the Indian wars of the Western Plains—the Custer Massacre. . . ." Indeed, what seems to be happening with this film is a shifting of balance from visual to verbal, with the verbal (titles) becoming more clearly biased as some aspects of the visual (e.g., weapons, uniforms) became more detailed and accurate.

Ince's impulse, nonetheless, appears to have been "historical"—to create a record, an artifical memory. Feasible as this might seem for visual data, it did not extend to the titles. Rain-in-the-Face, for example, is introduced as "a bloodthirsty Sioux brave, [who] ambuscades and kills sutlers Balarin and Dr. Hozinger." In fact, Rain-in-the Face appears to have found the two whites mining illegally on Indian land; the "ambuscade" is debatable, his "blood-thirstiness" a matter of which side of the fence you stood on.

Ince's film then follows the events leading toward the Little Big Horn, often with visual and narrative believability because of a careful inclusion of details, including minor figures (e.g., Tom Custer, the great man's brother). These sequences show Ince's command of his medium as well as his ability to direct actors, who look natural and who are helped by having real things to do (smoking, cooking). The advance over films like *Kit Carson* and *Leather Stocking* is remarkable. However, Custer, when he appears, looks like a fraying rope, with hair cascading seemingly from his nostrils down each side of his mouth, and from his scalp in an uncombed tangle. He is, according to a title, "Indian fighter and scout," those terms not defined.

The apparent credibility of the film evaporates, however, with the presentation of Sitting Bull as "the brainiest of the Sioux—High priest in the Council and Chief Medicine Man." The Sioux had no priests, of course, not even high ones. Sitting Bull was a rather more interesting figure—a mystic and a leader. No mention is made here of the days he had spent in a sweat lodge or of the great dream that resulted—white soldiers falling from the sky.[25] Rather, the film shows him as a clever coward who runs away when the soldiers come.

Custer, deploying to drive the Sioiux back to the reservation, wears—should we be surprised?—a fringed buckskin jacket and thigh-high boots. The buckskin jacket was by then historically accurate: Custer wore such a jacket. The boots, however, look too much like stage wear to be practical.

The sequence in which Reno's troopers wade the river and begin to fire on the Sioux village is stunning; for sheer visual beauty, it will stand with anything in black and white. It is surrounded, however, by uninteresting and sometimes ludicrous footage—the Sioux erupting into a cliché of savage dancing when the army is sighted; Sitting Bull waving his arms and running back and forth, the title sneering, "Sitting Bull, thoroughly frightened at Reno's attack, leaves one of his children behind." Then there is another superb piece of battle film as Reno retreats, his men wading the river without their horses, gunsmoke drifting, riders silhouetted.

Later, "Sitting Bull makes medicine from afar" (title), as the Sioux and

Cheyenne overwhelm Custer "with a red mass of destruction." Naturally handsome terrain and splendid cinematography combine to create wonderful long shots of the battle. Custer rallies on a hilltop; his men plant their sabers in a protective circle. (The real Custer ordered sabers left behind.) The final moments are intercut with long shots over the rugged terrain.

Custer's Last Fight is a sophisticated piece of cinematography, and a beautiful one. It is less successful as history: despite its promise of "actual reproduction," it is biased, its negative focus Sitting Bull. Its positive focus is the final stand, given nobility by the circle of swords, the isolation, the centrality of Custer. That the event did not happen this way was irrelevant; this is the way Ince wanted it to have happened, or believed it really had happened, thanks to its transmission through the paintings, the doggerel, the Wild West Show.

One may ask why an anti-Indian film was desirable in 1912. Is it significant that this was the year of the last run for the presidency by Teddy Roosevelt, who had built his image on a shaky claim to being a cowboy in a buckskin suit? Or was it the triumph of the West, now officially all white as Arizona became a state? Or was it, more simply, the soothing syrup of popular culture, repeating the comfortable line that taking America by force had been justified because the enemy was cowardly and perfidious?

Despite Ince's visual sophistication, little advance had been made in the presentation of Native Americans over *Kit Carson* and *Leather Stocking*. The simple signs of savagery were hardly bettered by the signs of savage dancing and "ambuscade"; these are Native Americans as the "fiends incarnate, highway robbers and midnight assassins" described by an officer in the Indian Wars.[26] Contrarily, one of the signs for "frontier hero," the buckskin jacket, gave Custer added stature as both racial and cultural figure. Despite its complexity and its artistic excellence, then, *Custer's Last Fight* was cultural myth, not history.

A similar sense pervades a related film, one that also puts the Native American in a context that seems both triumphal and closed. *The Life of Buffalo Bill* (1912) was produced by the Buffalo Bill and Pawnee Bill Film Company in the waning days of their existence; it is clearly a compilation of pieces from the Wild West Show, and thus history twice removed. Its frame is the Cody of 1912, an aging man on horseback, with rifle, white beard, elaborately fringed jacket, and high boots, who rides into view, indicates "looking," then lies down to sleep.

"A dream of the days of his youth," a title tells us, "Memories of the old Santa Fe Trail. The way to the West before the railroad came." Wild-West-Show bits follow, with a younger actor playing Cody in the same costume, among cowboys and cowgirls in much later (1912?) costumes. These include "Night on the Plains," with Winchester-wielding Indians attacking and Buffalo Bill frightening them off; another Indian–white battle, this time with a melee around two wagons and a pile of gear; a stage coach robbery; "With

General Carr, 5th Cavalry," the soldiers in Spanish–American War uniforms; an Indian scene, during which a tepee (about one-third correct size) collapses and is set up again by a participant; and "The Famous Duel Between Chief Yellow Hand and Buffalo Bill Which Prevented the Cheyennes from Joining the Sioux," a mild struggle that ends with "The First Scalp for Custer." The film then returns to the frame, and the aged Cody saddles up and rides off.

As a record of the Wild West Show in its late days, the film has some interest; as history it is hokum. To be sure, Cody did kill Indians, but not as his major activity. In fact, he probably spent as much time on the theatrical stage as on the trail; a tireless self-promoter, he toured for years in gut-buster plays before starting the Wild West Show (1883), and his killing of Yellow Hand—a mistranslation of "Yellow Hair"—within weeks of Custer's death (1876) led him immediately to a new play, J.V. Arlington's *The Red Right Hand; or, Buffalo Bill's First Scalp for Custer.*[27]

Cody wore costumes on the theatrical stage that were based on, but were more elaborate than, the working clothes of the West—hence the fringed jacket, derived from the Plains Indian war shirt, and the thigh-high boots, based partly on cavalry boots and partly on theatrical swashbucklers. So interlocked were Cody's theatrical and real lives, in fact (divided loosely into winter and summer), that when he killed Yellow Hand, he purportedly did hold the scalp up and shout, "The first scalp for Custer," but if he didn't he might as well have, for he was doing in life what in a few weeks he would be doing on the stage, in much the same costume. Life and art had interpenetrated, and so had the signs of history and the signs of myth.

Any history of Cody would have to question how he shaped the events in which he took part—that is, how much of his life was a deliberate Wild West Show. This film does rather the opposite: it unquestioningly accepts the Wild West Show as life.

It was not too long after the Little Big Horn that the young Theodore Roosevelt had a fringed buckskin suit made for himself to go with his Tiffany Bowie knife and his custom-made Winchester. By this time, it appears, no one knew where the frontier ended and fantasy began. It is no wonder that by 1912 filmmakers were unsure where history ended and show biz began.

A similar confusion appears in the historical Westerns of the period. *Martyrs of the Alamo* (1915) put almost every Anglo in Texas in fringed buckskin and an enormous coonskin hat. Its Santa Ana was not merely an enemy, but also a moral degenerate under whom "the honor and life of American womanhood was held in contempt." He was "an inveterate drug fiend . . . famous for his shameful orgies." The Texas rebels, on the other hand, were "liberty-loving Americans who had built up a Texas colony." While Santa Ana is shown surrounded by dancing floozies, the Anglos are family men, surrounded by wives and children. Utterly simplistic in its moral system, the film opposes the now familiar signs for "real American" (buckskin, coonskin hats, rifles) against those of "evil non-American"—swarthy skin, dancing women, elaborate uniforms, ranting.

Like *Custer's Last Fight*, the Westerns seemed to aim at "actual reproduction" of fact, often by using actual sites or what was left of them, sometimes by including still photographs of the participants (now and again as corpses), often by insisting on the exactness of dates and names. Sometimes, they had an agenda: justifying the badness of the badmen as part of a larger political agenda.

Of none is this more true than *Jesse James, His Life and Adventures* (c. 1914), a film whose titles glorify the "King of all bandits and train robbers" and damns his murderer as "the traitor and coward who for a reward of $10,000 treacherously shot Jesse James in the back." James is thus a martyr because of the manner of his death; he is already a hero because of the treatment of his family in Missouri before the Civil War. His step-father had been "suspected of being in sympathy with the . . . pro-slavery people of the South" and so was "subjected to many indignities and tortures" by Unionist militia. The indignities and tortures must be taken as read; little is shown on film other than the emergence of the militia from a cornfield and their confrontation with the stepfather. Yet, the soldiers "strike terror to the hearts of the family," and "the boy Jesse takes a solemn oath to avenge" such treatment. After practicing with an anachronistic cartridge rifle, young Jesse joins Quantrill, "whose whole life was embittered by the brutal murder of his brother" (not shown).

Thereafter, one mistreatment after another leads to the James's isolation and their turn to crime; yet they remain kind to the poor. In a long sequence, they give money to a woman tormented by her whip-wielding landlord; when she has paid him, Jesse retrieves it by holding up the landlord. So, "with all his faults, Jesse James was a good husband and loving father."

Jesse James, His Life and Adventures is execrably acted and poorly filmed. Half its length is taken up by the titles, whose frequent typos suggest a spelling dictated by regional accent (e.g., *Babtist* for "Baptist"). Yet, its badness embodies an idea: that the Jameses were the victims of antislavery government, and their turn to crime was a moral response. This idea—partly a defense of slavery and partly an expression of Lost Cause romanticism—is certainly Southern. It is noticeably different from the blandness of the Civil War films, therefore deserves attention because it at least sketches a historical hypothesis. To be sure, it lacks evidence, relying instead on hectoring (the language of the titles) and questionable assertions (e.g., Quantrell's motives).

Two films about the Daltons are less ideological but no less heavily titled. *The Famous Dalton Raid on the Banks of Coffeyville* (c. 1909) reenacts a gang's attempted robbery, using the actual site to give authenticity. *The Dalton Boys* (c. 1911?) is a story film that strives to show why the four Dalton brothers became, first, U.S. marshals and then criminals. The first of the films has little narrative drive and looks as if it was made for local consumption (the film-maker, Tackett, apparently owned the Coffeyville movie house). Its most interesting visual element is a 190-degree pan of central Coffeyville; the rest is a mix of reenactment ("Daltons in Camp Night Before the Raid") and still photos—four corpses, the Dalton homestead "showing stairway to Boys Room," "Emmitt [sic] Dalton at 18," and so on. Except for an interesting diagonal shot of "Death Alley," where most of the Daltons were killed, the film is as indifferent to composition as to narrative.

The Dalton Boys, however, has considerable narrative movement but poor directing and acting. "Evening Prayer" shows four kids around their mother's knees; they are also shown coming home from school. Then an interior, the marshal's office, is used repeatedly, filmed dead-on as if it were a stage set. Various Daltons enter, swear to be marshals, stand about, and leave. The oldest Dalton, Frank, arrests two rustlers, both black, but is killed by bootleggers, and the remaining three "resolve to get even" and so turn to robbery. The logic of this shift is never examined.

Thereafter, the film seems to depend on local knowledge: titles indicate otherwise inexplicable locales—"The M. K. and T. holdup at Adair"; "Chief Rogers' store Where the ammunition was purchased"; "Cubine's Shoe Store"; "The barber who wounded Emmett Dalton." With a picture of Death Alley, however, the film reaches "The Expiation"—Emmett Dalton, the only survivor, in prison stripes, banging his fist on his chest and communing with heaven, followed by his return to his mother. At the end, an unidentified man doffs his hat; context suggests this is the real Emmett Dalton, who, after release from prison, became the general manager of the Southern Film Corporation.[28]

The Dalton films, therefore, although not so ideologically insistent as the James film, seem to say that film can write history. Their use of real places, names, and stills implies that historical truth lies in images of the real. In fact, these seem to take the place of the signs in films like *Kit Carson*; costumes here look like the clothes of c. 1910, and "pastness" does not seem to be an issue. *The Dalton Boys* seems, as well, to end with an image that gives it a quality of authorization (the real Emmett Dalton), a visual analog, perhaps, to footnotes and a bibliography.

The Dalton films are a kind of history-writing: gather all the data; present it in a logical order. Lacking context, this is *histoire évènementielle* of an extreme kind.

FEW FILMS FROM the 1900-1919 period fall outside the area of traditional history—that is, male-centered power, especially politics and violence. Two such films, about creative men, perhaps "men of genius," were directed by D. W. Griffith, although one hardly looks it. *Edgar Allen* [sic] *Poe* (1909) is an early attempt to show creativity and its effect on personality. Static and melodramatic, it finds the causes of its effects (poverty, the death of the beloved) outside the arena (poetry) that makes the central figure worth examining in the first place. It has no sense of place, other than a room and a couple of offices, and little sense of period; it depends heavily on audience knowledge of Poe to make itself comprehensible—an understanding of "The Raven," of the Romantic idea of the poet—and on receptivity to indicative acting, which communicated states of feeling through poses. Strangest of all, it is a film in which the camera does no work, surprising even in primitive Griffith.

Poe uses three stagelike box interiors for all of its action. In one, a woman lies on a bed; a Poe look-alike (the face, as with Lincoln, a sign) puts his coat over her, indicates suffering, paces, then watches a portrait bust metamorphose into a raven. At once, he begins to write; he finishes the writing in seconds, shows it to the woman with poses of powerful emotion, and rushes out. The camera has never moved.

In an office, two men at symmetrically placed desks read the poem and refuse it. Poe emotes, then rushes into another office, where a man and a woman sit at a desk marked "Editor." The woman laughs at the poem, but the man buys it. (Everyone is a fast reader.) Poe kisses the money and rushes out. Back in the first interior, the woman, with the camera slightly closer now, emotes and collapses. Poe rushes in with food and a blanket, covers her, at last discovers she is dead, and collapses on her body.

The filmmaking is poor, but the problems presented are greater than those in, say, *Leather Stocking*. No bad "Indians" provide ready obstacles—no antagonists exist, in fact, except abstractions (poverty, creative block). There is no clear action, only the internal working of a mind, represented by the crudely materialized raven, and the attempt to sell the poem and turn it into food and warmth, crudely represented by the scenes in the newspaper offices. The film tries to ask, but cannot answer, difficult questions: What is creativity? What is the economic place of the poet? Given the unproductive use of the camera and the thrust toward extreme melodrama, its answers can be given only in terms of banality and cheap irony.

Griffith did much better five years later in tackling John Howard Payne, now recognizable only as the composer of "Home, Sweeet Home," which gave the film its title, but once an important American actor and dramatist who died while American consul at Tunis. This time, Griffith approached the creative experience as a problem of poetry rather than one of drama. A title says that the film is "not biographical, but photo-dramatic and allegorical, and might apply to the lives and works of many men of genius. . . ." The film was "suggested" by the life of Payne.

Home, Sweet Home is overtitled. Allegorical or not, its scenes have to be explained by words. And, as it turns out, Griffith's real interest is not Payne but the women around him. No one can ever have believed more firmly in the three female categories of Mother, Virgin, and Whore than Griffith; here, they are Mother, Sweetheart (Lillian Gish), and the Worldly Woman. Payne's life is seen as the withdrawal from Mother, a distancing from Sweetheart (whose relationship with a sister—Dorothy Gish—seems more real than any with him), and a carouse with the Worldly Woman.

Much footage concentrates on Gish, pacing, darning, waiting. Payne meanwhile goes into and out of debtors' prison (where? we never know), and Gish prays. "Adversity spurs the writing of the song" ("Home, Sweet Home"), and Gish is seen with the Mother, either as a memory or a vision. Then, "Evil News of Her Boy," and the Mother collapses; "His Death in an Alien Land" sees him lying on a couch, fanned by a man in a burnoose. "The True and the False Alike Went Into equal Silence," and there is Gish, also apparently dead.

"Home, Sweet Home" is the central idea of Griffith's poem, but "adversity" as its immediate cause is no better than the raven in *Poe*, and a good deal less visual. Creativity again escapes the camera; so does the relationship between creativity and money. What the film communicates most strongly is an intense sentimentality centered on Lillian Gish, who *is* home, sweet home—passive, endlessly patient, forgiving.

In both of these films, Griffith is willing that his women suffer and die and do nothing else; his men suffer, too, but have lives marked with crude explosions of emotion and bursts of creativity. Neither film can properly be called biography; neither has much interest in history, being indifferent to time and place, to signs of period or assurances of authenticity, and to cause or context. Yet Griffith cannot be faulted too much for failing at the enormous task of trying to show both the inner landscape of creativity and its outer effects. He would not, after all, be the only director to do so.

Two other films are interesting for their unique subjects. *The Black Hand* (1906) was concerned with a very different America, the Italian immigrant community of New York. Part actuality, it depended on audience knowledge of a contemporary kidnapping, with some dependence on "actual reproduction." ("A Clever Arrest. Actually as made by the New York Detectives," one title reads.) The Black Hand of the title was the signature of a purported Italian organization, obviously recognizable to the audience of 1906. So, presumably, were the signs of the immigrant Italian: dark, curly hair; full mustache; a wine bottle on the table. Although the film was probably commercial because of its crime story, it should be noted as another that equates immorality with "non-Americans."

The Molly Maguires (1908) was also a rarity, a film about labor. Now apparently lost, it was broken into eight scenes that can have been little more than quick takes; nonetheless, it managed to tell the story of a miner who refuses to go on strike when one is called by "desperate leaders who used their power over the simple miner folks for their own selfish ends."[29] He is "assaulted"; his "little cottage" is burned; there is a fight, and everybody goes back to work. The film seems to have shown no sympathy for labor organization or the strike, certainly none for the Molly Maguires. It is significant, however, that the narrative itself is about labor and is not a love story merely set against the period of the Molly Maguires. Whether the film conveyed (through titles, most probably) the condescension of the summary's language ("simple," "folk") is unknown.

WHAT WE CAN SAY about film and history at this point is that before 1920 filmed history was largely a matter of events and greatness and maleness, much of it communicated through visual signs, but much of it increasingly after 1910 through titles. The sometimes primitive filmmaking concerned itself with both authenticity ("actual reproduction") and authority (Longfellow), but it also depended on received signs and subjects. Film in these decades was a way of showing, but not a way of examining; it could be a virtual memory or a virtual record, but it also was drama (usually melodrama) and so subject to the habits of drama, the acting style of drama, and the emotional values of drama. These, derived from the contemporary theater, were far from neutral. What is perhaps most striking from a historian's point of view is the absence of cause. Except where, rarely, an agenda was being urged, as in *Jesse James*, the question Why? was not asked.

CHAPTER TWO

1920–1929: MAKING HISTORY HUMAN

Far fewer historical films were made in the 1920s; the films, however, were generally much longer. Centralization of production in a few locales pretty well ended the local film; the lengthening of films to at least five reels ended the short actualities and battle films; the beginning of a studio system and the appearance of stars changed screenplays, many of which became tailor-made vehicles. Some of the freewheeling openness of the first decade was lost to ideas of what made a successful picture and to commercial genre.[1]

Other changes visible after 1920 seem to have had causes in the culture itself. George Washington and Nathan Hale disappeared from titles, as did the American flag. The former abundance of Civil War films was not repeated. In part, this change may have been a result of the films' greater length; the moving portrait and the reproduction of historical painting became elements in something more complex. In part, increased cost was probably a factor. Certainly, the number of films about the Founding Fathers dwindled, and historical films (three or four a year) as a percentage of the total (854 in 1921)[2] were minuscule. The earlier thrust toward "actual reproduction" and authentic location gave way to a more self-aware, sometimes more thoughtful (often more cynical) goal of making story films with "accurate" historical environments. "History made human," the boast of *The Beautiful Mrs. Reynolds*, became a common goal (although it was hardly the goal of the so-called New History, then strengthening among historians).[3] The past was still reverenced, but increasingly as background rather than as foreground.

A number of major films dealt with events of the eighteenth century, but none earlier. In order of their historical chronology, *Winners of the Wilderness* (1926), is first. Directed by W. S. Van Dyke, it was a featherweight film in the Rafael Sabatini tradition, although it tried to put on historical poundage by including George Washington, General Braddock, Pontiac, Vaudreuil, and Dinwiddie of Virginia. Tim McCoy was an unabashed, if unsuccessful, Douglas Fairbanks imitator; a young Joan Crawford was a properly pretty and helpless heroine.

Winners of the Wilderness is concerned with that event we commonly call "Braddock's Defeat," the first of the stunning British reversals suffered in the early years of the French and Indian War, when British regulars were routed by Indians and French-led provincials in "that part of the Western wilderness which is now a suburb of Pittsburgh." [4]

Winners of the Wilderness turned the historical event into the context for an erotic romance; mostly for reasons of narrative momentum, it destroyed distance (i.e., Quebec to Virginia, Virginia to Fort Duquesne/Pittsburgh) and, by doing so, distorted the real complexities of Braddock's venture. McCoy plays an Anglo-Irish colonel, whom we first see in a mask and fringed buckskins on a balcony outside Governor Vaudreuil's chambers at Quebec. (Why is he masked? He's a spy.) He bursts in with drawn pistols, steals the Pontiac treaty, races up the stairs, bursts into Crawford's boudoir, exchanges verbal foreplay with her and vaults off into the night, a smile on his lips and a song in his heart. Her maid cries, courtesy of a title," Oh, Mistress, what manners—what daring, what wit—WHAT LEGS!"

Thus, despite its being an action movie, *Winners of the Wilderness* screams to have sound. Exchange after exchange is verbal badminton, fencing. The visual experience is constantly interupted by the need to read. As a result, this is a silent film only in its lack of sound; its dependence on language rather than on pantomime or symbolism or creative cinematography is complete.

The colonel races to Alexandria, Virginia. "How are you, George Washington?" he says to a tall fellow with a false nose; almost immediately, Braddock—fat and too old—cries, "We will move on Duquesne tomorrow." Duquesne seems to be just down the street. Most of what remains is the marching, shooting, and fleeing that was Braddock's Defeat—a replay of the 1909 *George Washington Under the British Flag*. Braddock is jolly but arrogant, dismissive of Washington's warnings with what a title assures us are "Braddock's own words." McCoy's colonel (now apparently commanding a regiment, an odd duty for a spy) warns that "this fellow Washington has the makings of a great soldier." No use; on and on goes Braddock with his regulars, the drums pounding (silently) away.

Native Americans (not rubberheads) dance and then hide along the line of march; when they open fire, the British fall and mill about. So terrible is the carnage that a buckskin-clad French-Canadian cries, "We Canadians came to fight—but this is a massacre!" and throws down his musket; so do all his buckskin-clad buddies, and they walk away. No matter; the villain (Roy D'Arcy), who sports a historically incorrect, thin mustache and thinner legs, emphasized by an inauthentically broad coat, sneers, twiddles with his mustache, and pokes at a British corpse with his sword. The British are routed; McCoy is captured; he meets Crawford again inside Duquesne and says, "Duquesne is still French, but God has spared me to see you once more." They exchange neoromantic blather in the grand manner—Sidney Carton meets Tosca—and he goes off to die but is freed by Pontiac (an old enemy who owes him a life), and there is a long take of the colonel and Pontiac shaking hands inside a tepee, their huge shadows cast on the walls.

Then there is a chase, the villain is overcome, and the colonel and the woman ride to safety and are married in Alexandria, with Dinwiddie saying, "She is French, you are British—what will the children be?" The colonel replies, prompted by a whisper from Washington, "They will be—AMERICANS!"

Clearly, it was difficult, only eight years after the armistice, to make either France or England an enemy. Yet the barely concealed subject here is the emergence of America at the expense of France and England. French enmity is mitigated by making most of the attackers Indians, although the prolonged handshake between the hero and Pontiac, and its larger-than-life visualization, suggest ambivalence. Too, the French villain looks and acts differently from the other French. The British are stolid and uncreative; as seen in other films, they wear overdecorated, stiff uniforms and they insist on marching in columns, with drums. Canadians are also exempt from enmity, for they disdain taking part in the villain's "massacre," and they wear buckskins like American frontiersmen.

The final lines (the offspring of England and France will be America) tell us what the film is finally about, the nature of Americans. We will be derived from Europe but new, of the frontier, woodswise, able to understand Indian honor. Europe, by contrast, will be no match—France foppish and self-centered, Britain inflexible—and will not deserve to claim the great wilderness of the West.

This flattering idea could also be applied to the American Revolution, the subject of two films, Griffith's *America* and a Marion Davies vehicle, *Janice Meredith* (both 1924). The Griffith film is the more challenging, the Davies the more engaging; the Griffith is contentious, extravagant, sometimes outrageous; the Davies is disingenuous, intermittently handsome, frivolous.

It would be pleasant to say that *America* is a masterpiece, but it is not. As so often with his women, Griffith here has an ingenue (Carol Dempster) who is a simpering idiot, which appears to be Griffith's notion of any young woman who isn't on the streets. Perhaps certain actors (the Gishes) could save him from himself; none is present here except the heroic juvenile, Neil Hamilton, who is handsome and workmanlike as Nathan Holden, "a noted express rider of the day."

America suffers from a mangling of historical framework of fact and a hackneyed story about a poor young man who loves a wealthy girl against her father's wishes. Most of the mangling takes place in the second half of the film, when the action (as in the 1917 *Spirit of 76*) moves to the Mohawk Valley, which is tormented, again, by Walter Butler (Lionel Barrymore). Griffith conceived him as middle-aged, power-mad, sybaritic, his real goal a wilderness empire. In thus shifting the villain's role from the British to an American-born Loyalist, Griffith may have been trying to avoid the fate of *The Spirit of 76*. The result, however, was ludicrous, both as film and as history; and it is bad history, as well, because of its insistence that history be melodrama, with villains and heroes.

America begins well enough, with interesting scenes in New England and Virginia, but with too much of the local-color cuteness that had marked the theater of Griffith's youth. In 1775, Nancy Montague (Dempster) is "of high degree" and the daughter of a Virginia Loyalist described as "a close confidant of the King." When Nathan arrives with despatches, she falls in love with him. A scene in London, however, shows George III as "the absolute and only ruling power" of Britain, a kind of Anglo Ivan the Terrible. "If [peaceful pressure] fails," he says in a title, "—the bayonet!"

There is a nice juxtaposition of parallel scenes, e.g., the House of Burgesses and the Iroquois Council, but the history is wrong and, in the Iroquois scenes, the visual signs are, as well: Walter Butler wears a uniform like a Ruritanian doorman's, and the Iroquois give him a beaded belt that looks as if it had been made in Taiwan. Then, "Later, at his hunting lodge," he is entertained by a dancing floozy in a buckskin bikini, and he "madly dreams" of an empire.

This degradation of visual signs is actually a result of Griffith's much greater attention to costume than in *Leather Stocking*, perhaps enhanced by a bigger budget; the more detailed costumes go beyond the simple signs of coat, breeches, and tricorn, but the greater detail shows up such anomalies as Butler's uniform. So, too, with Griffith's imagery of corruption (the belle in the bikini), which is more Elinor Glyn than eighteenth century—a sign that is itself an anachronism. Griffith appears, as well, to have conflated Walter Butler with both his father and Sir William Johnson, who had a "pleasure house" on the Sacandaga, although at his death what was found there was fishing tackle, not exotic dancers.

Butler, at any rate, is off to Boston to offer the British "thousands of savage warriors." (In actuality, the Mohawks were able to field a few hundred.) He is accompanied by two "chiefs" who look like used-up sparring partners for Jess Willard; later, when Joseph Brant comes on the scene, he is still older and more used-up looking, dressed in a rig that is based on a portrait of the real Brant but that makes him look like a Brazilian in a Drury Lane opera. Griffith's Brant is old and fat; the real Brant was in his thirties in 1775, fit, and Europeanized. Butler's madly glittering eyes fasten on Nancy, and he leers. If he had a mustache, he'd twirl it.

Paul Revere's ride and Lexington are duly reenacted, with Nathan and Nancy's foppish brother both involved. Again, as in *Paul Revere*, the militia are shown as spontaneous and undisciplined, mustering like the insurance-ad Minuteman in shirtsleeves and waistcoats. There is no hint that most were veterans of the French and Indian War and were drilled in line battle. Instead, the Americans are meant to be compared visually with the stuffed-shirt British—improvisation against rigidity, civilian clothes against military, the musket against the bayonet.

After Nancy's brother finds his manhood by joining the rebels and getting killed at Bunker Hill, still wearing his white wig, Griffith provides a tableau of the signing of the Declaration of Independence, and the film gets down to the machinations of Butler in the Mohawk Valley. The shift is marked by the introduction of a new, and invented, character, "Butler's infamous aide, Captain Hare" (Louis Wolheim). Wolheim had played the title role in Eugene O'Neill's *Hairy Ape* in New York in 1922. His ugliness is used here to expand Butler's evil, to make it more savage than the savage. Wolheim/Hare is Barrymore/Butler's moral self unmasked, his decayed portrait, and a brilliant touch by Griffith.

Butler has meanwhile got Nancy's father's permission to marry her. Stalwart Nathan is down at Valley Forge in the army (scenes out of the Brandywine School—snow, bare feet), where he has joined Morgan's riflemen. (But they were a Southern unit, one would object. No matter.) Off Nathan and his company go to "patrol" the Mohawk Valley; Washington says, "The North Country must be rid of Walter Butler!" (The real Washington sent General Sullivan and five thousand men in 1779, not to rid the Valley of Butler but to neutralize the Iroquois.)

Butler and Hare go from bad to worse to monstrous. Hare, now dressed as an "Indian," tortures prisoners. He and Butler raid local Loyalists, killing the Montagues' host. Butler, his good manners gone all to hell, dines in his shirtsleeves and orders Nancy brought to him. Like any good Griffith heroine, she faints. Butler carries her off to what should be a fate worse than death but is stopped by Brant—the good savage restrains the unleashed beast in the white man. Her father sees the error of siding with George III—not an entirely logical leap.

In a final confrontation, Butler's men attack "Fort Sacrifice," while Nathan and his riflemen ride to the rescue. (Where do riflemen get horses? Are they dragoons? What army is this?) In the fort, women cower and snivel. Butler, "maddened," is killed by his own men; Nathan and Nancy are united; and everybody fights the Battle of Yorktown.

As history, *America* is beyond criticism: it is a comic strip. It is inaccurate in its framework of fact, sometimes deliberately so; it pastiches history according to Longfellow (Revere's Ride, Lexington, Bunker Hill) with wildly coincidental fiction (Nancy turns up wherever Butler and Nathan are); it asserts a moral difference—high-minded rebels, vicious Loyalists—where none existed.

As film, *America* is often handsome. It has Griffith's touch with passing moments, the faces and bodies in hurrying crowds. It uses juxtaposition and parallel action well. Yet, because of its reliance on the clichés of melodrama, it is without subtlety, without intelligence, combining the worst aspects of the pageant and the soap opera. Nobody who has seen it will soon forget Barrymore's performance (and he does seem to be having fun), but most of the acting is unconvincing. So is the art direction, in which Griffith must have had a large hand: military uniforms, Native American material culture, and period behavior (e.g., movement) are simply wrong. It may be that the project was so large it got away from the master. More likely, reproduction of material culture and framework of fact were subsumed in the demands of moral melodrama: the purpose was not "actual reproduction," but moral assertion about American superiority, which could adapt history according to Longfellow to itself.

America is several quantum leaps beyond *Leather Stocking* as a piece of film-making. The mediation through film is infinitely better, but the idea of history is not. Nor, I think, is the use of historically meaningful signs. Hawkeye's fringe and Butler's gaudiness are pretty much of a piece. History for Griffith was not an idea or a set of questions; it was a moral environment, a setting for melodrama.

IF *America* is unsatisfactory, *Janice Meredith* is woeful. The effort of using the American Revolution as a vehicle for a female star was too much for all concerned, except perhaps the star herself. The action was, of course, a love story, again one across class lines, but Marion Davies's democratic charm seems wrong for the daughter of a New Jersey nabob. The hoydenish quality that usually worked so well for her—sexy self-mockery, pratfalls, an implied wink that showed she understood perfectly well what men were after—seems out of place, and it is only well into the film, when she is riding, running, falling down, and playing tricks on the British that her real skills come into their own.

The extravagant falsity of the plot may be taken as a sign that history is only a pretext: a British lord, down on his luck, has sold himself as an indentured servant and winds up in Davies's father's household—and is, of course, the most attractive man around. She is pro-Independence, however. When she overhears British plans to march on Lexington and Concord, off she rushes to warn the "Revolutionists," and His Lordship, already in love with her, changes his politics.

Historical accuracy of costume disappears in a smother of overdone fashion (by Gretl Urban). The signs have been elaborated to signify class, the visual idea of "eighteenth century" now a Central European one more appropriate to Mozart's Vienna than to America. Well-to-do men wear absurd wigs and inches of lace at throat and cuff; women drip lace down arms and bodices. On the other hand, the bondservant-milord first appears in an unbuttoned waistcoat, without neckcloth or hat, and a broad leather belt that looks piratical—all wrong; but it is significant that he is an aristocrat incognito. In this expensive film, clothing is "authentic" only insofar as it communicates period; beyond that, it is too upper-class and European. Nor are the settings any more careful: Paul Revere has a shop, but it looks like Lum and Abner's Jot-Em-Down store; it is too *lower*-class. Visual signs here widen class differences ahistorically, perhaps because the film wishes to proclaim the wealth of its backer

(William Randolph Hearst) and even, perhaps, the aristocracy of wealth in the America of the 1920s.

Janice Meredith is unabashed about bringing on historical figures (Revere, Washington, Cornwallis, Howe) and salting them into its trumped-up story. So too, with history bits: Paul Revere's ride gets major treatment, with a re-use of Longfellow to title some sequences. The British march toward Lexington with fixed bayonets, recalling *America's* George III. British fancy dress contrasts with American working-class plainness, the Americans' unbuttoned coats and waistcoats further emphasizing their vulnerability to the bayonets, which signal ruthlessness, even inhumanity.

The Americans' plebeian vulnerability becomes heroic immortality: after they are fired upon at Lexington, two ghostly drummers and a fifer rise from the dead and lead the living to victory, just like the painting and the 1905 *Spirit of 76*. And, although "we shall never know who fired first at Lexington, or why,"[5] it is clearly a British officer who gives the command to fire.

Hardly does Davies get back to New Jersey before George Washington drops by. Like many of the men in this film, he is unaccountably old. These greybeards set off Davies's youthfulness, to be sure, but much of *Janice Meredith* looks like a costume party in a nursing home. The aristocrat-bondservant announces that he is an ex-colonel of the British Army and wants to join Washington. Then Lord Howe, the British general, drops by. Then it is Christmas and Davies has made it to Trenton, where W. C. Fields as a Hessian sergeant does a bit with a hat. After much to-ing and fro-ing about spying and being caught and courtmartialed, Davies rides, trudges, and crawls through the snow to give Washington a paper that apparently tells him that attacking Trenton would be a swell idea. He does, in a snow scene of great spectacle that manages to recall both Valley Forge and Gates's dragging of the cannon to Boston. The crossing of the Delaware is stunning, a careful re-staging of the Leutze painting. The bad Brits and Hessians are about to put Davies's milord-bondservant-lover in front of a firing squad (indoors, yet—hard times for the wainscoting) when a cannon shot collapses the roof and he is saved.

"Thrice" the "tides of war" sweep over plucky Davies's house, "levelling its once proud glory," leaving it looking like Tara after the Yankees left. As Davies puts it in authentic eighteenth-century-speak, "Dad's lost everything." She almost loses everything herself; a particularly distasteful British nobleman pursues her with a zeal no American would be dastard enough to show.

History sweeps on and on—Ben Franklin at the French court; Mrs. Loring as a twenties vamp and former lover of the bondservant-milord-ex-colonel-spy-hero; the siege of Yorktown; and, at last, Mount Vernon. Her father's wealth is restored. Washington proposes a toast to Nancy's health. He couldn't have won the war without her, one gathers.

This delirium would be laughable had it not been so prestigiously presented. Deems Taylor composed the music for the New York opening. Joseph

Urban designed the often handsome settings. The production values screamed expense. Its howlers and contradictions are not mere accidents: where Griffith was trying to show history as moral melodrama, Hearst and his collaborators were trying to show history as economic moral comedy: more money is better than less. It is not a film concerned with equality. Despite sharing with *America* a romantic plot about lovers from what seem like different classes, *Janice Meredith* actually concerns two lovers from the same class. It has reverence for the past as the source of liberty, but it is a very different idea of liberty and who deserves it.

Davies's talents also illuminated *Little Old New York* (1923), a romance based on a play of the same name (and also the source of a remake in 1939). *Little Old New York* takes place in the early years of the nineteenth century and is as heavy with famous names as *Janice Meredith* is with history bits. Unlike the cameos in that film, however, these are not people important to the story, but men—they are always men—whose names (e.g., Vanderbilt, Astor, Irving) lend class. There is a plot about a will with an odd clause that requires that Davies, an Irish peasant, impersonate her own brother; there is a disappointed heir whose money troubles are so great that he has to settle for a town house and five hundred dollars a month (at a time when Jane Austen was writing, in *Sense and Sensibility*, that a house and two hundred and fifty pounds a year were adequate); there is a bet on a prize fight to raise money for Fulton's steamboat; there is Davies's love for a man who thinks she's a boy. It is a complex business; characters often drop out and must be dredged up from memory much later.

Much of the film's appeal is nostalgic, always about the quaint days of the little city on the Hudson. Some of the appeal is sexual: after Davies stops the prize fight with a false fire alarm, "The Hoboken Terror" (Louis Wolheim again) catches her, and, believing her a boy, ties her to a post and whips her in front of an all-male mob. Half-stripped, she cries, "I'm a girl!" and Wolheim leers. Some of the appeal is comic—not merely Davies's problems of masquerading as a boy (a device as old, at least, as Aristophanes) but also the funny-Italian antics of the first Delmonico, plus a lot of Irish jokes. And, of course, there is the patriotic appeal of Fulton and the *Clermont*.

Little Old New York at least looks like better history than *Janice Meredith* because the costumes are not so absurdly wrong. The settings, again by Joseph Urban, are wonderful, very stagey, one of the waterfront looking as if it had been lifted whole from the stage production. Despite this visual appeal, however, *Little Old New York* uses history as mere enabling environment, without concern for either framework of fact or meaning, and it is at last only an anachronistic romance in authentic clothing. The ultimate effect of both movies is to suggest that history happened so as to provide a vehicle for Marion Davies.

CIVIL WAR FILMS, so abundant before 1915, fell in the 1920s to even lower numbers than the eighteenth-century films. Only one was of real consequence,

The General (1927). It is one of the great comedies of silent, and indeed of all film. It is always worth watching, endlessly rewarding for the details it allows us to see of Buster Keaton's art. However, comedy does not suit history very well unless history itself is the object of the comedy. Such is not the case with *The General*, whose comic goals are universals—the intransigeance of objects, the workings of coincidence, the silliness of human beings, the follies of vanity and romantic dreaming. Nonetheless, its framework of fact is more or less intact— the same Andrews raid that also inspired *The Railroad Raiders of 62*. One aspect of *The General*, its Southern sympathy, should be noted. It is not pro-South, certainly not proslavery, but, as a matter of historical attitude—of the 1920s, not the 1860s—its tilt may be significant.

ALTHOUGH THE NUMBERS of films about the Revolutionary and Civil wars declined in the 1920s, those about the Indian Wars and the West did not. At least three major films were set in the Indian Wars: *Custer's Last Fight* (1925), *General Custer at the Little Big Horn* (1926), *Sitting Bull at the Spirit Lake Massacre* (1927). A fourth dealt with the building of the transcontinental railroad (*The Iron Horse*, 1924), a fifth, the struggle for Texas (*Davy Crockett at the Fall of the Alamo*, 1926). A sixth, William S. Hart's *Wild Bill Hickok* (1923) covered familiar Western territory and included famous figures of the Civil and Indian Wars. These may be clustered as Westerns, although a close look suggests that the caste marks of the Western are not clear in all of them.

    Davy Crockett at the Fall of the Alamo paraded fiction around real events and expected its audience to be interested in the fiction because the event had stature. It failed in good part because it was cheesily made, its American outdoors looking suspiciously like the weeds beyond somebody's back yard. The acting was dreadful, the story mostly about getting to Texas, not about fighting at the Alamo. Yet the film is interesting on two points: the use of the buckskin myth and the inclusion of slavery.

    When we first see him, Davy Crockett is not the conventional figure in buckskins and coonskin cap. Rather, he is a just-defeated politican in top hat and frock coat. However, when he decides to go to Texas (because "she is going to need all the fighting men she can get"), he changes into buckskins and coonskin hat. There is no suggestion that the coonskin hat was a political symbol or that Crockett and his party used it the way Nixon used the Republican cloth coat.

    Davy heads for Bexar, picking up along the way an odd lot of pals, gamblers, and helpless females, including one with an aged black slave. Mose runs into the Crockett party and recognizes power when he meets it: "I reckon I's your property now, Marse Davy." Later, when one of the film's several villains tries to make off with one of its several helpless women, he shouts at Mose, "Out of my way, nigger!" This leads to Davy's fighting with, shooting, or stabbing every bad man in the film before he rides off to the Alamo (the section of the film at the Alamo is now apparently lost).

A triumph of the unexamined, *Davy Crockett at the Fall of the Alamo* accepts without question both slavery and the idea of freedom symbolized by buckskin, the coonskin hat, and the Alamo. As embodied by this Crockett, the buckskin symbolizes courage, leadership, fidelity to friends, and the honoring and defense of women (good women, at any rate; a woman who has become pregnant by one of the villains has the good manners to die). It can be assumed that the missing footage showing the battle at the Alamo takes these virtues to their idealistic conclusion in death. It is unclear how it dealt with slavery.

Wild Bill Hickok (1923) starred William S. Hart and was a mixture of Hart's selective Western authenticity and an invented story. It included Bat Masterson, Calamity Jane, Lincoln, Sheridan, and Custer, but the framework of fact was shaky, most of all the amount of gunplay, "the high spots of Hickok's gunfighting career [having] been presented within 77 minutes. . . ."[6] Hart at least used a percussion (noncartridge) revolver, like Hickok, but deadeye shooting and ubiquitous handguns made this a fictional West.

Custer's Last Fight has a familiar look to it, and no wonder; it is an expansion and reissue of the 1912 film of the same title "under the Personal Supervision of Thomas H. Ince." Mostly, what have been expanded are the titles, now even more anti-Native American. The film opens with a portrait of Custer, then goes to American flags behind the credits, and ends with the flag again. By contrast, the very first title establishes the Sioux and Cheyenne as villains who "opposed the advance of the white man and civilization." The Sioux are filled "with pride and insolence" because the United States "gave them a vast territory," presumably the reservations they temporarily held in place of the truly vast territory they had once roamed. Still, a title assures us, "the Westward flow of civilization cannot be dammed. . . ." Rain-in-the-Face now thinks, "This is a good opportunity—two unsuspecting civilians." After he kills his victims, he is seen "boasting of the slaughter" at the agency's post, in footage from 1912 that also placed him there but without the slanted title. Apparently new footage then enlarges the size of the unit sent under Custer to arrest Rain-in-the-Face, now "a difficult and dangerous piece of work"; Rain-in-the-Face, escaping after his arrest, joins "hostile Indians, sworn foes of the United States."

Sitting Bull is "cowardly, but crafty and capable," rather than "the brainiest of the Sioux"; his "following is constantly increased by ambitious bucks, outlaws and disaffected braves" engaged in "robbing and murdering the defenseless. . . ." This language is juxtaposed with titles describing the encroaching whites as "settlers and adventurers . . . lured by the gold disovered in the Black Hills. . . ." with new footage of settlers fleeing a cabin, and a stampeding wagon train. A 1912 title about starvation among the Sioux has been scrapped. Instead, the Sioux are "better armed than the soldiers through unscrupulous traders." Interpolated footage reinforces the idea of the white soldiers' sacrifice: soldiers and women embrace and the woman suffer. A new title introduces a shot of Mrs. Custer, returning to the fort "with the paymaster" from bidding Custer good-bye; that good-bye seems to use a different actor for Custer from the 1912 footage.

New titles say that the Indians "lurk" along the Big Horn, and Gall's force is a "horde." Others have Rain-in-the-Face eating the heart of an enemy and attacking the soldiers with the Unkpapa Sioux. Footage of the mutilation and stripping of the white bodies by "the squaws and youths" who "swarm on the field" is followed by a sequence in which Custer's body is left untouched as "befitting a great and brave chief." A subsequent dance ("all night") appears to use unrelated ethnographic footage, the dancers wearing dance bustles.

Sitting Bull is "relentlessly pursued by the forces of General Crook, whose Chief Scout is Buffalo Bill." A completely bogus "Ghost Dance" shows women dancing around a figure in a white hood, with human skulls much in evidence.

The film ends with a rerun of the final sequence of Custer's battle and death, and the shot of the American flag.

The 1925 *Custer's Last Fight* represents a deliberate effort to redefine a historical film through titling and editing. The Indians are now a "horde" of "bucks" and "braves" who "lurk"; the word "hostile" is used several times; the Indians are "sworn" to oppose, not the loss of their land, but the United States. Custer and the whites, on the other hand, represent "civilization," and, through association with the flag, America. In sum, the film of 1912 has become an even more deliberate vehicle for identifying America and Americans with expansion, and Native Americans with anti-American nonhumanness. Custer has been made a culture hero. Native American power has been made the result of aberrant white action (i.e., "unscrupulous traders" have provided guns). Thus, the thirteen years between 1912 and 1925, rather than moving Ince from the beer-poster level of the first film, have moved him the other way. Native Americans, if anything, were even more powerless in 1925 than in 1912, so seem a poor target, unless this is mere triumphalism. More likely, it is a response to 1920s jingoism—the Red Scare, anti-immigration legislation, Wilson's failed internationalism.

General Custer at the Little Big Horn was hardly an improvement. It was a Custer film that lacked Ince's visual genius and wanted merely to be a Western. It featured "Roy Stewart and an All Star Cast," and if I say that Stewart did not play Custer, you will understand what sort of film it was. It is really a love triangle (Stewart, a young woman, and a cavalry officer, Captain Page), with Custer's last days as its environment.

Stewart was a cowboy star with the manner of a standup comedian telling Irish jokes. He played "Lem Hawks, Soldier of Fortune, official scout attached to Custer's staff," an overweight dude in a fringed shirt, a silk kerchief, and fringed and beaded gauntlets. The costume is that of a genre already removed from reality and history, the slicked-up or tight-pants Western, where the star's costume never wrinkles and his gun never runs out of bullets—a long jump from the proto-Western Dalton and James films.

The action builds toward the Little Big Horn, with the love triangle muted so that the captain can die in Hawks's arms during the battle. Nothing so embarrassing as death can happen to a tight-pants cowboy with fringed gauntlets, however, so Hawks rides away for help, firing his thousand-shooter in all directions. Meanwhile, the Indians have become the victims of one-sided titling and editing. Whenever a title mentions them, a beating tom-tom is shown. "Retreat was impossible. On every hand appeared the naked savage." All the Indians on view are wearing clothes.

Hawks, nonetheless, gets through this thicket of nudity, only to return too late to help Custer but in time to clinch with Betty and his horse. Custer's body lies by the American flag; nobody has been stripped or mutilated. "And so closed an event unparallelled in the history of Indian warfare. Sitting Bull escaped but was captured and confined on a reservation until his death."

The misstatements about Sitting Bull clinch the shift from near sympathy to condemnation—as if, having killed Custer as he clutched the flag, the Indians proved themselves the immoral savages the tom-tom and the titles made them seem. The heroic survivor—and in this kind of film the moral center—is the tight-pants cowboy, who, by implication, is Custer reinvented: Indian fighter, scout, American.

The miserable hamlet of Spirit Lake, Iowa, was attacked in 1857 by Indians; several whites were killed. The Indian leader was named Inkpaduta; Sitting Bull, a Dakota Sioux, was hundreds of miles away. Nonetheless, *Sitting Bull at the Spirit Lake Massacre* is a "thrilling epic of frontier days" that places him there, perhaps because "[no Indian name] of the past half century struck more terror to the heart of whites than Sitting Bull."

Here, far from his real home and people, Sitting Bull is an unimpressive Native American who walks rather like a duck. (All the Indians in this film walk; the whites ride horses.) He depends for evil inspiration on a local "white witch," who has two bad sons, one of whom wears thigh-high boots like Buffalo Bill's.

Opposed to this evil group are a truly sappy hero, tricked out in head-to-toe buckskins, a tiny mustache, and yards of teeth, and the townsmen. The hero's girl winds up a prisoner of the white witch and her sons. The good guys ride. Conventions of the Western movie seem to be well established here: all the men pack six-guns; their horses are all saddled and ready to go; nobody seems to have a job or any commitment that might distract him. It is like *Pastor Fido* with horses and guns.

Eventually, the Indians start to dance, and the hero says, "It's the Ghost Dance—that means trouble!" (Boy, does it! The Ghost Dance movement didn't start for another couple of decades.) The cavalry ride in; the girlfriend is saved from a fate worse than death; and the two bad sons of the white witch suffer "the vengeance of the squaws," which is so awful one can't make it out.

Clearly, this is a kids' movie, but, while this identification explains the film it does not justify it. *Sitting Bull at the Spirit Lake Massacre* takes two historically valid entities, Sitting Bull and Spirit Lake, and mashes them together like two wrecked trains, then drapes over them a romance plot as trivial as the one in *General Custer at the Little Big Horn.* A new detail is piled on, the fast-firing gun; although the action takes place in 1859, all the guns in the film, both handguns and long guns, use anachronistic cartridges.* I do not want to belabor this matter (yet), but the anacrhonistic use of guns has the potential to become a potent sign, like fringed buckskin.

One implication of this anachronism is that the whites have technological superiority over the Native Americans, many of whom brandish clubs and bows. Indeed, so enormous does the white superiority appear that it might be seen as unjust, but nothing else in the film allows that conclusion; rather, the superiority is itself seen as a triumph. The Native Americans, in reaction to it, turn to witchcraft and the Ghost Dance. The cartridge gun thus takes on a theological brightness: it is God's weapon.

JOHN FORD, ALTHOUGH younger than Griffith, shared with him the objectivist idea of realism practiced at the turn of the century and best exemplified in the American theater by David Belasco. Less theoretical and certainly less consistent than the realism of European avant-gardists (e.g., André Antoine), it nonetheless believed that if the surface of observable reality was correctly reproduced, truth would follow. Belasco in fact proved that the reverse could be true—that large areas of surface could be reproduced merely as a style to support the production of melodrama or romance whose plot was at base improbable.

When Ford made *The Iron Horse* in 1924, he was partly in the grip of such realism, partly in the grip as well of its stage and film uses; the result was that many of his natural exteriors were believable and beautiful, but many of his interiors were unconvincing stage sets. The dichotomy symbolized Ford's idea of character: the minutiae of everyday behavior were captured, but large matters of motive, decision, and act were unbelievable because based, not on life, but on conventions of stage melodrama. As well, like Griffith, Ford at this time seems to have accepted the already dated "local color" style of realistic acting, a matter of quirks and cutenesses as substitutes (mostly visual) for language, idea, and decision. Thus, *The Iron Horse* is an early Ford film with some great qualities and some serious flaws. Its historical claim, however—"Accurate and faithful in every particular of fact and atmosphere"— is moonshine.

---

* The first cartridge Colt appeared in 1873 and the first cartridge Winchester in 1866. Some revolvers were converted to cartridges in the 1860s, and there were percussion—non-cartridge—revolvers as early as the 1830s.

The first transcontinental railroad would seem event enough for most historians—technological achievement, milestone of expansion, high adventure. *The Iron Horse*, however, seems to need a legitimacy that could be conferred only by the participation of Abraham Lincoln. The film opens with a title citing Lincoln's "vision and resolution" to weld "with blood and with iron the East and the West," and it then flashes back to Lincoln's Springfield days and to a surveyor "dreaming of rails that'll reclaim that wilderness out there clean to California." A young Lincoln watches as the surveyor and his child head west, "impelled by the strong urge of progress." There is some sentimental slush about the boy's parting from his little-girl playmate, and then a beautiful shot of Lincoln watching the man and the boy ride away in the snow. Lincoln "sees the momentum of a great nation pushing westward."

This radically early point of attack now seems excessive, but it did give play to Ford's sentimental streak. Here, he is concerned with two events in the life of the little boy, although it is not clear in the opening sequence that it is the boy, not the father or Lincoln, who is the focus: first, the parting from the little girl, which looks forward toward their reunion, with the hidden reliance on coincidence that such a development implies; and, second, the loss of his father. When father and son are on the trail west, Indians, led by a white man disguised as an Indian, attack, and the disguised white man kills the father. The killer is missing several fingers on one hand, a clue that can be called up later if, again, coincidence cooperates.

"Years pass." Until 1862, in fact. Several long titles tell us of the preparation for building the railroad, of crews starting from east and west. Lincoln is seen (from the back) receiving people in a columned room; a young woman, pretty but simpering (played by Madge Bellamy, a species of Griffith handclasper, but without the waifishness) introduces herself as Miriam, the little girl we saw in Springfield. "And where is little Davy?" Lincoln asks, "a boy worth waiting for." Alas, Davy is forgotten; the simperer is engaged to a twit with a pencil mustache, and old enough to be her father, to boot.

"The far-seeing wisdom of the great rail-splitter President is the beginning of the Empire of the West." More titles plod by: 1864, and Chinese labor is brought in to build the western portion; 1865, and crews on the eastern end are made up of "chiefly ex-soldiers of North and South working peacefully side by side." A rather Soviet-looking sequence shows men pounding spikes in unison as they sing. When Indians ride by, the workmen snatch up guns and blaze away, then return to work: the former enemies are armed against a common foe, recalling the even-handedness of the early Civil War films.

After a beautiful establishing shot of North Platte, Nebraska, in winter, we are introduced to a pair of comic Irish workmen and "a young man named Cody, a crack shot . . . nicknamed 'Buffalo Bill.'" Scenes of railroad-building life follow; Cody leads a buffalo hunt. Hostile Native Americans try to stop a locomotive by stretching a rope across the track; they fall down when the rope snaps, and we are supposed to laugh. Other Native Americans on horses surround a burning train, a piece of splendid Ford spectacle.

At this point, the film turns from the epic to the individual and begins to resuscitate the fictional plot, moving the historical one to the background. The two remain linked, to be sure: the pretty simperer's fiancé is the civil engineer who must find a pass through the Black Hills for the railroad. The Indians burn a payroll train and the crews rebel, but the simperer sends them back to work with a gung-ho speech; Leroux, a big man who keeps hiding one hand (aha!) is a rich landowner who doesn't want the railroad to succeed. A rough, not always consistent division between interior and exterior scenes parallels the division between fiction and history: romance and greed indoors, progress and obstacles outdoors.Most of the interiors are shot at right angles to a back wall, often with a dividing line up the center (e.g., a stove and its vertical pipe), even a saloon ruled by a Judge Bean knockoff and the private car of the simperer and her father.

A newly arrived Pony Express rider (in 1865?) proves to be the very Davy about whom Lincoln asked (played now by George O'Brien), and not only does he now find his long-lost love, but he also just happens to know how to find the pass through the Black Hills. Davy, despite years with the mountain men, is dressed like a cowboy star in a fringed shirt and gauntlets, and he carries a six-shooter but no powder flask or bullet bag, suggesting that he is the possessor of one of the earliest cartridge conversions. Gun anachronisms abound, in fact: although Winchester's Henry model appeared only in 1866, Winchesters are everywhere in the film's 1865.

The Iron Horse now lurches forward on several tracks simultaneously. A rather mysterious herd of cattle keeps moving through breathtaking scenery; Davy is finding the pass and being done in by the wealthy landowner, Leroux, who proves to have fingers missing from one hand; he cuts the rope by which Davy is descending into the pass. In one of Ford's most brilliant sequences, the railroad moves its headquarters from North Platte to Cheyenne as hangers-on, gamblers, hookers, and workmen clamber aboard and the old tent-and-shack town comes down. "Hell on Wheels," a saloon on a flat car, barrels along; the new town springs up at Cheyenne; Wild Bill Hickok briefly appears. At the same time, "the Three Musketeers—Sergeant Slattery, Corporal Casey, Private Schultz"—join the work crews, early examples of the lovable, powerfully bonded, sentimentally conceived trios Ford will use in the cavalry films.

The storytelling is ragged as Ford attempts to bring these lines to a common climax; in fact, what he got was one small climax and one much bigger one later, necessitating the rather mindless continuation of one line (the cattle herd) and the dropping and then the renewing of another (Davy and Leroux). Davy, for example, has a badly directed fistfight with Miriam's fiancé that exists to justify Miriam's break from Davy. Davy—former mountain man and Pony Express rider—becomes head of a section gang, for which he has no qualification but which will keep him in the film. By this point, as well, it should have been clear to everybody from Lincoln's ghost to the Three Musketeers that somebody has tried to murder Davy and conceal the whereabouts of the pass, but, a title tells us, "Personal bitterness was put aside." How sabotage and attempted murder are "personal" is unclear.

Now, Ford sounds an ethnic, probably an anti-immigration, note. Crowd scenes and occasional shots have shown "foreign" faces among the workmen, signaled by curly hair and long mustaches, as in *The Black Hand.* Davy tells the Irish crew heads, "With those foreign laborers making trouble, we Americans have to stick together." Although this "trouble" is news to the audience, "foreigners" thus join the Native Americans and the villainous Leroux as the enemies of the railroad, of Lincoln, and of America.

"Meanwhile, the cattle herd nears the end of its long journey," and a handsome shot shows the herd swimming a river.

Leroux incites the Cheyenne against the railroad. Wonderful footage of Native Americans on horseback follow, with wide Western vistas and lines of riders snaking across the landscape and reflecting in rivers. Outdoors again, away from the phony interior sets, Ford is liberated.

Then the Indians attack; one of the Three Musketeers gets an arrow in the back—"My God, Pat! they've got Schultz!"—and utterly unbelievable feats are performed with handguns (galloping riders brought down with one shot at dozens of yards' distance). Many of the soldiers, however, take up the correct weapon for the period, the first breech-loading Springfield.

Davy runs the engine back to town and fills it with troops and civilians, including Buffalo Bill, but the "foreigners" refuse to help. "Yer Saint Columbus found this country—but it's our Saint Patrick who has to make it go," shouts an Irishman. And now the herd of cattle arrives, just in time to fill the town and be used by Wild Bill Hickok to drive the "damned shirkers" aboard the rescue train. The shots of frightened Italians scrambling on flatcars are demeaning.

The subsequent battle ends when the Pawnee scouts "like a sweeping wind" rush to the rescue. Davy has singled out Leroux, who is dressed as an Indian (why?), and they engage in one of the most inadvertently comic fights on film: first Davy's shirt is ripped, then torn off; then Leroux is stripped to the waist. The two men swing wildly, like children; they flail and roll in the dirt.

At last, however, Leroux is killed and Davy identifies him as the man who murdered his father. All would end well, except that Miriam still can't forgive Davy for fighting, so off he goes to join the western leg of the railroad. Both he and Miriam wind up at Promontory Point, however, where they are united as the golden spike is driven (some symbolism!). "The wedding of the rails. . . . The afternoon of May 10, 1869. Note: *The locomotives are the original Jupiter and #116."* Leland Stanford and Thomas C. Durant *(not* the originals, presumably) look on.

The film ends with a bust of Lincoln and a title, "His truth is marching on." We have come full circle, seeing history realized in the process: Lincoln has dreamed, and Lincoln's dream has come true. History, Ford seems to say here, is the big event; it happens because big men will it. Yet, what history contains is mess and opposition—hostile Indians, cowardly Italians, greedy two-fingered self-servers, who are battled by people and forces that promote the great man's will: romantic love, earthy Irish humor, femininity, boyhood sentimentality, manly idealism.

This notion of individual struggle as contained within historical movement is not necessarily wrong, although in story film the individual action (e.g., Davy's opposition to Deroux) has to be made disproportionately large. Ford has tried to solve this problem of overvisible personalization by multiplying subplots, a typically objective-realist solution: send in more examples. He has tried to solve it, as well, through objectivism itself, e.g., using the actual locomotives at Promontory Point.

The Iron Horse also suggests another problem, perhaps a contradiction, in historical film of this period. It is represented by the appearance of Stanford and Durant. Who are these men who are important enough to be named in a title but not important enough to be characters in the film? Why are the Presidential dreamer and the immigrant worker characters, but not the industrial-age businessman? Why can the American historical film of the 1920s show the President who dreamed of spanning the continent and the man who swung the hammer, but not the men who raised the money, fought the competition, lobbied the Congress, and earned the profits? America is a capitalist culture. It was so in 1924. Why were dreaming and hammering "history," while the workings of capitalism were not?

It is worth noting that Ford's version of history here accepts both the signs (buckskin, movie-cowboy costume) and gun errors (deadeye accuracy, anachronistic cartridge weapons) noted in other Westerns, and repeats an identification between "foreigner" and "bad." This identification is specifically Italian in *The Iron Horse* and is "bad" in the same ways that "Indian" is bad in *Sitting Bull at the Spirit Lake Massacre* and those Custer films that wrap Custer in the flag. It appears that Ford is using the West as a stand-in for "America," a place where the furtherance of "more West" (whether through population movement, war, or technology) is by definition good, and anything in opposition—Native Americans, foreigners, witchcraft—is anti-West, anti-American, and perhaps anti-God.

That this equation fails is suggested by the frequent appearance of "bad whites"—unscrupulous traders, the two-fingered Leroux, the witch of *Spirit Lake*. They inspire Native Americans to oppose expansion for what seems to be the same motive—desire for gain—that drives the expansionists. That is, what is bad about bad whites is not motive but act: they help the opponents of "more West." There may be in this quandary a partial explanation of Ford's inclusion of Stanford and Durant as images, not as characters: historical film of the 1920s may have been unable to focus on the place where the motives of the capitalist and the motives of the bad white overlapped.

Another film with Western resonances, now apparently lost, was *The Rough Riders* (1927), one of the few films to deal with the Spanish–American War and to include Teddy Roosevelt. It appears to have been primarily a love story, with the war and the Rough Riders as its environment.[7] Its ten-reel length and its direction by Victor Fleming suggest major treatment; its non-historical characters were a deliberately varied group with names like Happy Joe, Hell's Bells, Bert, and Van (a New Yorker among the Texans). Its ending brought the lovers together at a historical event, as in *The Iron Horse*—not, this time, the driving of a spike but the inauguration of TR.

THE EVENT THAT changed film most radically in the 1920s was, of course, the coming of sound, whose advent corresponded with a temporary lack of historical films (1927–30). Sound had the potential to change not only the way in which films were perceived, but also the amount and kinds of data that films communicated. Robert Rosenstone has pointed out that the amount of "traditional 'data'" in a film is thin compared to that in "a written version," but I think that he means here "data" as first-level (i.e., narrative) content; as he points out elsewhere, the data in film *images* are varied and copious and take pages to describe.[8] It remains to be seen if sound would increase such data or merely add redundancy.

Some films of the 1920s seem to beg for sound because of their profusion of dialogue titles. What they seem to want is the back-and-forth exchange of the stage, a use perhaps more likely to enhance fiction than history. The erasure of printed titles from the enacted sequence would seem also to have a potential for reinforcing the fiction by bringing the viewer farther into it, as well as removing the interruption of another kind of perception, reading, during which the fictional image vanished.

Music was a special case. Music had been used in the pre-film theater in ways we would still recognize: as "signature music," to accompany a character; as leit motiv, to encourage the linking of similar scenes or meanings; and as emotional arousal—all uses redundant with other aspects of the play. Music had also been specially composed or assembled for silent films, for the same purposes. We know, for example, that Deems Taylor composed music for the premiere of *Janice Meredith*; but where else was it played? Did most audiences hear it, or did they hear something cobbled together from a cue sheet, or merely some solo pianist's improvisations? And even if the music was specially composed, what kind of data was it? Was it mere redundancy? Did it add data? Did it comment?

Sound would make sure that all audiences heard the same music. It would also resolve these questions.

CHAPTER THREE

1930–1939: MOVIE MOVIES ——

The total number of historical films in the 1930s rose to more than forty. For the first time, another type joined traditional history (i.e., war, politics, "great men") and Westerns—the musical biography, made possible by sound. As well, films about business appeared. What was memorable about the decade, however, were films now popular in video—large-scale "epics," often in the new Technicolor, with sophisticated scores, big budgets, and compelling stars.

History was still the past, to be sure, but the idea of it expanded to include entrepreneurs, show people, even a few women. New kinds of protagonists also encouraged a focus on what the Marxist critic Georg Lukács called "pathology"—realistic works notable for their digression from norms rather than their heroic embodiment of norms.[1]

A marginal film of 1937 is worth noting first. It is notable because of its subject—the slave trade. *Souls at Sea* was alone in showing that the slave trade was part of America's history; only one other film (*Davy Crockett at the Fall of the Alamo*) showed blacks as white property.* Earlier films in which that fact could have been shown with historical accuracy (e.g., *Janice Meredith, America, The General*) had not done so.

Souls at Sea is a pseudonymous version of an actual maritime law case, but it is anachronistic and inexact. Still, it contains such lines as, "Get the stink of the slave-deck in your nostrils," and "The floor of the ocean is paved with the bones of slaves." Its protagonist (Gary Cooper) is a hater of slaving who wages a one-man war against it—and therein lies the film's weakness, for the idiosyncracy ("pathology") of his crusade mitigates the reality of slavery and slaving. Cooper becomes an agent of Britain, then (c. 1850) the enemy of maritime slaving. His idealism costs him the affection of his best pal (George Raft, in a decidedly atypical role). The film vitiates its points by showing only glimpses of the slave trade itself, nothing of American slavery. Nonetheless, in an industry that often retailed ideas of black menace, white-pillared mansions, and Southern moral parity (*The Birth of a Nation, Gone with the Wind*), *Souls at Sea* offered a very different view.

---

* *Slave Ship* (1937) was a fictional film about the slave trade; it quickly became a love and adventure story from which the reality of slaving slipped like snow from a warm roof.

THE 1931 FILM *The Great Meadow* was mostly fiction imposed on the westward expansion that was one of the causes of the Revolution. Daniel Boone was a minor character, his settlement in Kentucky a major location. Directed erratically by W. S. Van Dyke, it made a lip-service dedication to women— "WOMEN OF THE WILDERNESS, WE SALUTE YOU!"—which it then obscured behind a lot of plot about male adventure and violence. Its Enoch Arden story, examined closely, reveals a female protagonist and a female concern, but these keep disappearing behind wifedom, passivity, and male action. The problems of expansion are reduced to fake folk dialect—"Don't ya go theah! Don't a-go! The Red Injuns'll a-git ya! They'll take yer little girl chillun!" The men, including Boone, wear fur hats and deerskins that sprout fringe from every seam. They shoot Indians with anachronistic guns (trapdoor Springfields with fake frizzens), and the heroine writes home from Kentucky that she is "teaching the women to weave linen and wool," a double howler in that eighteenth-century women knew weaving perfectly well, and neither a sheep nor a flax plant has been shown anywhere in the vicinity.

Nonetheless, *The Great Meadow* is interesting for the way it treats two subjects. One is the continuity of Anglo-European culture, represented by the two books the heroine's father gives her as she heads west, to teach her children to read; Protestantism is attached to this visually (prayer, clasped hands). The other subject is women and their universe. Although women are generally shown as passive and male-centered, they are also shown as sharing a common group life, represented in the film by births. They take over male tasks—plowing, planting—when men are absent and they have "a women's law in this country" that "allows the woman to choose" a man when her husband has stayed away too long. This "law" is an implicit slap in the face of machismo, above all of the love of violence that takes the heroine's husband away from her for two years. It remains only implicit, however; the film lacks the courage of its heroine's convictions and makes a sudden turn to "love" at the last moment. Because of these two subjects, however, *The Great Meadow*, although not a good film, is a useful artifact.

The Last of the Mohicans was reinterpreted twice, first as a serial (1932), then in 1936 as a feature film. The 1932 serial suffered the usual serial distortions, above all a stringing-out of the plot that turned it into a long string of chases. The two white women were being constantly captured, lost, and recaptured by fiendish Hurons, a recurring sexual threat and release. Cheaply made, it had poor material history but the most Cooperesque Natty Bumppo in Harry Carey, despite his anomalous buckskins.

The 1936 version starred a laid-back Randolph Scott as Hawkeye, also in fringed buckskin and fur hat, and Binnie Barnes as Alice, whose scenes with Henry Wilcoxon as a British officer have so much crackle that you want them, not Barnes and Scott, to wind up together: they fence like adults and show real affection—the banter enabled by sound. Scott, on the other hand, sounds so Georgian and seems so unflappable that you suspect him of smoking something other than kinnickinick out there in the woods. Bruce Cabot is Magua, leader of a tribe of rubberheads who seem to have made little progress since Griffith's 1909 version.

Despite its relatively early date in the runup to World War II, this *Last of the Mohicans* seems to be looking out of the corner of its eye at what was happening in Europe. The story is more or less Cooper's, except that this Hawkeye falls in love; however, a political overplot first critiques the British as the class-conscious, overregimented subjects of a German king, and then brings Brits and Americans together in a common cause at the end with Hawkeye's "After all, we're fighting for the same thing."

The Native Americans are seen as both heroic and naturally moral, on the one hand (Uncas and Chingachgook), and evil and unredeemable on the other (Magua). Visually, they are anachronistic—mostly naked, in leather loincloths. The real Mohicans of the 1760s ("Stockbridge Indians") were so Europeanized that they furnished their own company of rangers for the war. However, implications of Native American–white sexual attraction must end in death: Uncas and blonde Cora (Heather Angel) die despite their goodness; Magua must die and dark Alice be saved because Magua's wanting "paleface squaws" was a racial nightmare. That this Alice also pleads for Hawkeye's life "because I love him" is Hollywood's further improvement of Cooper, made even worse by removing Cooper's own racial undertone: his dark sister was part African-American. This seems to have been too strong for Hollywood in 1936.

The film has other errors. Military orders and the exercise of arms are wrong. The historical massacre upon which much of the work is based is wrong; it happened after the British had left Fort William Henry, not inside the fort as shown; Montcalm, shown here as trying to prevent the killing, had a more equivocal role. Women are shown as having no part in Native American political life. Most of the Native American details, in fact, are inaccurate or anachronistic or both, including a duel according to "tribal laws," the use of wampum, and dress. Predictably, errors abound in the firearms: they are all too short, and the emphasis on sharpshooting and the use of rifles is from a later period and the Western frontier, c. 1800–1840; Northeastern frontiersmen of this period had little use for, or access to, rifles. Some of this error was Cooper's, to be sure.

The film's field of meaning is not Cooper's, either. His America was a romantically idealized wilderness; the film's is a prototypical United States, seen as having a natural alliance with Britain. Scott's Hawkeye and Wilcoxon's British officer are made to carry most of this ideological burden, with Alice's love for Hawkeye as a metaphor of Britain's love of democracy. Hawkeye at the same time moves toward the British position and agrees at the film's end to become a scout. "We've got a job to do," he says—arguably a reference to the rise of fascism, although remarkably early for it.

Much of the film defines Britain (personified by Wilcoxon) as rigid, America (Hawkeye) as improvisational (thus recalling ideas seen in *America, Janice Meredith, George Washington Under the British Flag,* and others). Theirs is a conflict of discipline and creativity. This difference is not resolved until Hawkeye joins his creativity to the army's discipline for "the job" that has to be done. There is more to the American spirit, however; earlier, Hawkeye has told Alice of another quality, a hunger for the new: "A man could spend his lifetime exploring this country and never walk the same trail twice. . . . I wonder if you can understand what it means to be *first.*" He dreams of marking trails for others to follow to "build a big city at its end." The hunger for the unmarked trail sounds right; the "big city at its end" brings one up short. This is another contradiction: the wilderness dreamer pulls destruction of wilderness in his wake.[2] This contradiction seems closer to the "more West" of *The Iron Horse* than to Cooper. However, it is a minor strain.

Allegheny Uprising (1939) would be merely another, lesser example of the same, except for its disturbing meanings. A typical B movie, it had John Wayne, George Sanders, and Brian Donlevy being, respectively, democratic, autocratic, and evil (and no nuances, please). Claire Trevor was a nonstop "fiery" woman.

The historical base was the resistance of settlers in western Pennsylvania, c. 1760, to central government. The immediate problem was trade goods, including weapons, reaching Indians. The actual historical conflict had at least seven sides, however, not the Manichaean two of the movie—the Indians (themselves divided into at least two factions); traders connected with Sir William Johnson; the Penns, proprietors of Pennsylvania; the traders of Philadelphia; the Pennsylvania Quakers; the British Army; and the settlers. The British Crown, to its credit, was making the most serious effort of the century to protect Native American lands, a major factor in the colonists' subsequent drive toward separation.[3] Thus, the Pennsylvania settlers were not proto-Minutemen who "spoke with guns in defense of liberty," as a title has it, but settlers fighting a government whose larger goals were not their own.

Wayne is a muscular settler who organizes a blockade of trade goods, disguising himself and his pals as Indians to enforce the ban. Bad Brian Donlevy passes goods through the blockade as military materiel, while aristo-snob Sanders builds a fort that looks like a post in the Indian Wars. When the new fort proves (unwittingly) to be harboring the contraband, Wayne and his buddies lay siege. "Their muskets won't fire this far," Wayne announces, "and our long rifles will." With that, the settlers brandish their "rifles" (actually nineteenth-century military muskets) and blast away. Again, the American long rifle has been backdated to the French and Indian War. The anachronism is not mere carelessness: by the 1930s, the long rifle was identified with a patriotic idea of America and had become a symbol—cultivated by the National Rifle Association, among others—of traditional, perhaps conservative ideas.[4]

Historical error is rampant: Wayne rejects a firearm because it is a "trade musket—they're no good"; in fact, trade muskets were quite functional. What he seems to mean is that it is not an anachronistic rifle. One settler boasts that he has killed "thirty Onondagas," not only an incredible number but of a tribe not known for its involvement here. The costumes are the usual cock-up, Wayne and his crew all in buckskin festooned with fringe, rubberheads wearing flesh-colored briefs under their breech-cloths, a British officer sporting more gold braid than Jeb Stuart. At film's end, wearing a new leather shirt with a cute fringed collar, and with Trevor beside him in a c. 1930s fringed jacket and open sport shirt, Wayne announces he is going off to "Tennessee"—like the rifle, a reference to an America yet to come.

To see *Allegheny Uprising* is to increase one's respect for *The Last of the Mohicans*, not least because, for a film made in 1939, *Allegheny Uprising* seems both anarchistic and hysterically anti-British. Although it seems to offer the same contrasts—America/Britain, democracy/autocracy, frontiersman/British officer—its espousal of raw force and vigilante justice mocks democracy. Its attitude toward Native Americans is itself savage: "The only friendly Indians are dead Indians." Its version of Hawkeye's trail with a city at the end is "Tennessee," by implication "more West" beyond the control of government. If it is a response to events beyond Hollywood, it is an isolationist one.

IT IS A MINOR irony of Hollywood historicism that the same year that produced *Allegheny Uprising* also produced a wonderful film with a very different idea and a very different star—Henry Fonda. *Drums Along the Mohawk* was directed by John Ford and was based on one of America's better historical novels (by Walter Edmonds), from a time when that genre was flourishing. The film suffers some from not having the novel's scope or its complexity, thus eliding matters of character and history that would better have been left intact; on the other hand, it is a canny film that gains in power by not showing scenes that a lesser director would have included without a thought (e.g., the Battle of Oriskany). Shot in beautiful technicolor, *Drums Along the Mohawk* is a handsome, enormously enjoyable film from the height of the studio period—although it is not always good history. The film was made in Utah and so does not look like the Mohawk Valley. Many of the Indians wear Plains Indian breastplates.[5] Too many of the Mohawk Valley farmers wear leather, especially a green outfit sported by Ward Bond. Some probably inaccurate fringe is used, and Fonda appears in an open-necked shirt rather too often. Yet these are minor concessions, considering Hollywood's record.

Two larger problems plague the film. Neither is simple nor simply solved. One is the elision of time in a work that covers six years but never specifies where we are in that time span. To be sure, there are indicators, especially a wife's pregnancies and the changes of seasons, but these leave room for fudging chronology. The other, greater problem is that of social interaction, the ways in which people of the eighteenth century, and above all a husband and wife, acted differently from us.

Henry Fonda is a young farmer in the Mohawk Valley at the beginning of the Revolution. Claudette Colbert is his Albany-bred, upper-class bride. At once, differences of city/country, upper/lower are suggested, as in *America* and *Janice Meredith*. These differences are not played out in eighteenth-century terms, however; rather, they are resolved by romantic–erotic love and by treating the wife's urban manners as aberrations. She is discouraged by the first sight of husband Gil's log cabin, then terrified by an old Indian who happens to walk in as a bolt of lightning flashes. "I'm going home!" she screams, but Gil cures her with a slap and an embrace, as if differences of class and environment have nothing to do with history but are male–female matters, to be resolved by mild abuse.

She loses a baby, becomes pregnant again and gives birth to a boy and says, "I prayed so hard it would be a boy." The behavior at least suggests the "heroic commitment to childbearing" described by Laurel Thatcher Ulrich.[6] Fonda handles the baby with movie-comic clumsiness, implying a universality of behavior that transcends history; I am not at all sure, however, that the clichés have been that enduring. "Wanting a baby" is presented here in nineteenth/twentieth-century terms, as the wish of sentimental people for marvelous toys, extensions of self, proofs of domestic bliss. But the young farmer of 1776 surely wanted children, and many of them, in part to work the farm, in part because so many died; the desire for children was not sentimental, but practical—no less loving, perhaps, but expressive of a different kind of love, and arguably a less narcissistic one. Here, it brings the young husband and wife together; she is still beautiful, young-looking, desirable, with no hint of what the ten or a dozen births Ulrich notes may do to her. *Drums Along the Mohawk* is not about that historical reality; it is about a nice young couple, with one child, of a much later period.

The chronology allows a bending of the framework of fact that hurts the film as history. Only two major raids on the Valley take place, one apparently the St. Leger raid of 1777, the other one of those of 1780. These cannot be pinned down, however. General Herkimer leads the militia in the defense against the first, as the historical Herkimer did, and he suffers the wound that leads to the amputation of a leg and his death; however, the heroic marathon run by Fonda in the film as part of the 1780 fight was actually run by Adam Helmer (played in the film by Ward Bond) in 1777. In themselves, these may seem quibbles, but they are part of a larger blurring of fact that then enables a blurring of historical meaning. Two matters above all are smudged: the role of Native Americans, and the role of Loyalists. The Native Americans, except for the old Christian, Blueback, who so frightened Colbert in the lightning flash, are the malevolent spirits of the wilderness, apparently called into being by the Loyalists. Chief among the latter is John Carradine as

Caldwell, one eye hidden by a patch, exuding untrustworthiness from the first frame.

Caldwell seems not to be the historical figure of that name, a captain in Butler's Rangers,[7] but an amalgam of John and Walter Butler and John Johnson. As in *America* and the 1917 *Spirit of 76*, a bogeyman is being conjured to explain the war in the Mohawk Valley, instead of going to the less lurid truth—a battle of increasingly desperate Loyalists to reclaim their lands. The film's implied historical argument is that the Loyalists had no claim; it turns their legitimacy aside by making them monsters. This is not entirely wrong, but it is only half right: *la petite guerre* was the result of mutual bitterness.

At a deeper level, Ford made a film not about war with Indians and Loyalists, but about war with chaos. Fonda is a farmer; he is shown in the fields; the fields are bounded with fences, beyond which are trees and darkness. The Indians come leaping out of these forests, jumping over his fences; they carry fire, like devils, and they not only kill humans but also destroy the farm itself. Fonda is the farmer as civilizer, an identification as old as the Puritans, who called the wilderness a "desert." This is not Hawkeye's trail with a city at the end; this is civilization as the taming, even the eradication, of wilderness.

Rather much is made of church-going in the film. A warning of attack comes when the people are in church; the final battle ends in the church; the minister is a major character. Here, Ford has made the same equation as some of the films about the West: civilization, Christianity, and white husbandry stand against demonic Indians and a hellish wilderness.

Drums Along the Mohawk is admirable for its inclusion of women. It is not merely about fighting men; it is in good part about women—not only Colbert, but also others, above all Edna May Oliver as a tough, soft-hearted, waspish widow. She centers every scene in which she appears. Her death is touching rather than mawkish, and her reminiscences of her husband, Barney, suggest that "strength and sensuality . . . which complemented [colonial women's] participation in the rugged family arrangement of an agricultural and frontier economy."[8]

The same cannot be said of Claudette Colbert, probably somewhat miscast here because of qualities of modernity. The given circumstances of class and urbanity at the beginning are not allowed to come to anything, as if Ford saw them merely as false attitudes to be stripped away to give play to the real woman underneath—an implication that "reality" and frontier life are the same thing. The issue cannot be made to go away so easily, however. Where, for example, are the effects of a genteel New York education, which would have "engaged in role definition, by class and sex"? Where are the effects of genteel sentimentality and the sentimental novel and their threats to "healthy sex"?[9] History, especially the shorthand history of the motion picture, should try to give the truth of the typical. In *Drums Along the Mohawk*, it seems to give the truth of the typical in Fonda and Oliver, but of the aberrant, or at least the questionable, in Colbert.

There is a temptation to say that men and women of another age were just like us. There is even satisfaction in seeing how like us they were (Washington had false teeth, Louis XIV a fistula). But surely it is a responsibility of history to ask how people were different. The answer can be fiendishly difficult, perhaps impossible, but it should be sought—but to ask it of John Ford here, and of few other films, is to admit how good this one is and how far above other directors he usually was.

IF AN ENTHUSIASM for George Washington had marked the early decades of film, an equivalent enthusiasm made the 1930s the decade of Lincoln: Griffith's *Abraham Lincoln* (1930), Ford's *Young Mister Lincoln* (1939), and *Abe Lincoln in Illinois* (1940) (this last actually just beyond the decade but considered here, in good part because it was the filming of a play of the 1930s).

Abraham Lincoln was Griffith's only feature-length talkie. It had Walter Huston as Lincoln, but it now seems painfully slow and formless, its principal virtue its use of vocal music. To be sure, this element alone is noteworthy for a film of 1930; it suggests, too, that Griffith was accustomed to using music. The opening, too, is memorable, a storm scene in which the howl of a dog is central, heard as the camera looks at a split-rail fence. A similar storm ends the film: Lincoln's life is enclosed in images of turmoil, death, work.

In between these richly atmospheric visuals, however, is too much old-fashioned melodrama and not enough old-fashioned plot: it is a film of effects without causes. Huston's acting has not yet accommodated to film; he keeps looking heavenward, smiling a little smile; his voice sings. Una Merkel as Ann Rutledge is vintage Griffith, saccharine and limp, cast to die bathetically. "Don't take me away—don't take me away! We'll meet—Abe—." And, unseen, a chorus sings "In the Sweet Bye and Bye."

The film races through Lincoln's middle years. "I'm fifty years old!" he exclaims all of a sudden; it's news to us. He is offered the Republican candidacy, but we don't understand why; suddenly we get the shadow of a bearded man in a stovepipe hat. Griffith hurries us to the Lincoln of legend.

There is little forward movement, however; instead we get a succession of episodes, the soldier sentenced to death for cowardice a particularly poignant one as, outside, other soldiers sing "Tenting Tonight." Finally, we are in Ford's Theatre, and Lincoln ahistorically recaps the Gettysburg Address for the audience. John Wilkes Booth rolls his eyes madly and shoots. The film ends with a shot of the Lincoln Memorial sculpture and a choral singing of "The Battle Hymn of the Republic." Again, we seem to have a film of history bits, obligatory scenes from the schoolbooks. Yet, some of the film is deeply felt and movingly shown—the storms, the dog, the vocal music—and, if *Abraham Lincoln* lacks context and internal cause, it has powerful character.

Young Mr. Lincoln is, by contrast, a wholly artificial film in which Henry Fonda has to work hard to be intermittently interesting. He is afflicted with a fake nose that seems to epitomize what is wrong with the film. Fake music tries to inflate the value of scene after scene. Fake significance inflates young Lincoln's importance. ("Father says you've a real head on your shoulders, and a way with people, too," Ann Rutledge says to him. She knows he has ambition "deep down underneath." But what we see is a naive dreamer and a bumbler.) Fake behavior inflates character: after Ann joins the angels, faster than you can say Little-Eva-Gone-to-Heaven, Abe talks to her gravestone.

The first half of the film lacks an action. It is Lincolniana, a string of anecdotes. The second half is active enough, but murky. By then, we have been told that Fonda's Lincoln has served in the legislature (unseen by the audience), served in the Blackhawk War (unseen by the audience), and studied law (unseen by the audience). The second half is a mystery on the way to becoming a courtroom drama. It looks excruciating for Fonda—acting mostly in a vacuum, moment by moment, wondering where in the world it is going. With the exceptions of Milburn Stone as Stephen Douglas and Donald Meek as a nasty lawyer, he gets little support; Ward Bond as a villain is leaden.

The *New York Times* found the film to be "Americana."[10] If by this the reviewer meant a kind of frontier kitsch, the term is apt, but if he meant something truly American, the point is mistaken. People—the American people, if one can extrapolate from the crowds in the film—are shown as unstable and violent; they go from being cute and colorful one moment to bloodthirsty and vicious the next. Mob violence erupts in an instant: "The rope!" they cry; men run around with torches and bring a battering ram to knock down the jail door to lynch a man who happens to be Young Mr. Lincoln's client. Later, when the American people become a jury, they are disorderly, stupid, and sometimes drunken. They are probably meant to be "real Americans," perhaps with a nod to George Caleb Bingham, but what they tell us is that the American people are an unworthy mob.

At the end of this false movie ("mostly fiction, and corny fiction at that"),[11] Fonda walks into the sunset as "The Battle Hymn of the Republic" plays. The wind rises; a lightning bolt flashes; we are meant to feel that something significant has happened. The similarities to the end of Griffith's *Lincoln* are marked.

The wonder is that the film was directed by John Ford, whose admiration for Lincoln (seen in *The Iron Horse*) seems to have got in the way of his good sense. Much that is right about *Drums Along the Mohawk*—crisp storytelling, honest performances, memorable cinematography—is simply wrong here.

Robert Sherwood's *Abe Lincoln in Illinois* won the 1938 Pulitzer Prize for drama. It was filmed with minimal changes, carrying with it the star, Raymond Massey, a talented actor with a superb voice and a craggy face that suited patriarchs and great men. That both play and film had him as Lincoln from adolescence to the brink of the presidency was a credit to his ability. As the adolescent Lincoln, he was probably more credible on the stage; the camera showed too clearly the deep furrows of his face. Yet, his body was convincing, gawky and long-armed.

Opposite him as Mary Todd was Ruth Gordon, an actress of many mannerisms, given to sticking her elbows out like a chicken shaking its wings, a stage gesture perhaps designed to capture attention but one distinctly odd in film. Like Massey, she was pre-Stanislavski, but he was by far the more believable; Massey had warmth, despite his sometimes ferocious exterior (after all, he would play Jonathan, the Karloff look-alike, in *Arsenic and Old Lace*), and he made good contact with other actors. Gordon, on the other hand, kept pulling away from him and others, taking scenes into solos. The difference hurt Massey in at least one scene, when he seems to be singing his lines to her solitude; on the other hand, Gordon's selfishness is not entirely wrong for the character. The two together suggest a man linked to the wrong woman.

Abe Lincoln in Illinois is a film about romantic heroism, about "greatness" conceived in terms of nineteenth-century size but expressed in twentieth-century folksiness. (It is hardly accidental that Sherwood wrote speeches for Franklin Roosevelt.) His Lincoln is a Romantic, not a neoromantic, hero: ugly, like Quasimodo; doomed, like Hamlet; different, like Werther. And he is "great," although here Sherwood ducks the definition of greatness; the film contains only snippets of Lincoln's speeches, pronouncements on liberty and slavery and union that ring true, not because of what we see this Lincoln do, but because of what we know the real Lincoln did.

The gunshot that martryed him echoes back to the first frame of this motion picture and is like a credit upon which Massey and Sherwood and director John Cromwell draw throughout the film. The final sequence exists only because of this credit—a beautiful shot of Lincoln, on the rear platform of a train, withdrawing from the camera and from us, headed for Washington and death, the engine's plume of smoke the brightest area, like a glory above him as he vanishes into history.

But has the film earned that ending?

Nothing is inherently wrong in relying on an event beyond the work so long as the audience knows all about the event (surely true in Lincoln's case) and the event is a culmination of things in the work. It is the latter point that is the problem, and probably for reasons peculiar to the changing view of Lincoln in the mid-1930s: in the course of creating the populist, humane Lincoln, Sherwood threw out most of what would have prepared Lincoln the statesman and martyr. *Abe Lincoln in Illinois* gives us the man's adolescence, his store in New Salem, Ann Rutledge and the sentimental twaddle attached to her, Mary Todd, a Lincoln–Douglas debate, but it only occasionally gives us Lincoln acting in ways that explain and prepare for the Presidency. And it omits much that historical truth would insist on—the kind of legal work he performed, the source of his income, his rise as a politician.

Sherwood was a serious writer at a time when Broadway, or part of it, was trying to be a more serious place. He made *Abe Lincoln in Illinois* seem more serious than it is because he avoided making it a melodrama (no villain, no threat) and he avoided cutting it to the measure of the three-act play. It at least touches on serious matters—politics, unhappy marriage, divided ambition. But it accepts at face value the things that Lincoln said, or is quoted as saying; it does not really look at Lincoln vis-à-vis issues like race; it is disingenuous about Lincoln the politician. Other people push him into office. The unintended result is that it seems to be about a man who did almost nothing and who then became President.

The Lincoln films suggest both that reverence for the past persisted and that there were urges to examine that reverence. Griffith, as we might expect because he was oldest, accepted reverence most entirely; the other two seem to be looking for contemporary justifications of it. Both fail at more or less the same point: they want to end with intimations of tragedy, but they have failed to show how or why Lincoln reached eminence. They suggest that a populist attack, no matter how well intentioned, would demystify.

SOUND MADE POSSIBLE a new kind of movie—the musical biography, in which, as it turned out, music would come first, biography distinctly second. As examples of history, a few will stand for the whole.

Harmony Lane (1935) was a B movie about that absolutely safe subject, Stephen Foster; its flaws illuminate the type. His music, which ranged from the art song to kitsch, was universally known; his life could be made dramatic (although not in this version); and, although a Northerner, Foster celebrated the stable South that Hollywood loved: massa-kissing blacks and sentimental whites. Plus, Foster's life had the essential element of the musical bio: lots of song cues.

"Don't cry for me, Susan," says the young Foster (Douglas Montgomery). Then inspiration strikes. "Wait! Don't cry—don't you cry—Oh, Susanna, don't you cry—." Song cue.

This is the seamy side of the musical bio, trying to show how those geniuses came up with the stuff. *Harmony Lane* didn't solve the problem. Creativity here seems little more than a lifestyle based on not liking office work; composition takes place out of frame.

The film is numb on the subject of creativity, blank on the subject of slavery, mythopoeic on the subject of the South. A plantation myth seems to be in force—gowns, white pillars, miles and miles of gentility. A montage of blacks working the cotton fields and the levee illustrates "Ring de Banjo." Hattie McDaniel looks on while Foster and his little daughter "play minstrels." Three white females in long gowns sing "My Old Kentucky Home" to harp accompaniment.

The minstrel show epitomizes *Harmony Lane*'s historical blindness. Christie of Christie's Minstrels (William Frawley) looks as if he would like to be W. C. Fields. When Foster dies, Christie announces the death from the stage, and the camera pans over the segregated theatre, showing without comment the balcony full of blacks, their real faces a strange counterpoint to the blackfaced whites on the stage.

Harmony Lane gives no hint of why the sentimental songs of an alcoholic Northerner who wrote about the South were wildly popular. It does not examine what the blackface minstrel represented or how he fit into the popularization of Foster's music. It was not concerned, any more than *The Jazz Singer* was, with a possible relationship among show business, blackface, and white success, or how these things might relate to a distortion of the American South. Another Foster biography, *Swanee River*, was released in 1939 with similar results.

The Story of Vernon and Irene Castle (1939) seems, on its surface, a straightforward biopic of a couple who made salon dancing an international craze. It is, one would say, a Fred-and-Ginger vehicle with no more authenticity than need be: as a title says, "With the exception of [the Castles, and others whose 'true names' are used], the characters and events portrayed are fictional." Which is to say that it is *not* the story of Vernon and Irene Castle.

It is, rather, a story about two people who happen to have their names. "In a fabulous and beloved era, near enough to be warmly remembered, two bright and shining stars. . . ." The fabulous and beloved era, of course, was the first decade or so of this century. The bright and shining stars, and everybody they know, are white (a black man in a uniform brings somebody a message, however). The stars meet, love, marry, and create the Castle Walk. Edna May Oliver, imperious here as a fuzzily delineated enabler (manager? agent?) fosters their career, one never quite knows how. Walter Brennan, as the bright and shining stars' loyal manservant, follows them everywhere, even into the Canadian Air Corps when Vernon enlists at the beginning of World War I; then he follows Vernon everywhere in the military, as if army life, like civilian, is a matter of personal preference.

Three matters are of historical interest. One is the view of women: in an early establishing shot, a bandwagon passes, decorated with a sign that reads, "Climb Aboard the Bandwagon for Women's Suffrage." Nobody climbs on, however, certainly not Irene, who is still "Mrs. Irene Castle" when she goes to Hollywood years later. A second is the concept of the entertainment industry. As in *Harmony Lane*, that industry is undefined but powerful, an entity visible in symbols (Broadway, the Palace) rather than as itself. The *business* of show business takes place behind a curtain, like Frank Morgan's manipulations in *The Wizard of Oz*. Connected with this opacity is a third matter, "success" and the way the Castles reach it. A montage shows "Castlemania,"—Castle shoes, cigars, even haircuts. What was the medium by which such salesmanship was achieved? Did the Castles profit? How? Why are the people who are shown responding to this salesmanship neither young nor pretty like the Castles, but older and frumpy? Was "Castlemania" a matter of youth and beauty by association? If so, what does this say about America?

The film, however, does not bother with these questions; process is not interesting—results are. *The Story of Vernon and Irene Castle* is really about the "fabulous and beloved era" only insofar as it unwittingly suggests questions about the era that it can't answer. "Mrs. Vernon Castle" is outside the concerns of suffrage; the bandwagon refers to other women, women of a different order, perhaps a different universe—the frumpy women, perhaps, who buy up Castlemania. Vernon Castle is caught up in the pursuit of "success" but is himself outside the machinery of business, the business of show business; he needs "luck," "the big chance," a fairy godmother (the Oliver character). Why, one may ask, must the Castles, like Foster, be bad business people? Why are we to have our attention drawn to Castlemania, its photos and objects and glamor, its *sell*, and to say, "Success at last!," but not, "What is the man behind the curtain doing?"

Such questions might have been answered in a film about "America's greatest showman," Florenz Ziegfeld. *The Great Ziegfeld* (1936) in fact did not answer them, but it was an enjoyable film, so long as one accepted its utter falseness in the way one accepts the utter falseness of Viennese operetta. *The Great Ziegfeld* is not quite operetta (Ziegfeld never sings), but it shares the same romantic-sentimental tone and the same visual signs of privilege.

William Powell was Ziegfeld, Luise Rainer his first wife, Anna Held; Myrna Loy his second, Billie Burke. Powell displays throughout the oily panache of a 1920s floorwalker; seen first as an entrepreneur at the Chicago World's Fair, he succeeds there as he does throughout the film, by cute tricks. Business, this characterization says, is a matter of bringing off charming falsehoods. The world of businessmen, as typified by Ziegfeld and a rival (Frank Morgan), is a world of hustlers, their charm a nervous, edgy one because it is based in a constant stress between expensive appearances and threadbare reality.

Luise Rainer got an Academy Award for this performance. She was an actress with a small bag of superb tricks—lilts, sad smiles, moues, tears, little laughs—but she had such control and such ability to vary the order of the tricks that her performance is, indeed, affecting. Far less convincing as the Anna Held of the stage than as the Anna Held of the dressing room, she is here a fine film actress. Nobody smiles through her tears like this any more.

Ziegfeld's greatness, it appears, lay either in raising business as trickery to a high art or in exercising triumphant bad taste. Because the latter fills the movie, it is probably the correct choice. Sets that look as if they have been sculpted from whipped cream, costumes that drip with sequins and swags, production numbers that are pastiches of pop and high culture: the film's version of Ziegfeld's taste gives us vulgarity as glamor, much if it in the name of "glorifying the American girl"— making T and A look expensive. Probably, this emphasis on expense is deliberate; for both Held and Ziegfeld, "love" is expressed as money—jewels, flowers, clothes.

Scattered through the film are real people like Fanny Brice and actors playing real people like Eddie Cantor, in blackface. The Broadway sterotype is relentless—openings, evening clothes, lights. "The glorification of the American girl," while ringing the changes on sex-fantasy costumes and phallic settings, erases female individuality: never *this* girl, but always *a* girl—any girl. And, to be sure, *my* girl. Ziegfeld is possessive; they are always "my girls and my stars." And possession *means* possession: Ziegfeld loses Held because he is caught possessing one too many of his girls. (You watch him, cigar in hand, lean toward one of these young, blonde, sweet women, and you think of what cigar breath is like.) Ziegfeld, however, changes wives the way he changes suits; one of the benefits of possession, after all, is the ability to replace things easily. And, as with his wives, his suits are absolutely gorgeous, or at least expensive.

At last, however, the Crash comes, and Ziegfeld sinks. Ziegfeld's valet, to cheer him as he dies, tells him that he has been responsible for "memories of the finest things ever done on the stage." Left alone, Ziegfeld plays out a death scene longer than Violetta's and fantasizes a Last Great Show—"I've got to get higher—higher—." And dies.

None of this answers the questions raised by the musical biography. However, by showing the other side of show business, it ought at least to imply something. For example, it is clear that Ziegfeld is a gatekeeper. "My girls and my stars" are his by mandate. So is his vulgar style. Unclear is how his gatekeeping is done and how things are financed, although there is a constant suggestion of operating on the edge of disaster, despite the silk dressing-gowns, cigars, jewels, flowers, and the Suit Parade. Indeed, conspicuous consumption *to the point of disaster* seems to be the mark of Ziegfeld's "greatness"; perhaps it is also meant to be in the nature of show business. Risk, then,—but not, apparently, manageable risk, as more mundane businesses know it.

Questions about women are embedded in "the glorification of the American girl" and "the Follies Girl," in Ziegfeld's sexual exploitation of "his" girls, as well as in Rainer's characterization of Held. Love is expensive gifts; femininity is tricks—like business. By these standards, Ziegfeld himself is almost female: the parade of clothes, the use of tricks.

Historically, *The Great Ziegfeld* is utterly out of touch with the period in which it pretends to take place. Teddy Roosevelt, Wilson, suffrage, The Great War, Lindbergh—phooey. What shows did they produce? Show business, *The Great Ziegfeld* tells us, is outside history.

These musical and show-business biographies are different from other historical films. Their memory is somewhat shorter. They look, too, at figures of popular culture, not traditional heroes of politics, war, "the winning of the West." If they are no better than those other films at presenting business, they are far more revealing at presenting women. And, like the Lincoln films, they suggest a populist crack in the stone of reverence.

EDWARD ARNOLD WAS one of those actors whom everyone saw but many people cannot now name, a "character" actor who was also a star. Arnold had great talent and star quality, but he was fat. This concentration of bulk and power often typecast him as what used to be called a tycoon (e.g., Jimmy Stewart's father in *You Can't Take It with You*) in an age when capitalists were called bosses and big bellies were called corporations.

Yet, Arnold was much more than a one-note actor, and in three films of the 1930s he displayed his range in businessman roles; in one, particularly— *Diamond Jim* (1935)—he gave a stunning performance as a risk-taker doomed to be successful but unloved. He ought now to be better remembered for this portrayal, in a script by Preston Sturges, of Diamond Jim Brady, "a personality so rich and typical of his time," as the film's first title has it, "that the story of his life reflects the portrait of his era." *Diamond Jim's* idea of the Gilded Age is very different from that of the films of expansionism and the Indian Wars; it is a perhaps welcome corrective to the common neglect of the role of business.

The film shows Brady in the mid-1880s as an ignorant Irish–American freight-handler, a man who has read a book on salesmanship and is determined to rise. He does so, with the help of rented clothes and diamond studs, recalling in his trickery the filmic Ziegfeld. Almost instantly, he is "making more money than I ever thought there was," and he buys a diamond to offer to a Southern belle (Jean Arthur), only to discover that she is getting married. "I'll never love anybody but you," he tells her anyway, a vow that he proves true when another woman played by Jean Arthur enters his life and he falls utterly for her. Sturges's clever script here makes the "you" apply to the actress, not the character—or to the actress as the shell of the character, as if that is all that Brady is able to perceive. Sturges, and the film, are not indifferent to Brady's commitment to a world of externals.

Late in the film (1906), the stock market plunges. The now wealthy Brady berates other businessmen for their fears, and his audacity becomes equated with patriotisim: "Only trouble with this country is you fellas. It was built up by a bunch of guys who had guts and believed in what they were doing. . . . I'll take a gamble on this [country] any day, any day at all." He then loses everything—and makes it all back. The scene does for him and the businessman what *The Great Ziegfeld* could not do for the showman—raises him to the heroic by identifying him with a major social force. By suggesting that the business of its protagonist is the business of the nation, *Diamond Jim* at least acknowledges what *The Iron Horse* and *The Great Ziegfeld* seemed unable or unwilling to admit: that the creation of wealth is central to a national agenda.

Brady's appetites have the same zest and heroic size, and they proclaim a vulgarity Arnold is able to make charming. "Where I come from, them as has 'em, wears 'em," he says of the signature diamonds that hang all over him. After meeting Lillian Russell (Binnie Barnes) he sends for "some roses—a hundred dollars worth!" His appetite for food has him buying an extra seat at the theater for the box of chocolates on which he feeds throughout the performance. A restaurant kitchen goes into a frenzy when a waiter cries, "Brady is here!"

A lesser actor would stumble over this self-indulgence; Arnold uses it to give the character dimension. It is impossible to say where Arnold's and Sturges's skills separate here; it is certainly to Arnold's credit that he was willing to go with the script and A. Edward Sutherland's direction to embody a self-indulgence that became rapacity and horrendous vulgarity, but that was never disgusting. In one sense, this part of the performance suggests a compensation for losses in the love action; in another, it suggests a parallel to, and a critique of, the business action. Remarkably, the three are integrated.

The appetites for food, diamonds, and money also play against Brady's startlingly undemanding relationships with Lillian Russell and the second Arthur woman; the first is a "pal" and the second a romantic ideal. Brady's appetites, we assume, do not extend to these women: it is clear that he would have a sexual relationship with Arthur if he could, but she puts him off; it is clear that he and Russell could have a sexual relationship with each other if she would, but she is "in love" with Cesar Romero. All this is, of course, utterly ahistorical.

The Arthur character, however, finally confesses that she is going to run off with Romero. Arnold the actor, despite scenes of joy, anger, trickery, ruthlessness, has managed to save something for this scene, for at last we see that Brady is capable of a heroic rage as huge as his heroic appetites. It is an almost crazed blend of self-sacrifice and outrage as he both forgives them and barely holds himself back from destroying them. "Now get outa here before I kick you downstairs—you're nothin' but a couple of double-crossin', two-faced—. Eatin' my food and pullin' this behind my back! Get out!" The words read rather emptily; the scene is all in the pauses. And then, when he in despair proposes to Russell, she, too, refuses him. "I don't love you, and you don't love me."

The film ends in Brady's lavish apartment, shot in an almost Gothic lighting with deep, velvety shadows. Brady's doctors have told him again and again that he must stop gourmandizing. Of late, he has been eating almost meagerly. Now, he orders a lavish meal for himself, and his black butler, taking the order, clearly understands that the meal is meant to kill him. Against his will, he takes the huge order to the kitchen, where four black cooks begin to prepare the solo banquet, the scene a macabre comment on that earlier one when the waiter cried, "Brady is here!"

Alone, Brady laughs at himself, at his world. He opens his safe, takes out objects that recall his beginnings (including a picture of his mother). He goes through a pile of IOUs, then burns them. The film's atmosphere is now thick, the tones not quite the chiaroscuro of the horror film, but a restricted range without highlights, a universe of shadows. Into this comes his black butler, who says nervously, "Dinner—ready—Mister Brady—."

Arnold is magnificent here. "Presence" in an actor is inexplicable: you got it or you ain't. Arnold got it. Tears in his eyes, he stands, says, "So am I, boy—so am I—." ("Boy" is Brady's usual slang, not meant racially here.) And he goes slowly into the dining room to eat himself to death, and the double doors close of their own power on him, and the film is over.

Much of this is bad history. Yet, *Diamond Jim* is a rewarding film—because of Edward Arnold, because of that stunning ending, because of the complex picture of the businessman that Sturges, Sutherland, and Arnold created—dreamer, vulgarian, raptor, idealist, feeder. It begins to give life to those figures who stand by the trains in *The Iron Horse.*

ANOTHER FILM OF the 1930s dealt historically with a businessman but is notable for its answer to questions about music in the sound film. *San Francisco* (1936) is "historical" for its treatment of the San Francisco earthquake; if ever a film deserved to be called a "movie movie," *San Francisco* is it, thanks in great part to W. S. Van Dyke, who directed it at a breakneck pace that makes the opening minutes absolutely crackle. There is a great sense of urgency, of life moving almost too fast to keep up, of people frantic to grab sensations as they race past. It is shlock, but it is first-rate shlock, very much of the 1920s–1930s (Anita Loos was one of the writers) with its tough talk, its unabashed sentimentality, its complete ease with sin and God and goodness, its complete confidence in its own ideas of virtue and of human nature. It is, in fact, these qualities that make it a document of 1935 Hollywood–New York more than of 1905 San Francisco. Two sequences do come up to the mark as history, the great earthquake and fire that end the film, and scenes from *Faust* at San Francisco's opera. These latter have the look of the antiquarianism and heavy-handed, operatic realism of that day. (Legend has it that Van Dyke invited the visiting D. W. Griffith to lend a hand with one of the scenes, and, indeed, a crowd scene does look like Griffith's work—although it does not look like opera.)

Jeanette MacDonald, Spencer Tracy, and Clark Gable are beautifully handled by Van Dyke, Gable above all giving a tough–tender performance that drives the film. MacDonald is surprising if you think of her as only Nelson Eddy's screen sweetheart; she looks handsome, sings well enough, has a "lady-like" quality that plays off Gable's vulgarity. When she applies to him for a job at his "joint," the Paradise, he has her raise her skirt so he can see her legs, says flatly, "A little thin for down here." He would play sexual predator if she would let him, but she does not: she is not a Follies Girl, he is not a Ziegfeld. They are Uptown and Downtown, Nob Hill and the Coast, the opera house and the Paradise, angel and sinner.

When they have met, lost each other, and have been reunited two days after the earthquake, their union is the symbolic rebirth of San Francisco. Tracy, as a priest, has called San Francisco "the wickedest, most corrupt city in

America." He has warned her that Gable is "unscrupulous with women, as he is ruthless with men." Gable himself has told her that he is an atheist, "me": politically conservative, self-assertive, individualistic. All this is crushed under the falling buildings. MacDonald, the figure of virtue throughout—her singing of the "Jewel Song" in one of the opera sequences does double duty as keystone in both the secular and the divine structures of the film—disappears, and Gable the secularist hunts frantically for her in the ruins, including the ruins of his ironically named Paradise.

He finds her in a vast tent city where dazed, dirty refugees wander. She is singing "Nearer, My God to Thee" for a child's funeral. The scene evokes photos of the frontier—a tent, a circle of bleak faces. If you can sit through this scene without a lump in your throat, you do not deserve to understand sentimentality; it is manipulative and glorious. More to the point, it is brilliantly conceived and directed (and not ahistorical). It is also resonant of the rest of the film, recalling her singing of "Jerusalem" in Tracy's church as well as of the "Jewel Song." Gable falls to his knees and thanks God; somebody shouts, "The fire's out!" and the crowd begins to sing "The Battle Hymn of the Republic."

Eight years after the coming of sound, San Francisco used the internal resonance of music (mostly the human voice) as a rich device to communicate "data." The film suggests, perhaps better than any other, what the new technology could do for or to the historical film; here, it is the principal source of internal resonance, therefore of meaning. The very banality of clichés—MacDonald's white dresses, the Paradise, Marguerite and Faust, a child's funeral, the threatened virgin, "The Battle Hymn," "Jerusalem"—overlaps into a communal and powerful body of moral and religious reference, which, buoyed by music, becomes idea. Regrettably, perhaps, it is also emotionally manipulative and an obstacle to thought.

Also, the ten or so minutes of the earthquake, the fire, and its aftermath are brilliant cinema. If Van Dyke had used Technicolor, we would now talk about the destruction of San Francisco rather than the burning of Atlanta.

THE HISTORICAL WESTERNS of the 1930s intensifed the signs and conventions of earlier Westerns; most were subsumed into genre, a process that ruined them as history. Several are memorable for their stars but are poor history: *The Plainsman* (1937), for example, deserves attention because of Gary Cooper and Jean Arthur, the latter as a memorable Calamity Jane. Nonetheless, the film, produced and directed by Cecil B. DeMille, is mostly foolishness, mangling history, reinventing character (above all Wild Bill Hickok). The screenplay now is camp: the death of Hickok, Arthur's final kiss and her reading of the line, "That's one kiss you can't wipe off." *Jesse James* (1939) had a tight script by Nunnally Johnson, but it is historical nonsense that blames the Jameses' criminality on the railroad; *Western Union* (1941) has an invented plot that uses the creation of the transcontinental telegraph as mere background.

History is not even a moral setting for these movies; it is an excuse, and one so frivolous that capitalism can be heroic in one (*Western Union*) and evil in the other (*Jesse James*) without altering the myth.

Annie Oakley (1935) was about the Wild West Show, with Buffalo Bill (Melvyn Douglas) as the Ziegfeld of America's mythic West. Oakley (Barbara Stanwyck) is a crack shot who shoots quail for a hotel until she has a chance to compete with the show's champion, Toby Walker (Preston Foster). She of course "falls in love" with him; she proves a better shot, and he leaves the show; Sitting Bull—here a comic dodderer—follows him to the wretched shooting gallery to which he has exiled himself and restores him to Annie.

Buffalo Bill here is warm and fuzzy; Sitting Bull is funny and sweet. Stanwyck is feisty, and because of her the film can be enjoyed, but only by turning off the brain: questions like the relationship among Cody, Ned Buntline, the West, and the business of show business are ignored; the comedy of this Sitting Bull and the tragedy of the real Sitting Bull are kept distinct; connections between "entertainment" and race are not faced. *Annie Oakley* reveals why the other historical Westerns of the 1930s are not worth discussing as history: they had consented to become a genre that put myth above truth in the name of entertainment.

EFFECTS OF SOUND

THE HISTORICAL FILMS of the 1930s do not answer the questions about the effects of sound, although it seems clear that a potential for more data per frame was not necessarily realized as historical data. Rather, music, now reliably consistent across showings, relentlessly urged emotional content: Griffith's *Abraham Lincoln* and Van Dyke's *San Francisco*, for example, used vocal music to wonderful emotional, but not historical, effect. Such music seems to have mostly narrowed audience options rather than broadening them: redundant with other content, it eased emotional access to plot and character or it inspired "ideas" that were feelings (e.g., *San Francisco*). This effect may have reinforced the rigidity of genre, as in the historical Western.

Sound also, however, satisfied a need seen in some silents (e.g., *Winners of the Wilderness*) to move toward larger verbal content. In most cases, that content was historically empty (e.g., erotic badinage), but in some films (the 1936 *Last of the Mohicans*) it expanded into overt statement aimed at clarifying, sometimes at narrowing, the film's field of meaning—for example, the "trail with a city at the end" speech of *Last of the Mohicans*, which is hard to imagine as a title, and the film's ahistorical message of Anglo–American cooperation.

Sound also allowed the creation of aural signs, most obviously the British speech associated with characters unsympathetic because of rigidity and class-consciousness (*Last of the Mohicans, Allegheny Uprising*); at the same time, American regional speech—Randolph Scott's Georgia accent, for example—seemed to have no power as a sign, although Brady's ungrammatical, colloquial

speech (*Diamond Jim*) did: it humanized his appetite. Accent, then, was sometimes an added kind of data and sometimes not, as was the content of some
speeches. However, I do not see the evidence for such a statement as "For the
historical film the new sound technology constrained location shooting and
directed attention to dialogue, characterization, and the heroic personality. . . ."[12]
A comparison of *Winners of the Wilderness* and *Drums Along the Mohawk*, for
example, will not support any of these points.

1939–42: EMBARRASSMENT OF RICHES

THAT THERE IS no real break at the end of a decade is nowhere clearer than at
the end of the 1930s. Production surged into the 1940s, with at least twenty-
five historical films (not counting B's) released in 1939–41. The studios had perfected themselves, "meshing into a vast interlocking system, unified by
standardized production and marketing practices, a code of acceptable content,
and an increasingly stable system of technical and narrative conventions."[13] Such
a system encouraged self-imitation—and stasis.

Some of the most beloved period films were released in these three years. An
unusually large number of them are now "classics" that continue to be popular as
videos. In good part, this longevity is due to their stars—Gary Cooper (*The Westerner*, 1940; *Sergeant York*, 1941); Henry Fonda (*Drums along the Mohawk*, 1939;
Young Mister Lincoln, 1939; *Jesse James*, 1939; *The Return of Frank James*, 1940;
Lillian Russell, 1940); Spencer Tracy (*Stanley and Livingston*, 1939; *Northwest Passage*, 1940; *Edison, The Man*, 1940); Tyrone Power (*Jesse James*; *Brigham Young,
Frontiersman*, 1940); Errol Flynn (*Santa Fe Trail*, 1940); Don Ameche (*Lillian
Russell*; *Swanee River*, 1939; *The Story of Alexander Graham Bell*, 1939); and one
woman, Alice Faye (*Lillian Russell*; *Little Old New York*, 1939).

Yet as a group, these films are not good history. They are immensely enjoyable, often beautifully made; they represent high degrees of skill in exploiting
stars, music, cinematography, myth. Yet they share common qualities that work
against good history: neoromanticism, which insists that idealism, usually as
erotic love, be an inevitable story element, with history bent to its needs; poetic
justice, whose meanings are preordained, almost a matter of casting; physical
beauty as a sign of moral beauty; a universe of good and evil (hence of the beautiful—Power, Fonda—versus someone like the lantern-jawed, gaunt John Carradine). The effect of these qualities is to shatter the films' internal probabilities, as
drama, and to wrench historical facts of character and event.

These films in fact represent the high point of neoromantic filmed drama;
they are the perfected heirs of Belasco. Like late-nineteenth-century neoromanticism, they see history itself as a moral system, in which America is the
good and, because it is good, the favored; the representative of America—the
hero—will therefore have beauty and will win. Like late-nineteenth-century
neoromanticism, they practice a kind of realism that is "real" only as far as it
suits perceived needs. Behind the film is somebody like Cecil B. DeMille,

willing to compromise matters of material history, character, or plot to further a neoromantic effect, often for purposes of sentiment (e.g., the death of Hickok in *The Plainsman*), but so skillful that even in 1980 someone could write that he was "a master at visual detail, gadgetry and period objects. . . ."[14]

There were exceptions. *Abe Lincoln in Illinois* played against beauty as morality; erotic romance disappeared early from it; poetic justice was not an issue. But *Abe Lincoln in Illinois* came almost intact from the stage, not from the factories that ground out star vehicles between 1939 and 1941 (nine from Fox alone, all produced by Darryl F. Zanuck) and in the process ground history to bits. The success of such films and the neoromantic formulae that produced them, however, made it possible for them to persist even after the world of the audience had changed.

CHAPTER FOUR

1940–49: GOOD WAR, NEW WORLD

The 1940s were marked most significantly by World War II, which split off the films released before 1942 at one end and those made after 1946 on the other. "War films" were a recognizable type, most of them celebratory; even the films made before 1942 often seem like preparations for war, if only for the antifascist spirit that Roosevelt urged in 1940 as "the arsenal of democracy." Yet, the experience of individuals outside the traditional foci of power continued to attract filmmakers, whether as the new sports films or the slightly older musical biographies. The war films themselves may have encouraged change as they concerned themselves not only with the generals, but also with the grunts and airmen.

If one looks for the significant 1940s film, however, it will not be found in traditionally conceived history, in new types, or in war movies. It is a black-and-white film made in 1946 whose subject is World War II but whose vision looked forward, not back. Made at the pivot of the decade, it was aware that the world had changed, probably forever, not necessarily for the better. It was called *The Beginning or the End?* (1946).

Just as war and policy are legitimate historical subjects, so, too, are power and its resonances. Attitudes toward the possession of power vary: at one extreme, the triumphalist view that power should be used, the view that at the personal level informs most Westerns; at the other, anxiety because power casts a new and brighter light on moral issues, one less popular as filmic subject.

If American possession of power is triumphalist through most of World War II, then, it smashes head-on into power anxiety with the dropping of the atomic bomb, a power so absolute that its illumination of moral issues cannot be ignored. *The Beginning or the End?* (1946) acknowledged this anxiety in its title. A small black-and-white movie, it managed to glance at many of the issues that would still resonate in the 1990s (e.g., the *Enola Gay* exhibit at the Smithsonian): Was annihilation inevitable? What was the obligation of the scientist—to science, to country, to moral ideal? Were there secrets too terrible to be discovered? Could a righteous nation live with possession of an ultimate weapon?

The Beginning or the End? is filled with familiar names: Hume Cronyn as Oppenheimer, Brian Donlevy as General Groves, Godfrey Tearle as FDR. It includes scenes burned into our retinas by repitition: the Groves–Bush handshake before the first dawn test; the mushroom cloud.

It is low-key, even tepid, but gains conviction from being so. It follows a young physicist (Tom Drake) who is present when Enrico Fermi's atomic pile under the University of Chicago is driven almost to critical mass by manipulation of rods and ropes, a scene so foreign to our high-tech consciousness that it jerks us back to those days. He helps to arm the first bomb; it is he who suffers radiation poisoning while playing with two chunks of radioactive material; dying, it is he who writes a letter to tell us all that "atomic energy is the hand [God] has extended to lighten the burden of war."

This small personalization of the historical is woven through real events that are "basically a true story," as a voice-over tells us, although "some rearrangemnt of chronology and fictionalization was necessary." The fictional hook is the burying of a time capsule in 1946 in a redwood forest that has "watched the rise and fall of many civilizations"; the dedication is itself a wonderfully dated fake event, the time capsule like a 1940s idea of a space rocket. The film we are watching is in the time capsule, and thus itself an image of the event that buries it—a cinematic Mobius strip that may represent the poetic license already cited.

Early scenes assume the rightness of America's cause in World War II and the wrongness of Germany's. Scientists appeal to FDR through Einstein; FDR consults Churchill; and then the project, after various Physics 101 chats about the basic science, gets off the ground. Robert Walker is a security specialist who asks the male scientists to "give your names to the girls" as they file into a briefing. When Fermi's primitive atomic pile almost goes to chain reaction, amid flashing lights as meaningless as those in Frankenstein's lab, Walker cries, "Hitler—here we come!" The scientists raise a toast in paper cups, Fermi praying, "God give us time."

"And God forgive us," Drake adds. A moment later, three of the scientists resign because of moral doubts.

Montage creates Oak Ridge and Sanford, Washington. Eighteen thousand people are moved to make room for the Sanford complex; "without question, without protest . . . they left." This dictatorial exercise of power goes unexamined in the film.

Even though the first test shot is without suspense (we know it worked; how could we suspend our disbelief in that event?), the black-and-white footage of the first fireball still appalls. The wonder and the horror of it justify the remarks about good and evil that follow. And they set up the questioning and the justification that still trouble us. Truman (Art Baker) talks about shortening the war: "A year less of war . . . will mean life for three hundred thousand, maybe a million, of America's finest youth." Nobody speaks for

Japan's youth or the Hiroshima maidens, but in 1946 could anybody here have been expected to?

Barry Nelson is Paul Tibbetts, the pilot of the *Enola Gay*. The flight is given a too deliberately dramatic buildup, perhaps, but it pays off in the expressions of revulsion on the faces of Nelson and the crew when Hiroshima is replaced by the mushroom cloud, and again when the plane flies back over the city and the men look down at miles of fire. The moment becomes the metaphor for Walker's musings about another war, "the whole world on fire, eating itself to ashes." This is not frivolous talk.

Within a few years, John Gunther had written *Hiroshima*, Karl Shapiro had redefined the Manhattan scientists as Faustus, and Walter Van Tilburg Clark had written "The Portable Phonograph." The Age of Fear had begun, an age of cynicism along with it, betrayal in the name of power pushing the Rosenbergs and Fuchs and others into our consciousness, with paranoia and suspicion of government to follow. Not all of this was foreseen by *The Beginning or the End?*, but there was enough of it to show that this was an admirable little historical film. Its framework of fact is not meticulous, sometimes deliberately so for security reasons, sometimes for reasons of necessary ignorance (the look of the bomb, for example). It is biased in its nationalism and its racism, but less so than some of the statements made on the same subject since. It misses the irony of justifying the Manhattan Project to beat Germany and then using the bomb to beat Japan; it is silent on the soul-searching of Jewish scientists vis-à-vis Germany and Japan. Yet it is serious. Given its subject, it was not being melodramatic in saying, "We know the beginning. Only you of tomorrow—if there is a tomorrow—can know the end."

NONETHELESS, MANY OF the films of traditionally conceived history ran on in the old ruts, the more so if made before the bomb. *Knickerbocker Holiday* (1944) was based on a Maxwell Anderson–Kurt Weill stage musical of 1938, but, after passing through several screenwriters, an adapter, and a number of tunesmiths who seem to have thought themselves better than Weill, it lost both its musical and its literary edge. What is left is tepid farce—Peter Stuyvesant (Charles Coburn) as a comic roûe, not a tyrant; Brom Broeck (Nelson Eddy) as a middle-aged liberal, not a young firebrand. Anachronisms abound: talk of "the colonies" and uniting them; entertainment by Carmen Amaya's flamenco troupe. "September Song" survives, but, in the context of Coburn's jowly leers, it has no sadness and no bite.

One sequence near the end seems distinctly odd—Brom's dismay when his revolution really happens, and the people pull down the stocks and attack the town guards; he moans, "I wanted to rouse the people, but this is mob rule." He does a turnabout and asks Stuyvesant to enforce the law, because what he wants is "a democracy—where you're governed by amateurs." This is ahistorical for 1647 but revealing for 1944, a view that "democracy" is defined by who administers power (amateurs), not by who is the ultimate repository of power (the people—or are they a mob?) In fact, the image of the people as mob had probably been erased by wartime ideas of solidarity and confidence in the productive mass; by 1944, *Knickerbocker Holiday* was archaic.

Northwest Passage (1940) again looked at the French and Indian War. Directed in gorgeous Technicolor by King Vidor from a novel by Kenneth Roberts, it has since become an icon in its own right, and it is probably churlish now to point out that it is wrong in its history and inaccurate in its details, and that its portrait of its central figure, Robert Rogers of Rogers Rangers, is laughable.

William Johnson, Britain's Superintendent for Northern Indian Affairs and the hero of the pivotal years of the French and Indian War, said of Rogers in 1766, "He was a soldier in my Army in 1755 . . . [who] became puffed up with pride and folly from the extravigant [sic] encomiums and notice of some of the Provinces, this spoiled a good Ranger for he was fit for nothing else. . . ."[1] Parkman called him "ambitious and violent," the modern historian Francis Jennings, "depraved."[2] Incorrectly thought of as the founder of the United States Army's rangers, Rogers has cast a very large shadow on the wall of American machismo. It was this oversized, pop Rogers whom the film chose to celebrate; with Spencer Tracy as Rogers, we are in the sphere of star-powered mythmaking, not history. The man who had just played Thomas Edison and H. M. Stanley brought an authority to Rogers that could hardly be questioned, and the film's script and direction hero-worshiped him from credits to fadeout. As contrast, Robert Young played a callow greenhorn and surrogate son.

The major action is more or less historical: a company of rangers trek north along Lake Champlain to the Abenaki village of Saint Francis, burn it, kill many of the inhabitants, and head back down through what is now Vermont, starving. The scenery is beautiful (although Western, not Eastern), many of the scenes thrilling. Walter Brennan is cute, in the local-color style; no women are present to spoil the fun.

Inauthenticities abound. For reasons best understood in Hollywood, Rogers and his merry men are costumed in fringed green outfits with little hats that make them look as if they're about to help the Jolly Green Giant bring in the peas. Their muskets are nineteenth-century ones. They march through the trackless forest carrying less kit than a backpacker would take for a weekend.

The film was not generous of time or judgment to anybody not blessed with white skin and testicles. Only one woman of even minor significance is seen, the Young character's fiancée (Ruth Hussey). A single black man is glimpsed, tending a spit at a tavern. The many Native Americans are either Mohawks, and so suspect, or Abenakis, and so damnable: "I don't need to tell you who the Abenakis are," Rogers tells his men. And he doesn't; instead, he gives a hair-raising account of torture. What he doesn't say is that the Abenakis were Roman Catholics or that they had been driven from the Connecticut Valley, so that the attack had elements of both New England anti-Catholicism and land war. "We're under orders to wipe out this town," Rogers says instead. And so they do, with bayonets—after we have been shown a scaffold hung with hundreds of scalps, but not the church that stood in the real town's center.

The Abenaki village, at least in the killing scenes, appears to be all-male; when a woman and child are seen, much is made of *not* killing them. (The actual Rogers and rangers were not so discriminating. Of the thirty killed, "many . . . were women and children.")[3] Despite their long association with whites and their proximity to the French, none of the Abenakis wears European clothes; instead, they display feathers, skins, seminudity, the same signs that denote "savagery" in films about Africa.[4]

Like the 1936 *Last of the Mohicans, Northwest Passage* uses the French and Indian War to show "Americans" fighting an immoral enemy. Although the nominal enemy are French, the real enemy are the Abenakis, "evil" like other Hollywood Native Americans. But there is none of the ambivalence of *Last of the Mohicans*; this is outright racialism—not necessarily wrong as history, but certainly wrong in failing to show the agenda of that racialism. It is doubtful, given such a display of triumphalism, that *Northwest Passage* is a prewar call to join Europe against fascism; rather the opposite, in fact.

What *Northwest Passage* lauds is male cohesion. Much of the film shows bonding experiences—shared hunger, shared killing, cooperation in crossing a river. The erotic romance of some early films (*Janice Meredith, Winners of the Wilderness*) has given way to a male superiority that virtually jettisons romantic love, and women along with it. It is male collectivization, not heterosexual love, that is idealized in *Northwest Passage*. It is subservient to a benign but monolithic power—Rogers's—that is inherently fascistic, as is the hero-worship of Rogers by the filmmakers themselves.

At the conclusion, Rogers stands silhouetted against the horizon, ready to walk off into a sequel (never made). Robert Young delivers a speech that sounds remarkably like Tom Joad's: "Every time we look across the river, we'll hear his voice, calling us through the wind. But he'll be within us, no matter where we are or he may be, for that man will never die." One understands, albeit a little woozily, what Tom Joad means by this sort of thing—the solidarity of common people. But what does it mean when applied to Rogers? *Eine volk, eine Amerika?*

Unconquered (1948) was a lavish serving of DeMille's brand of hokum, utterly improbable, spectacular, meaningless. Gary Cooper wore long buckskin fringe and carried two pistols in his belt, as if he were in a Western; Paulette Goddard did a bath scene, a burning-at-the-stake scene, a whipping scene; there was a ball scene, a siege scene, a rural fair scene, and all manner of things thought picturesque in 1900. The putative subject was Pontiac's War,

Before film, there was theater, in which early filmmakers (e.g., Griffith, DeMille) learned a style —commercialized realism—and a way of imagining human action—neoromantic melodrama. Here, Belasco's Broadway production of *The Girl of the Golden West*, 1905. (Dance Collection, The New York Public Library for the Performing Arts Astor, Lenox and Tilden Foundations.)

In Griffith's monumental *America* (1924), theatrical melodrama combines with myth to produce visual and dramatic untruth: the uniforms, the blackfaced white, the bestial Indians in Western fringed bucksin, the ubiquitous handgun. Center, Lionel Barrymore as a melodramatic and utterly ahistorical villain. (The Museum of Modern Art/Film Stills Archive.)

The West as the *real* America became a myth that triumphed over historical truth, even in so beautiful a film as John Ford's *My Darling Clementine* (1946), here with Henry Fonda. (The Museum of Modern Art/Film Stills Archive.)

Central to the Western myth was the hundred-shot handgun—fast, powerful, accurate—often, as here, provided with cartridges before they had been invented. Errol Flynn, ready to capture John Brown, in *Santa Fe Trail* (1940). (The Museum of Modern Art/Film Stills Archive.)

Fringed buckskin and handguns often conflated to push the imagery of the West back in time. Spencer Tracy as Robert Rogers fights the French and Indian War in *Northwest Passage* (1940).(The Museum of Modern Art/Film Stills Archive.)

Few directors had less respect for historical fact than Cecil B. DeMille; here, Gary Cooper makes like a cowboy star in the French and Indian war film *Unconquered* (1948), with Paulette Goddard and Mike Mazurki. (The Museum of Modern Art/Film Stills Archive.)

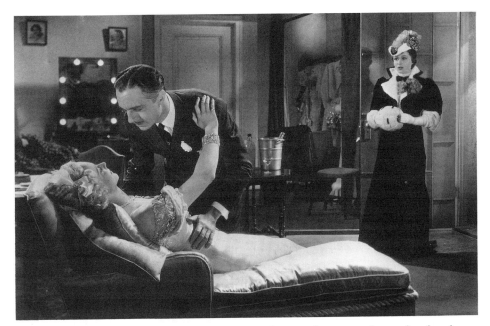

The show-biz biography, never strong as history, became a locus for female exploitation. Flo Ziegfeld (William Powell) stoops to exploit as his wife (Luise Rainer) happens by. *The Great Ziegfeld*, 1936. (The Museum of Modern Art/Film Stills Archive.)

The show-biz bio was also home to a lot of blackface racism with roots in immigrant vaudeville. *The Jolson Story*, with Larry Parks, 1946. (The Museum of Modern Art/Film Stills Archive.)

Paradoxically, it was in later show-biz bios that breakthroughs of both race and gender were made, not only in subject but also, as here, in brilliant visualizations of blackness and whiteness. *Leadbelly* (1976), with Roger E. Moseley. (The Museum of Modern Art/Film Stills Archive.)

Degrading women in the guise of biography was a major sideline in the 1950s—alcoholism, drug addiction, crime. Susan Hayward made it a speciality, as in *I'll Cry Tomorrow* (1955). (The Museum of Modern Art/Film Stills Archive.)

Aging male star/beautiful bimbo was also a 1950s cliché, but in *The Girl in the Red Velvet Swing* a surprisingly feminist tilt was given to the White–Thaw–Nesbit scandal. (The Museum of Modern Art/Film Stills Archive.)

Gary Cooper's face remained quintessentially "American" and quintessentially heroic to the end of his career; here, it serves the cause of air power in *The Court-Martial of Billy Mitchell* (1955). (The Museum of Modern Art/Film Stills Archive.)

but the model for the Indians and their tortures and ceremonies was Hollywood's idea of Africa. As so often, a bad white man (Howard DaSilva) was behind everything the Indians did: his desire for an empire was evil because, apparently, it frustrated everybody else's desire for an empire.

The Howards of Virginia (1940) returned to eighteenth-century conflicts of class to explain the obstacles to true love. It starred an unhappy-looking Cary Grant, in costumes that he never managed to make look like clothes, and Martha Scott, Sir Cedric Hardwicke—again, an English actor as an unsympathetic aristocrat—and Richard Carlson as a surprisingly lively Thomas Jefferson. An isolationist tilt casts the Revolution as a struggle between frontier levelers and anglophile aristocrats. If, like other movies of 1940, it has one eye on events in Europe, it is only to make sure that those events are kept distant.

THE 1940S SHOWED little interest in the Civil War, but two films early in the decade dealt with the years immediately before and after, both in a decidedly pro-Southern way, but without reference to the war in Europe or the "arsenal of democracy." *Santa Fe Trail* (1940) cast Errol Flynn as Jeb Stuart and Ronald Reagan as George Armstrong Custer, put them into the same class at West Point (changing the real Custer's age by five years), moved up the violence at Ossewatomie, Kansas by two years, gave Flynn and everybody else a cartridge-firing Colt (1873) for shootouts in 1859, and put Olivia de Havilland into a shirt and pants. It was not these anachronisms, however, that caused Bosley Crowther to say that "for any one who has the slightest regard for the spirit—not to mention the facts—of American history, [the movie] will prove exceedingly amazing."[5] It was, rather, the film's propaganda for slavery.

The focus of this agenda is John Brown, played with great authority by Raymond Massey, but presented as both cynical and mad: he abandons a settlement of escaped slaves, telling them that they are free and "there are good people in Kansas;" he sets fire to a barn that has three black men in it in order to flush out a white soldier; when the townspeople of Harper's Ferry gather to stare at the arsenal he has seized, he guns them down. His spokesman is Van Heflin, all but foaming at the mouth to embody abolition as fanaticism. By contrast, Flynn—dashing, gentlemanly—is the reasonable voice of the South—and of slavery. "All I ask is time," he pleads. "[The violence] will be stopped when we hang John Brown. Then the South can settle its own problems without loss of pride or being forced into it by a bunch of fanatics." To show that this is the wish of all sensible blacks, as well, we are given a scene in which one escaped slave says, "If this here Kansas is freedom, then I ain't got no use for it," to which another replies, "Me, neither! I just want to get back to Texas and sit 'til Kingdom come!"

Sitting, one gathers, is what slaves did.

There are many bad movies, few meretricious ones. *Santa Fe Trail* is heart and soul of this select company, a film that perverts history in order to rewrite it, with a result that is not amusing, but vicious.

Belle Starr (1941) does the same thing for Reconstruction. It transforms a law-breaking tramp (Belle Shirley) into a Southern aristocrat, and, as in the Jesse James films, turns postwar criminality into an offshoot of the plantation myth. At the center of this web of untruth sits Gene Tierney, the spider-woman as Southern belle.

Things get off to a handsome but false start with shots of a ruined mansion and a black man plowing; a black child finds a burned doll. "That belonged to Miss Belle Starr—a mighty fine white lady who lived in that house a long time ago, when I wasn't no bigger than you is. . . . 'Round here in Missouri, Miss Belle is what white folks call a *legend*." (The real Belle, née Myra Belle Shirley, was a tavern-owner's daughter.) A flashback takes us to the mansion in all its glory. The War is lost, but "it hasn't ended for me!" cries spunky Tierney as Belle. Reconstruction is signaled by a carpetbagger, overdressed blacks, a black couple under a sign, "Marriage legalized, one dollar," and glimpses of interracial cordiality. Much to-do follows about Confederate Captain Starr (Randolph Scott), whom Tierney hides in the mansion; then a Union officer (Dana Andrews) burns the mansion as punishment for her doing so, driving Belle to guerilla warfare and marriage to Scott. Their gang is shown triumphantly running three wagonloads of free blacks "out of Missouri."

However, guerilla war soon becomes gangsterism and Belle opts out; she flees to her former slave (Louise Beaver), who cries, "My baby! My baby!" and does exactly as she is told, as if slavery had not ended and slaves really did love their owners. Ultimately, for no probable reason, Belle is shot in the back by a bad man and the film totters to a teary end. That the real Belle Starr died far from Missouri; that she had a number of lovers, including one who styled himself the Blue Duck; that she married Sam Starr only in 1880,[6] none of this penetrates the Technicolor falsity of the movie.

Although less strident than *Santa Fe Trail*, *Belle Starr* is equally meretricious. The doll in the ruins, the mansion, the burning—these powerful visuals, handsomely filmed, signal ideas of value, loss, and injustice. The mansion, like the beauty of the female star, is as potent a sign here as in *Gone with the Wind*; both films mean to tell us that a culture that was valuable was wantonly destroyed. Beauty is the validater, in both house and woman, blinding us to moral questions about slavery and the narrowness of the class being favored. More cruel is the enlistment of black actors to signal Reconstruction as a sign of irresponsibility and to reinforce this deception with displays of love for former masters.

IF CUSTER HAD TO play second fiddle to Jeb Stuart in *Santa Fe Trail*, he got top billing when Flynn played him two years later in *They Died with Their Boots On* (1942). This movie is probably the all-time champion of the brewery versions of Custer's last stand, but it is also one of Flynn's great swashbuckling vehicles, teaming him with Olivia de Havilland in a courtship and marriage that glow with erotic love. De Havilland can never have been more beautiful, and, whatever they really thought of it or each other, in this film she and Flynn seem like two people only a heartbeat away from tearing each other's costumes off. On her wedding day, her father calls her behavior "positively unmaidenly," and she replies, "After today, that won't matter."

They Died with Their Boots On brought out the best of Flynn's limited talents, including a gift for self-mockery that is too easily forgotten. For its first half, the film operates as romantic comedy, exploiting comedy's lightweight sense of believability. There are many tricks and stratagems. De Havilland, having just met him, says, "That's the man I'm going to marry!" He gets away with striking a superior so as to continue an attack, and with stealing a superior's horse so he can have a mount to join the cavalry. He unknowingly insults De Havilland's father on the way to asking for her hand. He is made a brigadier by mistake, then takes command of a brigade and cries, "To the devil with the orders! We'll ride to the sound of the guns!" This is Robin Hood as cavalry officer, a child's vision of the ideal warrior.

But, if childish comedy tonight, then sermons and soda water after: the second half of the film is the doomed movement toward the Little Big Horn. Anthony Quinn is Crazy Horse, Arthur Kennedy the villainous white who sells guns to the Indians ("They're Civil War surplus," he snarls, but the guns we see are the common movie anachronism, cartridge-firing Winchesters). Now, Custer's goal is the building of a great cavalry regiment, creating men willing to "die with their boots on." When Kennedy gets the regiment drunk and they fall off their horses in a raucous dress parade, Custer smashes the post's saloon and gets himself cashiered.

At the same time, he puts himself on the side of the Indians: "The sanctity of the entire red race has been violated" by the Black Hills gold rush (which is more of villain Kennedy's work). Custer fights to regain his command in order to come between the Indians and the whites. "If I were an Indian, I'd fight next to Crazy Horse."

The hinged action has thus swung from the comic pursuit of love and glory (the Civil War years) to the melodramatic pursuit of glory and death (the Indian Wars). "There's one thing to be said for glory—you take glory with you when it's time to go," the mature Custer says near the end. It is a line that Flynn can make work. "Premonition of disaster," Libby Custer writes in her diary. Restored to command, Custer leads "the immortal 7th cavalry" out of the post, "Gary Owen" rising on the soundtrack. The end is pure suds (the beer poster), with Flynn the last man alive, gorgeous in his fringed buckskin shirt. We do not see him die but instead see Crazy Horse riding off with the flag next to which Custer had stood.

To suggest that much of this is history would be laughable; it is simply another in a line that goes back to 1910. Custer was a complex, sometimes a puzzling figure, so there is room for creative interpretation in his career; however, to make him a passionate spokesman for the Sioux is ridiculous. The film erases such embarrassments as the Washita River atrocities and Custer's fluctuations in rank. More significantly, it shifts responsibility for anti-Native American white activities (expansion, Manifest Destiny, "more West") from society to yet another "bad white man," turning one of the major causes of the Indian Wars into an aberration. Indeed, the Kennedy character's scheme to open the Black Hills replaces a scheme that the historical Custer may have been involved in.

They Died with Their Boots On is not history but modern pop culture's exploitation of neoromantic history, "the cinematic equivalent of the Budweiser Beer print."[7] It is colossal defeat as redeemed by the Wild West Show, the Last Stand as "one of Cody's most popular acts."[8]

In much the same way, *Buffalo Bill* (1944) made pop legend of bits and pieces of the life of the man who mythologized Custer, William Cody. With Joel McCrea as a virile, affecting Buffalo Bill, and Maureen O'Hara as a stunning reinvention of Mrs. Cody, this was entertaining movie melodrama that achieved one stunning image but little history.

Buffalo Bill is really about the West of the Wild West Show, not the West of reality; this disjunction shows most clearly in its depiction of Native Americans. Cody rides into the film, wearing a fringed buckskin jacket and waving a Winchester. "Ain't another rifle in the world with a bark like your Springfield!" an acquaintance shouts. He saves O'Hara from an Indian attack, then explains that "Indians are good people—if you leave 'em alone." Linda Darnell, as an Indian in tanface, is one who doesn't want to be left alone; eating her heart out for Bill, she steals into O'Hara's room to try on a dress "to find if I could be as beautiful as a white girl." There is no suggestion that a Native American woman at a trading post had opportunity to acquire European clothes—especially if she was the schoolmarm, as Darnell seems to be.

Native Americans are here the colorful figures of barnside posters and circus tents—homogenized, overfeathered, dehumanized. In a major sequence, Cody kills one, Yellow Hair (Anthony Quinn), "the first scalp for Custer." Yet this Cody, like Flynn's Custer, is pro-Native American. "The Indian is a freeborn American who'll fight for his folks, for his land, for his living, just like all of us. . . . You Easterners don't know what you're doing. . . . There's only one Indian you ever thought about, and here he is—." And he tosses an Indianhead penny on the plate of a railroad magnate, earning Eastern enmity. With the speech, Cody finds himself an outcast, broke and homeless in the flinthearted Northeast. Like Toby Walker in *Annie Oakley*, he ends up in a penny arcade, doing trick shooting. We see him teaching some kids—including a black child—to shoot, and then O'Hara finds him as he does his act on a wooden horse. The film lurches strangely: all of a sudden, it is deeply touching, this image of the displaced Westerner on the wooden horse, firing gallery rounds. Here, at last (and too late), director William Wellman has found the image that will contain both the Cody of the movie and the Cody of the Wild

West Show, as well as one that makes us question the historical Cody. The central sign of that image is the theatrical one peculiar to the arcade (and the one used later by Arthur Kopit in *Indians*), the wooden horse.

However, this is only a lurch. The film returns to itself by reuniting Cody and his wife and by having Buntline invent the Wild West Show: "We'll bring the West to the East!" Any connection between such a show and the degradation of the arcade is avoided; by implication, the arcade, the image of a debased West, is different in kind.

"His name came to typify frontiers and freedom, adventure and fair play—the spirit of the West!" We are given a montage of the Show: Teddy Roosevelt cries "Bully! Bully!" Audiences cheer. Kids love it. And then it is the final show, and McCrea, now white-haired, rides into the arena and makes an old man's speech aimed mostly at children, "my little comrades in the gallery." And a child on crutches actually shouts (*pace*, Tiny Tim), "And God bless you, Buffalo Bill!"

The wooden horse of the arcade has become the prancing horse of the old man in the arena; both are the cantering horse of the young buffalo hunter and scout. The effect is embarrassingly cheap, but it is beautifully done.

WAR MOVIES

HOW CAN A WAR picture be dedicated to peace? By having as its protagonist a pacifist, an Appalachian fundamentalist who takes "Thou shalt not kill" literally but whose minister persuades him that he must answer the draft: "The Lord will provide." *Sergeant York* (1940) was another recognition of the war in Europe and Roosevelt's "arsenal of democracy"—the story of a Tennessee pacifist who had become a hero in World War I. The producers dedicated it to those "who had [faith] . . . that a day will come when man will live in peace."

York (Gary Cooper) begins as a rural hell-raiser ("The devil's got you by the shirt-tail, Alvin!"), then meets Joan Leslie, determines to work to earn a piece of bottom-land so he can marry her, and goes on a drunken rampage when he is tricked out of the land. Coming home in a downpour, he is struck by lightning, knocked down, his muzzle-loading rifle destroyed. He staggers to the church, where "That Old-Time Religion" is being sung, and comes to God—and to Walter Brennan, the preacher. Embracing fundamentalist Christianity, he refuses to be drafted until Brennan resolves the conflict between God and Caesar; York then goes to France and becomes a hero.

All of this was shot in an artificial style defined ultimately by sound-stage rather than location shooting. The craggy hills, the twisting furrows, the skylines, while striking, are often more like the paintings of Thomas Hart Benton than like real landscapes. One in particular puts Cooper in profile against a cloud-piled sky. This was filmic realism trying to escape itself and become heroic, a visual equivalent of the tension between "great man" history and the burgeoning interest in "people" history. The acting style, on the other hand, was unadorned American realism—Cooper's simplicity, Brennan's local-color quaintness, and above all Margaret Wycherly's understated and unsentimental plainness as York's mother. The role rewarded such an attack with lines like "It's hard, gettin' corn out of rock."

So understated is much of this, in fact, that the film seems to miss its own climaxes—the lightning-strike conversion, the combat scene in which York shoots "about twenty" Germans and captures a company—and they are rather flat. However, if the film is viewed as York's growth to wisdom, rather than as a series of flashy events (not the lightning strike but the conversion, not the war but the pacifist's struggle with conscience), then this flatness makes dramatic sense. The high point of the film is not the heroics in combat but the quiet rejection afterward of attempts to commercialize his heroism— by, among others, Ziegfeld. "I ain't proud of what happened over there," York says. "Things like that ain't for buyin' and sellin'." And so he goes home to Tennessee.

The aspect likeliest to be of historical interest is religion. York's conversion, his mother's piety, his pacifism, are believable; on the other hand, they are presented by a commercial system with a poor record of depicting everyday faith in ordinary people. York's quiet faith thus gets less emphasis than Walter Brennan's ranting cuteness. Yet, the unmovable honesty of Cooper, supported by Wycherly's simple strength, bespeak the foundation of America and make the film a call to arms of a serious, even somber, kind.

Wilson (1944) was a big-budget attempt to be serious about recent history while making a plea for action in 1944. As a result, it has many of the earmarks of the earlier neoromantic films: an English actor (Sir Cedric Hardwicke) plays the hero's opponent, Senator Henry Cabot Lodge; patriotic music plays throughout, "The Battle Hymn of the Republic" being used four times and Wilson leaving the film to a choral rendition of "America, the Beautiful"; a great deal of footage is devoted to romance and domesticity; spectacle is an end in itself, so that political conventions are treated at loving length but the issues behind the candidates are virtually unvisited. Marching bands abound in the film; so do ceremonies, which, as in the 1912 *Coming of Columbus,* take the place of human action but reassure us of the importance of what is going on. Time is even wasted on Eddie Foy, Jr., pretending to be his father onstage; the act is followed by a blackface comedian who parodies Teddy Roosevelt's African safari.

Alexander Knox played Wilson interestingly and strongly; sadly, despite a talented supporting cast, he seems to be doing a one-man show because nobody else has an action. Many figures—e.g., Joe Tumulty (Thomas Mitchell), McAdoo (Vincent Price)—have names and a few lines but no characters; Hardwicke's Lodge has only hollow words to say, and he plays the role as if he had just been stuffed. The greatest omission of all is Theodore Roosevelt, who hated Wilson and whose hatred was a force of the times; to omit him is to distort history utterly.

Wilson is a wartime movie whose ostensible subject is peace. However, it is also a movie that generates its greatest enthusiasm for war; once Wilson takes the nation into World War I, happy military music strikes up and several minutes of patriotic newsreel footage flash past. The film would have been much more honest if it had dumped the bond-drive flag-waving and shown what happened in the trenches—the real reason for loving peace.

Wilson is better than most such films in giving us a glimpse of matters like the Fourteen Points, but it cannot see beyond maleness and whiteness and Hollywood to show us fundamental issues. Produced by Darryl F. Zanuck, the mass producer of neoromantic pseudohistory before the war, it is an expensive example of why this approach to historical film could not work.

A war movie of a very different sort tried to persuade American audiences that the Soviet Union was a worthy ally. *Mission to Moscow* (1943) all but dropped its trousers trying to show that it was quintessentially American while saying that the Germans were very bad and the Soviets were very, very good. The result was a well-made film that wore its attitudes like a conventioneer's badge, but one so biased that it cannot possibly be taken as seriously as it wants.

It opens with the real Joseph Davies, author of the book on which the movie was based, saying, in effect, Let me tell you what my biases and my credentials are. "My people were pioneers. . . . I think that I am peculiarly the product of our great country and its free institutions . . . a competitive society of free enterprise. . . ." He has come to have respect for "the integrity and honesty of the Soviet leaders" and is convinced that they want "to live in a decent world as good neighbors in a world of peace. . . ."

Retrospect tells us that he was wrong. Was he, therefore, a fool? A dupe? It seems clear he was not a liar.

Walter Huston then appears as Davies and takes up where the real diplomat left off: "No leaders of a nation have been so misrepresented and misunderstood as those of the Soviet Union." Moments later, in a scene with Franklin D. Roosevelt, he is saying, "Politically, I'm a liberal, but I'm also a capitalist." Seldom can a commercial movie have laid out its politics so carefully, or so carefully tried to defend itself against charges of anti-American, anticapitalist bias.

The ensuing film lacks an action. It has in its place an organizing principle (revealing the Soviet Union) and a noncausal structure (Ambassador Davies's trip to the Soviet Union). It could not have been a compelling film in the way that strongly plotted ones are; such suspense as it has is intellectual, and idea, not character, drives everything.

Seen from this distance, *Mission to Moscow* looks almost likably naive. Some of it is typical war-film propaganda: a stopover in Berlin is filled with marching soldiers, *Hitlerjugend*, Jews wearing numbers; von Ribbentrop—the actor Henry Daniell at his nastiest—says, "Germany has already turned her back on peace." Some of it is perfectly amiable shmaltz: Davies's daughter (Eleanor Parker) out with two nice Russians, meeting a nice ski regiment,

dancing at a nice cafe and drinking nice tea; Davies's wife (Ann Harding), visiting a perfume store that "might be on Fifth Avenue," as she says with admiration, to which the sophisticated Soviet manager replies, "Women are the
same the world over—they all want to please their men."

However, Davies's interactions with real Soviet leaders are harder to swal-
low. Litvinov is played by Oscar Homolka, an actor adept at conveying crafty
charm. Molotov (he of the cocktail) is played by Gene Lockhart, an actor who
occasionally played smalltime villains but who was at his best as slightly pretentious Babbitts. Neither actor projects here any sense of duping the American ambassador; on the contrary, they are evidently meant to be what they
seem. Huston's Davies, on the other hand, is so high-minded he seems a
divine fool. When an aide reports that the Italians have found listening
devices in their embassy and he would like to have the American embassy
checked, Davies turns him down. "Let's give [the Soviets] the benefit of the
doubt." He appears to accept Stalin's purges and the show trials at face value.
When he finally meets with Stalin, he says, "I believe, sir, that history will
record you as a great builder for the benefit of mankind." The great builder
smiles, says, "We want you to realize that we feel more friendly to the government of the United States than any other nation."

This picture of Stalin is intolerable, given the framework of fact visible
from the 1990s. However, it should not obscure some historical arguments
that he makes: e.g., that English ultraconservatives wanted to push Germany
and the Soviet Union into war. Davies repeats this charge in a meeting with
Churchill, this time citing "anti-Soviet prejudice in the [British] diplomatic
corps" and referring to the pre-Churchill British government as "the reac-
tionary government."

The final minutes of the film are devoted to the post-1938 world, with a
précis of the beginning of World War II. It includes scathing fictional scenes of
an American Congress cynically preparing to profit from sales to Germany and
Japan. There is footage of an America First (isolationist) float and the debate
over the 1941 draft bill, then montages of the Soviet invasion of Finland, the
Molotov–von Ribbentrop pact, and Pearl Harbor. The film ends with a stirring voice-over demanding, "Am I my brother's keeper? Yes, you are!"

Seen now, the film is astonishing, not less for its folly than for its willingness to engage intricacies of international politics that would leave most viewers cross-eyed with boredom. It is at once overt propaganda and historical
analysis, brash falsification and first-person documentation. It at least raises
questions about history and movies that are generally ignored: for example,
now that objectivity has been debunked and agenda is assumed, how much do
interpretive history and this kind of film overlap? To what extent does seriously intended propaganda qualify as history?

For all its problems, *Mission to Moscow* is the only one of the war films
that, by trying to show the causes of a war, gropes toward the understanding

that war is the final instrument of failed policy, not the instrument of success. For that, it deserves our attention.

Thirty Seconds over Tokyo (1944) was a morale booster about dropping bombs on Tokyo from carrier-based aircraft a few months after Pearl Harbor; without strategic or tactical value, the bombing was symbolic. The technological gimmick was the use of twin-engined bombers too large to land on the carriers; they could only take off, fly the mission, and then try to land—or crash—in China.

Spencer Tracy played Jimmy Doolittle, creater of the scheme; he is first shown in a Capitol Hill office with a view that suggests he is the Librarian of Congress. He gathers young pilots into one of those one-of-each fighting units—a Southerner, a Midwesterner, a rich kid—that includes Van Johnson, Don DeFore, Robert Walker, and Robert Mitchum. Tracy never smiles. He is their father; life is serious. "I want to emphasize the danger. . . . Bomb the military targets . . . and nothing else. . . . This necessary killing. . . ." His sobriety is balanced by a bevy of wives and girlfriends, including Laraine Day as Johnson's bride, who represent female uselessness. They sit in hotel rooms or on the beach, getting ready to breed, while the men work, learn, fly, fight. The women's talk of babies is endless and pointedly cute. Dropping babies is "the kind of job every girl takes on . . . once or twice in her life." Day writes lists of baby names. She never stops smiling.

Exciting as the attack footage may have seemed, it is fake; all the bombs, for example, hit their targets and result in huge destruction. After the attack, Johnson's plane crash-lands, and the rest of the film follows the survivors as they are cared for by Chinese. Johnson has a leg amputated in a makeshift hospital with only local anesthetic.

The film barely touches on the trauma of the wounded veteran. The amputation, hinted at as a symbolic castration, is dealt with quickly by Tracy's paternal brusqueness and Day's wifely cuteness (hugely pregnant, she looks like a padded six-year-old). Johnson rises from his wheel-chair and falls toward her; they end with an old lover's joke. Love and tender toughness, it seems, make everything okay.

God Is My Co-Pilot (1945) also left its women safely at home and got on with the serious business of killing Japanese. The father figure here is Raymond Massey, recently Lincoln and now Claire Chenault, founder of the Flying Tigers. And, although the film wouldn't say so, a heavy hitter in the old China lobby.

The movie has a comic-strip sensibility that makes for dumb dialogue, and a gung-ho racism (white Americans good, yellow Japanese bad) that makes for even worse ("That dog can smell a Jap at ten miles.")

Dennis Morgan is the protagonist. He is an agnostic, but we know he'll get straight before the film ends. Massey's Chenault is the same all-knowing, paternal, heroic leader that Tracy played in *Thirty Seconds over Tokyo* and *Northwest Passage*. Boyish Americans shoot down toothy Japanese; all American bombs hit their targets; Morgan kills hundreds every time he touches a trigger; and, when he finally prays to God that he be allowed to fly again after being grounded for malaria, Chenault gives him a new P-40 and tells him to go git 'em. The religious message has limited application: if you pray, God will overrule your medical officer.

Race is a key to both righteousness and godliness. The Chinese are rarely visible, perhaps because their presence would muddy the racial waters. There are no American soldiers of color. Back in Georgia, one faithful black man calls Morgan's wife "Miss Kathy." A place for everybody, and everybody in his place.

Thirty Seconds over Tokyo and *God Is My Co-Pilot* were wartime feel-goods that deliberately glossed the realities of war. But a film that dared to confront combat and the horror of combat injuries was quite different; rather, it said that bad things could not be made good easily, if at all. *Pride of the Marines* (1945) was an often honest film, thanks to John Garfield's gutty performance and Delmer Daves's direction. Written by Albert Maltz, however, it suffered from the soft-centered populism that crippled so much leftist writing of the 1930s, in part because of a writing-down that now brings thoughts of elitism. Garfield's lines, as a Philadelphia welder, are carefully ungrammatical, the settings carefully gritty and authentic. It is a film that wears its heart on its blue collar and that often looks like Depression agit-prop, although it is a patriotic, apolitical study of a severely wounded veteran.

Garfield is a deer-hunting working-man who winds up on Guadalcanal in a machine-gun crew. Guadalcanal was America's nightmare in the early days of that war, its Tet offensive, a jungle bloodbath that jarred the nation from any idea that war was glorious. *Pride of the Marines* tried to show that nightmare, and, for the 1940s, it succeeded, going to a form of surrealism to do so because convention and the Production Code would not allow a literal rendering. The studio sets, as in *Sergeant York*, are unfortunate, but Garfield's terror is palpable, the more so because war movies typically showed idealized courage, not true-to-life fear. The obscenity that is the language of war was also forbidden, and to the ear of the 1990s, the combat dialogue is unconvincing; it probably was to the veterans of 1945, as well. Garfield's fear is justified: his buddies are killed; he is blinded by a grenade.

It is at this point that the makers' concept of the proletarian hero gets them into trouble. Counterproductively inarticulate, Garfield's character is incapable of nuance, the more so because of Garfield's narrow range as actor. (Compare, for example, Brando in *The Men*.) He says things like, "You're educated; you're smart," to his doctor as he seeks an explanation of what has happened. The illogical equation of intelligence and education—and, by implication, class—confuses our understanding of his character: is he stupid, as well as bewildered? Insensitive because proletarian? Dumb because working-class? In Garfield's performance, his anguish peaks early and stays at one level; it seems to have no context but brute suffering.

As well, the film is slow. Everything is done to death, ridden until it falls over from fatigue—jokes, emotions, what pass for ideas. There are near-misses with such leftist ideas as the humanity of Mexicans and Jews, the evils of anti-Semitism. Unbelievably, Garfield's character has no racial or religious intolerance of his own.

The girl (Eleanor Parker) enables his adjustment to blindness by articulating his feelings for him—and for Maltz and Daves. She has a big speech that includes a complex metaphor; it is this rhetorical device (a typical solution to the quandary of working-class realism) that makes it possible for Garfield to change. We *see* the results of the change, but the change itself is actually in the woman's speech. In a film in which women are nurturers, we see that women also serve male film-makers as saviors: no dumb male ox without a female poet.

Pride of the Marines approached a difficult subject, the returning veteran, and dealt with it as honestly as it could within the context of an uncongenial style. The film might have cut to its harsh truths more directly if it had been able to jettison the inarticulateness, the *faux* working-class grit, the leftist correctness that forbade racial intolerance in working-class heroes. The mistake was an honest one, that of conceiving the common soldier as the common man of 1930s proletarian art. In fact, however, identity as soldiers transcended political or social definitions (a truth caught much better by Bill Mauldin). A sensitive communicator, not an inarticulate prole, would have served the film better. The trappings of Group Theatre angst—endless detail, repetition, half-baked Stanislavskiism—merely get in the way.

MUSICAL BIOGRAPHIES

IF WAR FILMS of necessity were mostly serious, however, the musical biographies were not. Granted that the level of seriousness of the typical performer's life is likely to be lower than that of the typical grunt, the possibility for the historical would seem more or less equal. What actually happened, however, was that the musical biographies derived more of their content, as well as their style, from the traditions of the musical than from the rigors of biography. This is true, for example, of *Yankee Doodle Dandy* (1942), the biography of George M. Cohan that starred James Cagney. It is a revered film because of both Cohan, whose statue stands in New York's Times Square, and Cagney, who sang and danced joyously for audiences more accustomed to seeing him as a gangster. The film itself, however, creaks, with typical elements of racism, mawkishness, and fractured fact. It accepts "the fabulous era" as fabulous and "Broadway" in the terms set down by *The Great Ziegfeld*. It accepts blackface and the "coon song." It accepts the idea of business as a clever trick.

Only in its relentless patriotism is the film substantively different from other musicals. A propaganda film for Roosevelt's "arsenal of democracy," it has FDR as a character seen always from the back—such was the awe of the office—and Cohan's performance as an FDR parody in *I'd Rather Be Right* as its springboard. Cohan is afraid that FDR has summoned him to the White House to chastise him. In fact, FDR wants to give Cohan "the Congressional Medal of Honor"—errant nonsense; what Cohan got was a special medal from Congress, quite another thing. At any rate, the entire plot device is improbable by all but the standards of musical comedy.

Flashbacks make up the bulk of the film, climaxing in a production number of "You're a Grand Old Flag" with Boy Scouts, soldiers, Teddy Roosevelt, Lincoln, the Capitol, and—as a distinct unit, suitable for easy excising—a black chorus with soloist singing "Glory, glory, hallelujah!" The actor who walked past, without lines, as Teddy Roosevelt, got screen credit; the black soloist who sang got none.

This is the white America of *The Iron Horse* and *Martyrs of the Alamo*, jingoistic and xenophobic. Blacks, all but excluded from its patriotism, are presented as loyal out of gratitude, apparently for being freed of the enslavement that the same nation imposed on them. Most of the songs—intended here, after all, to inspire enthusiasm for intervention in 1942—were written before 1920.

The other 1940s musicals mostly illustrate the genre's rigidity. Male-centered biographies (*Dixie*, 1942; *Till the Clouds Roll By*, 1946; *Words and Music*, 1948) were joined by biographies of women (but not women composers): *Shine On, Harvest Moon* (1944); *The Dolly Sisters* (1945); *My Wild Irish Rose* (1947). They are all bright, sentimental, and vapid. They signal period—usually the fabulous era—with establishing shots that use two signs, transportation (horse or automobile?) and skirt length (ankle or knee?). Most have a mentor with a European accent. Most are in color. Most are about "love."

Rhapsody in Blue (1945), however, attempted to deal with a serious protagonist, George Gershwin (Robert Alda); regrettably, he was shackled on one side to Joan Leslie, the love weight, and on the other to Oscar Levant, the wit weight. Trying to cause real biography to fly under such circumstances was a doomed enterprise.

Gershwin is first shown in a tenement boyhood with a loving family, in which the parents (Rosemary DeCamp, Morris Carnovsky) have accents but nobody wears a yarmulke or prepares a seder or ever utters the family name, Gershovitz. Young George (Dwayne Hickman) learns to play the piano by following a player piano, abruptly leaps to advanced classes with a teacher who has a Central European accent. "I want to be a composer!" says young George, but there is no hint of what such a statement might mean. In the context of the bearded teacher and his Biedemier salon, it seems to have a strong Romantic flavor, but we are given nothing more.

As the film progresses, this Romanticism becomes an undefined notion of "art," identified with Europe through a long meeting with Ravel and continued attention to the teacher. Sometimes, however, art is American—"This boy has a gift . . . he is from the people—he will write American music, great American music." What the makers of the movie may have been trying to do was assure the audience that in America, art is democratic and homegrown, an idea implicit in many of the musical biographies but one that certainly was not yet resolved. Gershwin seems to turn away from European models (the piano teacher dies as Gershwin plays "Rhapsody in Blue" at the famous Whiteman concert at Aeolian Hall), but his American models are never traced to their sources. They are hinted at, however, in a rarely seen short opera, known as both *Blue Monday Blues* and *135th Street* (for which, alone, the film is worth seeing), a precursor to *Porgy and Bess*. Whites in the film react to the opera with confusion and boredom, but blacks respond with tears. "He's sold on the blues—he won't give 'em up for anything," we are told—but what the blues are, or where they came from, is left unsaid. We are supposed to know, apparently: "blues" is a sign for black.

An early scene in the film can now be seen differently. One of Gershwin's earliest hits was "Swanee," the song identified with Al Jolson. The young Gershwin plays the song for Jolson, in blackface. He listens, hums, sings. It is a paradigm of ethnic amnesia: a Jewish star sings, in blackface, a Southern black song written by a Jewish composer.

After the success of the Whiteman concert, Gershwin goes to Paris and falls in with Alexis Smith as "Christine Gilbert," an apparently invented stand-in for the mysteries of Gershwin's personal life. Smith, always beautiful, classy, was able to convey either hardness or a softening self-irony. Her character here is a woman who wants to make art but lacks the talent. She seems meant to be a rich-bitch cliché but comes across in Smith's portrayal as something more, something both touching and annoying, a self-denying neurotic. A male-created type, she seems right for the period, although here she seems to be a sign, like a period automobile—of Gershwin's heterosexuality, at the very least, and probably of Europe's power to corrupt.

Gershwin rises and rises; he plays a white piano against a view of the Eiffel Tower; "An American in Paris" plays as picture-postcard views of Paris flash past. He begins to drive himself harder; he has headaches—uh-oh—and *Porgy* goes by so fast that if you blink, you miss the black folks. Then he dies, and boring Oscar Levant, who made twin careers out of Gershwin and nastiness, plays the "Concerto in F" under Walter Damrosch's baton. Still unsatisfied, Levant then plays "Rhapsody in Blue," free at last of a live Gershwin, with Whiteman conducting.

Rhapsody in Blue is middle-brow shlock. It wants a love story but has the problem that Gershwin never married; we get a good girl (Leslie) and a more or less bad one (Smith), and a story that has him behaving rather badly toward both. The result is a muddle about a man whose deepest relationship seems to have been with his brother, Ira (Herbert Rudley), and his publisher (Charles Coburn). The movie is unwilling or unable to go with the idea that he was a man so driven by ambition (or "art") that love was unimportant to him, and so what is on the screen as plot (the love stories) is neither interesting nor persuasive.

At a deeper level, *Rhapsody in Blue* pretends to grapple with two other questions, that of ethnicity and that of genius. Ethnicity is there mostly by default; Gershwin's debt to African–American music screams for attention it doesn't get. It is not enough to show a few feet of *Blue Monday Blues* and a snippet of *Porgy* and pretend that we have been told how a white composer absorbed black musical culture.

The matter of genius is more nearly the film's subject. The word is bandied about, and Ira's fiancè says, "Promise me something, Ira—don't you ever be a genius!" Ira Gershwin, however, already had shown himself a genius: if his lyrics are not proof of a special ability, what are they? But *Rhapsody in Blue* won't let Ira Gershwin be a genius. He is slow, smiley, stolid. He is allowed none of the signs of genius—self-destruction, speed, Romanticism. Genius is showy, this film tells us. In Paris, you play on a white piano. Not to be showy is not to have genius. This seems a fair conclusion for Hollywood to have reached, "show" there being connected with success, success probably thought a result of genius. Or something.

Rhapsody in Blue, then, is poor biography and fairly poor commercial cinema. It can only inadvertently raise questions, not answer them. Mostly, it buries them or gilds them. Too bad. Gershwin is a good subject. A film might have shown how his early drive to "get on," as this Gershwin puts it, affected American popular music—and commercial cinema, for that matter. It might have looked at what it really meant to be a lower-class Jew in New York, not as a set of signs but as culture, as reality; it might have looked at what show business meant to immigrants, rather than engaging in a feeble Eurocentric quibble about "art."

Rhapsody in Blue was at least more or less faithful to chronology. The same cannot be said of *Night and Day* (1946), a purported biography of Cole Porter. If I tell you that Porter and Monte Wooley were classmates at Yale, but in the film they are student and professor, you will get some idea of what has been done to the framework of fact. Cary Grant played Porter and was too old for the college scenes; Wooley played himself and was always fiftyish. A totally artificial film, it made even World War I look like a stage show.

Porter is seen first and last at Yale, an institution treated in the film as definitive, like the Supreme Court. He is loved by Alexis Smith (the ideal composer's love interest, evidently), who keeps giving him silver cigarette cases, a wonderfully dated symbol of the socially smart. Stylish and sophisticated musicals flash by in a montage, but not his first, *Hitchy-Koo*. The film ends back at dear old Yale, with the Yale Chorus or the Whiffenpoofs or somebody singing "Night and Day," and everybody looking rich and sad, Smith clutching Grant while he looks as if he's worried about his investments. Porter was still alive when the film was made; the real struggles of his life were not on film.

It was, however, neither Gershwin nor Porter whose bios would distinguish the musical in the 1940s; it was, instead, Al Jolson. *The Jolson Story*

(1946) and its sequel, *Jolson Sings Again* (1949), had Larry Parks lip-synching Jolson and giving enjoyable and hugely successful versions of the singer's life. It was really *The Jolson Story* that dramatized the Jolson everybody knew; the sequel brought his life from World War II tours for GIs up to the making of *The Jolson Story* itself. That two of his marriages were dropped in order to concentrate on the one with "Julie Benson" (Evelyn Keyes), for which we are to understand Ruby Keeler; that a brother who also went into show biz and was praised for his singing of "coon songs" was erased; that his reputation as a colossal ego was varnished over—these things are not supposed to matter. The songs are there; the voice is there; Ziegfeld and Broadway and Hollywood are there; the blackface, the Mammy songs, the hands on the heart are there: what more could history ask for?

And, in one important area, more is there than we get in the other musical bios: ethnicity and religion are there. They may be cuter than they should be, but this is the kind of movie in which deep seriousness must always escape into pathos or bathos or humor. One of the first scenes in the film has the child Jolson running to the synagogue, where his cantor father scolds him for being late. Years later, home from a tour, he makes a small joke about not covering his head: his father seems to acknowledge that he has become a different kind of Jew, no less loved.

Later in life, when a fiftyish Jolson has given up show biz ("I've been like a guy who's been drunk all my life;" show business has "cheated me all my life"), his parents come to visit him in California, and he sings for the first time in years—"The Anniversary Waltz," while they dance for their anniversary. They are happy and at peace; he is restless, really still itching for an audience and applause. Thus, religion and family love are themes that run unevenly through the film; sometimes they are successfully juxtaposed against his performing, but too often show biz is presented as a self-justifying end, and the themes of family and religion are simply dropped. The reward for being Jolson is—being Jolson. By implication, there is an expensive trade-off in accepting family and religion—you stop being Jolson.

Suggesting that Jolson's loss of family and religion was the price he paid for giving the world his genius is false but dramatically satisfying, a very old conflict of the public and the private; showing that it was the price he paid for satisfying his ego was probably impossible while Jolson was still alive. To its credit, at any rate, *The Jolson Story* preserved ethnicity and religion as important realities, something others of its type failed or feared to do.[9]

However, the now-familiar problem of the interaction between the performer and African-American stereotypes and music appears. In the film, Jolson dons blackface for the first time to take the place of a performer who is drunk. Nobody will be able to see the substitution, is the idea. A popular "coon song" of the period put it succinctly, "All Coons Look Alike to Me." Jolson gets a job with Dockstadter's Minstrels. What was the minstrel show?

What was blackface? What were that big mouth, those banjo eyes? The white gloves? Why did they carry Jolson to superstardom in a business that was supposedly marked by sophistication and glitz? The film is deaf to such questions. Blackface simply exists, part of the "fabulous era."

Yet, the film also shows the young Jolson in New Orleans, listening to black musicians so intently he misses his own show. He leaves the minstrel show, goes home, says he is "trying to make songs out of music I've picked up— music nobody has heard before, but the only kind I want to sing." He talks about "his kind" of music—and sings "Mammy." In blackface. Then he sings "Swanee." "His kind" of music, we gather, is some offspring of New Orleans jazz, but when "his kind" of music gets on the stage it turns out to be sentimental tripe about a whitewashed Southland, what the young Gershwin called "Southern songs" in *Rhapsody in Blue*, an established commercial category. As in *Rhapsody*, a very large step has been skipped: how do we get from those black musicians in New Orleans to the white genius and whitewashed "jazz"?

Can Jolson's drive to get applause and Gershwin's drive to "get on" be related to the often-shown immigrant attraction to vaudeville in the other musical biographies? Is "getting on," for example, the perhaps unconscious metaphor for secularization by assimilation, and the resulting loss of culture, represented here as family and God? In *The Jolson Story*, it is the cantor's son who runs away and puts on blackface and becomes a star; when Hollywood celebrates the star, it also acknowledges the something lost. In other musical biographies, the loss is shrugged away. In the Jolson films, it is intact; as a result, they may be pretty good history—source documents, at least, for useful questions.

The year after *The Jolson Story*, the musical Dorsey brothers played themselves in a miserable little movie, *The Fabulous Dorseys*. Its principal value here is the conflict between scenes of their improvisation with black musicians and those when they lead all-white bands. Improvising, black and white sit where they like and dress as they like. The white bands, however, are always in suits and ties, with one female singer whose head and shoulders emerge from her strapless dress like a flower from its stalk. This female look manages to be both phallic and erotic (about to be unclothed). Except for the woman, however, the signs communicate acceptability—musicians dressed as businessmen, regimented to stand, sit, and wave their instruments in unison—and conformity. Swing is thus visualized as black jazz under strict white control. Nonetheless, the woman sings sexually suggestive lyrics and threatens to emerge from the top of that dress. The older meaning of "jazz" as intercourse is implied, even promised by the singer and her lyrics. Yet the imagery and the sound communicate control: See, our white superego has this dangerous black and female sex stuff well in hand.

There is also a repetition of the Eurocentrism of *Rhapsody in Blue* and *Night and Day*, not in the Dorseys but in a concatenation of Paul Whiteman, an uptown venue, and a "serious" jazz concerto. Was jazz at Carnegie Hall *making it*?

WESTERNS

WESTERNS WERE NOW mostly locked into genre. The same names came up again and again—Hickok, the Earps, Billy the Kid, the Jameses, the Youngers. The titles have become interchangeable—*Bad Men of Missouri, Badman's Territory, Law and Order*. When one struggles to shake off genre, it is because of style, not better history (e.g., Fritz Lang's direction of *The Return of Frank James*). Indeed, as a genre Westerns are so contemptuous of framework of fact that Wayne Michael Sarf found them "unique among period films in their sloppiness of historical reconstruction and almost universal failure to ensure any accuracy of physical detail."[10] Two Westerns of the period, nonetheless, are inescapable.

The Outlaw (1943) gives us a West that never existed anywhere. Ostensibly about Billy the Kid (Jack Beutel), it was really an opportunity for Howard Hughes to sell tickets to watch the breasts of the young Jane Russell. Long notorious, the film is often dismissed as voyeuristic junk; so it is, but nothing with Walter Huston (here as Doc Holliday) can be dismissed. Thomas Mitchell, too (Pat Garrett), is quirkily interesting. Often pungent with sex, much of it sophomoric, the film has homoerotic undertones that seem at odds with the cheap exploitation of Russell.

Historically the film is a laugher. It is ears-deep in the firearms myth (there are six-guns and dropped holsters all over the place; crack shots make Annie Oakley seem a piker, including Holliday's dropping three men at a couple of hundred yards with three shots from a Winchester pea-shooter); the costumes are off the studio rack by way of B Westerns (Russell even wears silk stockings); this Billy the Kid has no connection to the framework of fact that props up the real Billy; and the presence of Doc Holliday is merely a means of dragging in another recognizable name. The Tchaikovsky-indebted score rises and falls like bedcovers; Russell acts like the lead in the sixth-grade play; rape is a male character trait; women are exploited and dismissed. "They're all alike—there isn't a thing they wouldn't do for you—or to you."

But *The Outlaw* has an eerie fascination. It has a reputation as a film that adores a woman. The reality, however, often is that it is a film that despises a woman—ogling her, but also raping her, battering her, rejecting her. Two men use her as a sex object, more or less by turns; she has less real value for them than a horse that one of them fancies. The real sexual rivalry in the film seems to be between Huston and Mitchell for Beutel. Androgynous, physically dangerous, Beutel is a pretty piece of rough trade fought over by the two older men. Russell is there for overt sex, whenever one of the men wants some. But, contrary to the film's hype, that overt sex degrades rather than honors her. Director Hughes's camera work seems less an act of voyeuristic desire than one of covert transference: he wants to be not in her pants, but in her shoes.

John Ford's postwar *My Darling Clementine* (1946), is a dark, moody film that looks at justice, revenge, and the establishment of law; its climax is the shootout at the O.K. Corral in Tombstone, Arizona, its focus the relationship between Wyatt Earp (Henry Fonda) and Doc Holliday (Victor Mature). It is a violent film whose most memorable sequences are about waiting and whose most memorable cinematography is its interiors. Its principals are a ferocious father, Ike Clanton (Walter Brennan), murderer of Earp's young brother; Holliday, a gloomy Romantic; Morgan Earp (Ward Bond), seemingly stolid but quick to impassioned action; Wyatt, careful, reflective, slow-burning. Ford used the interplay of these characters to create a beautiful, visually disturbing black-and-white movie whose interiors more than compensate for those in *The Iron Horse*: asymmetrical compositions, great depth and variety of tone, pools of blackness, a visual correlative for the principals' interior selves. The script, based on a 1939 B film, is not up to the acting or the direction, however; neither is the history. A reverie on the relationships among society, law, and private bonds, *My Darling Clementine*, as an example of Ford's idea of the West, has become a classic. It is an idea, however, that is merely tangential to the events of history.

SPORTS AND OTHER MATTERS

Knute Rockne, All-American is a deadly movie that only a football nut could sit through without laughing. It managed to star one of the dullest actors in Hollywood (Pat O'Brien) as a man who, one gathers from the film, was one of the dullest men in America. The result was a film whose biographical high point comes when Rockne suffers phlebitis. Along the way, of course, there is the famous (now camp) sequence about George Gipp; Ronald Reagan seems very fresh and young as Gipp and is the best thing in the film (although, apparently, nothing like the real Gipp.) To get itself off the turf, the film is pumped up with titles, the first against a choral background: "The life of Knute Rockne is its own dedication to the youth of America, and to the finest ideals of courage, character and sportsmanship. . . . Knute Rockne was a great and vital force in molding the spirit of modern America. . . ."

The great and vital force starts out as a kid in Norway, sprung from "simple, hard-working people from the old countries, following the road of equality and opportunity. . . . In the great melting pot of Chicago, the Viking boy added a rich sense of humor to his lust for life. . . ." Then O'Brien appears, looking forty and wearing more nose putty than Fonda's Lincoln; he displays all the humor and lust for life of a clam. However, he plays football, gets to Notre Dame and, the film would have us believe, passes up a chance for the Nobel Prize in chemistry so he can coach.

Donald Crisp has the thankless (and characterless) role of Notre Dame's president, a kind of motorized cassock with a golden voice for mouthing such pieties as, "[By coaching], you're helping mankind, Knute, and anyone who helps mankind helps God." And what God wants just then, apparently, is a national craze for watching boys run up and down a field on Saturdays.

Newsreel clips go on and on. The invention of the T-formation and the backfield shift are given more attention than Fermi's atomic pile. Matters come to an intellectual climax when some busybody commission or other has the temerity to investigate college football, and a smarmy official lobs Rockne a fat one: "Just why is football so vital to the public welfare?"

"Because," O'Brien intones in the voice of the recently dead, "every red-blooded young man in every country is imbued with what we might call a natural spirit of combat," leading to wars, as in poor old Europe. "We have competitive sport. . . . The most dangerous thing in American life today is— we're getting soft, inside and out. . . . We [coaches] have tried to build courage and initiative and tolerance and persistence. . . ."

Wild applause, end of investigation.

But Rockne's words are at odds with what we see in this film—newsreel clips with huge audiences in gigantic stadia, shots of newscasters, of people glued to radios. His words actually referred to the twenty-two young men on a number of fields on any Saturday; what we see are millions, sitting on their buns.

Unintentionally, *Rockne* is a historical document about the coming of mass media; unintentionally, it shows the contempt that manipulators have for those millions. "The people believe anything the newspapers print," says Crisp, apparently speaking for God. Unintentionally, it shows that the millions are white and male, as sequence after sequence goes by—stadia, airports, hearing rooms—without a female or a nonwhite face. Unintentionally, it shows the period when Americans began their slide toward the replacement of experience with entertainment. *Rockne* lies at one point on a Hollywood loop; it returns on itself to find Disneyland.

By contrast, *Gentleman Jim* celebrates physical life and focuses on the athlete, not the coach. Errol Flynn is wonderful as James Corbett, perhaps his best performance, full of self-mockery as the overweening but endlessly charming Irish boxer. Everybody in the film fights. Alexis Smith, as the upper-class woman he loves, adores fighting, and for part of the film she lives to see him beaten. He is not. At base a comedy, *Gentleman Jim* nonetheless has some of the best boxing footage ever filmed. In one fight, the camera looks almost entirely at the fighters' feet; another bores in on the brutality of bare knuckles. The script is good, funny and fast; period is there as background; family and personal relationships are a focus of great warmth. Of course everything ends well, and, when Flynn's Corbett beats Ward Bond's Sullivan, there is a sweet scene between the two men as Sullivan seeks him out at a party to hand over his championship belt.

Gentleman Jim offers no pieties about the youth of America and no fascistic twaddle about redblooded young men and the dangers of going soft, and it has roles—and regard—for women of wit and spirit. It is a comedy of character that happens to have sport as its matrix.

Were it not for Knute Rockne, Babe Ruth would have been the victim of the worst sports bio (perhaps the worst film) of the 1940s. *The Babe Ruth Story* is a sugary pack of lies about a man who loved children; resemblances to the real Ruth are mostly in the newsreel clips. As in *Rockne*, sport is offered as a good, above all for children—meaning boys. As in *Rockne*, mass media are natural components of the American scene, unexamined. As in *Rockne's* Gipper scenes, syrupy sentimentality is the key to understanding the central figure. Nowhere is there a suggestion that anyone connected with the film—writer, actor, director—said, "Let's cut through the crap and ask what Ruth was really like." Rather, like the other sports films—*Pride of the Yankees* (1942) included—it suggests that Hollywood had found a new kind of sudser for white guys.

THE 1940S ALSO took a couple of stabs at biographies of great writers. The titles pretty much said what they were: *The Adventures of Mark Twain* (1944) and *The Loves of Edgar Allan Poe* (1942). "Adventure" is not usually the first thing that springs to mind concerning Clemens; "love" may do so with the mention of Poe, although it would not be love as Hollywood understood it in the 1940s. Neither movie will meet the simplest tests of framework of fact, other than some rough dates and titles, and name-droppings like "Bret Harte," disconnected from anything the real figure ever did. More important is that they trash any intelligent, not to say noble, reasons for respecting literature; Mark Twain, for example, is presented as a writer for children. It can be said for *Poe* that at least it didn't make the same claim, but neither film is much of a step forward, except technically, from Griffith's *Home, Sweet Home*. If they are evidence for anything, it is a continuing discomfort with "art" and a contradictory attraction to literature as understood in schoolbooks: an after-image of "history according to Longfellow."

As for a new cluster of films about "little" people, it is worth noting that a number of them were about women and that most were made from books. *One Foot in Heaven* (1941) was a rather arch story of the travails of a minister and his wife, presented as charming and more or less comic, but in fact mostly pious mush. *Roughly Speaking* (1945) was a biography of a determined and gutsy but not always successful woman. Rosalind Russell played the woman, the undervalued Jack Carson her husband; regrettably, this film is virtually impossible to see now, a loss because it is said to be a rare instance of a strong woman's film.

Our Hearts Were Young and Gay (1944) and its sequel, *Our Hearts Were Growing Up* (1946), were lighter-than-air fluff about being young, white, and affluent in the 1920s, when going to Paris was the beginning of life—for a certain class—and young women wore dresses and hats to sightsee, and young men wore evening clothes to take them to dinner. The two films recall a time when chastity was a virtue, respect a glue that bound the generations, class an essential of genteel existence. The *Hearts* movies deal with the period of the Harlem Renaissance and *The Well of Loneliness*, but you would never know it. They are history as privileged nostalgia.

Fighting Father Dunne (1948), on the other hand, was a fairly serious look at the work of a priest in St. Louis, one of the few films to look more or less seriously at the problems of children, showing them living on the streets or with alcoholic and abusive fathers. The acting is terrible, not only by Pat O'Brien as the priest but by some of the kids, as well; the viewpoint is blindered—no women, no people of color. Bad as the film is, however, it is evidence of a postwar desire for a cohesive society, one that despises the abusive father and the wicked child not because of sentimentality about children but because of fear of threats to cohesion. Its bad kid ends in the electric chair, an object lesson of society's willingness to protect itself. The imagery is regressive, looking back to the gangster films of the 1930s; the point, I believe, is not.

IT IS DANGEROUS to generalize about these films: more than ninety historical films were released in the 1940s, of greatly different sorts. Many of the wartime films can be seen as reflecting the time, some of them with surprising seriousness and a surprising emphasis on peace; those released after the war—a smaller number—are harder to read. Most of those seem to show a return to business as usual, an attitude that would prove in the 1950s to be fatal.

In fact, the strains in the 1940s are so diverse and so numerous that I find it the most difficult of decades to understand, despite the war. What can be said is that a tendency within the industry to repeat its successes, especially those of 1939-42, ran counter to the direction of American society during and after the war. The war was a bursting dam, and it swept away much that Hollywood thought of as permanent. The industry's experience in the 1950s would suggest that it did not notice until too late that the dam was out.

CHAPTER FIVE

THE FIRST 1950s: HISTORY FROM THE TOP DOWN _____

The 1950s have a pop reputation for silliness and placidity, probably as the result of their having been the first full television decade. For any-one who lived through it, however, it was less a period of "Father Knows Best" than of unease: it opened with the Korean War, and men and women who had survived World War II found themselves in uniform again; the Cold War dominated politics, the primary effect a low-level, grinding para-noia. The civil rights struggle became a national one. Unanswerable ques-tions became the common coin: Who lost China? Was there a missile gap? How many Communists infested the State Department? Who would survive a nuclear war?

The total number of historical films almost doubled that of the 1940s —so many films that they have been broken here into two chapters to be manageable. The traditional and Western films continued to dominate (half the total), although musical and show-business biographies climbed to almost a quarter, with smaller numbers of sports, outsider, and, a new type, gangster films.

No film better captures the jagged nature of the decade than *I Was a Communist for the FBI* (1951). It is both bellicose and whiny, patriotic and antidemocratic. In black and white, it has the look of a 1940s cheapie, yet it actually got itself an Academy Award nomination—for feature documentary.[1] It is the flip side of *Mission to Moscow*, an anti-Communist propaganda film.

The film opens with an image of an FBI badge; serious music plays. Then, as female clerks file, serious FBI men sit at desks and give the women orders. This is the film's image of America: serious, efficient, autocratic, male.

Matt Cvetic (Frank Lovejoy) is an FBI informer and mole in the Com-munist hierarchy in Pittsburgh, "where the Commies had planted themselves to throw [America's industrial heart] off-beat." He is despised by his own brothers, suspected by his own son, a "slimy Red," as one brother calls him. He goes from an angry family gathering to a luxurious hotel room, where other slimy Reds are meeting Gerhardt Eisler; a huge spread awaits them. "Better get used to it," a local leader tells him, "this is the way we're going to live, once we take the country over." Eisler toasts the Soviet Union, offers

Cvetic caviar. They show no belief in Marxism or idealism; Communism here is a self-serving sham.

At a Communist labor meeting, most of the faces are black. This is one of the few films of the period to include blacks in numbers and to seem to take their concerns seriously. However, a white Communist says afterward, "Those niggers ate it up, didn't they?" He explains to Cvetic that if a black "goes out and kills a white man, gets convicted by a white jury, we can raise a defense fund." Eisler adds, "Just like in the Scottsboro case," and the speaker says with lip-smacking unction, "The Party raised two million dollars just to defend those six niggers, and all it cost was sixty-five thousand." The inclusion of black faces, then, is no better than their exclusion in other films; they are included only to be called niggers and to indict the civil rights movement as a Communist trick. Later, an FBI man tells Cvetic that Communists started "the race riots in '43 and the riots in Harlem the same year. . . . Those [who were killed] never knew that their death warrants had been signed in Moscow." All civil rights activity, and by implication all dissent, is a Communist trick.

Ultimately, Cvetic is to testify before the House Un-American Activities Committee. By then, it has become clear that dissent is itself an un-American activity, the act of a sucker who has fallen for the Party line. Any application of the First Amendment is a concession to Moscow. The Bill of Rights is part of Moscow's plot; as a CP official tells Cvetic, "We'll give 'em the usual runaround—stand on your Constitutional rights. . . ." Cvetic, however, is at last allowed to reveal himself as the loyal American he is, and he testifies against the Party: "Most of the members are traitors whose only purpose is to deliver the people of the United States into the hands of Russia as a slave colony." His brother and his son love him again; "The Battle Hymn of the Republic" plays; a bust of Lincoln appears on the screen.

There is the germ of an interesting little *film noir* in *I Was a Communist for the FBI*—the tale of a man undercover who loses the love of his family. It could even have been made to work within the same good-FBI, bad-CP context, but not with such thin characterization and such paranoid bombast. As made, however, it is improbable fiction whose origins are in fear. Those origins do not necessarily make it a poor subject of study, although they make it a poor film. It does give us one aspect of the period, albeit from a biased viewpoint; more importantly, it gives us insight into some American ideas— or at least some Hollywood ideas—of 1950–51: that the informer is a hero; that the Bill of Rights is for suckers; that civil rights activity is a foreign plot; that the mass of Americans (like the mobs in *Young Mister Lincoln* and *Knickerbocker Holiday*) are gullible and volatile; that the FBI, and such activities as covert penetration of labor and offensive political parties, epitomize America at its best. One would say it is very much of the Cold War, but the Cold War was only beginning; rather, it is very much of the paranoia of the late 1940s and early 1950s.

AMONG THE FILMS dealing with traditionally conceived history, a curious failure of nerve seems to have taken place. Despite their numbers, they do not include a single first-rate motion picture. Despite big budgets and lavish use of color, they seem the products of an industry that has lost touch with itself or with its audience. Films whose plots and characters seem to have sprung from the same sources that produced the neoromantic successes of the late 1930s now have glaring flaws, not least of them the discernibly lower level of directing, absent a few old masters. Part of the trouble may have been the sheer number of films—four times as many as in the 1930s—which required that the pool of skills be spread much thinner. Part of it was the aging of the male stars and a concomitant change in the idea of women, who are now more like the waiting wives of the war movies than like the roles played by Rosalind Russell and Alexis Smith. Again and again, these films combine a visibly over-age man with a woman young and passive enough to be his daughter. Indeed, the improbability of the female characters represents what is wrong with the decade. Whatever the cause of their troubles, these films seem joyless.

Some films appear to have been made almost reflexively. Sam Katzman reprised the Zanuck productivity of the prewar years (ten films, including The *Iroquois Trail* [1950], *The Pathfinder* [1952], and *Fort Ti* [1953]), but the films were vapid and perfunctory; one used footage from the 1936 *Last of the Mohicans*, one a set from *Plymouth Adventure*, made the same year; Rogers Rangers appeared in the same pixie suits of *Northwest Passage*; sets had anachronistic dressing—a display of percussion and revolving pistols in *Fort Ti*, Victorian knick-knacks in *The Pathfinder*.

However, what is perhaps most striking about this traditional cluster is what the films were not: none of them was about the nation's founding, none about the making of the Declaration of Independence or the Constitution, and only two, *The Scarlet Coat* (1955) and *The Devil's Disciple* (1959), were about even minor events of the Revolution. The French and Indian War was the subject only of negligible B's like the Katzman movies. Thus, historical subjects that had been important since the beginning of film were mostly ignored. The reverence for the past, or at least for the past of the Founding Fathers, seems to have collapsed. Not only are there no canonical events, but the respect that allowed the making of big pictures about Revere and Braddock and Rogers has diminished to the tepid enthusiasm of the B producer.

What had been found to replace the old canon? Commendably, one might think, three films about less examined subjects; regrettably, none was good history—or even a good film. *Captain John Smith and Pocohontas* (1955) was a cheap, dull piece, badly acted and directed, with horrendous anachronisms and ludicrous props—one blunderbuss, for example, was clearly an 1870s Springfield with a tin funnel soldered on the end. It had laughable dialogue ("yon gladsome Indian maids"; "I had never meant to fall in love with Pocohontas, but it happened.") That there might have been something other than erotic love in the twelve-year-old Pocohontas's saving of the aging Smith did not occur to anybody, nor did anybody bother to deal with the embarrassing aftermath, Pocohontas's early death in England.

Plymouth Adventure (1952) looked at the Mayflower Compact and also saw an erotic triangle—Spencer Tracy, stalwart sea captain; Leo Genn, genteel but of course sex-blocked Puritan; Gene Tierney, beautiful and of course frustrated wife of Genn. No matter that Tracy by then looked old enough to be Genn's father, so the title might better have been *The Old Man and the She*; no matter that the Mayflower crossing had events of real importance; no matter that the script was as wooden as Tierney's face.

Tracy is graceless and rude, playing a man who is graceless and rude; he drinks too much and shouts things like, "I'm carrying a cargo of madmen!" "There are no honest men!" and "Friendship—love—Rffff." The Pilgrim saints are played by English actors (the virile captain thus seeming the first American), apparently to show that they are not graceless and rude, but at the cost of sexual interest and perhaps pheromones: English niceness just can't cut the mustard in the sex department, whereas Tierney starts breathing strangely whenever she gets a whiff of Tracy. "What a foul man you are," she says, inhaling deeply. Eventually, she drowns herself.

Tracy, after her death, enjoys a change of heart. He casts off gracelessness and rudeness, spends the winter at Plymouth with the genteel English actors, and makes a most pious speech about having been alone and now being "with my fellows," and he and Genn have a buddy scene and talk about "her" and "love."

Seven Cities of Gold suffered the same reverse alchemy, from the precious metal of history to the lead of fiction, this time of both the pious and the erotic variety. Made, apparently, from a children's novel about Junipera Serra, it starred an English actor (Michael Rennie) as the padre, then slapped a heavy-breathing sex plot (Rita Moreno and Richard Egan) over his piety and threw on Jeffrey Hunter as a blue-eyed Native American. The only contexts were paternalism (good) and sex (bad); it shares with Selig's 1912 *Coming of Columbus* a conviction that the Spanish were good for Native Americans.

The American Revolution provided the environment for both *The Scarlet Coat* and *The Devil's Disciple*. The latter is by far the worse of the two, based on a lesser Shaw play that really exists only for its third-act tour de force by whoever plays General Burgoyne—in this case, Laurence Olivier, who could hardly do wrong in the role but who is surrounded by incompetence. The costumes, for example, are abominable—ludicrously inaccurate military uniforms, the men's coats padded like 1940s suits, Kirk Douglas in the little silk neckscarf brought over from the cowboy flick. It is not even funny—hard to do with Shaw. All these films suggest that the reason for doing history has been forgotten.

The Scarlet Coat tried to be better history but kept getting caught up in Hollywood myths. The firearms myth, for example, is hit bang-on: Cornel

Wilde, as a rebel officer, downs a man on a horse with one shot from a flint-lock pistol fired from *his* galloping horse, at night. Uniformed rebels—and Wilde—keep showing up in various versions of the fringed-buckskin myth. It keeps trying to be a Western. Wilde walks right through it all, apparently secure in the knowledge that it is an action film with costumes in which he looks good, whatever their inaccuracies.

He is an American who goes undercover to find spies operating out of then-British New York City, his character based on a real figure. Michael Wilding is genteely witty and humane as the historical Major André, the British officer hanged as a spy. His characterization works both for and against the movie, making it seem sometimes adult in its charm and intelligence, but too often childish in its derring-do. Anne Francis is a female rebel, both too modern and too American to be credible, yet she has great spirit. Both Wilde and Wilding romance her, the three usually surrounded by too much luxury, as if it were a Ross Hunter film.

At best, *The Scarlet Coat* is an in-and-out experience, both as film and as history, finally more committed to what happens in movies than to what happened in the past. Nonetheless, it is one of the few films to deal with Arnold's treason, a very old subject in American drama. And its version of Andre's hanging is touching and probably accurate. Yet it is significant that the same events that provided one of the most successful early plays of the American stage are here merely fodder for a romantic shoot-'em-up.

John Paul Jones was a naval pageant intended as a recruiting tool (it began on the deck of a modern aircraft carrier). As Jones, Robert Stack was as wooden as his ships. His contributions to the nation's beginnings are made to seem trivial here. The filming is so archaic that it includes a tableau vivant of Trumbull's signing of the declaration—an example of the outdated notion that reenacting events was writing history.

The President's Lady (1953) was less a parade of patriotic tableaux vivants than of romance novel covers. Charlton Heston, dripping leather fringe, is Andrew Jackson, Susan Hayward the woman he married in more haste than her other husband liked. *The President's Lady* recalls other star vehicles about women who were defined by the men who protected them (*Magnificent Doll*, 1946; *The Gorgeous Hussy*, 1936) and is perhaps interesting because it opens the situation of such male-defined women to historical scrutiny. These films, however, do not supply that scrutiny, probably because they are equally male-defined.

Fiery and tempestuous, tossing her hair and rearranging her bosom, Hayward is in hog heaven. "I've lost all respect for you," she cries when she finds her husband's mistress is a slave. Off she goes with Heston, poses for several romance covers with him, then fights the idea of divorcing her husband to marry him. "You're a man—I don't think you can understand what this means to me—it means I'm—marked for life!"

Passion is all, however; they do some more poses and then marry and pose some more, and then people stop speaking to her. He goes off to fight the Creeks; Hayward plows and plants and gets dark makeup on her cheeks; he comes home, fights a duel for her; she waits, suffers, weeps, nurses. It's 1812. It's 1825. Heston's Southern accent gets thicker and thicker. She dies. His inaugural speech is a voice-over for a montage of Hayward in action.

The President's Lady offers history as female trouble. Behind, or beneath, every great man is a greater woman.

Certainly there is history to be written about women who connected themselves to men who became "great." There is history to be written about ideas of marriage and divorce, about social pressures in the nineteenth century, about Jacksonian ideas of "honor" and the code of blood, about the sexual exploitation of black women and about white women's tolerance or contempt for it. But none of this is in the film. What is there is a male idea of entrapment in biology, of a destiny that paradoxically gave a gloomy heroism to the woman who devoted her life to it.

A related idea of women infected The Far Horizons (1955). One would think that the story of Lewis and Clark and the tiny group who crossed North America and returned in the first decade of the nineteenth century, losing only one along the way (to peritonitis),[2] has sufficient narrative force. Not so, apparently; the film must needs involve Merriwether Lewis (Fred MacMurray) and William Clark (Heston again) as lovers of the same woman twice over. One woman is Julia Hancock (Barbara Hale), the other, Sacajewea (Donna Reed), the Shoshone teenager who went with them on much of the journey and whose baby provided the portable proof of their good intentions. This Sacajawea, of course, is no teenager, has no baby, and is a sexy Anglo virgin in tanface. Like Susan Hayward, she is a prisoner of biology, often helpless, always self-sacrificing.

Much about the movie is appalling, including the dialogue ("Sounds like a big order, Mister President," is Lewis's response to Jefferson's idea to cross the continent), the costumes (fringed buckskin à go-go, modern beadwork that makes the Indians look like ads for a moccasin shop), an utter balls-up of Native American ethnology.

After the return to Washington (this Sacajawea goes with them, history be damned),[3] Sacajawea and Julia Hancock talk girl stuff. "A woman [among the Indians] cooks for her man, works in the fields, and has the babies. That is all," says Sacajawea. Hancock replies that a white woman "runs her husband's home, entertains his friends, tries to make him happy and successful and proud of being married to her." Sacajawea tries on a dress, just like Linda Darnell in Buffalo Bill. Whether it is the thought of all that entertaining, or a dislike of fashion, Sacajawea opts out; in a trice, she is headed west by carriage, and Julia has to read aloud her letter of farwell to the man both women "love." The scene is thus a double humiliation of the women in the film: neither, we see, is even worthy of trying to "make him happy and successful and proud of being married to her." (Why did Lewis and Clark cross the continent? To put women in their place.)

The Buccaneer (1958) was an overblown remake of a 1938 DeMille epic, directed this time by Anthony Quinn. Its costumes got an Academy Award nomination,[4] apparently for making the New Orleanians of 1815 look like the residents of the Emerald City. The nomination may be significant of what was going on generally: history was so little regarded, or so little understood, that costumes were considered as mere prettiness. So with the rest of the film; as a historian wrote of it, "It is hard to keep a straight face through an entire screening."[5]

The 1950s showed an unusual interest in the history of Texas, perhaps as patriotic response to the pressures represented by *I Was a Communist for the FBI*. Three films were released during the decade; a fourth (*The Alamo*, 1960) is related. *Lone Star* (1952) looked at Texas on the eve of the Mexican War but was anachronistic in material culture (guns and men's costumes) and dishonest in its human behaviors. *The Last Command* (1955) was a near-B film that pushed itself to a higher level with an intelligent screenplay. Not blessed with stars of the first rank (Sterling Hayden, J. Carrol Naish, Anna Maria Alberghetti), it nonetheless got good performances and the best backwoods Davy Crockett of the decade in Arthur Hunnicutt. *The First Texan* (1956) had beautiful photography, and Joel McCrea as Sam Houston, but little else. The three films taken together comprise a crude history of Texas, c. 1835–45, with more attention given to prior events in *The Last Command* than is usual. Naish's Santa Ana is a relief from the eye-rolling monster of some films. *Lone Star* is manipulative, racialist junk, full of Western clichés, but it has the only fledged-out women (Ava Gardner and Beulah Bondi), one a newspaper owner and the other a political activist; the women of the other two films are young enough to be the daughters of their male partners, the inequality seen also in *Plymouth Adventure*. The juxtaposition bespeaks again the male definition of women in these films, but it may also tell us something about the aging of Hollywood and its ideas.

The Barbarian and the Geisha (1958) was a beautiful film that mixed fact and legend and, when neither sufficed, invented action to fill the gaps. At base an account of the first official American representative to Japan, Townsend Harris (John Wayne), "it is also the story of a beautiful geisha girl known as Okichi and her place in Harris' life" (title). Okichi (Eigo Ando), however, is a legendary, not a historical, figure, and the meaning of "geisha girl" remains murky throughout the film (charwoman? tea maker? Avon lady?). Sam Jaffe is also present in an unexplained role (actually the German who translated for Harris).

Wayne looks ancient but interesting as the huge barbarian, but he has to do too many John Wayne things—fighting a local strongman, burning the town when cholera strikes—rather than Harris things. Okichi is a woman for the 1950s, so passive and weepy she can hardly get out of her own mincing tracks. Presumably she provides Harris with sex, but she and the script play this as "love." Ultimately, she is told by her overlord to help him kill Harris; told to mark his door so the governor, in full Samurai blacks, can kill him, she marks her own door instead. When the man discovers it is she and not Harris, he is so overcome that he kills himself. She flees Harris, watches his triumphal procession pass with a newly signed commercial treaty: "So he passed into our history, and from my sight. . . ."

The Barbarian and the Geisha was directed for maximum exploitation of the beauty of Japanese design and art by John Huston. The performances by many of the Japanese actors are superb: there really is a strong sense of an utterly different culture, and of people confused and even suicidal over the clash of their closed culture with an alien one. The film's second half, at the shogun's court, is intelligent and perceptive; the first half is marred by Wayneisms. To succeed on all levels, the film would have to be more frank about sex, less indulgent of machismo.

This, however, was 1958. Huston's version of the coming of Townsend Harris owes rather a lot, perhaps, to the coming to Japan of Douglas MacArthur. It notably has no way to refer to Hiroshima, being of the past and having no war in which we might see Japanese dying in American-made fires. Despite its anachronisms, all of them surrounding Wayne, and its bias, however, it is a good piece of historical film, not least because its visuals capture so truly and arrestingly a moment in another nation's time.

THE 1950S PRODUCED three Civil War films: *Seven Angry Men* (1954), about John Brown, again with Raymond Massey, this time in a performance that was a counterweight to the madman's portrait in *Santa Fe Trail; The Raid* (1954), about an anomalous Confederate attack from Canada on St. Albans, Vermont; and *The Great Locomotive Chase* (1956), about the same incident (as noted) that had inspired *The Railroad Raiders of 62* and *The General. The Raid* and *Locomotive Chase* were about incidents so minor as not, certainly, to represent the war. Both films are reasonably accurate. Both films gain entertainment value from their oddity and from the tradition of the caper movie. In the end, however, they remain anomalies, their historical value marginal.

Seven Angry Men, however, deals with a major issue of nineteenth-century America and with seminal events—Bloody Kansas, Harpers Ferry. It at least makes a stab at understanding Brown as other than a lunatic, trying to build a progression from the Brown of 1856 to the Brown of 1859. Massey works hard at this change, undoubtedly aware of what he had to undo from a decade and a half before. However, in trying not to show a crazed Brown, the film overdoes the villainy of proslavery whites in Kansas; now *they* are the fanatics and Brown the victim, an arrangement that is no more satisfactory than the reverse.

The film does capture Brown's relationships with his sons, and it is the deterioration of those relationships that best dramatize his turn from balance to excess. In so doing, *Seven Angry Men* picks up the patriarchal theme of several 1940s movies, not to replicate the evil father of *Santa Fe Trail* but to show a father moving from paternal love to authoritarian patriarchy to a kind of wisdom and forgiveness. Most of the burden of sonship is carried by Jeffrey Hunter and his relationship with the daughter of a Brown activist (Debra Paget). The history of Brown and what he represented can bear a partial focus on those close to him, but if their concern is merely "love" as Hollywood conventionalized it, having no matrix but itself, more is lost than gained: Brown is not contextualized; he is trivialized.

Somewhat the same problem affects the film's spectacular events (e.g., the sacking of Lawrence, Kansas). The imminent causes of the event are unclear, the larger contexts of abolitionism, slavery, and statehood inadequately examined. The spectacle, like the romance, is made to be self-justifying; the only contexts are "bad whites" (the Border Ruffians) and victimized blacks and whites.

Early on, Massey's Brown is more a loving father than an abolitionist fire-eater. "Not my work—God's work—that's what we're doing here," he says as he assembles his sons in his tent town, Ossawatemie. After the burning of Lawrence, however, he says, "The war has begun," and he reveals hidden crates of weapons. He leads his sons in attacks on men thought to be the Lawrence raiders. "An eye for an eye," says Brown, but the young woman (Paget) says "He's a murderer. He's made you [Hunter] one, too."

Brown's sons begin to drift away, unable to tolerate the father's bloody faith, leaving only Hunter. "We can't leave him to fight alone," he says; but, to stay with his father, he must accept an authority that now seems close to madness. "It is I who will decide what is wrong. . . . As long as a single human being is in bondage in this land, we cannot rest. . . . The Lord has appointed us to that task."

Harper's Ferry is the film's climax—the abortive "raid," with his sons returned to help him, and the brief assault led by Robert E. Lee. It is presented rather more critically than the first two-thirds of the film, in part because it rather carefully follows real events. The first in Brown's way is a black railroad employee, who says, "I don't need you to be free—I been free eight years!" Brown's belief that a thousand slaves would rise to join him is made to seem crazy. Perhaps, in 1859, it was not so, least of all in Virginia, but they do not rise, and Brown and his sons are no match for even a few Federal troops. "Can it be that the Lord has forsaken me?" Brown cries when the first son falls; then, when another is shot, "Thy will be done! And all men shall be free." In prison, waiting to be hanged, he prays for "God's despised poor."

Despite the banalities of the romance action, *Seven Angry Men* was a carefully made film. Its look is convincing; details like firearms are usually right. The performances, above all by Massey, are convincing. Directorial care shows most clearly in a visual device that frames the film: the opening shot appears to be mere landscape, with an unexplained row of shadows in the foreground; at the film's end, Brown's hanging opens out to show his view from the gallows, which is this same landscape, the shadows now explained as those of the soldiers who line the road to and from the hanging. "The Battle Hymn of the Republic" plays under the scene.

As history, *Seven Angry Men* is simplistic overstatement (Brown did not cause the Civil War), but, as a use of film to make a narrative history, it is impressive and a little redeems the 1950s films.

NATIVE AMERICANS

THE FILMS ABOUT Native Americans seem a welcome change from traditional history: many of them at least try to be about something. Only one, *Hiawatha* (1952), dealt with an America without whites; only one other, *Chief Crazy Horse* (1955), focused more on its eponymous Native American than on the whites around him. In all, about a dozen Native American films were released, most of them really about the white guy.

Hiawatha was Longfellow for teeny-boppers, debased by phony ethnology (Plains Indian war bonnets, beaded war shirts, painted shields), dreadful writing, and primitive acting by young performers who kept tripping over their urban accents ("Whadda dey doing in aah territoary?"). Hiawatha (Vince Edwards) and his buddies trek hundreds of miles with no gear, as if they are going to the malt shop to hang out, although they are in fact "a big waw pahty." Hiawatha's thoroughly California question about his mother and father is, "Were they happy?" Lacking as the movie does any contact with either history or Longfellow, it might better have been titled *I Was a Teenage Rubberhead.*

Broken Arrow, on the other hand, was a serious attempt to introduce liberal racial ideas to the Indian movie. Directed by Delmer Daves, it showed some of the tendencies of his *Pride of the Marines*, although it was standard 1950s in its depiction of an Indian woman (Debra Paget). And, as soon as James Stewart falls in love with her, you know her days are numbered, given Hollywood's proscription against what it insisted upon thinking of as miscegenation. And indeed, Paget is killed by bad (i.e., racially intolerant) whites, leaving Stewart's good white and the Apache Cochise (Jeff Chandler) to say pious platitudes to each other, like Tracy and Genn at the end of *Plymouth Adventure.*

Daves framed his story of a racially tolerant white man with a first-person voice-over intended to increase believability. What the audience is about to see "happened exactly as you are to see it," he says, except that the Apaches will speak "our language." And, he does not say, will be played by whites. This reinforcement of believability underscores Daves's apparent nervousness about his idea. That the film's discovery of "good Indians" was as old a subject as any other in American writing seems not to have occurred to anybody.[6] Given

Pride of the Marines, however, it appears that Native Americans are surrogates here for all objects of prejudice; the actual impetus in film may have come from a 1940s morale movie, *The Negro Soldier.*[7]

Stewart finds a wounded young Apache and helps him. When the boy says his mother "is crying" for him, Stewart muses that he had never thought of an Apache woman as crying over a son. "Apaches are wild animals, we always said." Later, he is confronted by bad man Will Geer, who will be responsible for the death of Paget: "You mean you found a wounded Apache and didn't kill him? If you don't fight against [Apaches], you're with them."

To a degree, Stewart's character is a setup by Daves and his writer. He has to talk too much, as in explaining that the Apache wars started when the army tricked Cochise. He has to be present at too many events by coincidence, from finding the wounded Apache to seeing the Apaches torture a white, to being present for the attack that kills Paget. Yet the character is internally consistent, and it causes most of the participation in events—learning to speak Apache, volunteering to find Cochise to talk him into letting the mail through his lands, marrying Paget for "love." It is, of course, Stewart the actor who brings needed credibility to all this.

Broken Arrow is not really good narrative history, and its visual history is not impeccable, either. The weapons are more or less correct: the Apaches have few, ill-assorted firearms, correctly, but Stewart wears a cartridge six-gun and a low-slung belt and holster, wrong for 1870. Jeff Chandler's Cochise wears leather clothes that look more Rodeo Drive than Southwest desert; an extended ceremony surrounding Paget's menarche looks generic Indian, although it is meant to show respect for the ceremony and the people.

The relationship between Paget and Stewart is "love" as Hollywood understood it, with matters of culture an irrelevance. There is a touch of child molestation about the relationship, Paget playing a girl in her early or mid-teens. This is not examined. It is hardly Paget's fault that she seems insipid; she is another non-Anglo woman conceived by white men, like Pocohontas, Sacajawea, and Okichi. As with them, she is conceived in terms of "love," which in the 1950s seems to have given women very little room to move. Biology has trapped her, but not in the passional showcase allowed Susan Hayward in *The President's Lady*; this, rather, is biology as second-class status, Sacajawea's "a woman cooks . . . works in the fields, and has the babies." As a character, she is created to do nothing; as a dramatic agent, she is created to die. She is wanted mostly to be the cause of the pathos that will condemn the film's racists and give stature to the closing platitudes. Women, clearly, do not have a part in the arguments against prejudice.

Much of *Broken Arrow*, nonetheless, is dramatically strong and visually effective—a defection from Cochise by Geronimo's faction; an Apache attack on an Army wagon train; Stewart's grief over Paget's death. As so often with well-intended seriousness, however, too much footage is given to words that arise more from the conviction of the makers than the characters. They are not the convictions of 1870, nor are they convictions that arise from studying 1870. What they tell us about most clearly is the hesitancy of the 1950s.

To see *Drum Beat* (1954) is to wonder how it can have been directed by the same man. Reflection suggests gross similarities: bad whites, mediation by a good white with a "bad" Indian, a Native American woman as romantic focus. *Drum Beat*, however, is driven less by idea than by the conventions of movies, and it is indifferent to both Native American ethnology and historical accuracy. It abounds in clichés—the thrown knife that kills (screenwriters, one gathers, have never tried throwing a knife); the bad white who sells Winchesters to Indians (and 44.40s, at that, the year before they were manufactured); "Indian fighter" as a designation of a profession; the hand-to-hand duel that will decide all the issues in the film—with tiny Alan Ladd of course besting large Charles Bronson.

Its supposed framework of fact was a rebellion by a group of Modoc Indians in Oregon in the early 1870s, led by a man called Captain Jack (Bronson), who took them to an impregnable natural stronghold. Ladd is John McKay, "peace commissioner" to the Modocs. He shows up at the White House in fringed leather and six-gun, and the President, too polite to comment on his guest's bizarre dress, sends him off to Oregon. Of course, Ladd quickly gives up being a peaceful commissioner. Of course, the Indian woman who "loves" him (Marisa Pavan) is going to have to die; after all, white Abby Dalton is after him. And the only really bad white is Elisha Cook, Jr., who smuggles a mule-load of Winchesters to Captain Jack's stronghold by night.

The material culture is wrong: all the Indians in *Drum Beat* use iron bits and bridles. Marisa Pavan wears a leather skirt that is see-through fringe from midthigh down. Ladd is costumed throughout like a matinee cowboy. As well, a stupid, purpose-written song, "And I'll answer the drums of love," clumps under the credits (For this, movies got sound?). It is as if *Broken Arrow* had been smashed into little pieces and Daves had tried to reassemble it blindfolded.

A more careful attempt to show a white man trying to help Native Americans was made in *Walk the Proud Land* (1956). However, like other attempts to do the right thing without providing adequate artistic (and financial) support, the movie fails; it is often dull, sometimes confusing, and in the name of historical accuracy it lacks an ending. Yet it is sometimes arresting in its desire to avoid Western cliché. John P. Clum (Audie Murphy) has been sent as Indian agent to an Apache reservation at the behest of the Dutch Reformed Church. A voice-over insists on the truth of what is to follow: ". . . the story you are about to see is true. It's my father's story, as he told it to me. . . ." Perhaps this insistence on authenticity is the result of some change in the idea of realism; perhaps it reflects nervousness about a departure from cliché, as in *Broken Arrow*.

Murphy arrives by stage, stiff and sore, dressed in a tight suit and a bowler hat. It is a good beginning, but the film falls somewhat into a type, the new-warden or new-teacher movie, and when we recognize this we expect—and get—hard-line opposition, unexpected support from the supposed bad-asses, and ultimate triumph. One of the problems for such a film is, of course, not to fall into the trap of its own predictability. *Walk the Proud Land* simply didn't have sufficiently good writing and direction; it adds cliché and dullness to its predictability. When an Apache widow (Anne Bancroft) is sent to "care for" the new agent, we know there will be a clichéd sex-tease; there is a lot of simpering and flirting and coyness, although to her credit Bancroft is skillful enough to communicate real sexuality through the dither, even though the script doesn't support her. When Clum's fiancée comes west and they marry and she moves to the agency, we know she will hate it, just like Caudette Colbert in *Drums Along the Mohawk*, and she does—even though the West was settled in good part by women. Nor is the visual framework of fact strong.

Yet, *Walk the Proud Land* tried to say things about both Apaches and whites that needed to be said. Murphy's Clum is a rarity, a layman of faith who talks easily of the Bible and God, a man who does not use a gun in a genre dedicated to the gun. The Apaches are shown in chains on the reservation, a people degraded, even bestialized. The cavalry is for once the enemy, not the savior. Even Bancroft's woman is a clumsy attempt at revisionism, and Bancroft works, against the grain of stupid lines and situations, to breathe real life into her; what she tries to create is an active, intelligent, sexually aware woman confronting an attractive but repressed man. It doesn't work, because the script and the (male) director (Jesse Hibbs) are frozen in a 1950s idea of coy and passive child-women, in part because that idea underlay the Production Code.

Although *Walk the Proud Land* was finally only a sincere muddle, it tells us that some filmmakers in the 1950s were seeking new directions. It is not a captive of the military but sees the military as the problem; it espouses a despised group; it is nonviolent; it at least acknowledges an independent woman. The movie is worth seeing, and we must take account of its serious idea, which is not 1930s leftist mush, but a real but under-funded, inadequately produced attempt at truth.

Sitting Bull (1954) had some of the same tendencies but sacrificed them to the demands of the shoot-'em-up. Yet another interpretation of the Little Big Horn, it muted the role of Custer and tried to look at things from the viewpoint of Sitting Bull (J. Carrol Naish) and a maverick cavalry officer (Dale Robertson).

The film was poorly made, certainly poorly edited, and dreadfully written. It is hardly surprising that the costumes were a mess. Historical framework of fact was weak: Custer is a bad officer who disobeys orders to attack the Sioux; President Grant himself comes west to make peace with Sitting Bull; General Crook and the other forces who marched against the Rosebud and its aftermath seem not to exist; and, after the Little Big Horn, Sitting Bull says, "They died like men—we will not scalp brave men."

Sitting Bull is at least rare in having a major black character, Sam (Joe Fluellen), a former slave who has been living with the Sioux and becomes Robertson's sidekick. And Naish's Sitting Bull, thanks to the actor, is a figure of some dignity, although not the mystic of history. It is the film's action that is improbable and therefore ahistorical, a kind of kid's Saturday movie built around the name, Sitting Bull. It looks backward, like so many 1950s movies, yet tries to incorporate a positive view of Native Americans and blacks. Of course it fails.

The warrior Crazy Horse was played in *Sitting Bull* by "famous TV star Iron Eyes Cody." He got a better turn in *Chief Crazy Horse* (1955) in the person of Victor Mature, who, despite an absurd wig and a padded bolero that made him look like Joan Crawford from the front and Judy Garland from the rear, gave the character real size. Again, a voice-over stressed the film's authenticity: ". . . a true story . . . [filmed] where it actually happened. . . ." The framing figure (John Lund) tells the story as a flashback, in the context of changes wrought by the coming of the whites, represented for him by the disappearance of game. Despite Lund's presence, this is a film that really does concentrate on the Native Americans, for all that they are played by whites.

The real Crazy Horse was a moody, perhaps neurotic man. *Chief Crazy Horse* makes this quality the effect of a childhood vision that he is slow to accept. The device is probably too linear, and certainly the music accompanying it is far too European, but it at least suggests a cultural gulf between Crazy Horse and most of the movie audience. Ray Danton is, despite an urban accent, an interesting figure near Crazy Horse—and his ultimate murderer: a Sioux detached from his people and detribalized by whites—although the cause of the alienation, a fight with Crazy Horse over a woman, is weak. Given a gun and a uniform, he becomes a "native policeman"; at the end, he bayonets Crazy Horse while taking him, without authority, to the reservation's jail. The real Crazy Horse was bayoneted by a native policeman, but not by one acting on his own; as so often, the truth was more complex than the film can bear.

Chief Crazy Horse knows it has a great story to tell but can't rise to the telling. Like Mature's wig, the material aspects of production fall short of the dignity they need: when, for example, he accepts his vision and dons a war bonnet decorated with the red hawk of which he had dreamed, the bonnet looks merely cumbersome and flashy, not significant, and there is no attempt to suggest how it might be significant to a Native American eye and not to an Anglo one. Similarly, the Sioux–Cheyenne village on the Little Big Horn is far too small.

Only once does the director (George Sherman) capitalize on his obvious lack of resources: we do not see the battle at the Little Big Horn, but a sky filled with thunderclouds; we only hear the battle. The brief aftermath—a somewhat sanitized shot of half-stripped bodies—says everything that needs to be said.

Regrettably, the same inventiveness was not brought to the problem of showing the experience of the Native American people and the fate of the Sioux and Cheyenne after the Little Big Horn, although the introduction has caused us to think about such matters. Presumably there were not enough extras or costumes or tepees to show the tragic decline into starvation and surrender. Reducing these to the experience of Crazy Horse does not suffice, in part because he has been presented as an individual, both in genius and in inspiration, and because of the tendency of narrative to focus on the individual.

Paradoxically, the general experience might have been encapsulated better by the Danton character. To have shown his suffering before killing Crazy Horse, to have given a more believable and more meaningful reason for the killing than spite, would perhaps have needed better artists than this film got. There seems to be no question that the potential exists in the work: both Mature's Crazy Horse and Danton's detribalized Sioux progress through the film, both changing over time, both moving away from the other and then back toward the other. But clichés doom any chance to make a great film about the Native American experience from these characters.

It is too bad. *Chief Crazy Horse* sometimes comes close to being more than just another Indian movie. It is to the director's credit that he visualized in some sequences what he and the writers could not create in plot—Mature's donning of the feathered bonnet, Danton's donning of the policeman's uniform; the free Sioux on horseback, the detribalized Sioux at rigid attention in his uniform; the free Sioux going down under the bayonet of the uniformed Sioux. He understood the tragedy of Crazy Horse and the history that killed him, but he could not make a movie about it.

Chief Crazy Horse is not alone among the Indian films in this failure. *Broken Arrow*, too, reached for something it could not attain. So did *Walk Proud the Land* and even, dimly, *Drum Beat*. Theirs were not merely failures of art. Mainly neoromantic melodramas, they tried to make racial tolerence a moral touchstone that was no more convincing than the Code'snotion of good and evil. At the same time, they crippled themselves with narrow ideas of women, especially Indian women. The frequent insistence on believability, on historical truth, suggests both didactic purpose and doubt of its reception.

WESTERNS

THERE WERE MORE non-Indian Westerns in the 1950s, but they repeated the earlier movement toward mere genre. Most of the films are negligible, but at least two—*Gunfight at the O.K. Corral* (1957), and *The Left-Handed Gun*

(1958)—are among the most important films of the decade, although for different reasons. One other, *The Lawless Breed* (1952) is marginally interesting for its return to the bad-guy Western as a way to push Southern victimization. Like *Belle Starr* and some of the James movies, it tries to justify lawlnessness as a Southern response to central government. "We were a proud people, ruled by a foreign army," says John Wesley Hardin (Rock Hudson). "There's no law in Texas—only Yankee law." And there's no history in the film—only Western cliché.

Gunfight at the O.K. Corral was probably the most psychologically probing of the many movies made about the Earp–Clanton shootout. It was also one of the few Westerns to try to break from established style. It starred Burt Lancaster as Wyatt Earp and Kirk Douglas as Doc Holliday; an affinity between the two actors enabled an exploration of "friendship," although the two characters are sometimes "friends" in ways that we recognize more easily in lovers. They come together and move apart; they have spats; they lack ease together but seem to be in a perpetual state of mutual wooing. Each is the most important figure in the other's universe, despite a female for each (Rhonda Fleming for Lancaster, the overwrought Jo Van Fleet for Douglas). The relationship suggests, in Joan Mellen's words, an "obsessive male friendship essentially homosexual in character yet sexually chaste," one exhibited by men "who temporarily fear women and prefer each other's company, yet indulge in excessive displays of machismo to [demonstrate their] heterosexuality."[8] The displays of machismo comprise the violence essential to the Western; much of the rest of this long film can be seen as the characters' (and perhaps the filmmakers') unconscious attempts to resolve their contradictions through excessive drinking, time-killing (cards, knife-throwing), and alternating appeals to and fights with women. Nonetheless, *Gunfight* does not remind us of *The Outlaw*; it is not homoerotic; there is no contest for a third male, no female stand-in for a homoerotic object.

The film has a very early point of attack, starting in Texas and moving to Dodge City before getting to Tombstone, site of the gunfight. The director (John Sturges) has imposed a stylistic unity on these places that implies endless repetition in the Earp–Holliday experience. The saloons in the three towns are virtually identical—same layout, same camera angles. Each town is approached past its Boot Hill, which has a sign with the town's name. This association with death and endless repetition is the opposite of a celebration of the Western life of violence.

Other scenes are haunting but inexplicable, as when Earp is first seen in Dodge City at a distance, walking and sorting his mail, but with only endless prairie behind him—no stage, no post office, no messenger. The effect is eerie, but such moments are set in the matrix of a conventional movie-Western look: silk neck scarves, tight shirts, big, anachronistic gunbelts, flat-topped hats, movie-Western sequences of shootings, lynchings, and chases. Indeed, there is a sense of two movies going forward on the same strip of film.

Despite its title, the real focus of *Gunfight at the O.K. Corral* is not the Earp–Clanton enmity but the Earp–Holliday friendship. The Clantons and the final gunfight merely provide active framework, and, perhaps, release from repressed tension. The centrality of the Earp–Holliday friendship is recognized by the carpet-chewing Kate (Van Fleet), who explains to Holliday why she conspired in an attempt to kill Earp: "I thought if Wyatt was out of the way, you'd come back to me." When, later, Earp comes to him and slaps him awake, crying, "Doc, wake up! I need you, Doc!" she says from the dark of the room, "Leave him alone. Can't you see he's dying?" Her appeal, however, is futile; coughing, near collapse, he goes after Earp. "If I'm going to die, at least let me die with the only friend I ever had."

Women are impotent against this kind of male bond. Yet these women are not passive: Van Fleet is a parttime whore, Fleming a professional gambler. Nonetheless, the impotence of women in 1950s films plays to the inability of the two to crack the death-centered male relationship. The women seem inadequate, at best, perhaps inexplicably unworthy—because they do not kill? Certainly, the men hold themselves away from them, Earp with a chilly "honor," Holliday with abuse. He even throws knives at Kate and verbally assaults her. When he threatens to kill her, she begs for her life; he collapses in a fit of coughing, and she holds him and croons, "It's all right, honey."

To a degree, self-abasement typifies both Holliday and Kate. "We don't matter, Kate. We haven't mattered since the day we were born." The implication is inescapable that it is Earp who matters, that he is admirable. The film is confused here, however, split between its images of repetition, sterility, and death, and its talk of law and honor.

Gunfight at the O.K. Corral is fairly accurate in its framework of fact but is led astray by both pop psychologizing and genre. Given the historical triviality of the Tombstone shootout, history might have been better served by using some of the footage to explore the event's historical context. Instead, it explores the central figures' psychological context and sporadically tries to go beyond commercial realism while still operating within the increasingly artificial limits of the movie Western. The result is a 1950s baroque, now stylistically puzzling because overwrought and overlong, a film trying to do mutually contradictory things.

The Left-Handed Gun was a very different film that had the enormous advantage of Paul Newman, probably the most important new actor to appear since Marlon Brando. His skills and appeal were combined with the talents of Arthur Penn, who brought to the Billy the Kid story a willingness to play with film style and a reluctance to cater to the conventions of the movie Western.

The Left-Handed Gun looks different from *Gunfight at the O.K. Corral.* The costumes appear to be real clothes copied from old photos rather than from old movies; the actors, even a veteran like John Dehner (as Pat Garrett), seem new. Derived from "a play by Gore Vidal" (apparently a TV script), the film is constantly surprising, a quality that played to Newman's ability to surprise. Script and actor work together, as well, in withholding—or simply not being interested in—what would formerly have been essential matters: the basis of Garrett's and Billy's relationship, for example, which is never explained; it merely is. This indifference to exposition, so unlike conventionalized realism, seems real and fresh, partly by contrast with familiar forms, partly by its similarity to experience. The practice really was new, comfortable with ambiguity and even ignorance. The same urge was at work in *Gunfight* but limited itself to the odd repetitions and eerie visuals; matters of action, character, plot were always explained.

Stylistically, Penn may have gone too far, understandable in an innovator; certainly, the film has been accused of mannerism. In part, this comes from some heavy-handed symbolism. In a key scene, Billy happens to be near a forge; reading that he is thought dead, he cries, "Now I catch fire!" and throws the newspaper into the forge and pumps to make it blaze. It is useful to see Billy as a "man afire," but the words and the gesture seem forced, as until then he has been presented as both illiterate and just a bit stupid. Shortly after, a dangling straw mannequin at a Mexican fiesta is set afire, and the camera lingers on it.

Even more than that sequence, however, a continuing character played by Hurd Hatfield seems to exist more in the realm of symbol than of life. Seen first as a small-town newsman, he reappears again and again in Billy's short life, metamorphosing into a seller of "souvenirs of the West," then into an obsessive collector of Billyana who betrays Billy to Garret because of his now-crazed disappointment in the real Billy the Kid. "You're not like the books. . . . You don't wear silver studs. You're not him!"

Yet, if we can look at *The Left-Handed Gun* as an attempt not to copy the hundreds of cowboy flicks that preceded it, most of the effect of mannerism disappears. In good part what we see is that this is not a film about the usual Western concerns, and one not made in the usual Western fashion. Its movement toward violence is not its reason for being, nor is the bringing of order out of disorder. Hatfield's character is central, as is Newman's quirky, now and then self-indulgent performance. This is a film about an atypical, not very bright, emotionally volatile adolescent who could not see the connection between acts and consequences. He became a media myth, the medium being print in the form of the dime novel. And the film is about the effects of myth-making, then more generally about the effects of mass myths and the idea of "celebrity." The myth creator and consumer (Hatfield) destroys the real Billy—hardly a brilliant insight, but a startling one in the hackneyed world of the Western.

The Left-Handed Gun adds to Billy the Kid's historical framework of fact but does not violate what we know of it. It touches base with the main points of fact (the shootout at a hideout, the killings of the deputies when he was a captive, his shooting by Garrett) and attempts to fill in gaps of motive. Certain scenes (e.g., the burning of a house and the looting of a store) look forward to the fast-cut, selective sequences of violence of later films. (Compare, for example, the house fire in this sequence with Huston's rather deliberate, literal fire sequence in *The Barbarian and the Geisha*.) The violent shootings presage the shooting sequences in films to come, as do the alienation from law and "niceness" of Billy, as well as the violence of people who follow the law and are "nice." By working against the grain of conventional filmmaking in visual style as well as character and idea, it actually accomplishes for history in the Western what *Gunfight at the O.K. Corral* could not: a revision that demands new examination of context.

THREE OTHER FILMS brought traditionally conceived, top-down history forward in time, although it is perhaps significant that their subjects are somewhat restricted. *Beau James* (1956) was a vehicle for a middle-aged Bob Hope that made a stab at the politics of New York City in the 1920s but couldn't face what it found. A voice-over by Walter Winchell gave the real message: corruption in "this cockeyed town" (New York) is supposed to be lovable. *The Magnificent Yankee* (1950) was a film version of a Broadway bonbon about Oliver Wendell Holmes. Its origins show in its repetitious interiors, its talk, talk, talk, and its obvious act curtains. Nonetheless, it is a small, literate, sweet film. One might compare it productively with *The President's Lady*; both are films about the domestic lives of "great men." This one, opting for sentiment rather than romance, and intelligence instead of musk, is more enjoyable as a work of history—and even arguably better.

The Spirit of St. Louis (1957), on the other hand, was a memorable tour de force, and a stunning reminder of an element essential to traditional ideas of America—individualism. It deals with Charles Lindbergh's 1927 flight from New York to Paris. The flight itself takes up half the film; its fascination is a credit to Billy Wilder's direction and James Stewart's acting.

The first half has flashbacks to aviation's early days, to Lindbergh's impulse to get into the race for a successful trans-Atlantic flight. Stewart is warm and funny. Wilder surrounds him with a densely textured visual world, convincing both as history and as dramatic environment. There is no girlfriend, no footage frittered away on a lesson in female passivity. That he was backed by the St. Louis businessmen who put up the money, and that he was helped by the craftsmen who designed and built his airplane in sixty-three days, is made clear and then put aside. This is a film about one man's achievement.

The smallness of the aircraft is made real by camera work: this was a plane smaller than a Piper Cub, and one that got slightly better gas mileage than a Land Rover. In the second half, the loneliness of the flight is perhaps overdone: he talks to a fly, tries to shout to a fisherman. The insertion of some heavy-handed piety is an embarrassment but presumably came from the book on which the film is based.

The hinge between the two halves—between, that is, the scanty group preparations and the solo achievement—is a beautifully realized sequence as the plane is rolled out in rainy darkness at Roosevelt Field, the air thick with moisture, the lights of rickety autos and motorcycles following. Lindbergh has these briefly for company, and then he is off.

Yet, for all its brilliance, *The Spirit of St. Louis* fails to put Lindbergh's flight into any context but the individual. To be sure, it contains an implied argument for aviation, but it does nothing to place Lindbergh or the flight in history. The landing in Paris, greeted by thousands (the scene wonderfully realized by Wilder) catapulted Lindbergh into the world at a time when achievement in one arena conferred authority in others; he became a man to be listened to, as H. G. Wells and Einstein were. He also became a man to be rendered tragic, as in the kidnapping of his child. And to oversell his own ideas—isolationism, for example.

The film does not tell us what this process of deification was or how Lindbergh arrived at the ideas he espoused; it does not help us to relate him to another such deified figure as Knute Rockne in the same years. It does not tell us what would be different had Lindbergh not decided to fly. Other than the individual—the adulation, the fame, the tragedy—what would have been missed if Lindbergh had not flown? The question, I think, relates to questions of transmission and deification, but also to questions about individualism on the verge of the corporate age.

THE MILITARY–CINEMATIC COMPLEX

OF THE HALF-DOZEN war films of the 1950s, several were major efforts. One of the decade's finest films came from the group; the rest were of varying quality, many of them deeply propagandistic as they apparently forged a symbiosis with the military they celebrated.

Lafayette Escadrille (1957) was the only film about World War I, a sad penultimate effort by William Wellman. It was supposedly a film Wellman had wanted to make for years—too many years, in the event.[9] One can see how its sophomoric ironies and profound sentimentality might have appealed to the young Wellman, and a silent film could have been made around them in 1920 or thereabouts. Wellman was supposedly ashamed of the final film. You would like him to be proved wrong, but it is a bad piece of work. His own voice-over tribute to his long-dead friends in the Escadrille is moving and worth hearing, and some useful snippets of history lie in his recreation of the machines and the flying he knew, and perhaps in the terribly dated idea of war and of young men that come through the mush.

The Court-Martial of Billy Mitchell (1955) was a slow work about the wealthy and iconoclastic proponent of air power (Gary Cooper) who tried to jump over his superiors and got court-martialed for his pains. The court-martial scenes prove that even Otto Preminger could screw up a courtroom drama; the suspense can barely keep us awake, in good part because the issue is so fuzzy and the consequences so meager. Cooper often seems lost, as if the lines are not worth his remembering, and his lack of a confidant robs him of chances to explain himself. His final appearance suggests what the film is really about: now in civvies, suspended from the army for five years, he looks up into the sky, where a flight of biplanes metamorphoses into a formation of jets. Read: defense budget.

To Hell and Back (1955) was an attempt to tell "the true story of the foot soldier as seen through the eyes of one," the one being the most-decorated soldier of World War II, Audie Murphy, who played himself. Produced and directed by the same director (Jesse Hibbs) who would make *Walk the Proud Land, To Hell and Back* has some of that film's mix of honesty and bad judgment, as well as its look of needing more money.

Murphy was an interesting figure, the genuine article among a group of young actors of the 1940s and 1950s. Physically small, a Texan, he brought a record of remarkable courage to the challenges of Hollywood and succeeded without any great talent; what he had, instead, was good looks, unquestionable masculinity, and intelligence. *To Hell and Back* is the story of his war, with what now seems insufficient footage devoted to his life before the army. The glimpses we get of it hint at an austerity, caused by poverty, that many Americans would no longer understand: a sick mother, an absent father, a kid who at twelve leaves school to support the family and who, when his mother dies, enlists to make enough money to support his siblings, by then in a church orphanage. Texas, 1937–41—one wants more of it, but it is shoved aside so we can get to the war stuff.

The rest of *To Hell and Back* follows the undersized kid through boot camp, seasickness on a troop ship, an implied introduction to sex in North Africa, and the horrific battle up the Italian peninsula. A lieutenant with a battlefield commission at nineteen, he is recommended for West Point, then rendered unfit by a wound; the film ends (as it began) with a march-past of soldiers, Murphy now on the reviewing stand to receive the salute. Despite the phony battle sequences that have preceded it (Murphy must have winced at some of the heroics he had to perform), the closing is deeply moving—the music, the young man, the knowledge of what it means to stand in harm's way. (Some of the marching soldiers are black, a visual lapse from the truth of 1945.)

It sounds strange to say that Murphy is not entirely convincing as himself, but his rather flat delivery and unemotional mien do not serve the idea of hell very well. Mostly, the life of the grunt seems too clean, battle rather neat; director Hibbs, as in *Walk the Proud Land,* has a tin eye for detail.

The film has an opening chat from General Walter Bedell Smith, suggesting that it got somebody's seal of approval for its presentation of the army.

Above and Beyond (1952) put its debt to the "officers and men of the United States Air Force" right up front, and its cheerleading for air power is clear. It's a film about Paul Tibbetts (Robert Taylor), the man who flew the bomb to Hiroshima, although "the events, characters and firms . . . are fictitious. . . ."

Eleanor Parker plays Tibbetts's wife. Her opening line tells us the role of women in military history: "Here I am, waiting, again. . . ."

Taylor is firm of jaw and double of chin, Parker more beautiful than most military wives ever dare to be. Everything they do is as serious as the Last Judgment and as false as, well, a war movie; all emotions call for Parker's "thrilling" voice; every act calls for Taylor's frown.

Women, as the film progresses, are worse than useless; they're a risk. "Women talk," says James Whitmore as a security officer. "Speculation about the project by wives . . . [in] grocery stores and bridge parties" could breach security. The answer: bring them to the secret base to live, so their husbands can keep an eye on them.

The actual Hiroshima drop is hyped to melodramatic breathlessness. Badly directed, it is all "playing attitudes"; the event is done far better in *The Beginning or the End?* But what *The Beginning or the End?* illuminates most of all in *Above and Beyond* is the irrelevance of hero-centered narrative to such a technological event. *The Beginning or the End?* captured the corporate nature of the Manhattan Project and carried that to the dropping of the bomb, whose importance was shown to be in Hiroshima and Nagasaki, not aboard the Enola Gay.

Above and Beyond also compares revealingly with *The Spirit of St. Louis.* The bomb was dropped only eighteen years after Lindbergh flew the Atlantic, but the flight of the *Enola Gay* and the flight of the *Spirit of St. Louis* are a universe apart. The two films comprise a cautionary tale for postwar film: Where is the heroic individual heading?

The McConnell Story (1955) also began with a general's harangue; the movie itself is propagandistic, air-power drivel. *Battle Hymn* (1957) similarly opened with a general who was pleased to introduce a handsome color film about the Korean War. It served up, in the name of air power, Rock Hudson, religious clichés, and Anna Kashfi as a non-Anglo woman who had to die because she would otherwise distract the hero from his blonde wife (Martha Hyer). It also offered acres of cute orphans. The film does have a black character, an air force officer (James Edwards).

The Gallant Hours (1959) used Robert Montgomery's TV-tested skills as producer and director to present James Cagney as Admiral William F. Halsey, a naval hero of World War II. It is big on pretentious music that recalls Richard Rodgers's *Victory at Sea* and on pseudodocumentary that uses ponderous voice-overs and fake-real footage. Most of the pseudo-real footage concerns the Japanese, who are thus distanced from the audience. The film's pace is glacial, perhaps even tectonic. The details of Halsey's world are taken so seriously that foot after foot of film is taken up with dithering shots of planes flying, boats floating, people walking. It all labors to be believable, but, with that intrusive musical score constantly haranguing us about our feelings, it is labor in vain.

The Gallant Hours is not good military history because of a lack of maps and related data, and the very insistence of the style makes the images suspect, as well. As a tribute to Halsey, it deserves respect, but as a commercial movie it is dull and finally meaningless. Montgomery's pseudodocumentary style speaks to a changed view of both Japan and the good war—the former enemy now an emerging ally, the former horror now becoming nostalgia.

Montgomery here uses style, therefore, to signal that *The Gallant Hours* is not a shlock war movie, as well as to protect Halsey and to redefine the Japanese. Yet, there is a major hole through the film, the lack of a human action on which an audience can hang its desires and its fear. *The Gallant Hours* is finally a cold film—the price of its false objectivity. It may be mere coincidence that it appeared the same year as another cold movie about a naval hero, *John Paul Jones.*

The Wings of Eagles (1956) acknowledged the "generous and full cooperation" of the Department of Defense and the United States Navy and was dedicated to "the men who brought Air Power to the United States Navy." It has many of the attributes of other military films of the decade: a male environment, with a woman in a waiting role; boys-will-be-boys hijinks, with lots of boozin' and fightin'; a pro-military agenda. It even has John Wayne and Ward Bond, both by this time carrying heavy political baggage. Yet, *The Wings of Eagles* escapes all the dangers that seem to surround it and soars. It is a fine film, certainly one of John Ford's finest. To be sure, it lacks the visual magic of *My Darling Clementine,* much of it taking place in uninteresting interiors— small houses, a hospital room, offices. It is not even, in fact, typical Ford.

The Wings of Eagles is about "Spig" Wead (Wayne), naval aviator, screenwriter, friend of John Ford. In the first half of the film, Ford implies that Wead was a man born to love Tailhook; masculinity is associated with alcohol and violence and the usual lame Ford humor. Structurally, this part of the film alternates between the low comedy of two signature military-brawl sequences in identical surroundings and the pathetic melodrama of a child's death. Maureen O'Hara weaves through this masculine hyper-activity as Wead's wife, oddly noticeable as a real woman.

It is, in fact, O'Hara who makes *The Wings of Eagles* so unusual a Ford film—that is, O'Hara as actress and O'Hara as embodiment of what Ford is doing here. A woman usually valued only for her beauty, she here shows range and subtlety in a rather difficult, sometimes unsympathetic role, for it is she who must reveal the harsh underside of the fightin', lovin', flyin' Wayne.

The film gives O'Hara opportunity for progression, and she seizes it, from a coltish young wife in the 1920s to a restless woman in the 1930s to a self-reliant individual in 1941. She suggests a woman giving in slowly to alcohol, a problem resolved and dealt with off-camera; she suggests infidelity, even a kind of weary trampishness, the response to her officer husband's perpetual absence. She suggests a very real physical desire for him without vitiating a constant and believable anger at him. When, halfway through the film, he comes home to her and her two children after a long absence, it is to a sloven's house. She is that supposed rarity in 1950s America, a rotten housekeeper, a lousy mother, a woman straining to find and be herself.

When Wead falls downstairs and is paralyzed, he sends her away to have a life of her own. We infer that he cannot conceive an emotional life without a sexual one, and that he believes his sexual life over; as well, in this mature film, he understands that she has a sexual life, too. Wead's accident thus strips him of everything he has valued and frees her, although, in a last long shot of her outside his hospital, we see that for her, too, the freedom comes at a high price.

Wead leaves the Navy, learns to walk with crutches, and makes it as a writer. He begins an assocation with "John Dodge"—Ward Bond, doing a John Ford imitation with Ford's own pipe and sunglasses. Wayne now wears, not a uniform, but a superbly relaxed tweed jacket and one of the coolest hats ever seen in film. In middle age, he again gets in touch with O'Hara. He tells her now what he could never say when they were married or when he was first injured: "I need you." But she has made a life for herself and says so. He pleads: "If it isn't a family, it's nothing," never specifying what *it* is.

The last time we saw O'Hara, it was in that long shot outside his hospital, where she stood unsurely after he had dismissed her. Now, in her own apartment, she circles behind his chair, puts her hand on his balding head, then kisses it, the encapsulation of mature affection perfect; she moves away toward a window and abruptly swings back to embrace him: mature affection become mature love and sexuality. It, too, is perfect.

But it is 1941. Pearl Harbor happens as he is preparing to bring her to his California home. He telephones her; she is packing, but, hearing of his decision to go to Washington, she weeps and begins to throw things. Machismo—history as male action—has done it to her again.

Despite his handicap, Wead gets himself reappointed as a naval officer, serves briefly on a carrier, has a heart attack, and accepts medical retirement. When he leaves the carrier and the navy, military men from his past form an aisle, including the army officer (now a general) with whom he had the glorious Fordian fistfights early in the film. The scene has great edge—Wead has not advanced in rank as the others have; their affection and respect isolate him between them rather than embracing him. They stand in two formal lines; he hobbles between them. Honor—with irony.

And the last we see of him, he is being borne away from the carrier by a breeches buoy to another ship. He dwindles from the camera, fading to near-unrecognizability, then to invisibility. He is gone. It is a magnificent close, sad and harsh, recalling his other isolation, and, in its angle and its length, O'Hara's turning away from the hospital when he told her to leave him.

Much of *The Wings of Eagles* is devoted to rather stereotypical sequences of flying and war. In the 1950s, it was probably seen much more as being about a heroic comeback than about the price of masculine history. Nonetheless, it contained that idea, and it contained the field of ideas generated by O'Hara and her character. It is as if Ford knew that his character's machismo was self-destructive but could not keep himself from celebrating it in a series of personal clichés—boozing, happy fights, practical jokes, bondings. However, he seems to have recognized Wead's paralysis as a means to critique the machismo. O'Hara's character embodies that critique, so astonishingly textured a portrayal, so complex in its conflicts, that it cannot be ignored: it is a light that illuminates everything else in the film. Ford was artist enough to use her character (and Wead's, through her) to say that sorrow is sometimes inescapable—and to give inescapable sorrow a visual correlative, the long shot of the dwindling individual, the shot that shows us both of them at their moments of loss.

In a very real sense, Ford in this film is more concerned with the impingement of history, conceived as military events, on individuals than in the films we usually associate with him. It is Pearl Harbor that destroys the Weads' last chance at "it"; it is war that drives Wead to his final loss and isolation. To be sure, this is history conceived as a male activity—one in which Wead participates but his wife does not. She seems to flee "history" (as do the military wives in films like *Battle Hymn* and *Above and Beyond*), but only to become a participant in another idea of history that we do not usually associate with John Ford or the military movies of the 1950s—a women's history that also has self-assertion and loss. It is in this other idea of history that *Wings of Eagles* is significant, not least because it shows us an important Hollywood figure trying to find a way to cope with a changing America.

1950S BAROQUE
THERE IS A FEEL to many of these films of no longer knowing how to do it right, as if confidence in making good movies had been lost. Many of the films have a quality of overelaboration, of excess, as if the rigidity of inherited forms was resented but could not be escaped, and embellishment and elaboration have been exploited instead of rebellion. Many of them pull in several directions at once. Certain new fields of interest show, as well: racial tolerance, above all, expressed most clearly in the Native American films, perhaps extended into other films by the occasional appearance of a black character. An age disparity between men and women suggests both that women were seen as children and that male stars were getting old, yet here and there a female characterization stands out sharply because it is so different. "History according to Longfellow" remains only as a set of techniques, even a set of habits.

Clearly, historical films as a patriotic response to stress do not have the cultural position that they had in 1939–45. These films are not celebratory. They are peripheral to the national experience, and they seem to know it.

PART II

Democratizing the Past

CHAPTER SIX
1950–1959 II: HISTORY FROM THE BOTTOM UP ─────────────

It is clear that even in the films of traditionally conceived, top-down history of the last chapter, history "from the bottom up" was intruding—as individual characters, as ideas—in the 1950s. As well, films devoted entirely to bottom-up history appeared in such numbers that they account for much of the swollen total of the decade. In all, these films about people outside traditional power are often more significant than those, many demonstrably impoverished, of the previous chapter.

The nearly thirty musical and related biographies of the 1950s can be seen, perhaps, as regressive, because they work so hard to repeat earlier successes. Many still were about the "fabulous era," but others looked at the people and culture of nontheatrical music of the 1930s and later. They seem to represent a generational change in Hollywood: the fabulous era had been the era of the first Hollywood generation's youth; vaudeville and Ziegfeld were formative memories. In the 1950s, those people were old, and the culture was changing fast.

ANNIE OAKLEY WAS one of Ethel Merman's memorable roles, and, if her performance had little to do with history, it had a lot to do with brass and Broadway and performing genius. When *Annie Get Your Gun* was translated to the screen in 1950, however, Merman did not get translated with it. Instead, Betty Hutton attempted Annie. The result was a disastrous but revealing look at Hollywood's notion of a woman with "manly" skills. Most of what is wrong with the film was wrong with the stage musical (a song, "You Can't Get a Man with a Gun," for example), but one forgave the theatrical version a lot because of

Merman. The reverse is true with Hutton, a grating and ego-centered performer; the vehicle has to make up for putting her before our eyes.

Stylistically, *Annie Get Your Gun* is pure movie musical, hard-edged, bright-colored, made entirely on a sound stage. "Movie musical" is not quite a style, like realism or expressionism, but it is an identifiable departure from realism, an imitation of imitation, not of life. In the opening scene, for example, the exterior set is obviously false, the flat "grass" something laid over a floor. It could be explained by dancing, but there is none.

Hutton first appears as Annie in dark greasepaint and rags; the paint is supposed to be suntan and dirt, the rags the clothes of rural poverty, but both makeup and costume shriek their contrivance. It is like watching seventeenth-century pastoral—shepherdesses in silk, bowers of fake roses. The dominant falseness finds its perfect proponent in Hutton, who is always on, always over the top, always noisy because she has no other level.

The character that Hutton projects is more interesting than the performance itself. In the 1930s, we had an Annie Oakley who was smart, sometimes shy, and pretty (Barbara Stanwyck); now we have an Annie Oakley who swings her shoulders like Big Boy Gwinn, seems to have her hands glued to her hips, and rolls her eyes like Eddie Cantor. She is, her performance tells us, a freak—a woman who shoots like a man because she hasn't learned to be a woman. Hutton works to make us understand that she is not pretty. (In one embarrassing sequence, she tries to get rid of her freckles, dress up, get pretty—it is like those sequences where Indian women try on European dresses.)

Women who are not pretty and behave like men must be punished. *Annie Get Your Gun* has two punishment sequences, the first the sadistic "I'm an Indian, Too." The second is the climactic contest with the man she loves, which she loses so she can win him. "Win contest, lose Frank," Sitting Bull tells her. "Lose contest, win Frank. Keep missing, you win." The message is, give up whatever you do well if you are to be a real woman.

The unrealism of the musical style tries to say that this is "all in fun," as is, we suppose, having Sitting Bull (J. Carrol Naish again) possess oil wells on a reservation that is "no good for grazing—too much oil—fifty thousand barrels a day." This is ephemerally funny, but not very; the real Sitting Bull was headed for a violent death after he was briefly with the Wild West Show; the Sioux reservations had no oil or anything else; when Sitting Bull was returned to one, he got meat by going once a week for a government handout. By 1889, the "Great Sioux Reservation" had ceased to exist.[1] Like its message about women, the film's message about Native Americans suggests that we should have a new category—harmful fun.

"There's No Business like Show Business" comes from *Annie Get Your Gun*. It is sung twice, in fact. The business of show business is glanced at, and three men—Buffalo Bill (Louis Calhern), Pawnee Bill (Edward Arnold), and the show's manager (Keenan Wynn)—worry because the show is almost broke. Sitting Bull saves it with his oil money, Annie with her jewelled medals. On, on with the show, as the song says. But if the business of show business is disciplining women and mocking Native Americans—why?

Hutton was again on view in *Somebody Loves Me* (1952), "suggested by the careers of Blossom Seeley and Bennie Fields," but apparently the part of the career in which Seeley was a blackface "coon shouter" didn't suggest enough to get itself included. The period is again "the fabulous era," established, as always, by a street scene with a carriage and women in long skirts. It is San Francisco, which is due to fall down at any moment, and does, using footage from *San Francisco*. Hutton is supposed to be so loud and energetic she fears she caused the quake, ha-ha. After more noise, she has taught Fields (Ralph Meeker) everything she knows, and he becomes a star, and she says, "Now I've got the billing I always wanted—Mrs. Benny Fields!" Funny how familiar the message seems—give up what you do best, and you can be a happy woman.

Equally noisy, and even more unconvincing, was Doris Day's *Calamity Jane* (1953), in which she did a knockoff of Hutton's Annie, and to the same male star (Howard Keel). She is so perky and bright-eyed in the role you would think the citizens of Deadwood would hang her on general principles, and there is no indication anywhere in the film that Wild Bill (Keel) will be dead any moment from a bullet in the back of his head. Instead, the movie ends with the ahistorical wedding of Calam and Bill.

The songs are all familiar ones because they are knockoffs of songs in *Oklahoma* and *Annie Get Your Gun*. Day jumps and prances and swings her arms and looks like somebody who's popped too many bennies; she wears a fringed buckskin shirt and tight leather pants, and the gag is that she's mannish. She's also a pathological liar, as a woman pretending to be a man might well be. It is perhaps for this reason that her singing of "Secret Love" has unintended implications, the more so after Katie, a visiting music-hall singer (Allyn McLerie) moves in with her. But what's the secret? Martha Boesing made Calamity Jane a lesbian in her eponymous play; it would certainly make more sense for the two women to love each other than anybody else on view here, but, given the film's insistence that all women will pair off with men, once they start dressing like ladies and give up the skills (mule-skinning, spitting, swearing) that make them employable, the love that dare not speak its name would have to be very secret, indeed. It isn't; Calam loves Bill; "Secret Love" just sounded good, folks.

These antifeminine musicals were joined by others that were focused on issues of class as well as gender. *Tonight We Sing* (1953) and *So This Is Love* (1953) put high-culture music (mostly opera) on film in contexts that gave it box-office value, in part by inserting false arguments about democratizing taste.

Tonight We Sing had David Wayne as Sol Hurok, almost swallowing his tonsils in an attempt to be glottal on all occasions. Produced by George Jessel, it is a schmaltz version of the life of a now-forgotten entrepreneur, its principal message that producers can have good taste, too. It reduces Hurok's Judaism to a character quirk (although somebody says halfway through, "I thought you were *meshuga*") and ignores his early leftism and his sponsorship of Russian-Jewish groups like the original Habima. Murky about Hurok's early days and why he left Russia, it shorthands him through childhood and youth as a music lover with no talent. "Resign yourself to being a member of the audience," says his teacher. Wayne wears wide pants and boots, like Tolstoy in the country, although he's in St. Petersburg; Anne Bancroft as his girl has so much hair in coiled braids she looks as if she's trying to bring in Radio Moscow.

A three-second establishing shot means he's gone to New York; another three-second establishing shot and it's Paris; here's Ezio Pinza as Chaliapin; an establishing shot, and Hurok's on a ship, meeting cute with Eugene Ysaye (Isaac Stern), and suddenly he's rich, and he and Bancroft appear to be living in the Summer Palace; she has better manners than the Queen Mother, he has a bigger wardrobe than Ziegfeld. We get Verdi, Puccini, Moussorgsky, Gounod; Pavlova (Tamara Toumanova) dances, Chaliapin sings, Ysaye plays. The film ends in the early 1920s with most of the real Hurok's career still ahead of him.

Essentially a comedy, *Tonight We Sing* is full of coincidences, warm hearts, and happy endings; its picture of the entrepreneur as tasteful eccentric suggests that Jessel thought he was looking in a mirror. It does show a different side of both immigration and show business, however—not the mean streets and vaudeville, but uptown and entrepreneurship. We never understand what it is that such a man does to make all that money, but what we do see is enthusiasm for high culture and a hint of how it was disseminated from Europe and New York.

So This Is Love had Kathryn Grayson as Grace Moore, "a little girl from Jellico, Tennessee" who made it at the Met in the 1920s. Grayson had a small but sweet singing voice and a strikingly pretty face, and she suggested an utterly unthreatening child-woman, a kind of idealized American high-school girl as conceived by an American high-school boy. It is a bit surprising, then, to find her playing a woman who tossed away "love" (even in the form of Merv Griffin) for an opera career. "Ever since I was a little girl I had a dream—I've got to make that dream come true." Griffin gives the only reply a sane man could, although it's most unmovielike: "Good-bye, Grace. No man can fight a dream."

Off she goes to Paris to study with Mary Garden; she returns to debut at the Met as Mimi in *La Bohème*. The scene as filmed is the dichotomous result of its having two ideas of the character, and perhaps Grayson: at this supreme moment in the life of a woman who chose to be herself, Grayson is costumed like the maid in a French farce, and you expect her skirt to rip off in the first doorway she passes through.

In its plot, the movie wants to be a biography of Grace Moore; in its style and chaste sexiness, it wants to be a vehicle for Grayson. The result shows considerable temporizing: Griffin does not weigh at all heavily against her dream; comedy is the model, if not the genre; real conflict, real emotion, real threat are avoided. Much of the opposition comes from an irascible father—fair enough, patriarchy is the enemy—but is trivialized: "If Daddy ever found I was wearing rouge, he'd be furious." Grayson's sweetness is the key to everything not absolutely required by Moore's life; if, as you hope, Moore was not that sweet, too bad.

In its trivialization and its girlishness, So This Is Love resembles Our Hearts Were Young and Gay, although at its center it is the story of a tough-minded and courageous woman. Seen in that light, the title seems ironic.

Perhaps high culture, represented here by operatic singing, was meant to have a value that sharpshooting (Annie Get Your Gun) and stage-driving (Calamity Jane) lacked. You can't get a man with a gun, but if you have a world-class operatic voice you don't need one. Something of that sort was implied in The Great Caruso by Dorothy Kirsten as Louise Haggar: "I gave up a life to serve a voice—but at least it was my voice."

Other musical biographies dealt with the popular culture more familiar to Hollywood: Kalmar and Ruby (Three Little Words, 1950), Jane Froman (With a Song in My Heart, 1952), John Phillip Sousa (Stars and Stripes Forever, 1953), Sigmund Romberg (Deep in My Heart, 1954), Eddie Foy (The Seven Little Foys, 1954), Eddie Duchin (The Eddie Duchin Story, 1956); there were still others, but a few adequately represent the lot.

One of the Seven Little Foys grew up to be the producer of I Was a Communist for the FBI, but this hardly seems a reason for making a movie, much less another about the fabulous era and vaudeville. The Seven Little Foys has a waiting wife who gives up her career to drop baby after baby and then die, a ferocious sister-in-law who stands in for a stage mother, and George Tobias as an agent who "discovers people." "I discovered Bert Williams," he says, without explaining to us that Bert Williams was the lone black star in a white industry. Bob Hope was too old for romantic scenes, so some of the film (like some in the last chapter) looks like a dirty old man at work. The kids are either darling or insufferable, depending on your tolerance. A racist Chinatown number is fairly disgusting. The framework of fact is in tatters: the real Foy was married four times, started in blackface, was doing a drag act when the Iroquois Theatre burned down, and was funnier than this.

In Deep in My Heart, Jose Ferrer was entertaining as Sigmund Romberg, and his two-minute encapsulation of a very silly musical—with songs—is a tour de force, but otherwise, Deep in My Heart was standard kitsch mit shlag. The European mentor this time was Helen Traubel, the triumphant finale a retrospective concert in a classy but unnamed high-culture venue.

With a Song in My Heart starred Susan Hayward, an actress so much herself (like Grayson but for different qualities) that the film necessarily became a vehicle. Froman did her own singing. The rather heavy, trained voice now sounds strange in the ballads and swing tunes, but the juxtaposition may be the film's major stab at history; otherwise, it has a typical 1950s falsity—hard edges, bright color, overdecoration. Froman lost a leg while flying to entertain troops in World War II, so there is a Hayward-tailored tendency toward the weepie, but of a glamorous variety: everybody's makeup is perfect, and even the wounds look pretty. The female star is flanked by two males of lesser magnitude (Rory Calhoun and David Wayne); she is attended by a woman without youth or conventional prettiness (Thelma Ritter). Given this degree of manipulation, alternatives are not supposed to occur to us, and irony, critique, and history are all out the window.

The Eddie Duchin Story followed the career and emotional life of a society pianist from his early twenties to his late forties, and actor Tyrone Power from his early forties to his early forties. (Oddly, toward the end he is made up to be middle-aged and begins to look like Richard Nixon.) Power was by this time no longer beautiful and young; he was beautiful and middle-aged, and determined to show he could act. The film is therefore a vehicle, but it is one that indulges in the 1950s tendency toward the baroque—length, elaboration, luxury, strain.

Kim Novak is his first wife; she dies and dies and dies in childbirth, the meaningful sadness of her going announced by a sudden wind that gusts through their elegant apartment, as if nature itself understands how important her death will be. Until then, Duchin has been bright and bushy-tailed, a kind of musical Sammy Glick with a lot more polish. "I can't lie," he tells her, "I hope money comes up and bites me." In a dinner jacket for his first job at the Casino in the Park, he asks, "How do I look?" and is told, "Like a second-hand Vanderbilt." She is "society," but he gets her. One thinks of Gatsby, and Daisy's "money in her voice." Power should have played Gatsby.

Standing on their balcony high above New York, he says, "Eddie's luck—I have it; I always have it." Then the wind blows, and she dies, and he sits in the post-Christmas rack of the Casino and weeps. Power makes this rich shlock work, but only so long as the shot lasts; despite the symbolism and the lighting and the hype, what is it all about? A death in cafe society?

The film then goes to suds, the cliché of the man who blames the child for the mother's death. The luxurious look, the tone, the forced emotions are those of long-gone dramas about princes and kings and the conflict of love and duty, but the actuality is a sad tale of a man on the make who lost his luck and got older. Was this worth a movie? Cafe society might be worth examining, but not uncritically; the life of a man who uses glossy pop music to rise from vague beginnings—his parents have accents; his mother says, "Mazel tov," when he tells her he is engaged—would be worth examining. History might be interested in the women he married, but not as presented; the first has a baby and dies, the second serves dinner. *The Great Gatsby* and *What Makes Sammy Run* plow the same furrows. They do not, however, take cafe society at face value, as this film does. There is a lack of context; there is also a lack of social acumen; it would have made a huge difference if somebody had seen that Duchin was attracted to glitter, not gold, and that his music reflected his mistake.

Finally, there were four musical biographies that glanced at the evolution of a popular music based in African–American music. The subject had been hinted at in the 1930s and 1940s; now it became specific, probably impelled by the same force that put black characters in *Battle Hymn* and *Sitting Bull* However, it was not until the last-made of the films, *St. Louis Blues* (1958) that a seminal black musician got the credit due him for original genius.

St. Louis Blues was a cheaply made little Paramount film that featured oustanding black performers in a version of the life of W. C. Handy (Nat "King" Cole as Handy, and Eartha Kitt, Cab Calloway, Ella Fitzgerald, Mahalia Jackson, Ruby Dee, Juano Hernandez, Pearl Bailey). It is a static film, not well directed, with many standpat camera setups and go-nowhere talk scenes. Economy seems to have dictated the repeated use of the same locations. Cole was not a very good actor; Kitt, as an ambitious and tough woman, was caused to play pretty much on one note, but Dee and Hernandez were talented pros and gave the film some spark.

It is not, however, for acting or directing that you go to this crude little film. You go to it because it is unique: a film about black genius, with a virtually all-black cast, produced by the white commerical apparatus.

Handy is a young man in Memphis "near the turn of the century." (The vagueness is endemic.) His father (Hernandez) is a stern clergyman who tells him that "your grandfather was a slave . . . but I became a man of God. . . . I will follow your coffin to the grave before I see you a maker of music for the devil." But the young Handy plays the organ in church, upsets his father when he begins to syncopate and Bailey and Jackson in the choir begin to clap and rock. Off he goes to study music; back he comes in a flash, now a young man with Ruby Dee on his arm.

Profane music still beckons, however, and before long he and a pickup band are installed at the Big Rooster, a club run by Calloway and Kitt. Shortly, Handy has left his father's house, written "Yellow Dog Blues," and got something on with Kitt, although it is impossible to say what; she slinks and sulks through every scene, and sex, greed, and defensiveness all come out the same. Nonetheless, hers is an interesting depiction of an ambitious black woman who wants to break out of Memphis and be somebody, and who sees Handy's music as her ticket. Juxtaposed against her, of course, is Dee, a nice young woman in a 1950s circle skirt (the costumes are dreadful).

The audience at the Big Rooster is all white. So, too, is the man who buys "Yellow Dog Blues" for six hundred dollars, although the irony of this exploitation is that a black man, Calloway, is the real buyer for whom he fronts. Handy meanwhile is having headaches and goes blind; a newspaper headline screams "Prohibition Here!" This invitation to check the date says it is 1919; by then, the real Handy was forty-six and had been blind since 1903, having written the blues tunes we now remember, conducted an orchestra, and founded his own publishing company.

The film is thus ahistorical. Its interest is melodrama—good girl/bad girl, vision/blindness, papa's music/Kitt's music. Astonishingly, it drives toward the cliché finish of the white musical biographies: a concert in Aeolian Hall, at which Constantin Bakaleinikoff and "the New York Symphony" play a terrifically overorchestrated version of "St. Louis Blues." Dee is there in another 1950s dress; Hernandez is reconciled to his son (high culture conquers all).

The film abounds in anachronisms: Ella Fitzgerald, for example, born in 1918, appears as herself, singing "Beale Street Blues" in the 1920s. It boxes its action in a universe where the only forces are religion and individual desire; economics, race, gender, class are unimportant. Handy is a genius, but in the Hollywood tradition; his struggles are not with music but with his father.

Yet *St. Louis Blues* has made a break that is significant. When we think of looking for history in the show-biz films that exploit blackness—in the jazz or swing films; in the minstrel or the coon-song films—we should stop and say, "Let's look at *St. Louis Blues* first, so we will remember that there was another version of the truth."

This truth is adumbrated in a scene in *The Benny Goodman Story* (1955) when sixteen-year-old Benny finds Kid Ory's all-black band on an excursion boat. Young Benny calls Ory and Co. "you boys," and he picks up his clarinet and jumps right in with them as if he had been studying jazz improvisation all his life. This is about all there is of Benny's apprenticeship to black music. Otherwise, Goodman is a nice white boy whose parents have accents and whose music teacher—the usual old male with the mittel-European glottals—says, when he learns that young Goodman has a job with a dance band, "No, Benny, not you! Not that ragtime!" Benny grows up to be Steve Allen, a terrible actor but a winning personality. The adult Goodman plays both pop and classical, and he at first offends rich girl Donna Reed with pop, then wows her with Mozart; high culture conquers all. The democratization of her taste as she comes to like pop is apparently meant to cause us to like her.

The film tracks Goodman's rise to the top of swing and to a concert at—what, again?—Carnegie Hall. Along the way, he meets and takes on Lional Hampton and works with Fletcher Henderson (Sammy Davis, Sr.).

Goodman seems to have worn a suit and tie everywhere, perhaps even to bed; Reed is always dressed in the height of 1950s fashion, no matter what year everybody else is playing. The film's direction is puerile, the acting limp. Nonetheless, one thing makes *The Benny Goodman Story* of historical value—its demonstration of the importance of radio and recordings, and the bacchanalian frenzy of adolescent crowds at swing concerts. When Goodman and his band open at New York's Paramount, they question whether anybody will come. They rise on a hydraulic lift to the pit, and mob mania breaks out. For those who think that rock 'n' roll was the first to bring teen-agers, sex, and Orpheus together, the scene should be studied. It gives us an early manifestation of several important American directions of the late 1930s—youth culture, group ritual, music as the dominant popular art. Another sequence recovers the impacted energy of the swing concerts in movie theaters of the 1940s, celebrations of a new community of young whites who had found the lively spirit of black music.

The focus on Goodman somewhat obscures the real importance of what was happening among the consumers of swing rather than its makers. The film only hints at what black music was for middle-class white kids—a forbidden sweet, difficult to find in some parts of the country, sometimes hard to identify, an experience whose language ("hep," "hot," "cool") marked a rebellion and an unease. For that audience, access was made through recordings and radio.

The Glenn Miller Story (1953) and *The Gene Krupa Story* (1959) also looked at this phenomenon. The first, with Jimmy Stewart, was an establishment film about the bandleader who became an icon after he was killed in World War II. June Allyson was his wife, cute as can be, saying "Honestly!" about things that were patently dishonest. Both she and Stewart were too old, but this was a movie for the early middle-aged who had listened to Miller in the thirties and fought in his war. Smooth, mindless, clichéd, indifferent to reality, the film was already a relic in 1953 but did not know it.

Of the swing films, nonetheless, this was the first to show white musicians routinely playing with blacks. On their wedding night, Miller and bride go to a party "in Harlem" and listen to Louis Armstrong and Cozy Cole, with Gene Krupa sitting in; Miller accepts a black player's trombone and joins them. One year before *Brown v Board of Education*, black and white musicians are shown as colleagues. *The Glenn Miller Story* also hints at the youth frenzy shown in *Goodman*, with its ritualized gathering of the audience around the bandstand.

After Miller is killed in World War II, his manager (George Tobias) tells Allyson that "if the band goes on . . . the kids'll be dancing to it for years and years." But, of course, the kids did not. Their parents did. The kids, even while this movie was in release, were hearing a still newer kind of music. Jimmy Stewart and June Allyson were their parents' stars, able to seem youthful only to those who had lost their youth. They enacted an America of niceness, of morality, of "Honestly!" The same week that *The Glenn Miller Story* opened, *The French Line* was released without a Production Code approval because it showed Jane Russell in 3-D. Change was coming.

The Gene Krupa Story (1959) was a modest result of that change, a "youth" movie that featured a new generation of actors (Sal Mineo, James Darren, Susan Kohner) and made its central figures seem eighteen and everybody else—especially parents—ancient. It took place in a perpetual not-just-now of late adolescence; there was no history, it said, because being young is a state outside time. Except for its youthful faces, the film was actually a step backward; it got the need to appeal to the young but didn't get (or didn't dare show) what they were really into. Only in Mineo's frenzied performance as Krupa on drums did it suggest why Krupa was an imporant figure, and why he might have served as a symbolic bridge from swing to rock, from the 1940s to the 1960s.

NONMUSICAL FILMS ABOUT actors and performers proliferated. *Prince of Players* (1954) leaned heavily on the assassination of Abraham Lincoln to explain why Edwin Booth was worth making a movie about, although the historical Booth was much more important, and was much less injured by his brother's crime, than was here pretended. Richard Burton as Edwin Booth all but came off the screen to devour the theater seats, suggesting that he was playing Kean, not Booth. Burton's fruity vowels and modulated baritone showed a fine but overtrained instrument, his use of tongue and lips threatening a spray of spit on everything within reach. He is so relatively good, however, that everybody else in the film except Raymond Massey as Junius Brutus Booth looks weak. As John Wilkes Booth, John Derek, a pretty young man without discernible skills, fails to suggest why this Booth was a favorite in the South or why his father prefers him to Edwin.

There is much in the film about boozing, some attempt to connect overindulgence with genius, and a more modern interest in addiction as a psychological problem. Consciously or not, too, the film seems to do a certain amount of finger-painting in the blood of its fathers: John Wilkes Booth participates in the hanging of John Brown—as, in fact, the real man did—that figure played twice by the actor playing his father in this film, Massey; and he kills Lincoln, also played in the 1940 *Abe Lincoln in Illinois* by Massey. The references seem typical 1950s baroque, rather wild, sensational but not necessarly meaningful; the film is baroque in other ways, too—expensive, lush, bad.

Man of a Thousand Faces (1957) gave a splendid role to James Cagney (Lon Chaney) but never resolved the quandary of how to show what was great about silent-film acting in a sound film. It also failed to answer the question of how in the world a biography of Lon Chaney could be made without even mentioning Tod Browning. The two matters may be connected: if you don't understand what Browning did, you'll never understand what Chaney did.

The film is a distortion that is suggested by its title, an emphasis on Chaney's makeups and prostheses, not his acting. For all the hoopla surrounding plastic scars and leather humps, the film really tells us nothing about what Chaney did onscreen. It focuses on his marriages, the first to a fragile woman (Dorothy Malone) who is appalled to find that his parents are deaf. The real Cleva Chaney was sixteen when they married, and Malone captures some of the near-child's vulnerability.

Malone's performance may be an instance of a growing interest in emotional instability in women, apparently as punishment for seeking their own lives. A singer, she cries, "They liked me tonight—and I liked them liking me!" and "I've got to make some kind of life of my own." Unstable, she breaks into his act and drinks acid onstage. Chaney blames himself, but the film would have it that she is really upset because a secret boyfriend has ditched her; there is a sense here of wanting to have things both ways, of wanting Chaney to play guilt but not be guilty.

From this point on, the chronology is all out of whack, and any notion of history is lost. He enters movies (which the real Chaney did in 1912), makes *The Miracle Man* (1919), and divorces Cleva (1914).[2] The rest of the film is a mess, mixing quick takes of Chaney movies (the Hunchback! the Phantom of the Opera!) with soap-opera emotions—the return of Cleva, a second marriage, estrangement from his son, their reconciliation, his death. The final footage, a pan shot of his makeup sketches, tells us what is wrong with the film: it glibly associates silent film with pantomime, makeup with acting, yet it always prefers the emotional involvement of its protagonist with another person to his emotional involvment with his art.

Films of Female Victimization

A MOVIE THAT was lush, set in expensive surroundings, and concerned with seduction, murder, and adultery would seem to be simply another example of 1950s baroque, but *The Girl in the Red Velvet Swing* (1955) was made with such intelligence that it rose above the type. It serves to introduce a subcluster of five films concerned with women, mostly in show business, but from a new point of attack—their victimization.*

The Girl in the Red Velvet Swing recounted the Stanford White–Evelyn Nesbit–Harry K. Thaw triangle and murder of 1906. Joan Collins was Nesbit, Ray Milland was White, and Farley Granger was Thaw. In a title, the film justifies itself as dealing with "a man of consequence, another of great wealth, and a girl of extraordinary beauty"; the statement seems in part a desire to escape a charge of sleaze.

Stanford White was, in the "fabulous era," America's ideal architect. Many of his buildings still stand, eclectic, Eurocentric designs that managed to be monuments to both past greatness and present power. White's architecture can be seen as a manifestation of a national culture that was expressing itself in the Wild West Show, the Sousa band, the Spanish–American War, and mass immigration: triumphalist, greedy to extend its grasp to include other people's history, other people's land, other people's people. The implied critique of it in this 1950s film seems another attempt to break from that past.

_____

* A related film, *The Snake Pit* (1948), is marginal according to my criteria; it has been studied from a feminist perspective by Leslie Fisbein (see bibliography).

The Girl in the Red Velvet Swing inserts a poor woman (Nesbit) into the structure of White's power and Thaw's wealth. The conduit is the theater, in which Nesbit's mother works as a seamstress. The film shows Nesbit as wanting to be part of the theater's onstage world rather than the backstage one; a model, she becomes a chorus girl purely on the basis of her looks. It is as a chorus girl that she is introduced to White when a more experienced performer takes her to him and he asks the older woman to bring Nesbit to "lunch." In this sequence, White is visiting the site of one of his buildings (apparently the library at Columbia University); the encounter suggests that the older woman, a former or perhaps current mistress, can be made his procuress merely by his willing it. Three entities are thus linked in the scene: the theater, female submission, establishment (male) education. The common link is male power, expressed mostly as sexual predation but also as money and as culture.

The theater of this film is rather different from the theater of the show-biz biographies. Here, it is more like the theater of the old *Esquire* cartoons and of Edwardian jokes about stage-door Johnnies, a place where older men eye, select, and meet very young women. "Twirly Whirly" is the title on a theater billboard, suggesting mere contrivance for displaying the women; it also suggests the whirling confusion of minds like Nesbit's, caught up in a rush of attention, gifts, self-display, and the trading away of sex (in Nesbit's case, of virginity).

When White is in the midst of his affair with Nesbit, he has a run-in with her mother in a dressing-room, and to escape her (the residual power of the mother is an interesting detail) he announces that he will "wait for [Evelyn] in the manager's office," and off he goes, displacing the manager simply by saying he wants the man's room. The sequence cuts two ways: it reveals the extent of White's privilege, but it also suggests that the theater exists for him and his predation—another way to look at films like *The Great Ziegfeld*.

Milland is splendid as White. It is a complex portrayal, a forty-eight-year-old man "obsessed" (his word) with a nineteen-year-old woman. He is charming, intelligent, conscience-stricken, but still predatory. He loves his wife and will not leave her; nonetheless, he wants and gets Nesbit. He maintains a mansion (for life with the wife, a complex symbol of rectitude, money, social belonging) but also has what the tabloids used to call a "love nest," a private apartment reached through a door inside a toy shop.

The red velvet swing of the title hangs in this apartment, in a room above the rest, a domed "forest glade" adapted from Watteau. It is here that the seduction takes place—the writers and the director, Richard Fleischer, are perceptive enough to see that the seduction is mutual—and is presented as a piece of 1950s, potted-Freudian symbolism: he pushes her higher and higher in the swing, her feet pointing toward a lunette in the dome, the rhythm explicity sexual, the moon-window referential and allusive; her feet touch it, and she has committed herself, symbolically deflowered herself (her phallic feet and the hymeneal lunette.)

Granger's Thaw is first seen expressing jealous hatred of White in a restaurant; later, he is seen giving out presents on the stage. He sees Nesbit, then in the early days of her affair with White, and wants her. Wherever he turns, however, White is ahead of him, until White and Nesbit have a falling-out. Thaw moves in; he takes Nesbit and her mother to Switzerland, proposes on a snowy Alp, beats Nesbit when she refuses and then wails in contrition—the perfect batterer.

Distanced from White by her own maturing, Nesbit marries Thaw, but Thaw is more jealous of White than ever. As a wife, Collins now looks like a tart; the more proper she becomes, the less proper she looks.

After the still-jealous Thaw shoots White, Nesbit is increasingly isolated from her husband and his wealthy family, and she is finally abandoned altogether after his acquittal for insanity. Leaving the courthouse alone by way of the Tombs, she is manhandled by prisoners who reach through the bars for her; outside, a crowd manhandles her again. When she gets into her carriage, an apparently sympathetic man joins her and seems to offer help. His "help" is a job in Atlantic City—and this is where we last see her, on a red velvet swing, legs bare, skirt high, swinging out over an audience of raucous men. She has become what White made her, the Girl in the Red Velvet Swing, without career, without talent, without husband, without family, living on the one thing men prize—her prominently displayed crotch.

The Girl in the Red Velvet Swing is an extraordinarily clever work. It has the look of glitzy trash, but it is much better than that. It has the visual sophsitication of a very good film, and it uses the devices of visually narrative art (e.g., the swing) with care. To be sure, it suffers from 1950s baroque—heavy-handed psychologizing, including dreams, and an opacity to its own causes. Too much of the cause is called "love," but "love" will not explicate the more intelligent aspects of the film. What, for example, is the cause of the role of the theater here? What is the cause of White's paired achievements as architect and predator? How was White, the arbiter of taste for a generation, the pivot in this tasteless event? What is the relationship among Eurocentrism and White and women?

Or, to put it differently, what cause links the event with the society of White and Thaw (expressed partly as style)?

Good as Milland and Granger and Collins are, the acting lacks self-awareness. They enact; they do not show that they know what they are doing. That is, they give typical Hollywood performances, essentially realistic, even though the film's style and the director's consciousness are not strictly realistic. Fleischer's direction is so good that I suspect that he let this "typical Hollywood" quality stand as a kind of protection. Some of what I see as the film's depth and questioning was consciously disguised, perhaps, by style, excess, sexual titillation, yet the glances at forbidden subjects may be more telling than other, more frontal attacks have been. It is easy to be put off by its resonances with Esky and Arno cartoons and Edwardian chuckles. It deserves feminist analysis.

Three show-business biographies also raised questions about women, their focus female victimization. Two of them included strong images of male abuse, even sadism. Two of them were also strong in their use of pop Freudianism, especially parental blame. *I'll Cry Tomorrow* (1955) starred Susan Hayward as the alcoholic, much-married singer–actress Lillian Roth. The film was an emotional bloodbath, a super-soap that let Hayward pull out all the stops as she progressed from young star, bedevilled by a stage mother (Jo Van Fleet), to boozing star, bedevilled by a sadistic husband (Richard Conte), to a down-and-out alcoholic, bedevilled by everybody in the vicinity. At last she meets Eddie Albert, who sponsors her recovery in an AA-like setting, and her apotheosis comes when she walks down the aisle of a TV studio and one of the then kings of smarm shouts about "a story of degradation and shame— This Is Your Life, Lillian Roth!" Hayward wears a meaningful face: we are supposed to see this as triumph.

However, one questions now how successfully Roth had escaped victimization: not only was she the victim of this hellish television show and its male host, but she was the subject of a lurid "autobiography" written with two men, Mike Connelly and Gerold Frank.

I'll Cry Tomorrow was not a cry for women generally. Produced and directed by men, it starred an actress whose persona seemed created by men—bosom and hair, thrilling voice and flashing eyes, sex and suffering. Hayward starred in another film of the same sort, *I Want to Live* (1958), about a woman on death row, but again it was a solo, a queen bee's story. Hayward in fact seems a ludicrous candidate for a women's representative; she is always a female individual (*The President's Lady, With a Song in My Heart*). When she triumphs over adversity, she triumphs within the context of the same idea of "woman" that first victimized her, and she triumphs only in ways that will show off her male-defined attributes. Thus, to suggest, as *I'll Cry Tomorrow* does, that the cause of a woman's adversity (here, alcoholism) is another woman (here, her mother) makes sense only until we look at all the men involved in making the suggestion.

Too Much, Too Soon (1958) had much in common with *I'll Cry Tomorrow*, including a sadistic man, a victimized protagonist, and the involvement of Gerold Frank. Frank even appears as a character in the film, offering salvation via autobiography at the end.

Diana Barrymore (Dorothy Malone) is the daughter of John Barrymore (Errol Flynn) and "Michael Strange," pseudonym of the writer Blanche Oelrichs (Neda Harrington). Malone is very good; early on, she takes risks as a homely, uneasy adolescent, then matures and plays a fragile woman destroyed by her inability to accept herself.

Her mother is cold; her father is absent in Hollywood, and she goes after him, moves into his strange house with him, has a brief movie career before following him into alcoholism. She marries an actor (Efrem Zimbalist), gives him up for a drunken fling, then marriage to a one hundred percent rat (Ray

Danton). Down and down she goes, and the film goes with her, becoming merely a sensational exposé of the weaknesses of the rich and famous. At the end, having hit bottom, she is on her way to tell all to Frank, who has convinced her that he "knows about" writing.

Too Much, Too Soon is the film version of the resulting book, "The Daring Story of Diana Barrymore, based on the Book by Diana Barrymore and Gerold Frank." Produced by a man, directed by a man, it is mostly a bad (male) movie about a vulnerable woman victimized by men, including those who said they could help her. It expends its creative energies in the first half, mostly in the sequences with Flynn, who in no way recalls John Barrymore but who commands attention. Bloated and lined (the sixteen years since *They Died with Their Boots On* had wrecked him), he projected sadness and charm and self-destruction.

Flynn has been surrounded with a mansion out of a horror film—Gothic doorways, a stone staircase, a tall iron cage with an ancient eagle in it, a male nurse. His daughter, pathetically optimistic, moves into this setting like a Gothic heroine moving into the haunted castle, and she suffers the horror-movie clichés we expect.

After John Barrymore's death, the movie, its imagination exhausted, careens from one hackneyed setup to another, one badly played husband to another, to the slimy pen of Mister Frank. Except for John Barrymore's personal hell, it never finds an image for its protagonist's suffering, and the responses it tries for seem limited to our saying, "God, doesn't she look *awful!*" Despite its hype, the film is not so much "daring" as exploitative—of Diana Barrymore, of John Barrymore, of Errol Flynn. Even more than *I'll Cry Tomorrow*, it was an example of the victimization it pretended to deplore.

Jeanne Eagels (1957) starred a beefy Kim Novak as the woman who created a sensation onstage in *Rain* in the 1920s and died young. The movie has one memorable moment. Charles Drake, as a football-playing husband, is killing time by showing a bunch of black kids how to pass the ball. "You hold it just like a watemelon, see?"

Victimization takes many forms.

BY CONTRAST, AT LEAST one film showed women as self-sufficient and happy people. *Belles on Their Toes* (1952) was a sequel to the successful *Cheaper By the Dozen* (1950). It removed the father (Clifton Webb) from the family and made the widowed Myrna Loy a self-reliant engineer, the move from father worship to female emergence perhaps consistent with other changes of the decade.

Edward Arnold was prominent as a male chauvinist. "Women are creeping in all over"; "No man who's worth anything could ever take instruction from a woman." Loy calls him "stupid, hardheaded, ignorant" and lambastes his "stupid male conceit," and in time he comes around, hiring Loy to teach engineering. He even tries to propose but can never get a word through the family chatter, and the film ends with its focus on Loy and eldest daughter Jeanne Crain, not on mature romance. More or less patriarchal ideas of family hang over the film like Papa's ghost, but what it shows is women making their own way and finding satisfaction without male approval.

SPORTS FILMS

THE SAME BRYAN FOY who was one of the Seven Little Foys and who produced *I Was a Communist for the FBI* made another foray into Americana with *The Winning Team* in 1952. This movie about Grover Cleveland Alexander might have had more luster if it had not been preceded by the most important sports film yet made, *The Jackie Robinson Story* (1950). As it was, *The Winning Team* and *Pride of St. Louis* (1952), a biography of pitcher Dizzy Dean, were made to seem trivial by the Robinson film and by two others later in the decade that transformed the sports biography.

The Jackie Robinson Story looked cheap and lacked anything as interesting as a novel camera angle or an innovative shot, yet it told more about its time than most were able to do with big budgets, Technicolor, and stars. It used a couple of old pros (Minor Watson, Billy Wayne) to give it continuity with other sports bios, but gave Watson a real role for a change—Branch Rickey. Ruby Dee played the wife of Robinson, who played himself.

In a sense, perhaps, the film is no less a distortion than other sports biographies, for its focus on race undoubtedly limits our understanding of others forces of the time; however, unlike other sports films, it took race instead of sport as its subject, and by doing so moved into the real world. What *The Jackie Robinson Story* said was, first, that race was an important issue in America; and, second, that sports could not live in a make-believe America where everybody with ability was white.

Robinson was better than most people who have played themselves in movies, certainly no worse than Audie Murphy. The story begins before World War II, takes him quickly to UCLA as a football player. Race is a constant subject. "What good will a college degree do? They're not hiring colored football coaches. Not our color, anyway. . . . Baseball's one sport they'll never let me in. . . ." Drafted, he becomes an officer, and after the war he returns to the same job rejections he had found before, except from the Negro Baseball League.

Traveling in the team bus, he learns the realities of segregated sports at the professional level: as the new guy, he has to go into the restaurants and ask the questions. "Three things—see if we can eat *inside*; see if we can wash up; if we can't eat inside, see if they'll fix sandwiches." On his first try, the sandwiches are permitted; washing up is "out of order."

Robinson is pulled from this kind of humiliation to a meeting with Branch Rickey. Watson plays Rickey as a serious, kindly, rather aristocratic man with a slow but real temper, another in a long line of Hollywood father figures. What he proposes is putting Robinson into the white minor leagues. As the first black player, "It'll take a lot of courage. . . . I want a ballplayer with guts enough *not* to fight back. . . . You can't fight back!"

The rest of the film is Robinson's rise to prominence through two years of insults, challenges, small triumphs, and humiliations. In Florida, a game is called because blacks and whites cannot legally play together. Some of his teammates won't let him warm up with them. His manager asks Rickey, "You think he *is* a human being?" The word "boy" is used often. Fans call him "shine" and "nigger"; other players call him "Sambo" and "liver lips." Boos greet Robinson's first appearance as a major-leaguer. As he helps Brooklyn to win, however, the boos become cheers. The film closes with a shot of a black kid walking, the Statue of Liberty superimposed on him, a voice telling us about "a country where every child has the opportunity to be President—or play baseball for the Brooklyn Dodgers."

The Jackie Robinson Story is naively told, although no more naively than most sports movies. It has many of the same staples—the supportive wife, the big game, the fickle fans. It relies more on subject than on plot. However, it has shifted that subject from sports itself to an aspect of the larger world that sports inhabit. It was made four years before *Brown v Board of Education*, only shortly after Truman integrated the army, a decade after Marian Anderson had been refused Constitution Hall. It was followed by *The Joe Louis Story* (1953).

Somebody Up There Likes Me (1956) also looked beyond sport. It gave Paul Newman one of his best roles as the boxer Rocky Graziano, who came from criminal beginnings, by way of the less-than-admirable route of desertion from the army, to the middleweight championship. It is also a film about boxing, with some of the most brutal sequences ever made, but it is also about maturing and learning to accept the responsibilities of one's acts. It marks an emergence of Italian–Americans from the old signs of mustache and curly hair.

Somebody Up There Likes Me was grounded in a new American acting (the Method or its derivatives), with the result that its extreme naturalism feels sometimes more like a challenge than a style. Steve McQueen is self-indulgently "real" as a friend, Sal Mineo surprisingly touching as another. The look is gritty, grimy, a Little Italy without glamor or joy.

As a child, Graziano is abused by a drunken father, who, in the guise of teaching him to box, beats him. Given these beginnings, it is comprehensible that the teen-aged Graziano leads a gang that steals tires, then furs, and blows the money on dreadful clothes. Then it is reform school, then Rikers Island for beating a guard, and then the army. But Graziano knows only the street, and he assaults a captain and goes AWOL, tries low-level pro boxing, is recognized, and does time at Leavenworth.

This is not a pretty picture of a hero, nor is Newman trying to paint a pretty picture with his twitches and jerks, his grunts, his thrust-out lips, the demotic accent we also hear from Brando in *On the Waterfront*. "Antihero" is too nice a term; Graziano is, to this point, a loser. For all the excess of some of Newman's mannerisms, however, he creates a character with room to grow. And, no matter what Newman does, he remains Newman, with his charisma and his talent.

Graziano now meets his wife-to-be (Pier Angeli). Angeli plays it simple and sweet, and not coy. It is not that love conquers all, or that behind every great boxer there is a thin Jewish woman; rather, marriage becomes the outward sign of maturity. Inarticulate, boorish—"Fighters ain't got much time for girls"—he nonetheless cannot get along without her, nor she without him.

The film ends with the second Graziano–Zale fight, with Tony Zale playing himself and, despite by then being in his forties, looking dangerous and capable. Fights are not edifying spectacles, and this one is particularly brutal. Graziano wins, and the film ends with a parade through Little Italy, signs hanging from the fire escapes, the Grazianos waving. Before this triumph, however, he has been through two moral crises, a reconciliation with his brutish father, and an appearance before the New York Boxing Commission to explain an unreported bribe attempt. He does not emerge from the film a hero; he does emerge as a man, and one who has learned to deal with moral issues, not always with his fists. This is history from the very bottom up.

Monkey on My Back (1957) was also about a boxer, although its real subject was Barney Ross's life after he left the ring and became a drug addict. It opens with a sequence in which Ross (Cameron Mitchell) admits himself to the "United States Federal Hospital" for morphine addiction; most of the film is flashback—winning the title in the 1930s, combat experience in World War II (badly overdone), his wounding, the military's use of morphine to deal with pain.

The rest of the film is a sometimes lurid depiction of an addict's life. Although sensational, this honesty about addiction is early days for movies or theater (*A Hatful of Rain*, play, 1957; *The Connection*, play, 1959). Things are overdone; his pusher, for example, is a sadistic tease, to no good dramatic purpose. Other addicts are made to seem addle-brained fiends. Nonetheless, the realization of the power of addiction is convincing. "I'm dirt. I stink," he tells his wife when he can no longer hide the addiction. "I ain't kidding myself now. The dope's stronger than me."

The film ends where it began, in the hospital where Ross has withdrawn from the drug; a title, "The Beginning," is hopeful. As Ross, Mitchell is believable, workmanlike, but not compelling; he lacks Newman's ability to make us see his value no matter what sins he commits. Still, *Monkey on My Back* can be looked at without flinching or smirking—more than can be said for *The Winning Team* or *Pride of St. Louis.*

SOCIOPATHS

THE TENDENCY TOWARD nonheroes or antiheroes was pushed several notches lower with a small, new cluster of films about urban criminals. They looked at bad men for their own sakes, something that the Western had been doing for a long time, but without the Western's self-justification. *Cell 2455, Death Row* (1955) was about the once-notorious Carryl Chessman, *Pretty Boy Floyd* (1959) about the Public Enemy Number One of the early 1930s. Both were "youth movies" that used newcomers, William Campbell as Chessman, John Ericson as Floyd. *Floyd* even had a primitive rock 'n' roll score, hardly enough to save it; the movie was slow and simplistic, but it was unabashed about showing a good-looking protagonist at odds with the world of adults—police, laws, honor, morality. It peels people (and responsibility) away from Floyd as he rises, takes part in the Kansas City Massacre, then goes on the run and is shot by police in a farm field.

Carryl Chessman was once something of a cause, one of the first Death Row criminals to focus interest on legal rights. The film insists that Chessman is a sociopath, an anomaly who should be executed. "Not society—not heredity—not enviroment—but the man alone. I alone am to blame." We see him move from petty crime to armed robbery, from reform school to Folsom Prison; we watch an extended sequence of rape-robberies that became known as the "Red Light Bandit" crimes, for which Chessman was sentenced to death, although stays kept him alive on Death Row for years.

The film refuses to use the word "rape" and refuses to tell us that Chessman is the rapist, so the force of Chessman's argument for capital punishment is lost. William Campbell's performance, contemptuous and egocentric, is much like Ericson's as Floyd; for all the ostensible difference in meanings, the two films are bound by a common fascination with handsome young criminals.

Characterized by cheap sets, unimaginative photography, and carefully edited sex and violence, the films seem to represent an attempt to reach a new audience with a new subject, but without shaking the old ways represented by the Production Code. Neither film has any use for women, except as objects of sex and violence; both see their protagonist as a victimizer but make no moral judgment. It is a little as if films had been made about the sadistic men of *I'll Cry Tomorrow* and *Too Much, Too Soon* and had given them heroic status.

BEHIND THE FAÇADE of 1950s conformism, these films tell us, America was suffering powerful strain. Father figures are seen as both self-important generals behind desks and sadistic brutes; women are seen as passive nebishes, as victims, and as independent creatures. After two wars in ten years, militarism is pushed hard in many films, but others undercut it. Many male stars are too old and are paired with women young enough to be their daughters, but another kind of film appears that features young men nobody ever heard of, often playing outcasts. Some films revere high culture; others reject it utterly. The large events of the decade happen outside these films—*Brown v Board of Education*, the Cold War, suburbanization—but aspects of them squeeze their way into certain ones. Perhaps what is most striking, however, is how cautiously they do so. These are not rebellious or innovative films. Symbolism, allusion, hint, suggestion are more often their devices than overt statement of things controversial—race, gender, sex, war. The Production Code, although losing some of its influence, looms at least metaphorically over Hollywood, still engendering an art of euphemism. However, earlier euphemisms seem to have sprung from an acknowledgment of a social conservatism out there in the sticks; the euphemism of the 1950s seems more a part of an atmosphere of suspicion and worry. Reverence for the past was going fast. Part of the worry was over what would replace it.

Native Americans had fared poorly in films through the 1940s; the 1950s revised some of that bad history. *Chief Crazy Horse* (1955), despite shortcomings, gave this devastating image: the heroic Crazy Horse, in buckskins, being murdered by detribalized Native Americans in uniforms. Victor Mature, center, and Ray Danton as his murderer. (The Museum of Modern Art/Film Stills Archive.)

Just as Jackie Robinson changed baseball, *The Jackie Robinson Story* (1950) changed the sports bio, propelling it into the real world. Robinson, as himself, faces his teammates. (The Museum of Modern Art/Film Stills Archive.)

The sports biography got underway with *Knute Rockne, All-American* (1940), with Pat O'Brien. The photo epitomizes the genre: no girls, a father figure and the boys, God, and a microphone—sport as white male entertainment as media event. (The Museum of Modern Art/Film Stills Archive.)

Robert De Niro's performance as Jake LaMotta brought the sports film to the far extreme of realism—a long way from Pat O'Brien and his microphone. *Raging Bull* (1980). (The Museum of Modern Art/Film Stills Archive.)

Independent women remained rarities in films, if not in history, until the 1970s. Rosalind Russell was an exception, although in *Flight for Freedom* (1943), a pseudonymous mock–up of Amelia Earhart's life, she got stuck in the glue of Hollywood romance. (The Museum of Modern Art/Film Stills Archive.)

Meryl Streep, Kurt Russell, and Cher in *Silkwood* (1983). Few films better represent the hypothesis that the closer historical events are in time to the making of the
film, the better the history is likely to be. (The Museum of Modern Art/Films Stills
Archive.)

Cooper's *Last of the Mohicans* is one of the most durable of film histories. The 1936 version, with Randolph Scott, Henry Wilcoxon, Binnie Barnes, and Heather Angel, was the basis for the less well-pressed 1992 version, with Madeleine Stowe, Jodhi May, Steven Waddington, and Daniel Day-Lewis. (The Museum of Modern Art/Film Stills Archive.)

Revisionism is sometimes essential to history, not only in subject but also in imagery. Here, African Americans as self-sacrificing American heroes in *Glory* (1988), with Denzel Washington and Morgan Freeman. (The Museum of Modern Art/Film Stills Archive.)

Two brilliant peformances lie at the heart of Oliver Stone's *Nixon* (1995), those of Anthony Hopkins as Nixon and Joan Allen as Pat Nixon. (The Museum of Modern Art/Film Stills Archive.)

A long way from Cooper and Tracy—interchangeable, corporate men as team hero. *Apollo 13* (1995), with Bill Paxton, Kevin Bacon, and Tom Hanks. (The Museum of Modern Art/Film Stills Archive.)

CHAPTER SEVEN

1960–1969: A CHANGING OF THE GUARD ─────────────

The conflicting directions of films in the 1950s may have been part of the change that became marked in the 1960s by a radical falloff in the total number of historical films, by more than two-thirds to barely forty. Musical biographies fell to four (with three more show-business biographies), Westerns to five (eight if films about Texas and the Indian Wars are included). These figures reflect a decline in film production itself (down to an average of 153 a year from close to 500 in the early 1940s).[1] They also reflect changes in the industry—the end of the Production Code (1966), the collapse of the studios, the internationalization of production (so that the definition of "American" film applies to relatively fewer of those released).

Nowhere does the diminution show more clearly than in the films about traditional, top-down history: nineteen 1950s films dealt with events before the Texas Rebellion; none of the 1960s films did so. The 1950s had produced seven films about World War I and II and Korea; the 1960s produced two, none about its own war in Vietnam. The 1950s were abundant with patriotic greats—Boone, Crockett, Bradford, Jackson, Pocohontas, Sacajawea, Lewis, Clark, Houston, Jones; the 1960s offered two—Kennedy and Roosevelt, neither as President, plus a minor explorer, John Wesley Powell, plus Crockett again, and the group hero of the D-Day landings. Like the 1950s films, too, they are often disappointing—backward, even stale.

JOHN WAYNE PRODUCED and directed *The Alamo* (1960) and also played Crockett. It is a long film, oddly talky for a man whose movie persona was terse and who, as an actor, communicated best through facial expression and the use of small properties. The talkiness had two immediate causes, one the urge to celebrate democracy, the other Crockett's urge to make verbal love to a beautiful woman (Linda Cristal) who otherwise had nothing to do with the film. The talk does not, on the other hand, come from any desire to provide exposition. The only background is provided by an opening title, "In the year of our Lord, 1836 . . . Generallisimo Santa Ana was sweeping . . . toward them, crushing all who opposed his tyrannical rule. They now faced the decision that all men in all times must face . . . the eternal choice of men . . . to endure oppression or to resist."

The emphasis on men indicates clearly what part of human experience will be dealt with. Virtually the entire large cast is male, and much of what they do is aimed, consciously or not, at defining how males are "men," including scene after scene in which men either get drunk or fight and make up. Jim Bowie (Richard Widmark) is drunk when we first see him. After Crockett and the Tennesseeans arrive, they repair to the cantina and get drunk; then they brawl. One man challenges Crockett to a contest he has already lost thirty-six times: each hits the other as hard as he can. "It's a kind of game the boys play back in Tennessee." Later, Bowie helps Crockett fight off a gang of thugs hired by Cristal's protector; then they sit down to drink. Much later, Crockett gets Bowie drunk to keep him and his men from leaving; next morning, he throws water on Bowie to wake him, the two have a good-buddies fistfight, and then they drink together.

This defining personal violence is not carried over into war, however, which is clean and pretty. After an early sortie against the Alamo, the ground is littered with bodies, but all are dead and pure; no men scream, no horses struggle to their feet with intestines hanging to the ground. War, like the good-buddy brawl, has no real hurt; it is all stuntmen and doubles—the only kind of war Wayne knew.

Historically, the film's visual framework is as shaky as that of most Westerns. Crockett, having arrived on a horse with no baggage, appears in a series of leather jackets, each more Rodeo Drive than the one before. The Alamo has its now-familiar curved top, in fact lacking at the time of the battle. Most of the men carry pistols, many in holsters, possible but not typical in 1836. A flamenco sequence is copied from a Sargent painting, but the original was Spanish, not deep-boonies Mexican.

The acting varies. Richard Boone should have been provided with a steel pick to get the shreds of carpet out of his teeth; "playing anger" is the overriding flaw in the cast's performance, the cause of the rage never clear, unless it is not knowing why they are in the village of San Antonio, or why fortifying an old mission will stop Santa Ana, or who all these men are, or why they are in Texas, or what "liberty" means to Anglo–Mexican citizens who own slaves, or in what ways Santa Ana's rule is "tyrannical." Certainly, Wayne as director has finessed the question of the Alamo's military usefulness, burying it in the Bowie–Travis rivalry over command (better handled in *The Last Command*). Some people view the battle of the Alamo as one of history's great cockups, on a par with Custer's Last Stand and the Charge of the Light Brigade. *The Alamo* will not let us consider these possibilites; Bowie's adumbration of them becomes more mere talk.

The talk itself is often of the abstract variety. Crockett says, for example, "Republic—I like the sound of the word. Means people can live free." White people, he presumably means. White men, anyway. Propertied white men, at least. As the battle nears, he emits two back-to-back paeans to Texas. The subject is reprised as the women and children leave the Alamo.

One character, however, is not allowed to speak on this subject: when Travis (Laurence Harvey) tries to make a speech to the newly arrived Tennesseeans about "freedom," Crockett stops him with, "They don't need any such speech. These men are from Tennessee." Flattering as this is to the Southern mythos, it does not explain why director Wayne cuts off his favorite subject. Hollywood convention does: for most of the film, Travis embodies the ethical androgyny often imposed on British actors. He is another antidemocratic disciplinarian who is not a real man because he prizes rules and does not drink or brawl.

When *The Alamo* is not talking, it is often visually rich, although not necessarily lifelike. The battle itself is athletic, full of stunts (including too many that endanger horses). Nonetheless, there is a look of obligation to the Hollywood way of seeing, to cavalry movies and cowboy movies, especially of the late 1930s. Visually and thematically, it would fit in that group of big films of 1939–42; by 1960, its moment was past.

The film's weaknesses—poor history, preachiness, talkiness—come from its trying to serve goals that the real events of the Alamo, noble enough in themselves, were not thought adequate to supply. This lack of trust in history, also reminiscent of the neoromantic blockbusters of 1939–42, is part of a larger distrust of intellectual rigor, not surprising in a movie whose one negative character, Travis, is unacceptable because rigorous. Rigor is bad; as the song that thumps under the final frames tells us, "They fought to give us freedom, That is all we need to know."

Red Runs the River (1963) was an unusual and serious film about the Civil War that managed to embody the profound religious feeling of many of the Civil War's participants. Starring Bob Jones, Jr., and Bob Jones III, with the "faculty and staff of Bob Jones University" and music by the Bob Jones University Orchestra, it showed in its credits that it was a message movie. The film can now be seen as an early example of the grasp of modern media by militant Protestantism.

Concerned with General Richard Stoddart Ewell, who "in his heart . . . warred against God," it is almost a good movie. What it lacks is a plot, perhaps an inevitable problem in a work that is waiting for most of its length for divine intervention, although most commercial films are able to build suspense on or toward equally gratuitous events—love at first sight, change of heart. In terms of action (in the Aristotelian sense), Ewell's conversion could as well happen in the first reel as the last; between exposition and crisis there is activity but no causally linked action.

The activity is the Civil War, whose reenactment here may please Civil War buffs for reasons of sentiment but not for dramatic ones, as it has no suspense. Only one side (the Southern) is shown, without cause or context, and the sequence of events seems random: it has neither dramatic nor intellectual (historical) structure, despite a good deal of activity by figures like Jeb Stuart.

In other ways, *Red Runs the River* shows its amateur origins, as in generally bad acting, bad fake beards, costumes that sometimes look cheesy, poor direction of a major battle sequence. On the other hand, the cinematography is more frank about the horrors of war than, say, *The Alamo*, and there is a nice sense of detail in the establishing sequences, sometimes frittered away on subsequent scenes of talk.

The film comes to a ringing end with Ewell's conversion after being wounded: "To surrender to God is victory, and to be defeated by Christ is triumph, indeed," and so it fulfills its evangelical goal. One may question, however, why that message must so completely accept a Southern bias, including mostly invisible but occasionally comic blacks, the plantation myth, the Glorious Cause, and a blind eye to slavery.

Ten Who Dared (1960) was, like *The Great Locomotive Chase*, an unassuming Disney foray into all-male history. Its treatment of John Wesley Powell's 1869 trip down the Colorado suggests that he was the first float-tuber. *Ten Who Dared* is not dreadful history; it is simply a dull little movie that tells us (incorrectly) that so little happened to Powell (John Beal) that the smarties at Disney had to make the good stuff up—a cute dog, a drunk, wrangles. That Powell's journey had meaning is invisible.

Sunrise at Campobello (1960) was a filmed version of Dore Schary's stage play about the pre-presidential Franklin Delano Roosevelt. It is concerned with the onset of polio, his loss of the use of his legs, and his courageous return to politics to nominate Al Smith. It includes interesting performances by Greer Garson as Eleanor Roosevelt and Hume Cronyn as Louis Howe, but their very excellence points up this lavish film's flaw: wedded to a stage realism that amassed trivial detail, it necessarily moves glacially and gives equal value to family evenings at home and the Democratic Convention. Garson is constantly occupied with details of domesticity, often seen knitting or sewing; the perhaps unintended result is an ahistorically disengaged Eleanor.

Roosevelt himself (Ralph Bellamy) is torn between realistic dithering and Big Moments; because of the first, the second seem false. Because of the attention to authenticating detail, always heavier in the first act of such a play, and because of a felt need to make Roosevelt immediate and "real," most of the early footage is given over to what seems like endless family warmth, fatherly concern, and foreshadowings that date to the plays of Scribe. FDR feels a little tired; "the first swim in years that didn't refresh me"; he stumbles; ominous music thrums, and so forth.

The visual environments are rich, the costumes admirable (although one doubts that Eleanor Roosevelt wore mascara), the Roosevelts' summer home enviable. What is left for the other two-thirds of the film, however, is predictable—more of the same, but with mixed sadness and courage. At the end, having struggled to the convention podium on his crutches, FDR accepts the adulation of a crowd gone wild. Ahead lie the White House, the Depression, history. Eleanor is at one side, knitting; ahead for her, we assume, lies more knitting. This is a severe disservice to a woman who in some ways was more courageous and more committed to ideals than her husband, and it is the inevitable—and contemptible—result of the emphasis on domesticity as a backdrop to male achievement: again, female history through male eyes.

Entertainment requires that we see the great man in his everyday roles, most satisfyingly when he is assailed by a leveler like polio. History is impatient with such matters, the more so when they bring ephemeral propaganda with them, including the imbedded gender propaganda that sees women as incapable of greatness even when the truth of that greatness is already known.

The Longest Day (1962) was Darryl F. Zanuck's version of D-Day. It starred everybody (male) who had ever spent a day in Hollywood; the faces go by so fast it's like watching history from the bullet train. Look! there's Henry Fonda—is that John Wayne?—Hey Richard Bu—Ray—Bob—Kurt/ Peter/Sean—! If they have accents, they must be Germans. Where are we? What beach is this? Where are those guys going? Huh? Only two-thirds of the way through does a movement map appear; until then, little of what goes on makes overall sense. Perhaps the intent was to simulate the fog of war.

The Longest Day is infantry war without the infantryman's life of terror, without screams and moans and prayers, without exhaustion and missing limbs and blown-off faces. It is, instead, war with an undue emphasis on atypical heroics—commandos and paratroopers and Canadian, British, French, and American rangers, out of all proportion to their importance compared to the thousands who never even made it to the beaches. It is probably accurate enough in its names and many of its details, being based on a well-researched book, but it also contains some Hollywood hokum: John Wayne as a paratrooper officer who gets an inordinate amount of attention for apparently wasting his men's time carrying him around the countryside instead of leaving him and his broken ankle behind; somebody saying to Henry Fonda as Theodore Roosevelt, Jr., "Your father was a great soldier!"; Sean Connery as a comic Irishman. What it does not show is the tactical reason for its blur of names: infantry war is anonymous because chance rules who will die, who will live; individuality disappears in statistics. Grant's "Send in more men" is the meaning of the D-Day invasion; Omaha Beach and Cold Harbor equally reduced the individual grunt to a dispensable atom.

PT-109 (1963) offered Cliff Robertson as John F. Kennedy in the same war, the film made before the Kennedy assassination but after his election. Richard Reeves called it "a World War II morale movie made twenty years too late," in which it was certainly no different from others of the decade.[2]

NATIVE AMERICANS

OF THE 1960S FILMS about Native Americans, *Cheyenne Autumn* is the best, but, as "John Ford's *Cheyenne Autumn*," as a title has it, the film is disappointing after *Wings of Eagles*. Like *Sergeant Rutledge*, Ford's fiction film about a black cavalryman, it seems to be trying to make amends. Here, the cavalry are weary self-doubters who try to protect a band of Cheyenne who set out from Oklahoma, almost without hope, for their old home in the North. As always, Ford makes stunning use of landscape, including a night scene when the Cheyenne move out under cover of a dust storm, and another in "the grim north of Nebraska" in winter.

Richard Widmark is an officer trying to protect the Cheyenne, but the film is so loose in its probabilities that we never learn how he is able to take a company of cavalry through several military areas without orders or coordination. The same looseness allowed Ford to include a lengthy saloon scene in which Wyatt Earp (James Stewart) shoots a drunk in the foot, then anesthetizes him with a mallet before removing the bullet. The scene's farce is simply wrong in this film; would we accept it if it were the ethical Widmark whacking one of the noble Cheyenne so he could perform surgery?

Some of the acting is good (Widmark; Victor Jory as a Cheyenne leader; Edward G. Robinson as Carl Schurz, reformer of the Indian Department), but some of it is bad (Sal Mineo bouncing off the tepee walls as a Cheyenne rebel). One sequence is refreshing: Mike Mazurki, as a Polish immigrant, now a cavalry trooper, tells Widmark he wants to leave the army because the Cossacks "kill Poles because they're Poles, the way we kill Indians just because they're Indians." This army is not Ford's usual troop of Irish comedians, but a mix of Poles, Germans, Irish, and others—a long haul from *The Iron Horse*.

Cheyenne Autumn is too long, too wobbly in its probabilities, too varied in its tone. Ford's admission that the Army sometimes did atrocious things would need a lot of rewriting before it could offer the perceptiveness of the Danton–Mature duality in *Chief Crazy Horse* or the depth of feeling of the final scenes of *Broken Arrow*.

The Great Sioux Massacre (1965) dealt ahistorically with the Little Big Horn, and was noteworthy only in that its sympathy had swung away from the army. The shift is a continuation of one already strong in the 1950s, probably an aspect of racial readjustment; by 1968 and the lackluster *Custer of the West*, it may have begun to reflect the tensions of Vietnam.

WESTERNS

IF THE INDIANS fared poorly in the 1960s, the cowboys did little better. One film was a Three Stooges farce (*The Outlaws Is Coming*, 1965), one a painful remake of *The Plainsman* (1966), with Don Murray in the Cooper role (Hickok) and Abby Dalton in that first taken by Jean Arthur (Calamity Jane), so dreadful she makes Doris Day's Calamity seem merely bad. A genuine stinker, *The Plainsman* has all the shlock and none of the charm of its predecessor; it reeks of television and contempt for the audience.

Hour of the Gun (1967), on the other hand, was the first of three Westerns that showed that the innovations of *The Left-Handed Gun* had been noted. It is also probably the best of the Earp–Clanton films, in part because it seems to be the most factually accurate and in part because it most carefully tracks the legal and juridical ramifications of the feud. In Robert Ryan, it has the most forceful Ike Clanton; in Jason Robards, Jr., the most believable Doc Holliday. In James Garner, the producer–director John Sturges has a believable, if understated protagonist. The same director's *Gunfight at the O.K. Corral* is more stylish, its examination of Earp and Holliday more tortuously "psychological," but its history is finally less probing.

Unlike most of the films on the subject, *Hour of the Gun* begins with the O.K. Corral and then follows Wyatt Earp's increasingly private vengeance. Here, Holliday—as always, a drunk—plays chorus to Garner's avenger as the action moves from legal killing as the extension of justice to extralegal killing as revenge. Earp, at first armed with warrants, shoots down Clanton's people with increasing coldness, then tracks Ike Clanton to Mexico and, warrantless, kills him. After the first round of killings, Holliday tells Earp, "Those aren't warrants you got there, those are hunting licenses. . . . If you're gonna kill like me, you might as well drink like me." When Earp kills, nothing shows—no disgust, no nerves, no shock.

At the end, Earp and Holliday part in a Colorado sanatorium where Holliday has gone to help his lungs. The scene has the terseness of the final one in *Gunfight at the O.K. Corral* but a very different point. It is not about tightly bonded men parting because their relationship is sterile, but about a man—Earp—who has become what Holliday said he would become. Just before Earp killed Clanton, Holliday told him, "[Your rules of law] are more important to you than you think. Play by them, or they'll destroy you." It is apparently because of fear of that destruction that Earp says as he parts from Holliday, "I'm through with the law." In fact, the law is through with him.

Hour of the Gun is an interesting reading of the Earp story. More literal than *O.K. Corral,* it lacks that film's lushness—and its women. *Hour of the Gun* is a male experience without being about male relationships. Less haunting than *My Darling Clementine,* less luxuriant than *O.K. Corral,* it stands as a clean, intelligent version of the events, and as a revisionist reading of the supposed code of the gun, which it sees as sociopathology.

Butch Cassidy and the Sundance Kid (1969) made as much history by bringing Paul Newman and Robert Redford together as it did by adding its bit to revisionism. It is widely admired, and certainly it has much about it that is enjoyable. However, its constant air of wanting to have things both ways—that is, to be both romantic and cynical, an essentially adolescent desire—undermines its value.

The two stars are splendid, no denying it. They give off sparks, and their performances and George Roy Hill's commercial version of New Wave directing give enormous comic value. The comedy, however, is at the root of the work's flaw: finally, nothing matters much, and when the two protagonists are shot down by hundreds of soldiers, our sense of loss is less for Butch and Sundance than for Newman and Redford: if they get shot, the movie's over.

It is, of course, ironic that a movie that pretends to be a revision of what Hollywood once meant by "Western movies" in fact exists only to be one. It swings between two attitudes, one of alienation (created by Marvin Hamlisch's I-wish-I-were-Kurt Weill score and the mannered camera work) and one of romantic yearning for supposedly simple values threatened by modernity. These are supposedly the values of a lost Golden Age. "It's over! Your time is over!" a sheriff tells the two stars.

What the audience is being caused to yearn for here is a Golden Age of the West that is an invention of the modern, urban (California) mind. We get some patently improbable acts: Redford shoots off another man's gunbelt with one shot, indoors, without regard to where the bullet goes next. The stars shoot people from galloping horses. When the two are wounded in the final shootout, they continue to make smart chat, like comic-book heroes. This falseness is apparently meant to be compensated (or apologized) for by the mocking music, which seems to say, "None of this matters, so it's OK if we cheat," but the loving caress of the two men by the camera tells us that it does matter.

It is in this manner that the film tries to have things two ways. It is probably a movie for upper-schoolers, having that level of sex and smirk: Katherine Ross is a schoolteacher (I wish my teacher did that!); nudity flashes past now and then (She was bare-assed!); Newman and Redford are gorgeous images of the never-was (It was all so sad.) And fun. But not history.

Also at the end of the decade, Audie Murphy produced a small movie that was director Budd Boetticher's last, *A Time for Dying* (1969). It was Texan Murphy's revisionist look at a real West, which he found to be different from the Westerns he had starred in.

Here, a deadshot kid who wants to be a bounty hunter (Richard Lapp) wanders for a few days through a Texas that includes a terrifyingly mad, toothless, and drunken Judge Roy Bean (Victor Jory), an almost benign Jesse James (Murphy), a young woman (Anne Randall), and a bad guy called Billy Pimple (Bob Random). Most of the acting is uninteresting, although Jory's has a repellant intensity. Boetticher's direction seems peculiar, as if he has something in mind but can't get it over to us: many scenes have too much light or too little detail; interiors sometimes look starved. The pacing is ragged, the action not always clear (that involving a James robbery, for example).

Yet Lapp has an appealing youthfulness that makes us want to follow his picaresque few days. These lead to his death, shot down by the first gunman he faces (Billy Pimple). The kid's achievements are quickly negated: the young woman, now his wife, is captured by the town madame, from whom he had orignally saved her; another young woman arrives on the stage and, without him there to rescue her, also heads for the whorehouse, as men congregate to end her virginity. *A Time for Dying* sometimes seems lackadaisical; yet one remembers Jory's crazed Bean and Lapp's hopeful boy, drawing his guns and seeing them fly from his sweaty hands in the instant before he is shot down.

Like *Hour of the Gun*, this is a film about the hollowness of the "code of the West." Its Billy Pimple is as affectless as *Hour of the Gun*'s Earp. The cool killer seems less attractive at the end of the 1960s than he once was.

MUSICAL BIOGRAPHIES

THERE IS A SOUTHERN type that Florence King pinned to the wall as the "mean good ol' boy."[3] Hank Williams had the look—lean, angular, hag-ridden—and perhaps the behaviors. George Hamilton, on the other hand, was an urban smoothie, and when he played Williams in *Your Cheatin' Heart* (1964), he seemed a city slicker acting out, rather than a country boy ridden by demons that killed him at twenty-nine. Like the swing films of the 1950s, *Your Cheatin' Heart* marked an important change in the musical biography: a move away from the Broadway-vaudeville nexus toward country music and a completely different commercial apparatus (i.e., Nashville, radio, the Opry).

Hank Williams was born in 1923 and died in 1953. He was on radio at thirteen and with the Drifting Cowboys at fourteen. The film's only glance at these beginnings is a scene with a black man (Rex Ingram) who sings blues and plays a guitar while young Hank shines shoes. Almost immediately, Hank is Hamilton and looks thirty. It is only now that he encounters the group called the Drifting Cowboys. Such playing with fact is fairly typical; costumes and settings are seldom helpful with dating, may be deliberately vague; audiences for the Louisiana Hayride in the 1940s are shown as integrated; Williams's songs come out of chronological order. Neither the Depression nor World War II is mentioned. The framework of fact is decidedly fragile.

What does get attention is the Hank Williams legend—the boozing, the populism, the music. Exhibiting the behaviors of an alcoholic from early on, Hamilton's Williams nonetheless seems more like somebody who "likes a drink" than an addict who goes through personality changes and lives in self-hatred. This failure to look at his sickness is a severe flaw; so is the failure to look at the allusions of country music and see what they meant in the South and in Williams's life—the mansion on the hill with the crystal chandeliers, the cheatin' heart, the honky-tonk, the rambling man, the whiskey.

Your Cheatin' Heart is nevertheless a landmark. Like Hank Williams or not, you must see him as an important figure in the emergence of the South from the shadow of its own myths, many of them perpetuated, as we have seen, by Hollywood. He, and the film made about him, signal a move that is at once geographical, ethnic, and social, a real democratization of American taste from the South, via recordings and radio.

A THEATRICAL VEHICLE for the mature Ethel Merman, *Gypsy* took a harsh look at the stage mother, here the one who produced the ecdysiast Gypsy Rose Lee and the actress June Havoc. Translated to the screen, the work was a weaker vehicle for Rosalind Russell, who lacked Merman's admirable vulgarity and brass-band voice but who brought a screen image of female independence.

On the stage, *Gypsy* worked in part by using the theater to question aspects of itself as an institution. On film, the theater is a step removed, and, either because of Mervyn LeRoy's direction or because of our associations with musical biography, the theatrical footage looks like the old "fabulous era" stuff. Nowhere is this more true than in the credits, where shots of a proscenium, an orchestra, a curtain, and the titles in lights suggest the glamor, not the grit, of the stage.

Given this weakening of the stage original, the film *Gypsy* (1964) still packs a punch. Its tale of an obsessive mother (Russell) determined to become somebody by making one of her daughters a child star, and its big, Merman-tailored songs ("Everything's Coming Up Roses") are well above the run of musical bios. *Gypsy* has none of the sticky shtick of mentors with shlock accents, none of the fake energy of Hutton, none of the sentimentalized "love" that drives most such films. Instead, there is a demonic, mature woman and her exploited daughters, and an ancillary man (Karl Malden) who wants to marry Mama Rose but finally can't stomach her ambition.

The fact that both daughters grew up to be stars gives the film added edge, not because it justifies Rose's ambition but because it questions the cost of that success—a ruined childhood, at the least. The supposedly talented daughter, Baby June, abandons Mama when she turns thirteen; Mama then works to make a star of her ugly duckling, Louise. Vaudeville is declining; the Depression grinds on; things get worse until they end up in a burlesque house and Louise, improbably stepping in for an absent stripper, finds that she is pretty and that she can strip.

Natalie Wood is good as the young Louise, but as Louise-cum-Gypsy Rose Lee, she lacks authority. One cannot see why Lee was a national craze, a synonym for sexy smartness in the mid-thirties. On the other hand, Wood's lack of authority makes a point: in her first strip number, Wood's residual sweetness is unsettling; what we watch is a very young woman giving up her innocence to a crowd of male strangers. The final images of *The Girl in the Red Velvet Swing* come inescapably to mind.

The sequence casts a dubious light on what has gone before, not only on Mama Rose but also on the theater and its audience. We see the sleaze, the maleness, the vulgarity; we place against them the sweet child who is pleasing them by taking off her clothes. Yet Mama, at first appalled, is now enthralled. Now she wants Louise to be a stripper. "Let's walk away a star!" There is an unmistakable sense of a woman selling her daughter to a group of men. It is at this point that the Malden character walks out.

The rest of the movie is Louise's rise to stardom ("I am Gypsy Rose Lee, and I love her!" a line that recalls the doomed first wife in *Man of a Thousand Faces*) and Mama's descent to hanger-on ("Scrapbook photos . . . with me in the background. . . .") Although finally sentimental (a reprise of "Everything's Coming Up Roses"), the end is both harsh and insightful, climaxing in her demented "I got me! I could have been better than any of you!" It is a beautifully written sequence that takes us through several emotions: satisafaction, that Mama finally gets what she deserves; pity, as we see she has been punished too much; reconciliation and uplift as we see that she has courage and hope.

Gypsy will not do much for our understanding of the arena of traditional history. However, it is probably the most revealing of the musical biographies about nontraditional history, because it raises a crucial question about women, about the aspects of society represented by the theater, and about men of power. Put narrowly, that question is, What is a stage mother?

We are sure we know: she is Jo Van Fleet, the monster mother of *I'll Cry Tomorrow*; she is the comic older sister of *The Seven Little Foys*. Anybody who has ever been close to the theater or television or film or beauty pageants has seen a pushy mother and her often disgusting child. But why is the stage mother such a stock figure of horror and mockery? We might look at the matter differently and ask, Who is it who mocks the stage mother? Who uses or used the term until it became a cliché? The answer probably is, the men with whom until recently she had most contact—stage managers, casting directors, stage directors. It is in the context of men that the movies typically show her: Van Fleet pushing her daughter to thank the man who has just rejected her; Mama pushing Baby June past a succession of casting directors.

The Malden character unwittingly comes close to an answer when he says bitterly to Mama, "Once upon a time there was a prince named Ziegfeld, huh?" The name conjures the image: instant success, fame, acceptance. The title—prince—conjures the metaphor: the fairy tale, the kiss that wakes, the glass slipper, the royal wedding, happiness ever after. "Prince Ziegfeld" is the magical, male gatekeeper. He defines the stage mother. It is not what she does, but the way in which she does it, that makes her offensive to him. She does too openly, too loudly, precisely what the prince wants the princess to do— tamely and quietly.

Gypsy cuts very close to the bone of social history in recognizing this situation. It shows us a world of men, both gatekeepers and audience, who offer fame, lights, glamor, and wealth to women; whatever the women get in return, the film argues, the price is too high.

Funny Girl (1968), on the other hand, was the old gang of ideas at the old stand—Broadway, Ziegfeld, show biz, biff-bam-pow! Based on the Broadway musical that made Barbra Streisand famous, it starred her and Omar Sharif, was again a hit, and made room for a sequel in the 1970s. Mostly a sticky amalgam of show-biz clichés, *Funny Girl*, coming at the end of Hollywood's period of immigrant-to-assimilant musical biographies, summed up and contained all of them and was finally too much of a good thing—chocolate-covered nougat dipped in marshmallow cream.

Most of the film deals with Fanny Brice's life with Nicky Arnstein (Sharif), another of those men in such films who have no visible profession. Most of the camera focus is on Streisand, and most of the characterization is hers; Sharif is a gorgeous feed, a second banana who stiffens slightly toward the end.

The songs do what Broadway songs are supposed to do, although their sense of period is lamentable. But so it goes; this is a Broadway musical on film; framework of fact is meant to be merely referential, more closely connected with advertising than with history. The real Fanny Brice was not named Brice, but her mother is "Mrs. Brice" here. The real Fanny had a brother in show business, but this Fanny has none. The real Fanny was in vaudeville, toured all over, and had a husband before Arnstein; none of that is here.

Unlike most musical biographies, *Funny Girl* has a star of the same magnitude as its subject. Like most musical biographies, however, it does not dare to grapple with the questions of its own concerns: it has the usual code to tell us that Brice is Jewish but no language for her to be Jewish, either ethnically, socially, or religiously. It has the usual ambitions—"I just gotta get on the stage somehow!"— but no hint as to why the stage was the preferred conduit for her ambition or how it was connected to the East Side's mean streets. It has the usual urbane Ziegfeld (Walter Pidgeon), but no sense of what structures Ziegfeld was a part of or why an aging "class" actor was chosen to play him, or why Ziegfeld's brand of garish bad taste was thought good. As always, there's no business like show business, and nothing else going on in the world at the same time—no war, no Bonus March, no Equity Strike—only show biz and love, love, love.

OUTSIDERS

THE SPORTS FILM vanished, perhaps temporarily, but films about ordinary people actually increased. All but one of these were released by the end of 1963, however, suggesting that they had affinities with the 1950s. Of the five, three were strong films with novel protagonists. Another, *One Man's Way* was about the then-famous clergyman Norman Vincent Peale, author of *The Power of Positive Thinking*. As presented in the film, his was a white-bread kind of fascism: "God gives us authority over all other creatures!"; "weaklings" are bad; people who complain of "bad breaks" are bad; "success" is the sign of God's grace. Everybody is white and Anglo, except for a sequence in an Italian restaurant, where a few Italians are presented as volatile and comic. The film was released about the same year that the term WASP was coined.

The Outsider (1961), on the other hand, offered Tony Curtis in a somber biography of Ira Hayes, the Native American who was one of the five men photographed raising the flag on Mount Suribachi, Iwo Jima, later the basis for the Marine Corps War Memorial. The title itself is significant, for it identifies both a type of historical film and a kind of role.

Ira Hayes, a much-hyped public figure in 1944, died in 1955, a troubled and almost forgotten man tormented by alcoholism. He had been an outsider in the white world of the Marine Corps; when he returned after the war, he found himself an outsider among his own Pima people. It now seems regrettable that he was played by a non-Indian actor, but the casting is itself significant of the time.

The Outsider begins with the young Hayes's desire to enlist during World War II and with his elders' warnings against going into the white world. "Those who fight [the whites'] wars are a traitor to the tribe," an old man tells him, angry because of a continuing Pima-government fight over water rights. When Ira enlists, his mother says, "You gonna be in the same uniform. That don't mean they're gonna be your friend."

The mother's warning is not completely accurate. It is not overt prejudice that makes Hayes an outsider, but something subtler. His platoon sergeant calls him "chief"; his platoon-mates go off on their first weekend without him. Yet, a white marine (James Franciscus) works to help him through the difficulties of basic training (not least swimming—the abundant water dazzles the young Pima). When, finally, he goes into San Diego as a reluctant companion of the others, the well-meaning young men literally pour alcohol down him; he gets quickly drunk, fights, makes up. "You're the first white man that was ever my friend."

The rest of the film follows a difficult interplay between Hayes and the white world, represented first as celebrity, then as degradation. An unwilling hero for his almost accidental part in the Iwo Jima flag-raising, he is brought home to do a morale-boosting tour. He is guilty about being mobbed by civilians, depressed by the loss of his friend in battle, degraded by binges. He is "the most famous Indian since Geronimo."

After the war, the Pimas send him to Washington as a member of a delegation trying to get them more water. He heads for a familiar bar. "I feel like such a phony. I feel like I stole something and nobody has caught me yet," he tells the bartender. He gets drunk, winds up in jail; a newsman photographs him. "That's all we need," a member of the Pima council says, "another drunken Indian. . . . He's no hero. He's a damned disgrace." The elder's warning has come true: he is a traitor to his people.

Now an outsider in both worlds, he wanders, goes down and down, gets a job cleaning the men's room in an airport; moves on, is seen doing a drunken "Indian" dance in a cheap club; moves on again, winds up in New York's House of Correction. Rescued by an older Pima, he attends the dedication of the Marine Corps Memorial at Arlington. He remains alone into the night and vows to the memorial that he will stop drinking. "I promise—I promise you—I promise myself."

It is part of the strength of *The Outsider* that this promise, which could have been a pious, easy key to redemption, is one that cannot be kept. He dries out for a while. He goes back to the Pimas. He becomes an almost manic worker, helping other people, working for others for free. But he is trying to find respect and position in Pima culture, and he tries too hard; now, pinning too much hope on an election to the tribal council, he is crushed by his failure to win.

The final sequence of *The Outsider* is perhaps too long and too slow, but it is powerful. Hayes, drunk again and still drinking, goes to a hill on the Pima reservation and drinks himself insensible. Both self-pitying and pitiable, he is a man lost, and lost now for good; when the dawn comes, only his frozen hand is visible above the rocks. The hand becomes the hand that reaches for the flagpole on the Iwo Jima memorial.

As *The Outsider* makes clear, Ira Hayes's failure was not merely the result of the war or the aftermath of his celebrity status. The man had a terrible naiveté, a terrible youthfulness, a terrible vulnerability to alcohol. Like the water that cascades over him when he takes his first shower, the abundance of the white world dazzles him; only another liquid gives him the illusion of clarity and of belonging. One of the most painful sequences in this painful film comes when he tries to talk to his mother on the telephone when he is falling-down drunk. She has had to travel for an hour to get to a telephone; he is in a Washington bar. The two cultures, one so easy and abundant, the other so rigorous and sparse, are too distinct for him; he cannot communicate from one to the other, but sinks into foolishness, drunken maundering.

The result here is an agonizing, valuable motion picture that proves that in this period there was a place for the serious film. It should be on any list of films about World War II or the 1940s or the 1950s, and it should be paired with *Pride of the Marines* in any study of the returning veteran.

Birdman of Alcatraz (1962) was also a study of an outsider, this time from the extreme of society, a prison. Robert Stroud (Burt Lancaster) spent most of his life in solitary confinement, had "never used a telephone or driven an automobile. . . ."

It is through relationships with other people that Stroud is seen to open as a human being. The film's early action is thus the replacement of his mother (Thelma Ritter), on whom he seems to have a fixation, by others: a sympathetic prison guard (Neville Brand), another prisoner (Telly Savalas), a stern warden (Karl Malden), the woman he eventually marries (Betty Field). The matrix for these relationships is an evolving interest in birds, beginning with a wounded one found in the exercise yard. Brand lets him keep it in his cell. He makes a cage from scrap wood, an effort that takes months. Brand's patience and (at first) grudging generosity make this possible. Only when Stroud cares for the bird does he begin to reciprocate any of Brand's humanity.

Stroud became famous as an expert on birds and bird diseases, all based on knowledge acquired in prison. This self-education is given a visual correlative in the multiplication of the cages, the expansion of his cell into a combined laboratory and aviary. Under pressure from a domineering warden, Stroud shifts from birds to prison reform partway through the film.

Birdman of Alcatraz was a tour de force for Lancaster. It is another example of the period's concern with the atypical, as if, in a period of supposed conformism (*The Lonely Crowd, The Man in the Gray Flannel Suit*), extreme nonconformity was fascinating.

The Miracle Worker (1962) was about a very different kind of outsider—and the only woman in the group. Made from an enormously successful stage play, it had the same star (Anne Bancroft) and director (Arthur Penn). It seems like something from the 1940s, a piece of very dated realism. Bancroft owned the role by the time the film was made, perhaps too much so. Perhaps she, like Penn, needed to have the text redone more radically for film. She is very good, but she seems deliberate, as Penn's direction seems regressive after *The Left-Handed Gun*.

The story of *The Miracle Worker* is an important and moving one, but it is told in the manner of *Sunrise at Campobello* and *The Magnificent Yankee*: its act break still shows; its stage-bound settings still show; its dated realistic conventions—e.g., Bancroft's reading aloud to herself so we can hear—creak. Its false suspense shows: Annie Sullivan (Bancroft) must achieve a certain success with the deaf and blind Helen Keller (Patty Duke) by a certain date, or she will have to give up. Its coincidences show: there just happens to be a building near the Kellers' house where Sullivan can work alone with Helen but where, when the playwright needs it, a member of the family can drop by to chat through the window. And when, early in the work, Helen's mother tells Sullivan (and us) that Helen as a baby had learned one word, "wa-wa" for water, we know that that word will ring through the play's climax. "Wa-wa!" says Helen, to let us all know that Sullivan has taught her to understand.

The script is a paean to tough love and socialization. Sullivan is presented as a young martinet who demands control. The ending would have us believe that Sullivan learns in the final seconds that in fact love and not control was what she was after; however, what we see is control.

Other than Sullivan and Keller, nobody else much matters. Most of the other characters are setups for Sullivan—to show how spunky, how strong, how single-minded, she is. In one sequence, such a character is a black child; there is a disturbing racism to Sullivan's (and the camera's) utter indifference to the child once they are through with him. Still, *The Miracle Worker* gives two arresting examples of outsiders who happened to be women. It is a refreshing change from the other films that show women mostly as wimps, exotics, or victims, and a portent of things to come.

SOCIOPATHS

NOWHERE IS THE examination or celebration of noncomformists seen more
spectacularly in the 1960s than in an eruption of movies about killers and
gangsters. The 1950s had produced five such films; the 1960s produced
eleven, despite the fall in overall production. A number of these were urban-
bad-guy movies of a type already familiar from fiction films and perhaps influ-
enced by the subject's success on television. With the 1920s as their focus,
they included *Murder, Inc.* (1960); *The Rise and Fall of Legs Diamond* (1960);
Mad Dog Coll (1961); *King of the Roaring Twenties* (1961); *Young Dillinger*
(1965); and *The Saint Valentine's Day Massacre* (1967). Another can be added;
The George Raft Story (1961), nominally a film biography but in good part
another gangster film. All were tunnel history—the world of crime without
reference to the world beyond it; most resurrected the threatening Italian. As
with the Western and the musical, genre was rapidly chasing out history.

Murder, Inc. was notable mostly for Peter Falk's performance as Abe Reles.
The putative protagonists (Stuart Whitman and May Britt) are so wimpy that
the film is tilted toward the morally repulsive, as the gangster genre is anyway.
Whatever poetic justice the ending achieves seems perfunctory; the straight-
arrow DA who delivers the moralistic voice-over (Henry Morgan) would make
dishwater seem fascinating. The film's real message seems to be that the closer
to the moral center you get, the duller people are.

Mad Dog Coll now has some of the camp appeal of an Ed Wood film.
Abominably directed by Burt Balaban, it nonetheless had a flash of originality
in calling up the visual clichés of the horror movie to tell a killer's story. At the
end, Coll is disguised in wig and false mustache and looks like a child playing
an adult; when these are pulled off his bullet-ridden corpse, he looks rather
like Chaney's Phantom of the Opera. Momentarily, the effect is unsettling—
within the child is a monster. This was another film in which the abusive
father was the cause of the sociopathology.

The St. Valentine's Day Massacre was a fairly classy production produced
and directed by Roger Corman, with Jason Robards, Jr., George Segal, and
Ralph Meeker. It told more about Al Capone (Robards) and the runup to the
"massacre" than most of us want to know, but (like all the others) without
telling us what we would really like to know about context and history. The
film is tunnel history of an extreme kind, disguised here as fake documentary
("A factual rendition. . . . Every character and event depicted herein is based
upon the truth") with "exact" times and even temperatures. *The Saint Valentine's Day Massacre*, however, is finally an exploitation picture in which violence, rant, and betrayal exist to titillate us. Like all films that insist upon the
roaring of the 1920s, it presents crime without context. Why, we may ask, do
these films ignore unionization, the Red Scare, the vote for women, progres-
sive education, mass production, and everything else that comprises a real history of the 1920s? One answer would be the 1960s' interest in outsiders,

which the urban gangsters certainly were; another might be the relative safety of the apolitical subject matter; another might be the ease which they were tailored toward a young audience with young actors (Danton, Whitman, John Goodman as Coll) and easy subject matter (sex, violence).

Four other films of this group, however, are rather different. Released in the same year (1967), *Bonnie and Clyde* and *In Cold Blood* were more than exploitation and more than youth movies; one has had a lasting effect on cinematic style, the other a short-lived notoriety as the filmed version of what was briefly fashionable as the nonfiction novel. In addition, two other films at the end of the decade joined *In Cold Blood* in presenting multiple murderers: *The Boston Strangler* (1968) and *The Honeymoon Killers* (1969). The last was a badly directed cheapie, but in its mindless way it replicated the gangster films by showing the morally repulsive as, if not attractive, at least banal.

Bonnie and Clyde starred Warren Beatty, who also produced, and Faye Dunaway as the Southwestern criminals of the early 1930s, Bonnie Parker and Clyde Barrow. Now something of a classic, it can be cited both for its style and its innovative content. The style is really an elaboration of director Arthur Penn's work in *The Left-Handed Gun*: altered motion, quick cuts, stills, unexplained events. The content matched this jagged and then-unsettling style, presenting two existential wanderers who redefined "love," lived by preying on others, and were opposed by an ultimately massive and powerful social tool, the police. Bonnie and Clyde and their followers (Michael J. Pollard as a screw-loose teenager, Gene Hackman as Clyde's redneck brother) are the ultimate outsiders; unlike the gangsters of the films about the 1920s, they have no organization, no gangster society, not even a home city: their venue is not "Chicago," but the Midwest, and they are not Italians but what historian David Hackett Fischer would call "backcountry borderers," the heirs of those who pushed over the Appalachians in the eighteenth century.[4]

Bonnie is first seen, nude, watching from a window as Clyde tries to steal a car. She throws on a dress and runs down; although strangers, in moments they are a couple. He shows off his gun, robs a grocery store to convince her he's bad, steals a car. When she kisses him, he says, "I might as well tell you right off—I ain't much of a lover boy." Still, he wants her to stay with him because they can cut a swathe together: "Because you may be the best girl in Texas." Later, after a scene on a bed that ends with Bonnie disarranged but frustrated, he says, "At least I ain't a liar. I told you I wasn't no lover boy." Yet they love each other.

The pair are pursued by an aged lawman named Hamer (Denver Pyle). Humiliated in his first attempt to arrest them—they force Hamer to have his picture taken with them, take his gun—he finally waylays them and, with a large force of other officers, riddles them and their car with bullets.

The film is different from the gangster films in that it does not make the morally repulsive attractive; crime is not presented here as morally repulsive, but as neutral. Despite some populist pieties about robbing banks because they oppress poor farmers, Bonnie and Clyde—Bonnie especially—are amoralists.[5] When asked what he does, Clyde says, "I rob banks," as if crime is a profession or a way of life. Beatty and Dunaway are physically attractive and their characters do many attractive things: they have fun, they make fun for others, they show affection—quite unlike Peter Falk's Abe Reles, for example.

Contrarily, the police are unattractive, not least because of their numbers. Especially at the end, the demonstrated difference in firepower between the police and Bonnie and Clyde is huge; it makes the two seem victims. It also robs the law of the kind of rectitude that the DA has in something like *Murder, Inc.* As well, the law, as represented by Pyle's Hamer, is old-looking, a deliberate falsification; the real Hamer was barely middle-aged, did not have Pyle's lined, craggy face.[6] Bonnie's mother is also visually old, older than in fact a twenty-year-old's parent should probably be. When Bonnie visits her "Mama" and family, she and Clyde move among them almost like ghosts. Even while there is an apparent acceptance of their lawlessness, there is alienation, in part represented by their youth. When, later, they are wounded, and the strange kid played by Pollard hides them at his father's farm, our first look at the father tells us he will betray them: he is old.

Bonnie and Clyde is not a "youth" movie like the gangster cheapies of the early years of the decade, but it is a film that uses youth to convey meaning. The youth and physical beauty of the two protagonists, like the beauty of the protagonists of *Butch Cassidy and the Sundance Kid,* are earnests of their value. Beauty has always been an earnest of value in historical films, but it was unified with moral value and poetic justice; now, it is merely itself. The protagonists also have qualities conventionally seen as negative: alienation, amorality, homelessness. These, however, become positives as Penn loads the scales in favor of Bonnie and Clyde.

Bonnie and Clyde was not very good at showing the real Bonnie Parker and Clyde Barrow of the 1930s. The real Bonnie and Clyde were not so pretty, although they were as lethal. I doubt if the real Bonnie Parker wore false eyelashes all the time, even in bed. I doubt that the real Bonnie Parker changed her clothes twice a day, as the filmic one seems to. In fact, what *Bonnie and Clyde* really shows us is a Bonnie and Clyde of the movies, conceived in an environment where casting is destiny. If you are young and beautiful, you can be heroic and doomed; if you are young and kinky (Pollard) you can be a sidekick; if you are a jittery screamer (Estelle Parsons) you can be humiliated and debased. If you are old-looking, you can destroy the young and beautiful, because that's the way central casting conceives you.

Thus, *Bonnie and Clyde,* despite its stylistic innovations, is really a Hollywood film about attitudes and ideas of the 1950s and 1960s. As history, it is an artifact of the day it was made, not of the Depression.

In Cold Blood was the filming of Truman Capote's "nonfiction novel" about the murders of a well-to-do Midwestern farm family by two strangers.

Capote's work was an acknowledgment, much ballyhooed at the time, that "narrativity" was itself a fictional act that implicated objectivity, the insertion of the observer into the thing observed, and so on—a recognition of what is now seen as an aspect of postmodernism.

Film was not in the same narrative position as the novel, however. It had no word for a fictional documentary; "nonfiction film" meant something quite different from "nonfiction novel" in the 1960s. In order to have translated the nonfiction novel to film, the makers would have had to be far more aggressive about showing, perhaps even destroying, cinematic narrative (as in, for example, *The French Lieutenant's Woman*).

What the movie delivered was not the book's formal novelty but its story, its two central characters—but not Capote as involved observer, a huge difference—and a little of its noncausal structure. The film does try to approach the book structurally, but this may be as much a result of the book's having tried to be "cinematic" as the other way around. It is to its credit that its structure is a correlative of the "absurd" action and the morally dysfunctional main characters, Perry (Robert Blake) and Hickock (Scott Wilson). As history, *In Cold Blood* brought the audience images of meaningless threat—the beginning of the era of the serial killer, the stocking-masked rapist, the wandering child stealer.

In Perry and Hickock, audiences see young men who traveled hundreds of miles in a night to murder strangers for no better reason than that one of them had heard the victims had ten thousand dollars. Other than their youth, the two have no appeal; they are not the beauties of some of the gangster films or *Bonnie and Clyde*; they do not take part in a famous event like the St. Valentine's Day Massacre. They are not identifiable types: one is an aspirin junkie and repressed homosexual; the other is a romantic sociopath who believes himself protected by universal criminality: "Stealing and cheating—the national pastime." One is haunted by memories of a brutal father and an adulterous mother.

The most obvious structural innovation comes with the murders. The killers arrive at night at the victims' farm. Perry says, "Let's get out of here before it's too late," and there is a quick cut to daylight, a doorbell, and the discovery of the corpses. Only late in the film do see what happened between those words and the morning. By then, the two have been arrested; Hickok has spilled. Driving back to Kansas with the police, Perry relates the murders: "It was like reading a story, and I had to know how it was going to end." What he tells becomes film: Hickok, acting out a fantasy of control but really helpless; Perry, capable of empathy for his victims, contemptuous of Hickok's fantasizing. "Ridiculous. Stupid!" Yet it is Perry who does the killing—cutting the father's throat, then shooting him and his son, then the mother, then the daughter he has earlier reassured: "They never hurt me. They just happened to be there."

At their execution, the two seem without feelings. Perry begs to be allowed to go to the toilet. "I'm afraid I'll mess myself." Hickok mutters, "No hard feelings." Perry muses, on the scaffold, "I think maybe I'd like to apologize. But who to?" An exaggerated heartbeat sounds; the bodies plunge.

Other events of the 1960s go unmentioned, seemingly as far from the film as they were from the Clutter farm. Yet Perry and Hickok (or Capote's perception of them) express related strains: the mobility of violence; the apparent meaninglessness of events beyond the personal; a threatening idea of youth; an inability to distinguish among fact, fantasy, and fiction; a separation from history.

The Boston Strangler similarly looked at a series of brutal crimes and tried to make narrative sense of the man who committed them. The film dealt with a type of crime then relatively hidden, the serial murder of women. Innovative in ways different from *Bonnie and Clyde*, it used split-screen to show simultaneous events and disparate views of the same event, and withheld one of its stars—Tony Curtis as the strangler—until halfway through the film. Beautifully directed, it was the work of Richard Fleischer (*The Girl in the Red Velvet Swing*).

The Boston Strangler remains a difficult film to see. Despite its avoidance of the gore that splatter movies have accustomed us to, it is genuinely disturbing for the signs of violence it uses and for the breadth of its victimization. Victims are old, young, white, black—anyone, so long as they are female. Some are mutilated; one is "raped with a wine bottle." The film is the apogee of 1950s–60s victimization of women.

The witholding of Curtis extends the sense of unease; the audience knows he is a star, knows he is in the film, knows he must therefore be the murderer; yet we see only gloved hands, feet on a stair. And when, at last, we see the actor, it is in a perfectly conventional setting, with a female child on his lap, watching the John F. Kennedy funeral on television.

Part of the film is now foolish, however; changes in general knowledge and attitudes have rendered its parade of "deviates" more quaint than either amusing or horrifying. One cop's remark that "this kind of mutilation goes with a queer" seems stupid. Indeed, the parade of supposedly deviate suspects looks so ordinary in the 1990s that you wonder if, even in 1969, some of it did not get hoots from the audience.

The strangler is caught soon after he enters the film; almost immediately, the investigators—Henry Fonda, George Kennedy, and Mike Kellin—realize that when he says he is innocent, the man is telling the truth as he knows it: he literally has no memory of his crimes. It becomes Fonda's task to reveal the man to himself.

This cannot have been a rewarding role for Fonda; there is not enough there. Only toward the end, when he understands that he is destroying the Curtis character in order to get the truth, when he says, "I'm *enjoying* this," do we get any sense of complexity, and by then it is too late. This blandness does serve, however, to concentrate our focus on Curtis and on his gradual and horrified glimpse inside himself. The progression is masterfully done; indeed,

Curtis is so good, and the opening of his psyche so compelling, that it might well have taken up more of the film—that and an expansion of Fonda's character; those things could profitably have replaced the freak show.

At the film's end, Curtis begins at last to reenact one of the murders. He is horrified. His suffering is filmed in closeup against a plain white background, in the white room where he and Fonda have had most of their scenes. The camera pulls back. Curtis is all in white. He stands in a white corner, and slowly his image fades, fades, until nothing is left of him.

The Boston Strangler, like *In Cold Blood*, brought unpredictable violence into film. Nothing really explained either the victims or the criminals. Unlike *Bonnie and Clyde*, these killers had no purpose and no compensating beauty; the Strangler was not even youthful. Related more closely to the somber banality of *The Honeymoon Killers* (all three films were in black and white), they made such killing frightening rather than entertaining: that is, whereas the killings in *Bonnie and Clyde* are arguably beautiful as film, those in the other three are not. Random, violent death is not even pretty. *The Boston Strangler* has the further horror of the killer's ignorance of himself: is it a figure for film's ignorance of its idea of women?

MANY OF THESE historical films of the 1960s have a postmodern feel. Many, for one thing, are about fairly recent events; not only does none look back to the nation's founding, but a few deal with events within a few years of the film's making. A few, but certainly not a majority, embody recognizably contemporary ideas like alienation, randomness, nonlinear structure. Many more, on the other hand, assert older ideas like linearity and causality. A rough division can perhaps be made at about the middle of the decade between films that seem to look back to traditional ideas of structure and morality (e.g., *The Alamo, Funny Girl*, even the gangster films) and those that question or reject such ideas (*Bonnie and Clyde, A Time for Dying, The Boston Strangler*). These suggest a turning away from traditional history and from traditional heroes, not necessarily toward antiheroes but toward the formerly disempowered—the outsiders.

CHAPTER EIGHT

1970-1979: THE NINETEENTH CENTURY ENDS AT LAST ────────

Total production of historical films in the 1970s was about the same as that of the 1960s, with fewer films of the oldest types—traditional history and Westerns—and more about people and events beyond war and politics. More importantly, the idea of history changed: history was no longer a moral paradigm about poetic justice and the rightness of America; the idea of history that had been inherited from the nineteenth century was over. Only three films, other than revisionist Native American ones, even dealt with events before 1900, and two of those were negligible (*Hawmps!* and *The Lincoln Conspiracy*). The third was a witless attempt to capitalize on the nation's founding: astonishingly, the only film to celebrate the bicentennial was a musical, *1776* (1972), and a bad one, at that—insufferably cute, inaccurately costumed, clichéd. The delegates to the Second Continental Congress were a divided lot, but here they dance together like the Rockettes. Even in a nation depressed by Vietnam and Watergate, did people really want to see Franklin as a standup comic, Lee as a howling good ol' boy, Jefferson as a mooncalf?

Traditional history fared better when the past was not so distant. *The Wind and the Lion* (1975) is one of the rare films to make a character of Teddy Roosevelt (Brian Keith). It is also one of the rare historical films to have a short, well-argued, professional's article as a basis for point-for-point comparison, Barbara Tuchman's "Perdicaris Alive or Raisuli Dead."[1] It is also a wonderful motion picture. It is also wonderfully flawed, so much so that I am torn between saying it is brilliant and saying it is bad. Its creator (John Milius, who wrote and directed) made two grievously wrong decisions but then made an intelligent and beautiful film on their foundation. For once—thanks to the Tuchman article—we can see that the decisions that were wrong for art were also the ones that were wrong for history.

The film concerns a kidnaping in Morocco in the first years of the century of a purported American citizen named Perdicaris. The kidnapping became a *cause célèbre* and in TR's mouth a battle-cry—and the title of Tuchman's essay. Some symbolic saber-rattling followed, mostly for home consumption, and the kidnapper, a Moroccan leader named Raisuli (sometimes the Raisuli), "lord of the Rif and last of the Barbary pirates,"[2] who simply wanted a cut of the local action, returned Perdicaris unharmed. At some point before the release, according to Tuchman, the American government discovered that Perdicaris was in fact not an American citizen, but it was too late for Roosevelt to withdraw his bombast—not to mention "seven American warships [sent] to Tangier,"[3] and so it all came to a satisfying—and ironic—close with Raisuli paid off, the secret of Perdicaris's citizenship held close to the vest, and TR renominated for the presidency.

Milius did some remarkable things with this story. Perdicaris became a woman (Candice Bergen)—first bad decision—and gained two children. Raisuli became a charismatic embodiment of masculinity (Sean Connery). And the American navy became an invading force in a contest that finally pitted American marines against German soldiers—second bad decision.

These changes have made for some gorgeous cinematography. As well as sweeping views of Morocco and wonderfully directed processions and charges of horsemen, there are excitements like the opening sequence, when the camera alternates between a garden, where Mrs. Perdicaris (Bergen) pontificates about wine, and narrow streets through which a group of horsemen gallop. The horsemen crash through a wall, then into the house, slashing and breaking. Mrs. Perdicaris is captured; her small son (Simon Harrison) stares, wide-eyed, then is taken, too. When, after a certain amount of bloodshed (invented by Milius), the woman is taken out, there is Raisuli, sitting by a fountain, a figure from romantic legend, all robes and handsomeness. A horse is brought from her stable, an English saddle on its back; he tries to ride it and is thrown. When she laughs, he strikes her. "I am Raisuli! Do not laugh at me again." And away they go.

The wrenching of history has provided what seems a promising situation: a beautiful, spirited woman; a vainglorious man of another culture: *The Sheik* with protofeminism.

At this point, Teddy Roosevelt is brought in. He is to be a major character, but one presenting a problem: what does the president of the United States *do*? Milius's answer is that he kills a lot of time (shooting, boxing, talking). As a result, dead spots are filled with authentic witticisms inauthentically spoken by the wrong people (e.g., John Huston as Hay). Thus, the Roosevelt scenes lack action but have talk. Keith is splendid, but he is not given the material to show what TR did—only how he behaved. And talked: "The road traveled by great men is dark and lonely and lit at intervals only by other great men—and sometimes they're your enemies. . . ." Roosevelt talks; Raisuli acts.

Back in Morocco, the spirited woman and the romantic man bicker; she protects her children, hears Raisuli's boasts, sees a beheading and is sickened. Yet the beauty of Raisuli and his world tells—most quickly and most fully on the little boy. Raisuli, it is clear, is a little boy's dream.

Roosevelt shoots a grizzly, meditates on power; Raisuli saves Mrs. Perdicaris and her children from another kidnapper, who wants to make slaves of them. The sequence is wild, medieval, as Raisuli uses a sword to behead horsemen who rush at him. And then Milius brings in the marines. Impressive as the sequence is as a piece of film, it is utter nonsense. As Tuchman wrote, "[The American consul] knew that leathernecks would have as much chance against Berbers in the Rif as General Braddock's redcoats against the Indians in the Alleghenies, and besides, the first marine ashore would simply provoke Raisuli to kill his prisoners."

But Milius has committed himself, and he punches forward: the Germans (an utter invention; the Germans had no importance in Morocco) capture Raisuli and start to torture him; Mrs. Perdicaris, the marines, and Raisuli's forces attack; she frees Raisuli, and he gallops off into the sunset.

The point that Tuchman found in the history of the Perdicaris event was, the complex politics aside, the comic irony of Perdicaris's citizenship and Roosevelt's use of it—and victimization by it. The point that a Moroccan historian would make would no doubt be quite different. Milius makes yet another, but an utterly false one because detached from the framework of fact. Perdicaris cannot become a woman with two children without severely altering the meaning; more importantly, the matter of citizenship cannot be erased without completely losing the irony. Nor can the marines be sent in—against the Germans, yet—without shifting the entire matter from one of bluff and negotiation to one of *force majeure*. Milius wants the latter; he wants to show the projection of force; this is where his meaning lies—but it is false.

Yet, Milius's falsification enables two moments, one brilliant, one missed. The first occurs at the end of the violence surrounding Raisuli's escape from the Germans. We see the little boy from the back, crouching in the dust of a Rabat street. The battle swirls around him. A rider appears far down the street—Raisuli. He gallops toward the boy, and the boy watches and watches, transfixed, seeing the hero of his boyish dreams. It is an epiphany of a kind that Wilfred Thesiger wrote about from his own boyhood in Ethiopia, the sight of the last savage magnificence of Northern Africa's Middle Ages. The moment is breathtaking if you know the frame of reference, those men who fell in love with Africa and the Middle East and Asia because of childhood moments like these.

The missed moment is our last sight of Roosevelt. He is sitting, in a formal rotunda, at the feet of the now stuffed grizzly. Milius has a chance to show us TR—alone with his bear, with his idea of himself. Instead, he uses the moment to have TR read us a letter from Raisuli. It is too bad: this often visual director goes to words, as he inevitably does with Roosevelt in the film; at best, the sequence is redundant. Perhaps Milius intended a cautionary tale about direct action, about learning the heroic nature of direct action (Raisuli and the boy), and about the failure of presidents to come up to the heroism of marines and desert chieftains. If so, what is significant is that he had to invent history to make the point.

Yet *The Wind and the Lion* is almost a good film. It pales, however, next
to one that may be great—*Patton* (1970).

"What an asshole," Paul Fussell quotes himself as having said about General George Patton.[4] Most of us might well agree. He was bombastic, vain,
romantic, jingoistic, mystical, and perhaps self-deluded—all of which has
been caught in this long film, thanks largely to the performance by George C.
Scott as Patton. Credit also has to go to the director, Franklin J. Schaffner, and
to those responsible for the settings (Urie McCleary, Antonio Mateos, Pierre-
Louis Thevenet), which become a visual metaphor of Patton's grandiose sense
of self. Seldom have architecture and interior design been used so powerfully
to wrap a character in imagery—here, the imagery, sometimes ironic and
sometimes celebratory, of glory.

The key to the film is its beginning. Scott, in uniform, walks into the frame
from the bottom, climbing steps we cannot see. Behind him is an enormous
American flag, so large that when he stands in front of it his head reaches only
the third stripe. Scott wears riding boots, breeches, a helmet. His chest is covered with medals. The stars on the helmet catch the light ferociously, and when
he tips his head back to jut his chin forward—a typical Scott stance as Patton—
these reflections create the illusion of a spike; the helmet becomes a *pickelhaube.*
Scott looks uncannily like Mussolini. He begins to speak. The words have no
context except the uniform, the flag, and the chin—they sound mad. "All real
Americans *love* the sting of battle. . . ! Americans love a winner and will not tolerate a loser. . . ! Americans have never lost—and never will lose—a war. . . !
This indiviudality stuff is a bunch of crap."

The rant goes on and on. It is eerily like the Chief of Police's speech in
The Balcony, an absurdist monologue on power, very European. I must confess
that I thought it was written for this film, a brilliant bit of invention. Not so,
says Fussell; Patton really said all this. Nonetheless, the sequence is absurdist
theater. Everything has been pushed beyond the limits of reality—the size of
the flag, the medals, the helmet, the posture. The words become absurd, and
so does the man. The sequence in turn becomes the context for the film. To
see the rest of it otherwise—for example, as straightforward realism—is to
mistake a part for the whole.

We see Patton next as a military administrator in Rabat, smiling at a sul-
tan he clearly despises; pulled from that post by Omar Bradley (Karl Malden)
to shape up the Second Corps after the disaster of the Kasserine Pass, he
appears with a gunbelt loaded with two pearl-handled revolvers over his trench
coat. "This is a barracks, not a bordello!" he snarls, ripping down a girlie
photo; he tears into soldiers for sloppy uniforms. And, alone with an aide at a
Carthaginian battle sight, he recites poetry—his own—and says calmly that he
has been there before as a soldier in the Carthaginian battle.

Patton's ego has no limit. He loves sycophants; hot and cold running
colonels flutter about him, their adulation repaid with his affection. In one

sequence, Patton and his aide (Paul Stevens) lean toward each other like lovers. In another, they chat in French; the language sets them apart, gives them a romantic, perhaps an erotic tone. He is a man in love—with war. "God help me, but I do love [war] so. I love it more than my life."

The event that caught American headlines, of course, was Patton's alleged mistreatment of a wounded soldier in a hospital. Here, it becomes part of a larger love of the good soldier: visiting a badly wounded man, he pins the Purple Heart to the man's pillow, then whispers to him, again like a lover, weeps. When, however, he finds a wounded man who wants to go home, who is sick of fighting, he rails, orders him taken out. "I won't have sons-of-bitches who are afraid to fight stinking up this place of honor!" He slaps the man.

The incident costs him command of the Seventh Army. Eisenhower orders him to apologize, and he does so, from a stone landing on a complex outdoor stairway, in a Mussolini-like pose. The last word—used only once—is "apology."

Later, in a red-and-gold bedroom in a baroque palace, he learns that Bradley has been given command in Europe. Patton is disgraced, shunted aside; he is languishing in Sicily while the war shifts to the assault on France. "Glory," the soldier's ideal, is all around him as decor; glory is the ironic setting for his judgment on the mistake of having slapped the wounded man: "I wish I'd kissed the son-of-a-bitch."

Ordered to England, he becomes the decoy commander of a nonexistent force to distract the Germans. Now a general without an army, he stalks through a windowed gallery in an English great house, only his valet to hear him: "I will not let this happen! I am going to be allowed to fulfill my destiny! His will be done!" And it is. He gets command again, makes the famous tank drive across France, then stalls when his gasoline is diverted to supply Montgomery. "A moment like this won't come in a thousand years!" he rages, believing Germany is his to take. Then comes the Battle of the Bulge, and Patton's lightning swing north. His relief of Bastogne is a triumph.

The rest of the film is foreshadowing and decline. "The end of the war will kill him," a German intelligence officer predicts. "Magnificent anachronism." The cuts become shorter, sometimes ragged; the film takes on an "underdetermined" feel, as if it is not meant to be read easily or clearly. He meets the Soviets and hates them; he insults a Soviet general; he is censured by Eisenhower and removed from command. Montgomery, on the other hand—the sequence is intercut with Patton's leaving—is received by the King as the new head of the Imperial General Staff.

The brilliant sequence is pure film; the monumental scale recalls the absurdist opening. In a long shot, Patton emerges alone from a baroque facade and starts to cross its endlessly repeated architectural details, which, in their identity and their formalism recall soldiers at attention. The camera pulls back for a still longer shot, and we see the same facade, another close by, a solitary tree, and a fragment of arch. There is no sound. Patton is in there but almost invisible, dwarfed by the architecture of glory.

We see him then from the back. He is walking away from us toward distant, snow-covered mountains. His voice is heard. He describes the return of Roman conquerors, with slaves coming behind them; the voice whispers that "all glory is fleeting." His figure dwindles; the shot opens out, now including a windmill; the angle changes to make more of the windmill, then changes again so that the windmill dominates the picture as, distantly, Patton walks out of it—an evocation of Quixote.

Paul Fusell points out that there are factual lapses in *Patton*, omissions, in good part about his personal life. These may reduce the historical interest of the film, although the military history seems right and heaven knows the character is. Complex, visually stunning, magnificently performed by Scott, the film *as a film* is little affected by biographical omissions. It is an error to ask if one must like Patton, or even respect him; in that *Patton* is a work of art, liking and respect are irrelevant; this is one of the discrepancies as between film and history, perhaps. This is the function of the absurdist opening.

What an asshole! What a film!

If eccentric George Patton was worth a movie, why not Douglas Mac-Arthur? "When Japan attacked, he led us back to victory. . . . When Korea exploded, we turned to him again. . . . To this day there are those who think he was a dangerous demagogue and others who say he was one of the greatest men who ever lived." This opening title from *MacArthur* manages to be both dishonest and falsely objective, however: MacArthur did not really "lead us" to victory, and it is no use telling "us" that some people think he was a windbag and others think he was a hero unless the film is to show us why.

Perhaps it is unfair to place *MacArthur* next to *Patton*, but their subject matters and their dates invite the comparison. Much of their difference lies in the portrayals of the central figures. Scott is brilliant; Gregory Peck as MacArthur is fairly perfunctory. As well, *MacArthur*'s direction (by Joseph Sargent) shows none of the use of place or the resonating imagery of *Patton*, and its script is pedestrian.

Peck lacks the public MacArthur's hamminess. The original sounded like John Huston doing a sendup of Orson Welles; Peck sounds like Everyman. MacArthur larded his speeches with Victorian rhetoric: toxin, thundering, ominous, the captains (for commanders); Peck is a modern. His readings of the lines that MacArthur made famous ("Old soldiers never die . . ." and "The corps, the corps, the corps!") are flat.

What *MacArthur* shows, unintentionally, is the archaism of the man. Already retired from the army when World War II began, he was five years older than Patton, ten years older than Eisenhower, essentially a Victorian with Kiplingesque ideas of manhood. "I think of West Point as home—the football fields where I became a man," he says to FDR; serious music plays under this, without any ironic reference to his age or FDR's handicap. Later, he speaks of "the Holy Grail of righteous victory."

Sometimes, the film makes him seem as bizarre as Patton, but never as interesting: "It's my destiny to defeat Communism, and only God or those Washington politicans will keep me from doing it." "Who are those who seek to humiliate me and undermine my authority?" He seems a paranoid martinet when he nixes a medal for General Wainwright because Wainwright had surrendered the Phillipines; he seems a vainglorious fool when he promises an officer that if he does well, "I'll release your name for newspaper publication." On the other hand, the film is fairly honest in showing that the sycophants who surrounded him were not "a staff [but] a court," as one character puts it. This is a minor strain, however; mostly, the film is loaded MacArthur's way: MacArthur is the hero of a realistic film, but his enemies are caricatures: Dan O'Herlihy as Roosevelt and Ed Flanders as Truman are extended impersonations, not characters. Truman, in particular, is shown unfairly, always surrounded by cronies, too often with a glass in his hand.

MacArthur's legacy is modern Japan. Oddly, the film shows relatively little of his work there as the American shogun. As history, it would have been a much better film if it had.

NATIVE AMERICANS

Films about Native Americans had by the 1970s swung completely to revisionism, some of them too far—a tendency also to be seen in the Westerns. Used as a surrogate for other minorities in the 1950s, Native Americans in the 1970s may have become surrogates for Southeast Asians, as well. None of the three films used the pre-1940 rhetoric of ethnic hatred; all three showed Indians who were noble, sometimes wise, victims rather than victimizers. Where there were massacres, they were perpetrated by whites: My Lai may have been a referent.

Little Big Man (1970) shows Custer as a madman and the Native Americans as victims, and it is a one-sided argument, in that way not very good history; essentially a satire, it is perhaps entitled to its distortions. And in Dustin Hoffman as Jack Crabb, it has a splendid young actor in a role that takes him from youth to extreme old age and shows him as white Indian, soldier, bum, gunslinger, and lover.

If the film has serious flaws, they are most visible in the idea of women, and, by extension, the idea of sex. There is not a solid female character in the film; those that exist do so within an adolescent male definition. A repeated joke about Crabb's sister's fear of rape is more than not funny; it is offensive. A clergyman's wife, played by Faye Dunaway, is a cliché that telegraphs its every titter (She Has to Have It). His white wife, Olga (Kelly Jean Peters) is a giggling nincompoop who is captured by Indians and then shows up later as another male cliché, the termagant. In an extended sequence, the Hoffman character is caused to service his wife's three sisters in one night. "The Great

Spirit was with me, and I survived." Little Horse, a man who chooses to live as a woman, is played as a female impersonator, homosexuality implied. These clichés seem odd as the work of Arthur Penn, director of *Miracle Worker* and *Bonnie and Clyde.*

The film's comic strength comes from the speed with which it rushes Jack Crabb from life to life and from famous event to famous event; he is present for the murder of Wild Bill Hickok, the massacre at the Washita River, and the Little Big Horn. The events, however, are all out of order; any historical notion of cause is lost, except for the white madness that is the cause of most of the film.

This idea, and the spine of the film, is embodied by Grandfather, Old Lodge Skins (Chief Dan George). He excepts only "the Human Beings"—the Cheyenne—from his bemused contemplation of human craziness. All whites are crazy; blacks are "black white men," not as ugly as whites but "just as crazy." But the madness of the whites and their like is unstoppable: "Whatever else you can say about them, it must be admitted, you cannot get rid of them." Grandfather is a splendid character, warm and amusing; Chief Dan George plays him with delight. His humor relieves the pretentiousness we might be tempted to find there in his philosophizing, his mysticism, his occasional delving into magic.

Grandfather is compared with two others, Little Big Man and Custer (Richard Mulligan). Custer is white craziness itself; he rants about the "poison of the goo-nads" rising to the throat; at the Little Big Horn, he is a raving looney, entirely detached from the reality of defeat. Little Big Man is less crazy, but his many lives suggest kinds of white craziness. As a black-clad gunslinger, he is death-crazy (but less comic than a similar figure in the 1965 *Cat Ballou*); as a bum, he is a falling-down, mud-wallowing alcoholic. As the very old man who narrates the film, he is a hairless, beady-eyed skeleton, very different from the picture of age we see in Grandfather. Even more pointed is the visual comparison of their environments: Grandfather, in the skin lodge or in the hills, lying in grass as raindrops begin to fall; Jack Crabb in a nursing home, lying in a white bed in a landscape of death.

Buffalo Bill and the Indians (1976) was a disastrous film made, ostensibly, from Arthur Kopit's *Indians*—arguably the most important American play since *Death of a Salesman.* The film has nothing to recommend it, not even the facts that it starred Paul Newman and was directed by Robert Altman. It was so formless it managed to be even worse than *The White Buffalo* (1977), which had at least an interesting Hickok in Charles Bronson and some gorgeous cinematography, ruined by a pretentious screenplay and a mechanical buffalo that suggested a killer rabbit.

THE WESTERNS OF the 1970s suggest that the same revisionism that informed the Native American films had affected them, but that the conventions of the

Western were more resistant to revision. Despite new stylistic elements, despite revisionist pressure, they seem like more cynical versions of other shoot-'em-ups—and, thanks to the end of the Production Code, more graphically violent ones. One, *Butch and Sundance: The Early Days* (1979), was not even that; a film that tried to be cute rather than funny, it apparently existed only to exploit the title of the earlier *Butch Cassidy and the Sundance Kid.*

Doc (1971) was an attempt to film the O.K. Corral story with a cast of characters who were all down-and-outers, no-goods, or exploiters. Presumably, this made for an attempt to show the West as it really was. If, however, when the myths are stripped away, all we have left are scruffy losers, not much of a movie results. If you want to make a film about a new take on the real West, but you insist on including Earp, Holliday, Kate Elder, et al., it might be wiser to center the film on the life of a grocer or a grain dealer and turn the violence into marginalia—as it *really* was. Failing that, you are involved in a contradiction: saying that not very bright, amoral, feckless people are worth all the attention of a film whose core event (the gunfight) has traditionally been used to examine questions of ethos and intelligence, or at least skill.

Stacy Keach is an unwashed, opium-smoking Holliday, Harris Yulin an unusual Earp (skinny, endowed with two huge six-guns that seem to be wearing him). Everybody is miserable. Love doesn't conquer all. Politics are crooked. Life in the Old West was hell. In revising the myth of the O.K. Corral, what the film offers as a substitute is a view of human existence: man is vile, so is woman, and you need a bath.

Paul Newman did far better in *The Life and Times of Judge Roy Bean* (1972) than he had in *Buffalo Bill and the Indians.* Bean, the bloody-minded eccentric who called himself the only law west of the Pecos, was a film favorite (*The Westerner, A Time for Dying*). Directed by John Huston, the character this time around is presented as a violent loner who moves from near-death to myth-heroism. Along the way, he encounters—or is encountered by, as he mostly sits still—cameos by Tab Hunter, Huston, and Stacy Keach.

Newman/Bean arrives at one of those godawful, end-of-nowhere saloon-cum-whorehouses that movies believe lay at the end of every gulch and canyon; there, he is set upon by the whores, tied by the neck to a horse, and driven off into the desert to die. He doesn't; instead, with a gun supplied by a Mexican child, he goes back, shoots everybody in the place, christens the spot Vinegaroon, and names the dive the Jersey Lily, after Lily Langtry.

Bean makes himself a judge and appoints five failed outlaws as his deputies. When Tab Hunter appears, Bean hangs him for killing a Chinese ("I'm very advanced in my views, and outspoken . . ." and will hang a man for killing "chinks, greasers, or niggers.") When a group of prostitutes shows up, he sentences them to one year of protective custody each, to be spent with one of his marshals. Huston arrives as Grizzly Adams (come south to die) and leaves a bear. Keach bounces in as Bad Bob, an albino killer all in black, with silver-mounted gunbelt and gauntlets (another afterimage of *Cat Ballou*); Bean shoots him in the back with a telescope-mounted rifle.

But real enmity arrives with prissy Gass (Roddy McDowell), a lawyer who claims the land on which Vinegaroon stands. Bean puts him into a cage with the bear, but Gass survives and gets himself elected mayor; the whores turn respectable, the town gets civilized, and Bean rides off into the nowhere.

The town finds oil and turns into a 1920s boom-town hell, all rusty metal and overcrowding. When things are worst, Roy Bean rides back into town, now grizzled, perhaps a ghost, and burns the place down. It is Vinegaroon's apocalypse: Bean chases Gass through the fire and is last seen, still on horseback, on the second floor of an inferno that had been the whorehouse.

Much of this is intermittently entertaining. The attempt at myth is strained, but it makes some sense; Huston is trying to replace one myth with another. It incorporates his usual views of men, women, and alcohol. It gives Newman opportunities to perform. What it fails to do, however, is create either a unified film with a discernible action or a revised view of the West that makes sense. Like *Doc*, *Judge Roy Bean* is really about a revisionist idea of movies, not of history. Like *Doc*, it selects a familiar cast of characters and familiar behaviors (above all, violent ones) and treats them differently from earlier movies. It seems to be saying, This is revisionist history, when what it is really saying is, This is revisionist filmmaking. And this stylistic change is mostly an intensification of realism—dirt, violence, language—actually a reversion to naturalism and its "morbidity."

Pat Garrett and Billy the Kid (1973) was violence as usual, with the odd bit of sex, both group and individual, thrown in. It tells us that in the Old West all men were alcoholic and all children were so inured to bloodshed that they used the hangman's noose for a swing and played in the dust next to a shotgunned corpse. The power of religion and the power of community, both so important in forging the real frontier, are of no importance in this filmic one. There is the usual foolishness with weapons and a good deal of degradation of women, as well as not a little pretentiousness: after shooting Billy (Kris Kristofferson), Garrett (James Coburn) shoots his own reflection in a mirror. The film ends with a nasal Bob Dylan song blaming "businessmen from town" for Billy's death. I'd blame the director, Sam Peckinpah.

The Great Northfield, Minnesota, Raid (1972) got an engaging performance from Cliff Robertson as Cole Younger in an account of the Minnesota foray by the James–Younger gang. The James brothers are first seen side-by-side in an outhouse, a clue to all that is to follow: man is vile.

The film lurches from the comic to the somber and back again. Jesse James (Robert Duvall) is a near maniac who goes into a religious frenzy when he outlines a plan to the gang. "A place called North—a place called North—a place called North—North*field*!" Opposed to him is an equally manic Pinkerton of the detective agency: "This is war to the knife—to the hilt!" There is no moral center—no justice, no ethos; the West is a mere muddle of pathology, folly, cupidity, and caprice. If this is meant as revision- ism, it fails; what it says is that the alternative to the West of movie myth is a West of black comedy, one peopled by psychopathic killers, venal bankers, sadistic posses, and buffoons. As with *Judge Roy Bean*, this just won't do: one can't replace melodrama with black comedy and call the result revisionism. To be sure, it reverses the older view of the Jameses, utterly demystifying them; to be sure, it is part of a revisionism seen in other Westerns and Native American films. It is not merely that the old certainties are gone, but that they are savaged, as if the very impulse to make historical films has changed from reverence to attack.

THE FIRST LABOR film in decades was *The Molly Maguires*, based on a notori- ous nineteenth-century incident leading to a trial, famous as a story "repeated incessantly in penny dreadfuls and dime novels," according to J. Anthony Lukas.[5] Directed by Martin Ritt, it has its best moments early in showing the rigors of life in the coal mines. A blazing yellow sky gives way to the mine; silence and flute music give way to mechanical rumble, the tap of picks on the coal face, running water. The tunnel is claustrophobic. Men cough. Their lunch pails clink, metal on metal. Nobody speaks. A workman (Sean Con- nery) and some others plant a charge of powder and run the fuse, then light it. They get into a tiny car and are pulled slowly to the surface, nothing to be seen but six headlamps glinting in the dark. They walk away from the tip, going separate ways, the sounds diminishing as the camera follows Connery, who walks in silence until the underground blast comes.

An apparent police spy (Richard Harris) comes to the wretched coal town, and the rest of the film is devoted to bonding with the violent group called the Molly Maguires and then exposing them. In the end, Harris reveals himself as a detective. Having caused the hanging of Keogh (Connery) and the others, he calmly walks away, his desire to rise having overpowered the desire to bond, although he has shared their misery; in his first week of posing as a miner, he earned twenty-four cents after paying the company for drills, food, even the explosive powder to loosen the coal. "I'm tired of always look- ing up; I want to look down," he says early in the film.

This story is played at the expense of context. Brilliantly as the physical background is photographed (by James Wong Howe), it does not become part of the drama. The deeply felt pictures of working children and laboring ponies, of boys and old men picking out slag, are powerful communicators; however, they are like pictures without captions, not directly related to what the Maguires are doing and Harris is exposing.

The problem extends to Connery's character; arresting as Connery is, his Keogh is an enigma, his motives unspecified, his objectives opaque. If the film is to have meaning, it is through Keogh that it must express it. Ritt no doubt wanted to avoid the traps that sentimental leftists had fallen into in the 1930s, above all their hollow rhetoric, but in the name of doing so he unwisely channeled Keogh's passion into bitter near-silence. One wants outbursts about labor and the bosses and black lung and Victorian legalized slavery, but they do not come.

In part, Ritt's dilemma is that of the historical film itself—the conflict of the particular nature of dramatic character and the generalized nature of historical argument. In part, however, the problem is peculiar to this film and perhaps to another of Ritt's decisions; in focusing on the relationship between Harris and Connery (will they bond?), historical analysis, critique, and argument go by the board. It is too bad, for there is much in *The Molly Maguires* to admire. Frank Finlay is fascinating as a policeman, done up in a thick cloth coat that makes him move like a man in a straitjacket. Scene after scene is compelling. But it is all wonderful pieces that never come together, lacking the cement of context and the armature of impassioned speech.

GANGSTER AND CRIMINAL films continued in the 1970s as a relatively large group, and they continued to be mostly uninteresting. As before, they divided into two types, one featuring recent immigrants, especially Italians, in urban settings; the other featured "backcountry borderers" in the Middle West.

Bloody Momma (1970) was an exploitation film that offered Shelley Winters as a redneck grotesque who hits the road with "momma's boys" to provide producer–director Roger Corman with opportunities for T and A, incest, sadism, and bloodshed. The framework of fact is wrong. The final bloodbath involves an army of policemen, now a cliché of the gangster film.

Dillinger (1973), directed by John Milius, set the famous bankrobber (Warren Oates) against a determined and violent FBI man, Melvin Purvis (Ben Johnson). Their rivalry is far more than one of law-breaking against law enforcement; because both men are publicity-seekers, it is a rivalry of superstars. (The newly married Purvis sends Dillinger a bottle of champagne in a nightclub; Dillinger calls Purvis on the telephone to brag of an escape from jail.) For much of the film, Purvis is shown pursuing and killing other criminals (e.g., Machine Gun Kelly) with ruthless, apparently affectless violence.

Oates is a likable and believable Dillinger. He sees himself as a kind of businessman; he has contempt (as the real Dillinger purportedly had) for such violent interlopers as Bonnie and Clyde and the Barkers. This Dillinger lacks the existential quality of Beatty's Clyde Barrow; rather, Oates's ordinariness is a foil for Ben Johnson's power. As in *Bonnie and Clyde*, the lawman is again significantly older; again, he enlists large numbers of backup gunmen, although he prefers to go into the final shootouts alone, armed with two Colt (1911) .45s. He kills Dillinger that way, although with a momentary hesitation that suggests awareness of their long-distance relationship, even their similarity.

The character touches lightly on 1970s figures and ideas—J. Edgar Hoover, the abuse of power, the use of fame and media by lawmen.

Dillinger includes the high points of the Dillinger story—the Lady in Red, the gun carved out of soap, the banks. It also includes, however, period elements that look right but may be Milius's invention—the enlistment of American Legionaires to defend against the gangsters, for example. Certainly, the level of violence is ahistorical. The film brings Dillinger together with Baby Face Nelson and Pretty Boy Floyd (mostly invention), and the final shootout has them dying on the same day and in the same place— quite untrue. Again, as in *Bloody Momma*, the number of cops is enormous, and the cold-bloodedness with which they kill (e.g., the execution of the already wounded Floyd) makes the lawmen seem more amorally violent than the gangsters.

Dillinger gets a good feel of the period in newsreel clips, costumes, and weapons. It is questionable, however, that it is any more successful in giving the context of 1930s crime than others of its type, except in one area: the use of mass communications.

The three immigrant-gangster films are unremarkable, except perhaps for Peter Boyle's fine performance as the title character in *Crazy Joe* (1973) and that of Rip Torn as his brother. Too, the film has a suggestion of context. *Crazy Joe* at least brings the gangster film into the contemporary world with its quotes from Sartre and Camus, its scene (based in fact) of a gangster's brief fling with the liberal wing of the New York glitterati, and its awareness of minority rights, the collapse of established social and cultural barriers.

The criminal films of the 1970s lack the psychopaths of the 1960s. With the exception of *Bloody Momma*, there is very little that is reminiscent of the randomness and the horror of *In Cold Blood* and *The Boston Strangler*. The end of the Production Code may have allowed those demons to be exorcised, or perhaps they expressed themselves more generally in the "morbidity" of the naturalistic Westerns and the black comedy of other films.

WITH ONE EXCEPTION, the musical biographies and show-business films were acts of recovery—steps toward historical revision, like *W. C. Fields and Me* (1976). It tried to be a warts-and-all biography, but its chronology was a mish-mash and it was unable to show how Fields was great, despite Rod Steiger's excellent performance. As so often, there was no context—for which filmmakers might have had to look at themselves. Fields's alcoholism was in the foreground but too often treated lightly.

The exception to the revisionist tide was the last of the traditional musicals, *Funny Lady* (1974). Again starring Barbra Streisand as Fanny Brice, *Funny Lady* was a better musical than *Funny Girl*, if only because it used authentic Brice songs and thus had better music. It was better, too, perhaps, because it had no stage original; it was free to be film. And show business here is business, at last: James Caan as Billy Rose actually has a scene where he talks about negotiating rights, percentages, rollbacks. And the fabulous era is put to rest, as Ziegfeld fades and Rose takes over Ziegfeld's money man. The film ends in the 1940s, with Brice in her fifties, smiling into a mirror, thinking big show-biz thoughts after years in California as Baby Snooks.

It is a fitting end for the show-biz musical. Ziegfeld is dead; the fabulous era is over; radio has come, and television looms. More to the point for the filmed musical biography, America was at last ready to make major films about black musicians.

Leadbelly (1975) was a densely textured film, directed by Gordon Parks, that presented both men and women in a story without the easily scored points of a romance plot. It was not about "show biz" but about a way of life in which music was a nutrient part. Regrettably, it was also in part fictional, and its chronology was sometimes shaky.

The central figure, Hootie Ledbetter (Roger E. Moseley), is a violent man and a womanizer who spends a good part of his life in prison. He is also an extraordinary blues musician. Leadbelly is first seen at work on a rockpile, muscles huge, temples graying. "This nigger's a real bad one," says a white onlooker. Taken to a visiting room and given a guitar to play for a musicologist, Leadbelly begins to reminisce.

What he first remembers is an idyll: rural, black Louisiana at the turn of the century, the fabulous era from a decidedly different viewpoint, "no white folks ten to fifteen miles." Young Ledbetter rides his father's fine horse, carries his guitar with him. When, however, he shoots at another man during a fight, the white sheriff comes to his father's house to arrest him, and he takes off for Shreveport to become the man of a "parlor house" on Fannon Street—a marvelously conceived place of varied humanity, dirt, and color—and the lover of Miss Eula (Madge Sinclair).

"You're born to trouble," Eula nags him, "and you're hurryin' to meet it like it was the train to New Orleans." Leadbelly is young and self-centered and foolish; he boasts he is "the king of Fannon Street!" In a saloon, he puts up ten dollars as a challenge to anybody to outpick him on the guitar. The challenge, taken up by an apparently drunken old man with a twelve-string instrument, is interrupted by a police raid; out they go, Leadbelly without his guitar, to wind up on a freight train bound away from Shreveport. When Leadbelly jumps the train in the cotton country of East Texas, he takes the twelve-string guitar with him.

He picks cotton and takes up with a new woman; tired of it, he heads off again on the train and, in a Jim Crow car, meets the blues singer Blind Lemon Jefferson. They play together and travel, making money by making music until, playing for a white party (against a Confederate flag for background), Leadbelly stands up to a redneck and is beaten and jailed. Blind Lemon heads off to Memphis to make records.

Most of the world of the film to this point has been black. As Leadbelly comes into sharper conflict with white law, however, whites invade the imagery. He is sentenced to a chain gang for killing another black man; now the pictures are of whites on horses whipping chained black men, the enmity naked but unexplained. He fights with a guard, is whipped with a cat-o'-nine-tails; he escapes and is pursued by dogs, treed, shot from the tree by a guard; the song "Old Rattler" plays sardonically under the sequence. As punishment, he is locked in a box in the prison yard. His father, now old, tries to buy his son's freedom; when he cannot, he leaves the money so Leadbelly can buy himself a guitar.

Summoned to sing for the governor, he is whimsically promised his freedom when the governor leaves office. "Ain't nothin' can sing like a darkie when he puts his mind to it," the governor says. He tosses Leadbelly the rest of his cigar. It is a cruel scene: the governor sits in the precise middle of a symmetrical construction, behind him a white house framed by two expensive cars, in front of it tables loaded with food; blonde young women lounge near him, while, beyond a fence, black prisoners work. Astonishingly, when the governor leaves office, one of his last acts is to pardon Leadbelly.

This quixotic gift of freedom (like the imprisonments, freedom seems unpredictable, less a gift than an accident) leads him back to Fannon Street. The life has gone from it; it is a dry, windy, brown place. He finds Miss Eula on a curbstone (a terrible straining of the limits of coincidence). "Nothin' more pitiful than a broke old whore," she says. His life is moving in reverse now; he goes back to his childhood home, finds his father's house lived in by crackers. One orders him away with a single-barreled shotgun, then sends three other whites after him who try to beat him. Leadbelly stabs one, and it is back to prison, this time to Angola.

The flashback ends; the beginning of the film is its ending. A title tells us that he later sang "a'' across America . . . to Carnegie Hall." The film's triumph, however—and this is a triumphant film, despite its sadness—comes not from the show-biz films' association of Carnegie Hall with success, but from Leadbelly's mature pride as he breaks rock. "You ain't broke my body—and you ain't broke my mind—and you ain't broke *me*!"

If *Leadbelly* is not splendid history, it is at least acceptable history. If it is skewed, it is no more so than any of the all-white musical biographies that preceded it, with their trivial love plots, their winks at ethnicity and race, their unthinking acceptance of gatekeeping, success, and show. If it is lacking in their bounce and brightness, it has a seriousness they never attempted, and a far greater depth. It is a splendid film in its own right, its music rich and moving, its central figure fully fleshed and deeply sympathetic, and one that, because it deals with a man so far outside power, brings its context with it.

Lady Sings the Blues (1972) was a less serious, more commercial vehicle for Diana Ross as Billie Holliday. Like *Leadbelly*, it has harrowing scenes of black life—a white cop taking the twelve-year-old in tow because "she shouldn't be hanging around by herself in this [white] neighborhood"; a Klan lynching. However, it quickly settles down to being about her drug addiction, and both the biography of Billie Holliday and the history of black music are submerged.

Bound for Glory (1976) took seriously another kind of music until then ignored by Hollywood. Based loosely on Woody Guthrie's book of the same name, the film is about the brief period in Guthrie's life between his leaving of Texas in 1936 and his later leaving of California for the East. Whereas *Leadbelly* shows the black world of the first quarter of the century, *Bound for Glory* shows a part of the white world of the Depression. The crossing point of the two lives came after the events of the films, but the two men had a common appeal for the political left and were, perhaps, alike used for political ends. Those matters, however, are not in either film.

Bound for Glory is an easy film to watch. It has superb photography and a wealth of Guthrie music. David Carradine as Guthrie is utterly believable and likable. The film has, however, a just faintly irritating air of smugness. The poor are generally so good, and the mostly unseen rich are so oppressive, and "greed," as the film calls capitalism, is so simplistically hated, that all that righteousness inescapably comes to seem just a little like self-righteousness. "Seems to me something ought to be done about this," Guthrie says about an Okie camp in California. Extolling the common people, he says, "You meet some man's got some money, and the human thing's just gone—cause he's afraid he's gonna lose something." Of Texas and the Dust Bowl, "It does seem that it was easier to put up with nature and dust storms and all, than it was with greed." Explaining why he walked out on a chance at big-time performing,"I just had to touch the people a little bit . . . I always feel as if I oughta be somewheres else [than a fancy club]." "The worst thing that can happen is to cut yourself loose from the folks."

What saves this from sappiness is the honest picture of Guthrie, and Carradine's playing of it. He is what contemporary country and western would call "a rounder and a rambler," something of a womanizer and an idealist who often thinks more about his music and its subjects than he does about his wife (Melinda Dillon). "Gone to California—Will send for you all," is all the note he leaves her when he goes. In California, he charms his way into the bed of a well-to-do and well-meaning woman (Gail Strickland); even there, however, he cannot keep from being honest. "Don't you ever get embarrassed . . . about having so much?" he asks her. She says she is sorry that so many people have nothing. "Sorry don't get the hay in," he says, and a little later, he is gone from her, too.

The film seems a little disingenuous about Guthrie's relationship with "Ozark Bill," an organizer, and the union he represents; although Bill is introduced as a man who "comes to sing for us" in the Okie camp, it is clear that he has a very real agenda. However, it is not quite clear enough, nor is Guthrie's connection with him. Bill gets Guthrie a job at a radio station, which turns into a weekly show; however, he blows this away when he insists upon singing protest songs. "I don't need you! I can sing while I'm walkin," says Guthrie. He does not mention—or think of, apparently—his wife and kids, whom he has by then brought out to California. His wife needs only one more idealistic gesture to send her back to Texas, and, on the loose again, he heads east.

This is a fairly slow film, one that indulges the luxury of careful development of both character and environment. For once, too, it is a film rich in context. It is denser than most films as a way of achieving this context, with great attention to material culture and landscape and a wide array of characters.

The handsome cinematography, the slow pace, and the texture almost "normalize" Guthrie's attitudes, as if they are historical truth. Guthrie's was an absolutely sincere but blindered vision, and *Bound for Glory* espouses it. The film would have us believe, for example, that the Okies were expressing a desire for equity that would abide—a fair shake, a sufficiency, and no more. Time, however, has shown that in a consumer economy, the Okies and everybody else wanted to consume; they wanted two cars, a boat, and a line of credit. They did not really want to challenge capitalism; they wanted to join it. Given this truth, it is no good calling capitalism "greed."

This notion of capitalism is the film's principal failure of context. It is simplistic, rhetorical, narrow; it begs the question of how to have democracy—surely part of Guthrie's ideal—with any other economic system. Failure to deal with that question results in mush, the very sort of thing that led the political left into sentimentality rather than rigor, an intellectual soft-headedness based on a willingness to accept answers defined by compassion alone (for which, ironically, we can look to the 1969 *Alice's Restaurant*, starring Guthrie's son Arlo).

Yet, Guthrie himself was admirable in his idealism, and his music—plain, American—caught that idealism and made it irresistible. Guthrie was above all an American musican, like Leadbelly. He was the real thing, and at its best *Bound for Glory* shows him—and his music—that way.

The Buddy Holly Story (1978) brought American music up to the 1950s and the emergence of white rock 'n' roll. Gary Busey was praised for his performance as Holly, the young musician who was killed even as he was becoming a star, although parts of that performance now look rather like a put-on—Opie Forms a Band. Perhaps the look was deliberate, an attempt to emphasize the very American and very young nature of this revolution.

What *The Buddy Holly Story* fails to capture is the mid-1950s, except in Holly's music itself. It is neither a very sophisticated nor a very well-made movie; it has no sense of how Holly was himself a creature of the 1950s, except insofar as he listened to black music on a New Orleans radio station and had parent trouble. The film has a historical point to make, but it is undercut by its insistence on being tunnel history, in the hope of appealing to a certain audience. The subject itself is so dangerously near camp (hence Busey's performance) that it could entirely escape it only by being ironic; it is not. As an attempt at history, it is probably useful for its celebration of the arrival of "youth culture," but as a history of that culture and its context, it is far too thin.

Lenny (1974), on the other hand, is a flawed film that itself stands as an artifact from a moment when the world turned upside down. Once notorious, now a name less recognized, Lenny Bruce was the embodiment of the social revolution of the 1960s, his weapon "obscene" language. "Don't take my words away from me!" he cries to a judge near the end of the film. Time has done what the judge could not. Bruce's words—*fuck, shit, cocksucker*—are now the throwaway slang of schoolchildren.

Just as it is difficult now to see why Buddy Holly was dangerous enough to provoke sermons in 1956, so it is difficult now to see why Bruce was dangerous enough to provoke jail sentences in 1964. The film is too interested in Bruce as a victim to make that danger clear. It does even worse with the self-destruction that now seems to have been Bruce's real subject, although there is a hair-raising sequence late in the film when Bruce (Dustin Hoffman) goes onstage high, wearing only a raincoat, and can only mumble and throw out scattered fragments of his once-glib chat. The film seems not perceptive enough to see that drugs, not a judge, have taken his words away. Perhaps the problem lay in the symbolic power of those drugs; like the words, their aura, inescapably associated with Bruce, was a weapon. To suggest that that weapon inevitably destroyed the wielder would not have been cool, and being cool was this revolution's goal.

The film's structure is a series of taped interviews, mostly with Bruce's wife (Valerie Perrine). It jumps back and forth in time, showing the young Lenny as a not very good standup comedian trying to make it on the Borscht Belt, then showing the Bruce of the 1960s saying "Fuck you" over and over onstage, grinning, loving the shock, the risk; back to scenes with Perrine as a raunchy stripper, as a lover waiting naked for him on a bed, as a broken body hanging from a wrecked car. Surprisingly, the film is really Perrine's. She is so good that she comes between the camera and the man she talks about, often being more affecting, more interesting than Hoffman. Some of this is the script (Bruce's routines are often boring), some is Hoffman's oddly detached performance, some is her skill at showing Honey's own fifty-seven varieties of degradation, dope, and decline.

Bob Fosse's direction places a premium on *cinematic* realism—black-and-white, grainy, sometimes apparently handheld: cinematography itself has become a sign—here, of authenticity. The direction does not always help Hoffman. In some sequences, especially those of Bruce at his height, Hoffman is fresh and believable, but in others he is uninteresting; Fosse may have been at fault here, trying to get too much grunge. The late sequence when he goes on in the raincoat, for example, is filmed entirely in long shots, robbing Hoffman of the nuance that closeup can give.

The film does cause you to ask if Lenny Bruce was an important figure. It does remind you of what was shocking and even illegal only a generation ago—saying "nigger—niggerniggerniggerniggernigger" to a black man in a public performance; saying "blah-blah" as a euphemism for "cocksucking" because a judge has prohibited his using the word. "How many guys like blah-blah? If you like blah-blah raise your hand." He was, the film makes clear, an early performance artist rather than a standup comedian, obsessed with himself and with saying the unsayable—a narcissistic infant, perhaps.

Vincent Canby expressed the distinctly odd view that *Lenny* was "no more profound than those old movie biographies Jack L. Warner used to grind out about people like George Gershwin. . . . [Genius] is principally defined by the amount of time spent dealing with disappointment."[6] Canby seems not to have paid very close attention to either those old movies or *Lenny*. He didn't like the interview structure either, finding it "full of simulated *cinema-verité* irrelevancies." The key to these attitudes may be found in his complaint that the film didn't show Bruce's unhappy childhood and his father: Canby wanted a film of the 1950s, perhaps a period he was more comfortable with—at least until Buddy Holly and Lenny Bruce came along. In a way, his criticism validates the film: Bruce really did help to drive a wedge between the 1950s and the 1970s.

Yes, he was a historical figure.

OUTSIDERS

THE FILMS ABOUT people outside traditional areas of power are remarkable in several ways: all of them are about men (in the 1940s, they were mostly about women), two are deeply narcissistic, and one is about two men who became so famous that they seem to contradict the idea of "outsiders." Reflection will show that they were, however, outsiders, and that their movement toward power, by way of notoriety, is part of what was happening in the 1970s.

All the President's Men (1976) was, as William E. Leuchtenberg put it, "ostensibly about politics but . . . actually about journalism."[7] It is an account of the roles of Bob Woodward and Carl Bernstein in getting the Watergate story. Derived from their book about themselves, it risks the dangers of all autobiography and apparently succumbs to them. It is tunnel history and narcissism, "How We Got That Story," with overtones of "How We Brought Down the President of the United States," and implications of "What Great Guys We Are!"

The movie has Robert Redford and Dustin Hoffman as Woodward and Bernstein. Alan Pakula's direction accepts uncritically the importance of the two and of what they did, confusing it with what the Constitution and the

Congress did. To be sure, the story of *The Washington Post*, its two newsmen, and its keeping the Watergate story alive is an interesting one, but it is not as pivotal as the film pretends. *All the President's Men* would have us believe that Woodward, Bernstein, and Ben Bradlee (Jason Robards, Jr.) were all that stood between the republic and its end.

The film begins and ends with devices that reveal its self-congratulation. At the opening, a typewriter key descends on a sheet of paper; the resulting sound is a gunshot. The typewriter types a date; each digit is another gunshot: the typewriter, by implication the press, is a weapon of war. At the end, Nixon's second swearing-in is playing on a television monitor; bands play; cannons boom. A typewriter continues right through all of it and begins to produce terse sentences to describe the events up to and including Nixon's resignation: the typewriter, by implication the press, has won the war and brought down the president.

The one area in which both book and film might have given real revelation is, regrettably, fictionalized. "Deep Throat" is played by Hal Holbrook as an unidentified nutcase who insists upon meeting Woodward in places that suggest the reading of too many spy novels. Nobody known to fame could be made to match this characterization. When Deep Throat finally growls to Woodward, "Your lives are in danger," and Woodward hurries home, looking worriedly over his shoulder, you want to laugh out loud.

What *All the President's Men* tells us about most notably is the vanity of the filmmakers and of two newsmen who could get the story right but who could not get right their own place in it—or not in it.

Sitting through *Midnight Express* (1978) is like sitting next to a wailing child on an airplane: it won't shut up, and you can't jump out. Like the infant, the hero of *Midnight Express* goes on and on about an injustice he has suffered, and his indignation is most impassioned because he is himself the cause of it.

Brad Davis plays a young American caught smuggling hashish out of Turkey. His rationale, once caught, is, "It was my first time. I'm not really a smuggler. It was only two kilos." Then, "I was only gonna sell it to my friends. I'm not a pusher." He later refers to this crime as "my error." He is sentenced to a horrendous prison, where, to his horror, everybody in power is a Turk. When his sympathetic father (Mike Kellin) shows up, the worst insult he can think to hurl at a guard is, "You Turkish bastard!" Both dad and son believe dad should fix things, as apparently he has fixed everything else in this spoiled child's life. Ultimately, the child escapes by way of a plot device that would have embarrassed Buster Crabbe. It is probably a key to the film: some— much? all?—is fiction. Whatever the real events on which this film is based, only a self-serving version of them seems to be here.

Escape From Alcatraz (1979) was certainly not narcissistic. It was basically a caper movie, with Clint Eastwood as a rock-hard con with a determination to get off Alcatraz Island. He is countered by the warden (Patrick McGoohan), a martinet who says smugly, "Knowledge of the outside world is what we tell you." (Historically, he appears to be the same warden as the one in *Birdman of Alcatraz*.) Terse, often nonverbal, the film has enough interesting detail to make up for its lack of real suspense. You can learn, for example, how to silver-solder with common matches and filings from a silver dime (if you can still find one).

Escape From Alcatraz is so much a Clint Eastwood movie that not too much should be asked of it as history. However, in a consideration of American ideas of legal punishment, it might be useful. Alcatraz, as shown here, was a place for the killing of men from the inside out, not at all a pretty historical insight for a nation that forbids cruel and unusual punishment. That Eastwood made it and that it was successful suggests unease with that penal system and perhaps with the nation that supported it; it seems consonant with the pictures of the FBI and the police in all the "backcountry borderer" crime films.

THE FILMS OF THE 1970s were technically attractive ones, most made in color, most with effective cinematography. The feeling of pointless excess found in the 1950s is gone; the direction is confident, skilled, usually post-realistic in the use of changed motion, altered sound, and camera angle. Some films show changes in filmmaking itself, not least the use of cinematography as a sign (*Lenny*). Cinematography had typically pretended to be naive, thus to authenticate its content; now it began to signal that some kinds of cinematography were more authentic than others. These changes in the form of films match changes in attack. All reverence for the past is gone. The Native American and Western expansion have been turned upside-down. The military has gone from heroic to amoral, or worse. The Jameses have gone from culturel heroes to buffoons. Western examplary tales of law and order have become tales of corruption and cynicism. In the crime films, the police are violent and self-serving. Contrarily, racial ideas have been radically revised toward a more idealistic and noble level—fairly isolated instances of a change toward the positive, rather than the negative. It is a decade of ironic revisionism and black comedy, one working to cut itself off from the ideas with which film began treating history. The nineteenth century was dead, at last.

CHAPTER NINE

1980–1989: PALIMPSEST⎯⎯⎯⎯⎯

There is a great freshness to many of the historical films of the 1980s, a sense even of starting over. Yet the slate is not really a clean one; old genres and ideas persist, perhaps as an irreducible minimum. For the first time, for example, the traditional–Western combination is a minor thread. More important, however, it is becoming difficult to separate insiders from outsiders; as a postmodernist might have predicted, walls were turning out to be membranes.

FOR ITS TECHNIQUES as much as for its notion of history, *Walker* (1987) remains a startling film. It comprises a critique of both, and its take-no-prisoners, slash-and-burn treatment of an audience's expectations is unsettling—so much so that the film's achievements easily get lost in one's annoyance or even revulsion. It also sets new records for gore; not since Shakespeare's actors wore bladders full of blood under their doublets has so much patently fake bloodshed been seen, its quantity horrifying, its quality funny—many wounds spurt blood the way soda fountains used to spurt chocolate syrup—so that *Walker* both mocks other films' violence and appals with its own. Robert Rosenstone called it "black farce."[1]

William Walker led a kind of invasion of Nicaragua just before the American Civil War. He has been a footnote to American history, and a mostly unread one. What director Alex Cox has tried to do is elevate that footnote to a headline and give the headline contemporary relevance.

To do so, he has cast Ed Harris as Walker (and got a brilliant performance from him), has employed sparing but wild anachronism, and has used many of Walker's own words to light the film with flashes of rant, rave, and obsession. Harris's Walker embodies the expansionist zeal of Southerners seen in the Alamo films, but with the religious righteousness seen in *One Man's Way* and *MacArthur*. "It is the God-given right of the American people to dominate the Western hemisphere," he says, defending himself early in the film for having invaded Mexico.

Cox does not proceed directly from this boast to the invasion of Nicaragua, however. Instead, he gives us an extended sequence in which Walker communicates with and for his beautiful, deaf fiancée (Marlee Matlin). The scene, superficially "normal"—realistic interior, recognizable social behaviors,

signs for "mid-nineteenth century, South, U.S.—" is made bizarre by his signing, then by his refusal to translate accurately her obscene and anachronistic
insults ("Go fuck a pig," to a bore). When they are alone, she reviles him in
sign, with subtitles; the subject careens suddenly to slavery and he cries—in
sign—"Ellen, you know I despise—I *despise* slavery!" The jagged rhythm of
the sequence, Matlin's obscenity, his subservience to her, crack the expectations for the sequence; the signing itself and the subtitles are alienating; they
set us back on our heels, refuse to let us off easily.

Walker then goes off to answer a call from Commodore Vanderbilt (Peter
Boyle); when he returns, his fiancée is dead from cholera. He is enraged,
orders everybody out of the room where her coffin rests, and—after putting
his hat on her feet—rants at her in sign, says aloud, "I—oh, God! I can't—oh,
you bitch!" He weeps, collapses on her, chews his fingers. The sequence is
absurd enough as it is, but it is also played against the immediately preceding
scene with Vanderbilt, who has received Walker under an umbrella in the
desert near his private railroad car. He wants Walker to go to Nicaragua so
Vanderbilt can control pan-isthmus trade. "Do you prize democracy, Walker?"
Vanderbilt has said. "More than life itself," Walker answered. And Vanderbilt
roared with laughter. "I like him. Get him a new hat." The two scenes, utterly
discontinuous, both with absurd elements (the umbrella, the hat, the signing,
the "Oh, you bitch!") do not "make sense," yet each is entirely satisfying as art,
therefore demands to be made sense of.

Walker of course takes up Vanderbilt's challenge. What follows is a stunning contradiction between Walker's vocabulary of idealism—enlightened,
civilized, hygiene, science, God—and brilliantly filmed scenes of carnage.
Walker and his "Immortals" are met by a fusillade, through which Walker
marches without a scratch. Blood spurts; men fall; limbs fly apart. On he goes.
This is battle without its own sounds; rather, we get only music and an occasional voice. When things become hopeless and Walker and his band are bar-
ricaded in a house, he plays the piano, then tells a wildly hairy officer (René
Auberjonois) to blow a hole in a wall to make a diversion so that they can
escape. The officer lights the fuse with a modern cigarette lighter.

A liberal ally of the invaders prays among the corpses for the Americans
who came "to improve our civilization and strengthen our economy." God
apparently answers the prayer: so devastating is Walker's defeat that it becomes a
victory; he has "broken the enemy's spirit." Walker takes over the government.

Now magazines such as *People* and *Newsweek* appear; he is delighted to find
himself on the cover of *Time*. He talks of himself in the third person. When
problems arise (cholera, foreign invasion, economic collapse), he has a solution:
slavery. He keeps his ideals: "I'm not an aristocrat. I'm a social democrat."

Everything falls apart. "Instruct the men to burn the town," Walker says.
The city becomes a madhouse. Men shoot each other, trundle flaming carts,
run from nowhere to nowhere. Walker, looking exactly as he had in the first

battle, marches through all this to the cathedral, now a hospital; there, he goes to the altar, where a wounded man lies bleeding, calmly carves a piece from the man and eats it.

He then delivers a sermon from the pulpit. "It is [America's] destiny to be here. It is our destiny to control you people. . . . We'll be back time and time again. We will never abandon the cause of Nicaragua." He and his men sing "Onward, Christian Soldiers," and march out, a priest sprinkling holy water, soldiers flanking Walker and shooting.

We hear the familiar chuffing of a helicopter motor; brilliant lights shine from above. A helicopter lands, and modern American soldiers jump out, automatic weapons at the ready. A plump little man in glasses says that they have come to remove all U.S. citizens to safety. Walker, as president of Nicaragua, is not a U.S. citizen and so cannot be saved. After shooting most of the people in the vicinity (including one already on the helicopter), the soldiers jump aboard and the machine flies away.

The film ends with Ronald Reagan on a television screen: "There is no thought of sending American combat troops to central America," followed by images of American military, of weeping Latino children, and of corpses.

This is history as phantasmagoria. The film has great detail, dense texture, although much of the detail and texture are redundant. It has context, both of its time (Vanderbilt) and of the present (Reagan), but the context is neither textured nor detailed and so seems simplistic, compared to the body of the film.

Rightly and richly, the film touches on puppet governments, "liberal" supporters of Walker's invasion, self-seeking among his own people, the inevitable corruption of revolution. Yet the overall effect is of excess for its own sake, excess as a language of art—that is, black-comic satire.

Glory (1987) is a very different kind of picture in almost every way. Essentially an act of recovery, it puts on film the heroism of black soldiers in the Civil War, heretofore erased from popular culture. Although in part a film about the white guy who led them, Robert Gould Shaw (Matthew Broderick), it succeeds in showing some of the obstacles faced by black troops and their heroism in battle. The style is strictly realistic, which probably enhances authentication, although it brings the usual restrictions and the usual manipulations to avoid them—overdetermined music, occasional symbolism.

Broderick seems an odd choice for Shaw because of his youthfulness; on the other hand, he is believable, and, in wartime, colonels come very young— especially colonels in despised units. We see Shaw take the command of the newly formed Massachusetts 54th despite the doubts of even close friends: "Issue guns to a thousand coloreds?" says another New Englander. If we ever thought that Northerners wanted armed African Americans, we are quickly disabused of the idea.

The film focuses on one lot of tentmates, a varied group that is not entirely exempt from the war-movie law of distribution: a tough cynic, Trip (Denzel

Washington); an educated Northerner, Thomas (Andre Braugher); an older ex-slave (Morgan Freeman). They suffer the indignities of drill under an Irish sergeant; lacking uniforms, they are in the beginning a sorry lot. Yet, when they are offered release from their enlistments after the Confederacy declares that all black prisoners taken while bearing arms will be put into slavery, none leaves. "Glory, halleleujah!" says the young and worried Shaw.

It is Shaw's fervent intention that his men will be combat troops. He therefore insists upon rigorous training, despite advice to let up. In a telling sequence, we see him at a distance, riding down a line of posts; a half-watermelon rests on each post. He canters past, slicing each watermelon with his saber: no more black stereotype. When the tough young cynic goes AWOL and is caught, Shaw has him whipped, even though it is pointed out to him that this is exactly the punishment he would have received as a slave. The white officer and the whipped man look each other in the eyes, one accusing, tears running down his face, the other guilty and determined.

Shaw finally takes his trained troops to South Carolina, finds himself serving under superiors who are using the war for their own ends. When he is unable to get combat orders for his regiment, he threatens to reveal the truth about his commander—smuggling, accepting looted goods—unless they are allowed to go. The orders are given. Marching to the theater of action, the black troops are again mocked by whites: "Stripes on a nigger! Like tits on a bull," says one to Freeman, now a sergeant. Even among themselves, some are still doubtful; the cynic tells the educated man that "he ain't never gonna be nothing but a colored chimp," but Freeman, readying them for combat, makes a stirring speech, repudiating the word nigger: they are men, and they are preparing to die like men. In their first action, they turn back a white Confederate assault.

Broderick looks weary and almost middle-aged by the time he volunteers his men to lead an assault on Fort Wagner—the act that would make them famous. A year after that real event, Thomas Wentworth Higginson would arrive at what was already called Fort Shaw with his own black regiment. Shaw and the Massachusetts 54th would be his inspiration, and the rest of the film shows why.[2] The gallantry of the 54th, a huge number of them killed with their commander in that action, is the history that the film aims to recover.

The night before the assault, Freeman prays, "We want [our people] to know that we died for freedom." The cynic, Trip, at last makes connection with the others: "You-all's the only family I got. I love the 54th. We *men*, aren't we!" And even the intellectual, Thomas, begins to sing: he has become black at last. As they go forward to certain death, they are cheered by the white troops who line the way. Shaw, pausing with a newsman, says, "If I should fall, remember what you see here." He rides down to the edge of the sea, dismounts, and sends his horse splashing away without him. Films seldom dare to show the soldier's fear of death and its consonant acceptance. The horse here is life itself, vigor, possibility; he sends it away and stands, seeming to weep, looking at the sea, the birds, the sun—for the last time, as he knows.

The battle footage is appalling. They have to lie for hours, unprotected, under artillery assault, then run uphill at a strongly defended position. Most never make it. Next morning, Shaw's body is dumped into a sand pit with his soldiers. Another soldier's body comes down on his in slow motion, and the dead man seems to nestle his head against Shaw in sleep.

Restorative acts of history are needed sometimes. This one was long overdue. It can be faulted for its manipulations—its music, its too-easy fit into certain niches of the war movie—but not for its sentimentality, for the emotions it evokes are appropriate ones. *Glory* is a grand movie, although not a great one. It sets a record straight—about historical fact, about participation of blacks in that war, about the manliness of former slaves, about their utter lack of nostalgia or affection for what Higginson called "massa time"—and does it stirringly.

Reds (1981) is also a grand movie, and, if not a great one, surely one that deserves attention. Its most serious flaw is probably also its greatest popular virtue, a sweeping romanticism that engages the eye and the ear with emotional riches. Unlike *Glory*, it is not content with realism; like *Walker*, it has gone to a nonrealistic device, in *Reds'* case the inclusion of "Witnesses"—survivors of the era of the film. Shown against black backgrounds, these aged people recount often conflicting ideas, opinions, anecdotes, related to the film: history as memory.

Reds is about "Louise Bryant [Diane Keaton] and Jack Reed [Warren Beatty]," a female dilettante and a male journalist–artist who covered revolutions in Mexico and Russia and died in the Soviet Union. It is about many other things and many other people, to its credit—an American bohemia in the second decade of this century, Emma Goldman (Maureen Stapleton), Eugene O'Neill (Jack Nicholson), leftist idealism, the Russian revolution, disenchantment with Lenin and his followers. Yet the principal action is the relationship between Bryant and Reed, with the usual problems that attend the reduction of events to individuals.

There is almost the danger at certain points that historical events are to become mere background for the Bryant–Reed story. That this does not quite happen is the result of two wise choices by Beatty as director: the Witnesses, whose skepticism and antiromanticism distance the pair; and the romanticizing of leftism and the Russian Revolution, with a choral singing of the "Internationale" a correlative of the love between Reed and Bryant.

Nonetheless, it is questionable that Bryant should have had a major place in a study of Reed. This is not to question whether she was herself a historical figure, nor is it to deny her importance because she was a woman. Undoubtedly, a compelling film could be made about Bryant both before and after she knew Reed. But in a historically accurate film of the years covered in *Reds*, Bryant's would be a supporting, not a starring, role.

Reds begins with their meeting in Oregon, quickly gets them into bed ("I'd like to see you with your pants off") and almost as quickly into a fight about her status; when he asks her to come to New York, she bristles. "What as?" "It's almost Thanksgiving; why don't you come as a turkey?"

When we see her arrive in New York, having left her husband, we hear the Witnesses. We see with our own eyes; we hear their conflicting views: we write the history using these materials. We decide she is a person in her own right. When, however, dialogue and action replace the Witnesses, Bryant seems a dilettante, in ideology as much as in art. Surrounded by argumentative ideologues (Goldman, Floyd Dell, Big Bill Haywood), she seems out of her depth. Reed seems very much in his.

She cannot bear the difference. "I'm just living in your margins," she says. "I can't work around you. I'm not being taken seriously when you're around." In fact, she hits on the film's and Beatty's problem: they do take her seriously. This is a complex issue, to be sure—male vs. female, the kinds of activity we think important, theories of history itself. But in the political terms that Beatty has set himself in his title, Bryant was, in fact, in the margins; in the romantic terms he has set himself in his narrative, she is central.

An extended sequence deals with the art theater that began in Provincetown, Massachusetts, and became the Provincetown Playhouse; like some other aspects of the film, it lacks context (e.g., Why was it avant-garde? Why was it art? Why does what we see of it look like mundane amateur theatricals?). Central to this section is Nicholson's O'Neill, a bad piece of casting but probably a commercially necessary one. Nicholson as star builds Bryant's importance: O'Neill and Bryant have an affair; when it is over and she has married Reed, O'Neill tells her, "You're a lying Irish whore . . . and you used me so you could get Jack Reed to marry you." Then there is more Bryant: she is unsatisfied in the marriage; her writing goes badly; they split and then come together again in Europe, go on to St. Petersburg in 1918.

The scenes of the October Revolution are the top of the film. Bryant and Reed unite again; the camera opens scene after scene to show crowds, marches, songs, meetings that signal enthusiasm and hope. (All that hope!) We are meant, of course, to compare it with what we know came after, but the emotions of that moment are made deeply moving. Beatty never implies that the later Soviet Union satisfied those hopes, but he does direct these scenes so that we feel a twinge of loss that such hope was possible. It is impossible to disassociate the revolution from their love affair. Their silhouetted heads meet as the "Internationale" is sung. Not a very Marxist moment, but we have to assume that this is the romantic image Beatty wanted.

And then one of the Witnesses sings the "Internationale" in English. Quavering, alone, the only image the old face—the moment is a sad and wry reminder of "history" since 1918, as well as of what happens to youth and love.

The rest of the film runs down toward Reed's death: the Red Scare begins in America—Emma Goldman jailed and deported, Bryant testifying before a Senate committee, George Jessel as a Witness singing "It's a Grand Old Flag" and "Over There" and "I'm a Yankee Doodle Dandy." Reed joins the Socialist Party; the party splits; leftist politics in this half of the film become like the Greenwich Village parties of the first half—chatterings, bickerings, divisions. Reed goes to Russia for his wing of the party; once there, he cannot get out; he is a useful propaganda tool for Zinoviev (Jerzy Kosinski). Bryant goes on an overlong search for him, more *Doctor Zhivago* than history, across the snow on foot. Goldman, already in Russia, is disillusioned and trying to leave. "We have to face it. The dream we had is dying. . . . Nothing works! Four million people died last year!" Reed falls back on empty arguments. "It's a war, E. G. . . . It's the beginning. . . . It's not happening the way we thought it would, but—." Sent to Baku for propaganda purposes, Reed has a set-to with Zinoviev, the romantic against the ideologue. Unable to budge Zinoviev, Reed tries to escape.

At last, Reed and Bryant meet again. It is too late; soon he is dying in a hospital of disease. Even then, she is not with him when he dies; she returns from getting some water and finds the doctors closing his eyes. This ending seems to acknowledge the defeat of the love plot's romanticism; certainly, it acknowledges the failure of Reed's role in the Soviet Union.

Beatty, a romantic, saw Reed as himself a romantic. However, the interpretation does not necessarily justify an erotic romance to embody Reed's romanticism. Least of all does it justify so much concentration on his love for a woman who is presented here as decidedly unromantic, even self-serving and trivial. Yet the film is so rich in historical figures, so well acted, so beautifully filmed in its Russian sequences, and the Witnesses are so inventive a device to achieve distance, that it is an important historical film despite its flaw.

Fat Man and Little Boy (1989) covered the same ground as the 1946 *The Beginning or the End?* but, surprisingly, with less satisfying results. The film is a distressing example of a failure to make a better historical film despite better information and better performers. Certainly, in Paul Newman as Groves the film has a huge potential advantage, which it dribbles away on a script that has no real role for him.

A little way in, *Fat Man and Little Boy* seems to decide to be about J. Robert Oppenheimer rather than Groves, and Groves becomes a bogeyman—rather the role that liberals have assigned him in the morality play of the Manhattan Project. Oppenheimer (Dwight Schultz) is a Eurocentric elitist who at first appears to be wrong in his elitism and his contempt for Groves—"a meatball . . . [who will be] eating out of my hand in a week." Shortly, however, his arrogance comes to seem a justifiable pride as we see that the real basis of his conflict with Groves is to be his affair with Jean Tatlock, a purported Communist. Because Oppenheimer and Tatlock are presented intelligently and sympathetically, and because Groves is presented stupidly and unsympathetically, what promised to be a real probing of that complex tale becomes merely loaded drama.

The film seems to get more one-sided as it goes on. When Oppenheimer kisses his brother good-bye, two watching security men are disgusted: "He just kissed his brother." "Gotta be a Communist." This sort of cheap shot, more appropriate to satire, gets us nowhere. Later, the film seems to return to some attempt to make Oppenheimer a complex character rather than a knee-jerk hero; when Germany is defeated, he wants to back out of using the bomb. Defeating Hitler is rather murkily equated with helping Jews, an idea the film implies but never explores. Yet, when he is made to stay, he seems to reverse direction, then to revel in the bomb's success. Again, real complexity of character seems about to operate here, but it is too late, and too little comes of it.

John Cusack is Merriman, a young scientist who dies from radiation (the film's version of the Tom Drake role in *The Beginning or the End?*). His lingering death is harrowing. It is not enough, however, to establish historical context or to set the terms for the profound argument that the contrast of Groves and Oppenheimer represents. When next this piece of history is filmed, somebody should have the wit to see to it that Groves is given his due, thus balancing the dramatic and historical scales; as well, the debate over dropping the bomb—limited here to a relatively short Washington scene, albeit one in which an admiral threatens to resign over the issue— must be given more time and more reality. And such people as Vanavar Bush need to be included.

The Killing Fields (1984) was a historical film about the war in Southeast Asia and a newsman who reported it. As with *All the President's Men*, it was too much about the man who got the story (Sam Waterston) rather than the Cambodian (Haing S. Ngor) who was the protagonist of that story. Only in the second half is his story allowed to run uninterrupted; it is harrowing, the experiences of an intellectual trying to survive under the Khmer Rouge. Even this is interrupted so that the American journalist can receive a man-of-the-year award; the Cambodian is meanwhile hiding in a mass grave of skulls and tibia and the blue cloths with which those who are about to be executed are wrapped. Ultimately, the Cambodian escapes and the American goes to meet him. This is both a painful and an irritating film, one somewhat more free, but not entirely so, of the self-congratulation of *All the President's Men*, probably more useful to a history of journalism than to one of American imperialism. Like certain other films about the Vietnam era (*Alice's Restaurant*, *Conrack*), it may assume an audience attitude that can no longer be counted on—an assumption that is itself historical evidence.

The Right Stuff (1983) took the air force movies of the 1950s and 1960s into the space age, but not without irony. Based on Tom Wolfe's book, the film benefits from his insight that Chuck Yeager (Sam Shepard) could be contrasted with the first group of astronauts to show how the tradition of the courageous loner—*The Spirit of St. Louis*—gave way to corporate culture. The film is over-long and intermittently comic, but it is a good look at American social history of the 1950s and 1960s.

Yeager is first seen in 1947 in a desert bar where the photos of pilots killed trying to break the sound barrier are posted on a wall. Yeager then rides his horse, a fixture of a number of his scenes, with resonances of the West and the cowboy; he circles the new X-1 on horseback before taking it up. When he flies the aircraft, he wears an old-fashioned leather helmet. Thus, Yeager and the test pilots at Edwards Air Force Base are established as the old way, with continuity to barnstorming and the Wrights and the independence of the West.

By contrast, after the Soviets launch Sputnik, a new kind of man is want-ed. Yeager himself is rejected by the two bureaucrats who come to Edwards: he has only a high school education, "doesn't fit the profile . . . too independent." Instead, Gordon Cooper (Dennis Quaid) and Gus Grissom (Fred Ward) vol-unteer; they, too, are at Edwards but do not fly the X craft. They are joined by John Glenn (Ed Harris), picked in part because of his nice-guy performance on a television show.

The film then moves too slowly through the testing of the astronauts, the selection of the final seven, and the progress of the space program up to Cooper's launch in 1963; by then, Shepard (Scott Glenn) has been the first man in space; Grissom has blotted his copybook by opening the hatch after splashdown and causing the loss of his capsule; Glenn has gone three orbits and survived a re-entry with a damaged heat shield. Many of the sequences alternate with others about Yeager—flying faster, flying higher, always at Edwards. The desert bar burns, the photos of the dead with it. The astro-nauts get publicity, money, book contracts, free houses in Texas; Yeager and his wife stay in the same scruffy quarters at Edwards. When the X-15 is rolled out for Yeager, we learn that it is the last. "The astronaut boys have the only ticket now."

The space program moves to Houston. Lyndon Johnson, then vice-presi-dent, hosts a huge barbecue in an indoor arena. This remarkably vulgar dis-play— "Miss Sally Rand" does a fan dance as the contribution of high culture—is intercut with sequences of Yeager's taking the X-15 to the near edge of space. In Houston, Cooper, asked who was the greatest pilot he ever saw, hesitates, begins to describe the wall of photos of the dead, and you know he is leading up to naming Yeager; then an interruption turns him aside and he says with a grin, "You're lookin' at him."

Then Yeager takes the X-15 up and up; he looks like a spaceman himself now, the leather helmet long since replaced by a plastic one, his flying suit now sleek and shiny. He has a flameout near the record altitude and the plane plunges.

In Houston, the astronauts smile covertly at each other and eye Sally Rand. Yeager ejects and we see him struggling with his face shield and his chute. On the desert, black smoke towers from the crashed X-15. The crash truck heads out. As they near the crash, the driver says, peering through the smoke, "Is that a man?" It is Yeager, walking toward them, his head bloody and burned. "You're damned right it is," says his companion.

The Right Stuff does not denigrate the astronauts, but it glorifies Yeager's quiet skill and courage. It reminds us of the differences, not the similarities, between the loner on the desert and the seven corporation men beside the sea: Yeager takes the X-15 up without any fanfare, without even any backup on the ground; we see the astronauts with the vast Canaveral complex, the mission control munchkins, the constant contact between earth and space. Yeager is always alone; the astronauts are always in groups. Yeager is always in jeans and casual clothes; the astronauts' clothes evolve into the IBM–FBI look, short hair and white shirts and ties. Everything the astronauts do is weighed for PR effect; nothing Yeager does is measured for anything but his idea of his goal.

Some of *The Right Stuff* is funny, not all of it at a very high level. Some of it is serious. The wives of both the test-pilots and the astronauts get more time than wives usually have in air-power movies; they are not treated as sweet attendant angels but as grownups who suffer. Early on, a wife confesses her fear of "the sound of the crash truck. . . . Nobody ever wants to talk around here." After Grissom has botched his landing, his wife cries, "Why didn't we eat in the White House [like the Shepards]? I wanted to talk to Jackie—! Oh, Gus, they owe you—they owe me, too—." They are pestered by journalists (all male) who climb over their fences and lean in their windows. They often look nervous or unhappy.

Harris has managed to create a John Glenn who is adept at public relations, courageous in flight, and crazy about his wife. A little bit square, he is a full and believable human being; he slides into the corporate image because he was a straight-arrow to start with; yet, at the end, he seems to be the one who is keeping a wary eye on himself for signs of dehumanization. It is a fine performance; the others, except for Glenn as Shepard, seem to be pretty much on one note.

The picture of Yeager walking out of the smoke of the burning X-15 is a picture of the end of a way of heroism. The picture of the astronauts watching Sally Rand is a picture of the new. The contrast of the two reminds us that the corporate image of the space program is a recent matter, as history goes, and not an entirely cost-free one.

THE FIVE WESTERNS of the 1980s were unexceptionable; genre was all. *The Long Riders* (1980) reprised the James–Younger story, this time with various sets of brothers playing the various sets of brothers, an idea that must have seemed good at some point but surely was not. In the event, which Keach or which Quaid or which Carradine played which whoever was so confusing that it was quickly not worth worrying about; nor were the magical, ever-shooting six-guns or the gratuitous violence. *Tom Horn* (also 1980) was a hodge-podge of fiction and history, something about a cattleman's association and a hired gun (Steve McQueen) and too much killing being a bad thing. The film might have histori-cal value if it meticulously reproduced Horn's later life and gave the cattlemen some sort of context, but it does not, and it lacks internal probability, to boot. Michael Cimino's *Heaven's Gate* (also 1980) has become famous for its expense and little else. This notoriety obscures some very good things, including a visual reproduction of the West in 1890 that is staggering. Some of the images are so compelling that I was reminded of the work of theater director Robert Wilson: a saturated visual universe, fully imagined, needing no "meaning"; regrettably, when character and plot appear, they seem inadequate. The opening sequence at Harvard in 1870, where we first see Kris Kristofferson and John Hurt waltzing with their classmates in a dazzling shot, creates context—the involvement of Eastern wealth in "more West" and the oppression of immigrants. ("Harvard" is recognizably Oxford, in fact, a resonance within a resonance.) Immigrants are also given life in this film; they are confused, fearful, defiant, riven by European divisions and politics. At film's end, Kristofferson looks back on the bloody events in the West from a yacht, an extension of context beyond those events into the future and back to the wealthy East. Like *Tom Horn*, *Heaven's Gate* serves to remind us that when the frontier closed, "more West" meant taking internal space. Immigrants were also trying to claim it, and the resulting disputes made for a different sort of winning of the West. *Heaven's Gate* gives us this despite its generic stupidities, and it is deeply satisfying as pure picture, as well.

THE MUSICAL AND SHOW-BUSINESS biographies, which had produced impor-tant films in previous decades, seemed mostly perfunctory in this one. They did, however, recover their former function of providing roles for women. They celebrated musical diversity, with three films about country music, one about black jazz, and one about the early Latino rock singer Richie Valens (*La Bamba*, 1987). Three nonmusical, show-business films provided roles for women but cannot be said to have done much for women's history; *Mommie Dearest* (1981), particularly, seemed regressive, looking back to the queen-bee screamers of the 1950s.

Bird (1988) is a long but memorable examination of the life and music of Charlie Parker (Forest Whitaker). Full of Parker's music, it is relentless with his drug addiction. Clint Eastwood's direction is uninsistent, willing to spin things out so as to get it all in. Much of the film is about Parker's marriage; his wife (Donna Verona) is often irritating, rather arch, a jazz groupie who says "man" so many times you want to shut her up. Yet Eastwood's and the film's honesty keeps bringing us back from such irritations.

Parker's life is presented as a constant tension between creativity and addiction. The addiction may be the result of having his creativity pushed to the outside of the society, rather than to its center with other arts: when he rings the bell at the gate of a famous European writer he reveres, the man comes to the door, sees that Bird is black, and shuts the door without even going to the gate—shutting him out of "art." Yet Bird cannot find another way and still be a black American. In France, he plays to ovations, gifts of flowers; another black jazz musician who lives there says, "Over here—you don't get rich—but they treat you like a *man*." Bird gives his rueful smile. "My country. Whether they like it or not." His life spirals down; his health gets worse. "They gonna shovel you under, Bird," Dizzy Gillespie (Samuel E. Wright) tells him, "and then talk about you. . . ." Bird dies in a woman's apartment. The doctor who writes the death certificate says, "Approximately sixty-five years of age." "He was thirty-four," the woman says.

Eastwood locates Parker on the fringes of white society: most scenes take place at night; many have implications of hustling. Drugs are usually accessible. Whites are the "they" of both this world and of Gillespie's remarks: they are the gatekeepers; they are the killers.

Eastwood seems to be an objectivist who amasses detail on a chronological structure and accepts the overlong result as truth. He has no interest in the devices of a Penn or a Cox. The music saves the film from its own length; so does Whitaker's performance, which embraces aging, great complexity, self-destructiveness. The result is an absorbing, if overlong, film about both music and race in America's 1940s and 1950s, an essential corrective to all those films about Benny Goodman and the rest.

Coal Miner's Daughter (1980) is the best of the country music films because it is the best at showing that music as part of a larger whole. Some of this expansiveness comes from the early part of the film, with Sissy Spacek as a fourteen-year-old Loretta Lynn in the Kentucky coal country after World War II. The wooded hollows, the unpainted houses, the look of coal miners and coal country are very convincing; so is the picture of a society in which patriarchy was all.

Loretta is wooed by a much older war veteran, Doo (Tommy Lee Jones). Married almost at once, she is miserable. The wedding night is a rape; he strikes her next morning; she goes home pregnant—"He throwed me out, Mama." He leaves to go to the West Coast. "There ain't nothin' for me in Kentucky, except a chest full of coal dust. Ask your Daddy."

Three more kids later, she is singing a Patsy Cline song with the radio, and then Doo is pushing her to sing with a cowboy band, and then she is off and running as a singer, and he is staying up nights to take her picture, write letters, mail out records, anything to get her ahead. Her father's death takes her home to Kentucky, and the setting of this sequence makes the connection between her songs and her father: music is "going home." From there, it is a short move to Nashville, Ernest Tubb and Minnie Pearl, the Opry. The rest of the film is about her relationship with Patsy Cline (Beverly D'Angelo), her husband's return to a working life of his own, and a career crisis as she works herself into a breakdown. It is not first-class drama, but it enables the music and it rounds out the film. The closing song, "Coal Miner's Daughter," recalls the early part of the film, her father, and the working life of the South. If you do not like country music, however, the music's contact with authentic lives of work will probably be lost in what seems an irritating style.

Like *Leadbelly* and *Bound for Glory*, *Coal Miner's Daughter* captures the connection between a kind of music, a place, and the life of that place. It is a film about the real South and its working class, not about the plantation myth.

Sweet Dreams (1985) was a less satisfying film about Patsy Cline (Jessica Lange), despite a good performance from Ed Harris as Charlie Dick, her second husband. The film never quite engages, despite Lange's saying things like "All of it—I want it all!" and, of Dick, "Sweet Jesus, it just feels so good." As in *Coal Miner's Daughter*, the problem of the suddenly successful Southern woman and the blue-collar husband is examined, and the husband continues to be what he is (he batters her); a real South of honky-tonks, hypocrisy, and new-money vulgarity is very much there. What isn't there is Cline's genius— what it was, how she worked at it. She seems in this film to be what her husband saw her as, a good ol' boy's wife who sang.

Great Balls of Fire (1989) has Dennis Quaid as Jerry Lee Lewis, who starts as a small kid sneaking out with his cousin Jimmy Swaggart to listen to boogie-woogie ("It's the Devil's music! I can feel it!") at a black honky tonk in 1944. A closeup of a black hand on the keyboard changes to one of a white hand, and there is Quaid as Lewis, chewing bubble-gum and playing stride piano with lots of glissando.

Quaid pops his gum and burns rubber and bugs his eyes and throws his head forward, and that's about the extent of the performance. His maniacal work at the piano is fairly convincing, but overall he does more mugging than has been seen since Milton Berle left the tube. As in *The Buddy Holly Story*, the expression "nigger music" is used. As in *Coal Miner's Daughter*, an adult male romances a girl barely out of elementary school, only this time the male is the subject of the film and the thirteen-year-old is his cousin Myra (Winona Ryder). "Can't we just wait three or four years?" she says wisely. He can't.

Too much of the film is cynical pandering. Jerry Lee Lewis is an interesting man, and his relationship with Jimmy Swaggart has far more depth than this movie hints at. Here, instead, parents are squares, teachers are stupid, a cute ass is better than a good mind, and religion is pretty much a joke. The film merely skates over the surface of this strange figure's life: his marriage, his drinking, his relationship with evangelical Christianity. ("If I'm goin' to Hell, I'm going playin' the piano!")

For a few years, back in the 1950s, Jerry Lee Lewis's demonic energy gave another dimension to then-young rock 'n' roll. Both he and his music, and their meaning, are worth a better historical examination than this film gives them.

OUTSIDERS

FILMS ABOUT PEOPLE outside traditional power continued; the films themselves were generally lackluster. *In the Mood* (1987) and *Melvin and Howard* (1980) both condescended to their subjects by staring at blue-collar life while pretending to admire it. Both had what must have seemed dynamite premises (Howard Hughes meets Everyman and leaves him a bundle; fifteen-year-old boy makes out with older women). *Mrs. Soffel* (1984) and *84 Charing Cross Road* (1987) both provided roles for women, and the former took a feminist look at a woman (Diane Keaton) who committed a decidedly nonpatriarchal act.

Zoot Suit (1981) was made from a stage musical and showed its source too obviously. The failure to become film damaged it severely; behind the merely acceptable acting, the inadequate sets, and the stagebound visualization is a dynamic piece about Chicanos and the Zoot Suit era. Edward James Olmos is striking but monotonous as El Pachuco, the spirit of *pachuco*, mostly demonic in black zoot suit and hat and scarlet shirt, partly angelic. Directed by Luis Valdez from his play, it would have been better given to a different director with less commitment to the stage. As a document, on the other hand, it is a valuable rarity, evidence of social history in World War II and a neglected, even erased, group.

REMEMBER WHEN YOU thought Cheech and Chong were funny? Remember when you thought Chevy Chase was funny? *Where the Buffalo Roam* (1980) will take you back to those dear days. Bill Murray plays (barely) Hunter Thompson, "gonzo journalist," as he is always called, another minor artifact of the 1970s. The kicker is that he's outrageous. He's so outrageous you won't believe it. He's so outrageous you'll barely be able to sleep through the film. Based largely on contempt for Richard Nixon, the film ambles, yawns, and limps through dumb episode after dumb episode, relieved now and then by flashes of Peter Boyle as a far more interesting figure than Thompson, and by René Auberjonois in a truly funny bit. Much is made of drug jokes; the winks and nudges and would-be shocks now seem as trying as the behavior of preadolescents as they discover sex.

Where the Buffalo Roam is an all-male film, except for a few women in the subject position who barely even have names. It is a film without relationships: Thompson is a loner; even his encounters with Boyle are accidents. The structure is aimless. An attempt to celebrate a journalism that was subjective, forced, and irresponsible, it is worth bearing in mind when looking at *The Killing Fields* and *All the President's Men*. Where do nihilistic subjectivity and ego-driven "objectivity" overlap? Why are both typical of the 1970s and 1980s? What do both have to do with Nixon as an authority figure?

I'm Dancing as Fast as I Can (1982) at least had a female protagonist (Jill Clayburgh), a kind of Blanche DuBois with an Emmy. Confessional but glitzy, it takes us through the high- and low-life of a TV producer who gets hooked on Valium, takes up with a rat (shades of the weepies of the 1950s), hits bottom, and rises to become—a TV producer! As a sign of the times, attention should be paid to the film she is making through most of this, a soppy study of a dying poet (Geraldine Page) who hates the original ending showing herself slow-mo-ing through surf. After suffering, learning, and rising with the help of a tough-love female psychiatrist (Dianne Wiest), the Clayburgh character proves that she is a new person by changing the ending so it shows *her* in the surf. I mean, wow, man. Is that wisdom, or what? Is that narcissism, or what?

The Falcon and the Snowman (1984) had a wonderful performance by Sean Penn and little else. "Based on actual events," it follows a supposedly idealistic young man (Timothy Hutton) who decides that the way to protest the evils of the world is to be a traitor. That he and the Penn character are both the spoiled products of rich, suburban, California households seems not to interest the filmmakers a whit. Both young men, of course, have dreadful parents (Hutton's father is a former FBI agent). The Hutton character keeps a falcon, apparently so he will have a symbol when he needs one.

Selling random secrets gleaned from his low-level CIA job to the Soviets, he uses spaced-out Penn as his courier. Penn is reprehensible, nasty, and absolutely fascinating. He proposes a heroin buy to his Soviet control, leaves his message mark at the wrong place, and uses his Dick Tracy spy camera to take nude shots of his girl.

The Falcon and the Snowman is reminiscent of *Midnight Express*, another film about a young American oppressed by reality. Like that film, it seeks to absolve its hero, in part by skipping or distorting essential data. It won't wash. What we see between the frames in both films is infantilism, a scream against life for requiring that boys grow up. At the end of *The Falcon and the Snowman*, as the FBI close in, the Hutton character loosens the tresses and the falcon flies free. Could we possibly be surprised? Must we care? Hutton doesn't seem to; he looks slightly pained, as if one of these crude people had broken wind. This is narcissism turned against the establishment; *I'm Dancing as Fast as I Can* is narcissism as part of the establishment. The attitude is the constant.

LABOR AND BUSINESS

IT IS UNUSUAL that two films about labor appeared in the decade, more so that both were unusually good films. *Silkwood* (1983) is the tighter and more unified of the two; *Matewan* (1987) the more emotionally powerful. Both have superior actors and superior directors (Mike Nichols and John Sayles).

Silkwood is the history of a young woman's growth, of involvement with labor organization, and of managerial retribution in the nuclear industry. Karen Silkwood (Meryl Streep) is a pretty, nervous young woman, divorced with a couple of kids she never sees, and a live-in boyfriend, Drew (Kurt Russell). She is a technician at a Kerr–McGee nuclear materials laboratory where radiation "can't hurt you unless you're careless," but where the company seems to ignore its own procedures and there is a constant, low-level fear of radiation.

Silkwood's life is a blue-collar limbo. She lives in a rundown house shared with Drew and another woman, Dolly (Cher); her job is a boring dead end. None of them likes the work; there is no identification with it, no fulfillment: Dolly cleans the labs; Drew quits. "I quit. . . . I just don't give a shit." But he has an alternative, an auto-body shop. Most of the workers, especially the women, have none, and the company "owns the state."

They smoke pot and drink. After Drew has moved out and Dolly's lover has left her, Silkwood says, "Maybe we should quit—get out of here—move somewhere it's clean." But they do not; they are held by their jobs, by their horizons, by their hopelessness.

Frightened by a friend's being "cooked" (exposed to radiation), Silkwood begins to educate herself about the company and about radiation. "All that about 'acceptable levels' is bullshit." Then she is cooked; the showering and vigorous scrubbing with brushes suggest a form of torture. By the time she is cooked again, she has involved herself so deeply with the union that she is covertly copying proofs of the company's mishandling of fuel rods; also involved as a union negotiator, she finds herself rejected by the very workers she thinks she is helping. They fear for their jobs. A woman blows up at her in the cafeteria for raising safety issues rather than concentrating on wages.

By the time that Silkwood sets off a radiation alarm coming *into* the plant, it is clear that the company knows what she is doing. The film's probabilities suggest that she has been deliberately poisoned: her urine is radioactive; tests show lung contamination. Her house is torn apart by a decontamination team in strange masks and uniforms, like alien beings. Everything goes—dishes, detergents, pictures, clothes, even the wallpaper. The sequence resonates with the imagery of invasion. Drew visits the house, to find it like something long abandoned, its memory erased, its lives expunged—the company as owner of history, of truth.

Silkwood agrees to meet with a *New York Times* reporter and turn over company data. She waves to Drew and gets into her car, drives away. On the road, lights come close up behind her, and abruptly we are looking at the wreck of her car, the dead Silkwood slumped in it. Cher weeps by a headstone. "1946-1974." A title says, "A year later the plant shut down."

Streep is remarkable in evoking this sometimes flighty, even exasperating woman. The script gives her variety, and she uses it to create a complete woman. Yet, the tone is remarkably muted, for such a controversial story. As a

labor film, *Silkwood* is singularly without rhetoric; it is also without the sentimentality that so often crops up in populist films. Despite Karen Silkwood's
demonstrated courage, there is no inflated idea of heroism. The film is a singu-
lar example of realism's ability to communicate searing truth when a director is
good enough to show how a mundane way of life is more than "mere pathology"—for example, an early scene when Dolly and Silkwood go to East Texas to
see Silkwood's children. We see refineries, a landscape of clean industrial hell.
"Stinks around here," Dolly says. "That's my home. That's why I left," answers
Silkwood. And then we come to see that she left it for the Limbo of Oklahoma
and the job, for a life lived between cancer and TV. This is context.

    Matewan is more recognizably a labor film. Set in West Virginia just after
World War I, it is about the beginnings of horrendous violence that tore
through the coalfields. Its central figure, a union organizer named Joe Kenehan (Chris Cooper) is fictional; the surround is not. "The company" is unseen
but represented by "detectives"— toughs, enforcers, killers.

    The film's terms are overdone. The most visible detective, Hickey (Kevin
Tighe), is a sadistic thug. In the same way, Kenehan is too good, and a black
miner, Few Clothes (James Earl Jones) is too easily a moral center. Like the
union songs of the time, *Matewan* sentimentalizes the goodness of those on
the union side, and it turns "union"—oneness—into a racial idyll. Few Clothes
and other blacks have come as scabs, with immigrant Italians from Milan. Few
Clothes, however, breaks into a union meeting, says, "I ain't never been no
scab!", and Kenehan preaches a unity message: "This is a *worker!* We got to
work together—*together.*" They have to take in everybody. "Coloreds and
dagos?" asks a West Virginian. Everybody, is Kenehan's and the film's message.

    Evicted from their company-owned houses for striking, the union mem-
bers set up a tent village in the woods. There, blacks, Italians, and West Virginians slowly come together, their fragile unity suggested by their music,
mandolin and harmonica joining fiddle and banjo. Hickey and his goons try
to evict others from houses in the town itself, but the local policeman, Sid
(David Strathairn) prevents them, less a man fighting the company than one
defending his jurisdiction.

    These forces come finally to group violence when Sid faces the goons,
with the West Virginians backing him with rifles and shotguns. After the gun-
battle, the wounded Hickey makes his way to the yard of his boarding-house,
where Elma (Mary McDonnell)—until now a patient, silent sufferer—kills
him among the hanging washing with a shotgun. Kenehan, too, is killed in
the battle, and, when Elma bends weeping over his body, we sense that she has
loved him, although in this film individual desires have been peripheral.

    Matewan has a complex plot; there are betrayals, spies, tricks, fights. Its mes-
sage of ethnic—actually class—unity is somewhat lost in the final violence, when
the blacks and Italians stay out. It has some splendid acting (Cooper, Strathairn,
Jones, McDonnell), although no role is allowed to develop any complexity. It is

rare in showing religion as part of the texture of its characters' lives; it is rich in the sad hymns and the bagpipe-like singing of hill gospel music.

Like *Silkwood*, *Matewan* shows working people set against each other by fear. Both films show the dangerous working environment of its characters, although *Matewan* is inferior in this to *The Molly Maguires*. Both suggest company indifference to those dangers, although *Silkwood* is much better at suggesting that the indifference is not so much callousness as wishful thinking. *Matewan* puts its unionizing struggle in more accessible terms, good guys and bad guys, tolerance and hate, although that accessibility seems to come at the price of oversimplification. Neither film gives the company anything like equal time—not surprising, perhaps, in the antiunion atmosphere of the 1980s.

THE LONE BUSINESS film, *Tucker* (1988), is a bright, brisk, enjoyable work about an incurable optimist and entrepreneur who tried to bring America "the car of tomorrow—today!" Today was 1946, the car was the Tucker, and the story of how this innovative part of the consumer revolution was squashed by the automobile industry is the subject of Francis Ford Coppola's film.

As Tucker, Jeff Bridges is breezy and forceful, so convinced of his own ideas that practicality (and financing) sometimes get brushed aside. He is a salesman in love with his product, a visionary, an optimist, a madman, sometimes a liar. His conscience—or at least his superego—is Abe Karetz (Martin Landau), ex-con man, worrier. Karetz finds himself swept along in Tucker's wake: "My mother used to say, Don't get close to people, you'll catch their dreams. How was I to know—if I got too close, I'd catch your dreams." Outsider Davids taking on the Goliath of Detroit, they come up against a Michigan Senator (Lloyd Bridges) whose message is very clear: "Stay out of the car business." But they go into the car business, and they get crushed.

If seatbelts, rear engines, and headlights that turn with the steering sound ordinary, you should see *Tucker*: he tried to introduce them. If "streamlined" means nothing to you, see *Tucker*: before there were intercontinental missiles, before Sputnik, before jet travel, there was the Buck Rogers look of the Tucker car. If you have forgotten those little-guy-against-the-bosses movies of the 1930s, see *Tucker*: he takes on the auto industry and the SEC and almost makes it. And his final defeat is a victory, as all fifty of the only Tuckers to roll off the improvised assembly lines drive in convoy.

On trial for securities violations he didn't really commit, Tucker tries to make his own closing statement; when the judge tries to stop him, a juror cries, "Let the man speak! Let the man speak!" And Tucker delivers one of those speeches that we used to hear from Jimmy Stewart and Gary Cooper as simple men caught in the complexities of corporate and bureaucratic America. "Rags to riches—that's not just the name of a book. It's what this country was all about." He pleads for a nation in which innovation is possible: "One day . . . we're gonna find ourselves buying our cars and our radios from our former enemies!"

He is found not guilty. On the street, where the fifty Tuckers are surrounded by admirers, Karetz says, "Look—they love the cars, the people." And Tucker, already thinking of something new, forever hopeful, says, "It's the idea that counts, Abe. And the dream." It is as joyous in its ending as a Frank Capra film, bitterwseet but triumphant.

This is a business film about entrepreneurship, not about corporate culture. Corporate culture, the government–industrial complex, are the enemy. Tucker's workers love him; some of them work for nothing when things get tough. Set next to *Silkwood*, it seems to be about another planet. Set next to *The Right Stuff*, it again questions what we meant about individualism in America in the 1980s and what we meant about it earlier.

SPORTS

TWO SPORTS FILMS appeared in the decade. One, *Raging Bull* (1980), has been placed on the National Film Registry and therefore is something of a classic. It is, however, a long, repetitive, often monotonous film that accumulates power only if you indulge it. Dealing, like *Somebody Up There Likes Me*, with an inarticulate near-thug (Jake La Motta), it uses repetitious dialogue with paralyzing effect.

La Motta (Robert De Niro) is a brute. That is the point of the film. He is a brute as a fighter; he is a brute as a husband; he is a brute as a brother. He is jealous; he ultimately beats up his brother because he thinks there is something going on with his wife. "You fuckin' wacko. You crackin' up!" the brother (Joe Pesci) says. But all La Motta knows is brutality; at the end of a punishing beating by Sugar Ray Robinson, at the end of his career, he says, "I never went down, Ray. I never went down."

There is a question as to how compelling a film centered on a sexist, inarticulate, brutal peasant can be. That question is made more acute by the film's hermetic concern: La Motta. There is no context; despite a bit of hackneyed Italian–Mafioso–neighborhood-don stuff, the subject is entirely La Motta. De Niro's performance is stunning, but it is stunning in ways that may be irrelevant to public performance. Introverted, subverbal, meticulous, slow, it is a demonstration of fine acting without being a fine dramatic performance.

In the 1840s, Dickens's Mister Crummles bought a pump and a tub to lend realism to his theatricals, advertising the innovations with bills that proclaimed "Real Pump! Real Tubs!" Some of the early attention given to *Raging Bull* concentrated on De Niro's having put on extra poundage for the film's final sequences: *Real Fat!* It is also, perhaps, real history, but of so small a compass that it tells us nothing—the apotheosis of American realism.

Eight Men Out (1988) dealt with the Black Sox baseball scandal of 1919. The director (John Sayles) seems to have made a fatal error in casting four or five young actors who are difficult if not impossible to tell apart; their similarities are emphasized by their wearing uniforms and performing many of the same tasks. The film has no center, and thus its group protagonist seems uninteresting.

David Strathairn stands out as Eddie Cicotte, partly because he doesn't look like the others. Michael Lerner is an interesting Arnold Rothstein, although the role leads to nothing; Clifton James is old and fat as the Sox' owner, Comiskey, implying perhaps an age–youth antipathy, but nothing much comes of that, either. John Anderson appears in the late stages as Kenesaw Mountain Landis, first baseball czar; it is mentioned in passing that he had something to do with "cleaning out the Reds" during the war, but nothing is made of that, either. This is a pity, because at this point *Eight Men Out* seems to promise something other than tunnel history (i.e., What do the national pastime and red-baiting have in common?).

If you love baseball, *Eight Men Out* may have some transitory interest. However, it keeps picking other subjects up and dropping them—corruption at the top mirroring corruption at the bottom, rich owners and underpaid players, love of the game and love of camaraderie and love of money. Sayles's apparent dislike for strong dramatic centers showed in *Matewan* but did not destroy the film; here, it does.

SEVERAL NEW THINGS were going on in the 1980s. For example, Richard Nixon is a character in *Where the Buffalo Roam*—in a men's-room scene ("Fuck the [little people]!"), as a rubber mask worn by Peter Boyle, and as a dummy that Thompson's Doberman is trained to bite in the crotch. John Kennedy appears in news footage used in *The Right Stuff* and also seems to interact with one of the characters. Lyndon Johnson (as vice president) is a comic character in the same film. Ronald Reagan appears on television at the end of *Walker*. The references are both immediate and, usually, disrespectful.

The labor and business films, combined with *The Right Stuff* and the presentations of working-class life in *Coal Miner's Daughter* and *Sweet Dreams*, suggest a new interest in questions of work, class, corporate culture, and individualism. The films do not resolve the questions; rather, they explore them from several points of view, possibly as responses to newly dominant conservatism. A few films, by contrast, concentrate on affluence and seem to accept narcissism as a kind of ethos.

Historical context seems more visible in some films than formerly. *Walker* and *Reds* tried new styles to get at it; *Raging Bull* pulled back into an extreme example of an old one. *Heaven's Gate* used saturated period imagery. Style, these films suggested, is related to the matter of presenting historical context, although they offered no clear explanation of how.

The repeated interest in individualism suggests that it was perceived as under attack, in the examples given by both internal narcissism and external collectivism; the matter was certainly not resolved.

CHAPTER 10

1990–1996: WORLD WITHOUT AWE, AMEN

The 1990s included the five hundredth anniversary of Columbus's first voyage. It is only a little surprising, therefore, that two films were made about the event, but a little surprising in that only one had been made for the bicentennial of the Declaration of Independence. At least neither was a musical.

Christopher Columbus—The Discovery (1992) has a piety and an unreality that suggest it was actually written by the sodality for the sixth-grade play. Paper-thin characterization, archaic Catholicism, stodgy direction—it might as well be Selig's 1912 *Coming of Columbus* with color stock. Marlon Brando is in there somewhere as Torquemada. Columbus is escorted to him through a torture gallery that recalls both Charlton Heston's in *The Three Musketeers* and Monty Python's soft pillow torture. When found, Brando seems asleep, as who can blame him? It is not that he cannot illuminate a film with a brief appearance (see *A Dry White Season*, for example), but he must have something to work with. Here, there is nothing.

1492: The Conquest of Paradise (1992), on the other hand, is a beautifully mounted film with remarkable spectacle and a bewildering babel of accents and acting styles. Inside this cacophony is a good film struggling to get out, but it is swathed in overproduction and internationalism. It is often difficult, for example, to know where we are, not least because set dressing has gone mad with detail: in order to have a brief scene with his son, Columbus (Gérard Dépardieu) crosses a courtyard that is so visually demanding that one wants to know what it is trying to tell us—but it is merely a courtyard. So, too, with a scene in which Columbus watches witches being burned at the stake; the scene becomes about witch-burning, not Columbus. And so does scene after scene become about something else—beautiful tendencies, spectacular distractions. The story is pretty much the usual one; the result is more or less the one we have seen back to 1912, although this one has far more awareness of the downside of discovery. Taken together, the Columbus films suggest that the point of attack is wrong, almost certainly too early; the story is in the new world, not the old, however much traditional piety values Isabella and Spain; the voyage and near-mutiny are mere melodrama. Probably, the story should be told from the Native American viewpoint.

The Last of the Mohicans (1992) also came around again, graced this time with not only Native American actors in small roles but also the Native American activist, Russell Means, as Chingachgook. This casting presumably lent authenticity, and indeed, the film is an ethnological treat, handsome and in most cases authentic, although I have doubts about a Huron village, and the canoes look like leftovers from the 1936 version.

It is not the Indians whose identity is at risk in this film, however, but the whites. Cooper had something in mind in creating Natty Bumppo as he did, in giving him that funny name (sounds like bumpkin) and that funny speech pattern, and in making him no longer young. Among other things, these qualities gave Bumppo a past and a future; they identified him with nature and with America, and they made him noble in a way we no longer much honor. He was also distinctly rural and lower-class Yankee.

In 1992, however, Natty Bumppo has become Nathanael Poe (Daniel Day-Lewis). In the age of the nose job, why not a name job? A perfect yuppie, he has gone to daycare with the Mohicans and then to Dartmouth (called "Dr. Wheelock's school" here with pedantic accuracy), and now he has come back to live with his surrogate dad in the woods. Long haired, gorgeous, and mostly nonverbal, he is a perpetual late adolescent who seems about to say "no problem" to any moral quibble that approaches him. Whatever.

Nat Poe and his friends live in a land of perpetual summer where the rain never falls and the hillsides are covered with rhododendrons. To be sure, both Day-Lewis and rhododendrons are exotics in the Adirondack foothills, but both photograph handsomely. The rhododendrons and Nat epitomize the film: beautiful visuals, dramatic dreck; splendid cinema, laughable history.

This is also the workout version of *The Last of the Mohicans*; everybody looks in such terrific shape, especially Day-Lewis, that you expect to see their personal trainers peeping around the trees. The film begins wonderfully with Day-Lewis running and running through the woods, joining Chingachgook, then Uncas, and finally running down a buck and shooting it. This is arguably the best sequence in the film.

However, when Major Heyward (Steven Waddington) appears, we are back in the us/them, laid-back/uptight dichotomies of the 1936 film—and indeed, this one credits its predescessor's script. Waddington is remarkably good in an ultimately thankless role as a foil for Poe: the beautiful Cora (Madeleine Stowe) turns him down (for Poe); he gets burned at the stake and shot as an act of mercy (by Poe). Waddington soldiers through all this manfully, nonetheless, giving us a rather foolish, not awfully pretty, extremely brave, fuddled British officer.

As in 1936, there is an entirely made-up, ahistorical tiff between the colonials and the English about fighting for the Crown. These colonials act like draftees and don't look as if they've ever heard of militia or train bands or drill. They are, it appears, *frontiersmen*, and they don't care about the Crown, so there. The real colonials at this 1757 battle were mostly Massachusetts farmers, of course, and were contract troops under provincial officers, although not without distaste for the regulars.[1] Cooper's apolitical novel has again been twisted to be about American independence, although this version does not drive, as the 1936 one did, toward British–American unity against a common enemy. In 1992, there is no common enemy—itself a bit of historical evidence, perhaps.

The film pretty much follows the 1936 plot to its conclusion, although it eliminates Colonel Munro (Magua cuts his heart out), Heyward, Uncas (killed by Magua), Alice (suicide), and Magua himself (killed by Chingachgook with an enormous war club). To do so, it again savages geography (how do you get to Huronia from Glens Falls in one day?) and trashes probability (wet gunpowder is a big issue in one scene; in the next, everyody's powder is dry). It also gets hokey in the way of action movies: Nathanael kills two Hurons with two simultaneous muskets, one in each hand. It also mutes the Uncas–Alice subplot, switches the women's names back to Cooper's, and erases Cora's descent from "the daughter of a gentleman" of the West Indies who was "descended remotely [from] that unfortunate class who are so basely enslaved."

Nonetheless, this *The Last of the Mohicans* has some powerful virtues. Wes Studi is a splendid Magua, so passionate that he makes Nathanael seem a wimp. Consumed by hatred, physically powerful, mature, he dominates much of the film. As well, the physical production is often superb. No fringed buckskin makes an appearance. Costumes and material culture are mostly correct. The battle scenes are excellent. Considered as a film about American history, then, *The Last of the Mohicans* is an intellectual dud but a visual winner. Considered as a version of Cooper, it's a laugher. Considered as a film about Native Americans, it puzzles, precisely because of changes from Cooper that tilt the film toward Magua, so that what we seem to have is a reversion to the Native American as demon; on the other hand, we have Native American actors and somewhat accurate ethnology. Arguably, the film may represent a maturing of Native American representation, but the presence of actors like Means and the erasure of Alice's African–American genes suggest a wish not to risk offense.

THOSE PERIOD FILMS aside, the remaining films that deal with what I have been calling "traditional history" are all about the 1960s and 1970s. Significantly, the categorization itself has become almost meaningless: although all are about men, one is about a radically antiestablishment black man, another is about a violently antiestablishment union leader, and in the third the establishment hero is demystified.

Hoffa (1992) tried to place Jimmy Hoffa in the history of the 1960s and 1970s. To do so, the director (Danny DeVito) used a frame and flashbacks; the frame comprises the invented events of the day when Hoffa disappeared;

the flashbacks range from Hoffa's early career as an organizer almost to the frame itself. DeVito cast himself as Bobby, a confidant and bodyguard, and Jack Nicholson as Hoffa.

The resulting film is complex and visually rich but oddly short on character. Neither Hoffa nor Bobby seems to exist outside the world of power. Almost by accident, we learn that Hoffa has a loving wife, then grandchildren; Bobby is seen with a couple of hookers. But private life and its potential for revealing character are missing. We are given incidents and acts, placed in time by elements of historical capital (Khruschev, Christian Herter); some are dramatic in themselves, some violent. But they never quite engage us. The film is like reading an encyclopedia entry on "Hoffa, James": we learn everything—and nothing.

Three narrative lines concern DeVito: Hoffa's genuine commitment to working people and the union; Hoffa's deals with Italian–American organized crime; and Hoffa's hatred of the Kennedys, and theirs of him. The union scenes are done with scope, and a march that turns into a bloodbath watched by company executives from the safety of an office building is excellent. So is the change in imagery as Hoffa builds the Teamsters Union and its wealth until, surrounded by Las Vegas-style glitz, on a stage hung with gold curtains, flags, and a huge photo of Hoffa, he tells a cheering teamsters convention, "We have led the working man into the middle class, and we intend to stay there!"

This scene—convincing and historically important because it raises questions about both the democratization of American culture and resistance to it—is not very well integrated with the gangster and Kennedy lines. Hoffa's deal with an Italian gangster, d'Allesandro, has union drivers taking half their trucks to mob warehouses to be robbed. If this is an example of the price paid to bring the working man into the middle class, we should see some attempt to wrestle with the question of whether or not it was worth it, and, more importantly, of what Hoffa went through in reaching it. Instead, we see results—investigations, more involvement with crime, enrichment of the union.

The Kennedy line is a fascinating one but is inadequately explored. We see a young and fairly inept Bobby Kennedy try to take Hoffa through congressional testimony; Hoffa blows him away. Privately, Hoffa calls Bobby Kennedy a "little fuck born with a dick in his mouth" whose attacks are "union-busting." Later, he insults Kennedy in his office, unawed by the name or the power. It is one of the best scenes in the film, one of the times when Hoffa comes alive and seems admirable for his guts, and we wait to see his contempt for the Kennedys justified—were they the agents of wealth, seeking revenge on the man who brought working people into the middle class? Were they really union busters? Was their unthinking anticommunism also antilaborism? Was their hatred of Hoffa based in class? But we get nothing.

Ultimately, the frame becomes the murder of Hoffa and Bobby by a hit man. The last we see of them, their bodies lie in a car that is driven into a sixteen-wheeler that disappears into the sunset. Hoffa has apparently been killed by the criminals with whom he once made deals. Perhaps this is what happened. But missing is the deeper question of cause, obscured by the emphases of a narrative film that relies too much on cliché pictures of Italian–American crime and of violence. DeVito and scriptwriter David Mamet were insightful in looking at the convergence of Hoffa and the Kennedys, but they obscured that insight with too much obeisance to Hollywood's habitual violence. It as if DeVito took as a given that Hoffa was an amoralist for whom ends justified means, when what his film cries out for is an examination of that very idea.

Malcolm X (1992), by contrast, is a stunning examination of a moral life—that of the man who died as Malcolm X. Spike Lee has directed it to concentrate maximum visual attention on elements that become symbols of Malcolm's intellectual and spiritual progression: clothing, from zoot suit to the dress of a *haj*; hair, from the lye-straightened hairdo of his youth to the sparse, natural hair of his maturity; weapons, skin colors, backgrounds. At the same time, the film is more attentive than most biographies to intellectual statement, and there is some conflict between the visual potency, especially of the early scenes, and the verbal content of the later part.

Lee himself is an actor in the early sequences about Malcolm's youth in Boston. Malcolm (Denzel Washington) swaggers through Boston with him in a powder-blue zoot suit and broad hat with an enormous feather. These scenes are visually exciting; they would be counterproductive—too pleasing—if not for brief flashbacks to Malcolm's childhood. His Garveyite father defies the Klan in Nebraska; their house is burned, his father murdered; his mother "hated [her] white complexion, her white blood." The family was broken up. "We were parceled out . . . [made] invisible. . . ." A white teacher tells him, "You're a nigger, and [being] a lawyer isn't realistic for a nigger."

Still in his zoot suit phase, Malcolm has a white girlfriend. He moves up by becoming a numbers runner, starts doing drugs, falls out with his black-gangster mentor and becomes a mean, mocking, self-destructive hood. Arrested for robbery, he is sentenced to ten years at hard labor. Prison is an experience of spiritual change. He meets Baines, a follower of Elijah Muhammad. "What makes you ashamed of what you are? What makes you ashamed of being black? Putting all this poison in your hair, in your body. . . . The white man sees you and laughs!" Baines warns him against the white man's "smoke, his liquor, his woman, pork. . . . God is black. . . . You've got to take everything the white man says and use it against him. . . . If you take one step toward Allah, he will take two steps toward you." Malcolm has a vision of Elijah Muhammad; then, freed from prison, he meets Elijah Muhammad and weeps.

Lee now shows the evolution of the Malcolm most whites recognize, into the stern, thin man in the dark-rimmed glasses, white shirt, and tie. He exercises military discipline over the Fruit of Islam. He meets a Muslim woman and, as he moves up within Elijah Muhammad's hierarchy, they marry. The idea of womanhood that is offered here is a difficult one—her head covered, her mind on having babies, submissive. It is made more so by a sign at a Muslim meeting, "We Must Protect Our Most Valuable Property—Our Women." This antifeminism is played, however, against earlier scenes of the despairing descent of black women into prostitution.

Malcolm becomes a national presence. He is humorless, dedicated, tough. Lee has directed this sequence as a series of public meetings in which the halls get larger, the audiences bigger and more attentive, noisier and noisier; the audiences are all black but segregated by sex, men and women wearing different colored clothes. Baines warns Elijah Muhammad that "the ministers" think Malcolm is "of great benefit to himself."

Inevitably, Malcolm's growth collides with limitations others want to put on him. Baines has been lining his own pocket and tells him, "One hand washes the other." Elijah Muhammad has had affairs with two former secretaries and justifies himself by saying, "I must plant my seed in fertile soil." Malcolm violates an order to be silent about the assassination of JFK and instead says, "The seeds of violence" planted by whites have become weeds that "have choked one of their own best gardeners . . . . I say it's justice." Elijah Muhammad orders him to be silent for ninety days, and Malcolm leaves the Nation of Islam. "I speak my own words, I think my own thoughts."

His progression now becomes, again, a spiritual one. He goes to Mecca. "I no longer subscribe to sweeping indictments of one race. . . . I am not a racist. . . . The true practice of Islam can remove the cancer of racism. . . ." The change makes him a threat; his house is fire-bombed; black men are shown loading guns. Whites eavesdrop electronically as he says that his enemies are not only in the Nation of Islam. His assassination is less interesting visually than the rest of the film because we seem to have seen it so many times; the "seeds of violence" have sprouted too often in film.

The film ends with a sequence in an African school, a teacher telling children about Malcolm. He should not be read out of black history, is the message. "Malcolm is our manhood—our living black manhood . . . our own black shining prince, who didn't hesitate to die because he loved us so." The teacher turns into Nelson Mandela.

Malcolm X is not flawless. It may be guilty of too much compression, of over-simplification, of too much editing of Malcolm's words.[2] Yet its seriousness speaks for its importance. To see it, and then to think of a film like *Mississippi Burning*, is to understand how much better it is than any white-centered, exploitative, white-accessible film about race can ever be.

So much so that, by contrast, *Apollo 13* (1995) seems to be a kind of sitcom about a lot of white guys. There is one black face fleetingly present late in the film, that of a newsman (in this film, by definition an outsider). Other than that, this is America as the Land of the Bleached. Malcolm had been dead only five years when *Apollo 13*'s events took place; where is the black America he addressed so vigorously?

The film begins with horn music, more than a little reminiscent of other recent space movies. Tom Hanks is Lovell, the astronaut, waiting to make his moon-walk and hosting a moon party as Walter Cronkite recalls "serious doubts that we could beat the Russians to the moon," but "Armstrong is on the moon." Alone in his garden, Hanks looks at the moon. "Christopher Columbus and Charles Lindbergh and Neil Armstrong," he says. The statement is a key to director Ron Howard's misunderstanding of what his reverence for NASA means. *The Right Stuff* saw it more clearly— Columbus and Lindbergh and Chuck Yeager. Indeed, although *Apollo 13* seems to take up where *The Right Stuff* left off, it takes up with no memory of the point that *The Right Stuff* made about the corporate culture of the space program. This lapse seems hunky-dory with Howard, who is as happy with tunnel history as a kid with a new computer game. Context? What's context? Vietnam? Riots? Individualism? Jimmy Hoffa? Lenny Bruce? Martin Luther King? Betty Friedan? Politics?

Apollo 13 is a strong narrative film, beautifully made, with a surefire plot: three presold heroes head for the moon and their spacecraft goes bad. Can they make it back to earth before their air becomes unbreathable? Howard uses three principal settings to tell this story—the spacecraft, mission control, and Lovell's house in Houston. All are clean and modern. The spacecraft and mission control are high-tech; the house is pretty, livable, low-tech, an environment for love and family.

The accident is an intrusion into all this. It messes up the spacecraft; it disturbs the regimented rows of mission control lookalikes; it brings anxiety into the home. Still, nobody in mission control loosens his tie or dares wear a colored shirt. Ed Harris, as Krantz, the honcho of mission control, is as rigid and flinty as an FBI man. When, at the film's triumphant end, his personal mission control slips and tears come to his eyes, it is as if one of the faces on Mount Rushmore wept.

The ending, of course, is a happy one. Everybody gets back safely; technology has triumphed, thanks to the grounded astronaut, Mattingly (Gary Sinese) and a team who figure out how the stranded trio can improvise an air filter from materials in the capsule. Lovell will not get to the moon, but, as Hanks's voice tells us at the end, he can see other landings "all from the confines of mission control and our house in Houston."

Apollo 13 is a feel-good movie for true believers. Anybody who questions military–industrial culture, jingoistic techno-fest, or conformism is not supposed to be in the audience. Set at the moral level of the Longfellow-inspired films of the teens, it posits an America without context, an America of "mission control and our house in Houston." Like the 1992 *Last of the Mohicans*, it assumes an America defined by affluent white life in the 1990s, classless only in that it will not look at questions of class, racially calm in that it shuts out reminders of racial unrest. The Americans of *Apollo 13* have given up their individuality for a large enterprise, and this has to be a Good Thing. By implication, so have (or should) the Americans of the 1990s—but what is the Good Thing in the 1990s? the free market economy? endless suburbia, America as our house in Houston?

Hoffa and *Malcolm X* show Americas of diversity and tension. *Matewan* shows an older America where a large enterprise, unionization, could overcome diversity and unify Americans, but without turning them into droids. *Silkwood* shows an America of workers caught between poverty and poison, and of management—in a high-tech atmosphere rather like that of *Apollo 13*—who have given up their ethical individuality to an enterprise that causes them to do unjust things in the name of the enterprise. Imperfect as those films are, they offer better images of America than *Apollo 13*'s bleached, bland, virtually interchangeable white guys, an America full of people without a past or a history, living in an endless suburb of body and mind.

And that is why, in a deep sense, *Apollo 13* seems to me the most anti-American film since *I Was a Communist for the FBI*.

JFK (1991) and *Nixon* (1995) were directed by the same man (Oliver Stone) and have in common the American presidency and an acrid sense of recent history. They are very different films, however, one rabble-rousing and foolish, the other almost Shakespearean.

JFK should have been written by Molière. It has at its center an essentially comic character of the kind Molière specialized in, the obsessive for whom reality exists only in terms of the obsession. One thinks of Orgon, obsessed with Tartuffe; when the maid tries to tell him about problems in his family, he can only say, to each new bit of disaster, *Et Tartuffe?* So it is with Stone's Jim Garrison (Kevin Costner), whose obsession with a conspiracy theory of the murder of John Kennedy spirals up and up and out and out and is made finally to encompass the universe.

Behind Stone's notion (it cannot be called a theory) is an apparent conviction that if the charismatic but lightweight Kennedy had lived, the world would be a different place. There is no good evidence that he would have been any less bellicose than his successors, some evidence that he might have been more so. Can a historian argue persuasively that Kennedy's death had as much lasting impact as Johnson's decision not to run again, or Nixon's resignation? Stone, evidently, would so argue, and much of the momentum of his conspiracy-building depends on that argument.

Kostner simply hasn't the abilities to carry the role of the New Orleans district attorney. Tommy Lee Jones, on the other hand, is remarkably effective as his principal target, Clay Shaw, whom Garrison went after for years and finally took to trial, only to lose. Between Garrison's first suspicions and that trial, Stone takes us through a bewildering and numbing parade of "evidence"—the amateur assasination film; reenactments of the killing; fictionalized statements; meetings in which Garrison's assistants rattle off suspicions, rumors, hints, connections between the unconnected. This notion-building is hyped by Garrison's increasing obsession: "What's that old saying? Once ONI, always ONI?" (As a one-time munchkin in naval intelligence, I must admit I never heard this old saying.) "Doesn't add up, does it?" "We don't know if he's CIA. Call him Oswald's handler." "You gotta think on a different level, like the CIA does. . . . White is black—and black is white." "Can't you *see?*"

He is abetted by equally obsessed, perhaps nutty types like "X" (Donald Sutherland), a "black ops" person who says, "That sound to you like a coincidence, Mister Garrison?" "Those of us who had been in [intel] since the beginning knew that the Warren Commission report was fiction." "Why was Kennedy killed—who benefited. . . ? Bell Helicopter . . . and General Dynamics of Fort Worth, Texas!"

Garrison replies, "The size of this is beyond me." He's right.

Stone abets this silliness with footage that often looks like documentary or hand-held camera-work, both black-and-white and overexposed color. This manipulation of signs and audience expectations lends a spurious authenticity to speculation. It is the equivalent of offering invented data as evidence in print.[3]

Kostner's Garrison is unaffected by the not-guilty verdict on Shaw, which says, in effect, that a jury does not believe his elaborate and boringly enunciated conspiracy theory. He does not say, "I guess I was wrong." Rather, Stone leaves us with more notion: "Dedicated to the young in whose spirit the search for truth goes on." *Et Tartuffe?*

Nixon is another kettle of fish. The level of acting in most cases is several notches higher, and Anthony Hopkins's Richard Nixon is a brilliant, a dazzling performance. It is complex, varied, subtle; it ranges from rage to near-madness to gnawing unhappiness. Whatever one thinks of Nixon, Hopkins's portrayal is so good that one feels, if not sympathy, at least understanding, and a kind of infuriated pity.

Stone uses the same filmic devices as in *JFK.* (They appear to be what Henry Kissinger objected to as "the triumph of technique over substance.")[4] This is a detailed portrait, and the first film since *Wilson* to go inside the White House to study a recent president in great depth. None of the old awe is here—no showing the president only from the back, no seeing him as a marble bust.

A title tells us that *Nixon* is a "dramatic intepretation of events and characters based on public sources and an incomplete historical record." Some of those sources are the White House tapes, with the result that some of the dialogue is direct quotation and much of the rest sounds like it. Indeed, one can fault the film for not distinguishing between the two, although to do so is to put on a requirement that has been made of no other film.

Beginning with the Watergate break-in, *Nixon* tracks back and forth from Nixon's childhood to the Cambodian incursion to his college days to his resignation. It includes most of the horrors that we associate with the Nixon White House—misuse of the FBI and the CIA, wiretapping, the plumbers, paranoia, abuse of the Constitution. But it also includes a psychological, even a poetic, analysis of Nixon—his lifelong oppression by his mother's rigidity, his social unease, his self-pity, his dreaming, his desire. We see him sober, drunk, weeping, falsely smiling, triumphant, defeated. We see him make the terrible journey from the run against Helen Gahagan Douglass to that final helicopter ride, and Hopkins is so good that you want to say to this pathetic, apalling man, Get off the horse; do less; be happy. But, of course, he could not.

Joan Allen is superb as Pat Nixon. You learn a lot from her portrayal—a woman of great courage, great understanding, surely a larger person than her husband. Toward the end, she comes to him as he stands in front of a portrait of Kennedy. It is night. He has been weeping; he has just signed his letter of resignation. "I'm so afraid," he says. "It's dark . . . I've always been afraid of the dark. . . ." They walk away, leaning on each other. Much of the emotional depth of the scene comes from her presence; because of what she has been up to this point, she lends his self-pity dignity, in a sense authenticates it for us.

Stone has caused his Nixon to say some things for the benefit of the little microphone attached to his desk. In the famous exchange when John Dean says, "There's a cancer on the presidency," this Nixon is playing for the tapes when he sends Dean to do a thorough investigation and when he says, "That stuff I don't know." This bit of direction, too, is speculation that is offered as truth.

Other scenes are apparently fiction. Late in the film, in a brilliantly conceived sequence, Nixon and Pat sit at dinner at opposite ends of a long table. When she begins to question him, he rings a handbell; the sound cuts through her words. A servant appears. "Mrs. Nixon's finished," Nixon says. The words seem to have a double meaning; the first-level one is so rude a dismissal that it shocks. The servant takes the plate away. Leaving the room, Pat says to him, "Dick, sometimes I understand why they hate you." Can this have happened? Can he have been that awful, she that brave? Yes, probably.

Some scenes are part of the Nixon legend. Just before the end, he is with Kissinger; he is irrational. "You're the only friend I got, Henry." (He has earlier had Kissinger's telephone bugged.) He gets on his knees and causes Kissinger to do the same. "Let's pray, Henry. Don't be too proud, Henry." He weeps. "How can a country come apart like this? What have I done wrong. . . ? Why do they hate me so? It's unbelievable—it's insane—Oh, Mom!" His voice tails off in a garble of sobs and half-words.

"Hate" and "love" are important words. He is a man who wants love. The specter of the love-denying mother haunts him: "I have to see this through. Mother would have expected no less of me." He apparently sees votes as a kind of love but is himself unlovable, partly because he is himself so filled with hate. "It's not the war, it's Nixon!" he cries. "It's not Vietnam—!" He rails at "the elite—top chicken-shit faggots!" It is Pat who sees his terrible truth. "You want *them* to love you. They never will, Dick. No matter how many elections you win, *they* never will." Late in the film, Alexander Haig says, "Can you imagine what this man would have been had he ever been loved?"

But Pat has loved him; so have his daughters. It is not enough.

Nixon can perhaps be faulted for including too much. Stone hints at something connected with Cuba that frightens Nixon—perhaps some complicity in Kennedy's death—that seems extraneous; scenes with an obviously gay Hoover (Bob Hoskins) are irresponsible. Nonetheless, length and inclusivenes are in good part what make the film so powerful. *Nixon* is undoubtedly the best film ever made about an American political figure—because of Hopkins's performance, a political *Patton*.

THE 1990S WESTERNS are a sorry lot, the one Native American film hardly better. *Wild Bill* (1995) is yet another look at Hickok (Jeff Bridges), meandering through the usual territory but also dragging in opium dens and dreams. It is an attempt to solve the questions of Hickok's violent character by looking at his violence, rather than his character; it thus becomes about the violence, another shoot'em-up. *Geronimo* (1993) was directed by the same man (Walter Hill, who had also done *The Long Riders*) to little effect. Modern dialogue ("The Apaches are *special*") hurts the often arresting cinematography. The film fragments into disconnected sequences, probably from trying to include too much (also a problem in *Wild Bill*). The nominal point is to show the Army's sympathy for Geronimo and the justification for Geronimo's rebelliousness, but the amount of violence, as in Hill's other films, suggests that it is the real reason for being.

Most of the labor, gangster, and show-biz films were mundane. *Newsies* (1992) was a kind of musical about a newspaper boys' strike that was less enlightening than *Fighting Father Dunne* (1948). The music of *Newsies* was deadly, the dancing derivative, the plot superficial. As a prolabor film, it had all the courage of a monarchist shouting invective at a statue of Napoleon. *The Babe* (1992) was a more careful look at Babe Ruth than he got in the 1948 *Babe Ruth Story*, but the principal difference was really one of changed mores: now, he can break wind, say four-letter words, and have sex. *Mobsters* (1991) was a dreadful attempt to draw more blood from the corpse of the Italian–American mob movie. *Chaplin* (1992) was another failure to film genius, the result unenlightening.

Ed Wood (1995), on the other hand, was a successful attempt to film a few years in the life of a man once voted the worst director of all time. Perhaps the selection freed director Tim Burton from the burden of adulation; certainly, he made a fresh, amusing, likable film that is the antithesis of *Chaplin's* tedium.

There is usually a line between parody and the thing parodied. This film has a terrible time finding it. It may be just as well; the rather off-the-cuff look of *Ed Wood* both hints at Wood's terrible movies and lets Burton work freely. Wood (Johnny Depp) is an utterly dedicated would-be director who happens to like to wear women's clothes, including those of his live-in girl friend (Sarah Jessica Parker). When he finds a producer of exploitation flicks planning a film on Christine Jorgenson, he offers himself as director. "You a fruit?" says the vulgarian. "No! I love women. . . . I even paratrooped [in World War II] wearing a brassiere and panties." Depp says this with a chipper smile and a tilt of the head. His Wood is entirely likable—and, you realize, entirely untalented.

The film has opened with typical items from the Ed Wood *oeuvre*—horror-movie music, a casket, a plastic octopus, flying saucers. It is no surprise when Wood passes an undertaker's and realizes that he is staring through the window at Bela Lugosi (Martin Landau), who appears to be trying out a coffin. Wood accosts him on the street. "I'm just an ex-bogeyman," says Lugosi.

Landau's Lugosi is a great creation. Looking sometimes like Raymond Massey, Landau is wonderful as a confused, sometimes witty, bitter old man. He is thoughtful: "The pure horror both repels and attracts [women] because in their collective unconscious, they have the agony of childbirth." He is outrageous: of Karloff, he cries, "That limey cocksucker!" He is pathetic: he calls Wood in the middle of the night. "Eddie—help me—." He has collapsed, a syringe and tubing next to him. The needle tracks on his arms look like monster makeup. "Bela—what's in the needle?" "Morphine. With a Demarol chaser." The old bogeyman and the young director forge a curious relationship, part buddies, part father and son. Lugosi appears in a Wood film. It is worth the price of admission to watch him wrestle with the plastic octopus.

Wood is joyous in his badness. Lack of talent in fact liberates him; he doesn't care about polish, surface, technical proficiency, hence doesn't care about cost. Getting it on film is everything. When a grip says, "Don't you want a second take, for protection?" Ed Wood wrinkles his brow, says with that sweet smile, "What's to protect? It was perfect!"

Burton has directed this with slyness and something like love. The black-and-white film stock recalls Wood's movies. The women in the film look like women in Ed Wood films; the sets have some of the underdecorated look of his sets. Certain sequences are echoes of Ed Wood sequences: at the cast party to celebrate the completion of a film, Ed appears in bra, panties, and a denture he removes. His girl, now angry with him for having given her role to another, shouts at the crowd. She is standing in front of a room hung with beef carcasses (the backer is a butcher). The peculiar setting, Ed's getup, and her reading of the scene suggest all those movies in which an ingenue tries to warn the kids about the monster that is about to destroy them. "You people are *crazy*! These movies are shit! Terrible! You're wasting your life making *shit*!"

Yet other aspects of *Ed Wood* question the ideas of "good" and "bad" art. Lugosi is a distorted validation of Ed's idea of himself as a director: if Bela Lugosi is in the film, can it really be shit? Ed runs into Orson Welles in a bar—a sequence treated as reality, but surely not. Welles talks to him as one great artist to another. "Ed—visions are worth fighting for. Why spend your life making someone else's dreams?"

Lugosi dies. Ed had shot a home movie of Lugosi, only a few seconds, Lugosi looking at the sky, smelling a flower; now, he incorporates this into a new movie, suggesting that Wood has the artist's ruthlessness; art comes before everything, even grief. But Wood is not an artist—is he? "This is the one! This is the one I'll be remembered for!" Ed burbles. He finds a dentist to do the rest of Lugosi's scenes, thus bringing Bela back—"like Dracula." The film is *Plan Nine from Outer Space*. It is, indeed, the one he is remembered for.

Ed Wood is a "postmodern" movie. It jumbles genres, mixes seriousness and farce, history and camp. It has two splendid performances, Depp's and Landau's. It takes itself frivolously, unlike the lugubrious *Chaplin*. It asks a new question: What is the relation between talent and art? It both asks and answers a related question, What is important about the worst director who ever lived? *Ed Wood* does not give the answer; it is the answer. It turns its back on success as a criterion—no Carnegie Hall concert, no Ziegfeld telephone call—and looks at a man who was utterly dedicated, inventive in his own way, ruthless in the name of the artistic product, and—a failure?

FINALLY, OF THE few films that dealt with the ordinary and the disempowered, only *Quiz Show* deserves more than passing interest. *Swoon* (1992) was a gay film that outed Leopold and Loeb (surprise!), already the subject of several mostly fictional films (*Rope, Compulsion*). Full of gay in-jokes, avant-garde in a derrière-garde way, it quickly wears out its welcome. The film may, in fact, offer a different contextual view of Leopold and Loeb and their murder, but its style is so precious that the points are not very accessible ones.

Quiz Show (1994) was another look back at the 1950s, this time at a scandal that brought a man named Charles Van Doren brief notoriety. The Van Doren name and elitist aura are important to the film: Carl, Pulitzer Prize winner, literary critic; Mark, poet, novelist, critic; both former literary editors of *The Nation*. It seems odd, therefore, that the director, Robert Redford, chose to communicate the date of his film's action (1957) with such elements of popular culture as "Mack the Knife," a car, and Sputnik but not anything from nonelitist literary culture—*Howl* or *On the Road,* for example.

A television quiz show called "Twenty-One" has a long-running winner whom the producers want to get rid of because he is "an annoying Jewish guy with a sidewall haircut." Played with wonderful nerdishness by John Turturro, Herbert Stempel is a smart but self-deluded jerk who thinks he's a wit. He's also lower-middle-class—and Jewish. The TV executives want to replace him with a good-looking WASP.

Ralph Fiennes is the good-looking WASP—Charles Van Doren. A Columbia University lecturer like his father, Mark, the younger Van Doren lives in an anglophilic world of tweed, books, polished wood, private clubs, and cleverness. He is a setup for the crooked quiz show. Why, is unclear. Vanity? Greed? There is a hint of desperation in some of Fiennes's playing of him, as if he fears or knows that under his handsome hair there is not a mind equal to that of his father or his uncle. There is also a hint of symbolic patricide, although the idea is never carried further—one of several motivations hinted at and then left to lie there.

When the producers lift the shell a bit to let Van Doren have a glimpse of the pea of truth—that "contestants" in fact know the questions in advance—he is hesitant. "I'm just trying to imagine what Kant would make of this. . . . It just doesn't seem right. I'd have to say no." But put a little differently, he can say yes: at a crucial moment on the show, when he is closed into his isolation booth, they toss him a fat one. And he, instead of saying, "I'm sorry, I had this question in a practice round," goes with it. And he's hooked.

Stempel is outraged, because he saw himself as an incipient television star. "Why now? What did I do?" he says, wrinkling his nose and pushing his glasses up his face. To his wife, he says bitterly, "Watch Charles Van Doren eat his first kosher meal. . . . They can put me in an isolation booth and pump in cyanide." Van Doren is now "the egghead turned national hero." His lecture hall is full; undergraduates look at him with adoration. And he is not above delaying his entrance until he has a big audience—a suggestion of mere vanity that gives Redford another possible answer to the question of motive.

"That big uncircumcised shmuck is on the cover of *Time* magazine!" Stempel rages. "That should be me on the cover of *Time!*" He's broke and wants the television producers to get him something, but they won't help him. He's yesterday. So he goes to the district attorney and says the show is crooked.

Richard Goodwin (Rob Morrow), a Washington staffer, sees an opening for his congressional committee when a grand jury investigates Stempel's charge. The grand jury probe fizzles when the judge (after a telephone call from the producer) orders the presentment sealed, but Goodwin goes ahead. He seeks out Van Doren. The two like each other; there is a sense of affinity, of a wary circling of friendly enemies—Van Doren, establishment credentials,

WASP; Goodwin, first in his class at Harvard, clerk for Felix Frankfurter, Jew. Taken by Van Doren to the Atheneum for lunch, where Mark Van Doren (Paul Scofield) stops by and makes a joke about Reuben sandwiches, Goodwin says mildly, "Unfortunately, there don't seem to be any Reubens here." "Touché," is Mark's humbled response.

This sequence is followed by a Goodwin meeting with Stempel, in which Stempel spills everything—"It's a fix, it's all a fix. Nail Van Doren, it'll be bigger than Sputnik!" When Goodwin again approaches Van Doren, it is to be taken to the family summer home—a birthday party, intellectual games, literary jokes ("Jesus shared an office with his father"), warmth and culture and comfort. Later, Goodwin tells his wife about it, that they call the literary critic Edmund Wilson "Bunny." "That doesn't mean you have to," she says acidly, pulling him back from the lure of the Van Doren world.

Goodwin confronts Van Doren before that world comes crashing down. He likes "Charlie," as he now calls him.

"Jesus," Van Doren says, "if somebody offered you all this money, instant fame, to be on some rigged quiz show, would you do it?"

"No, of course not."

"And I would?" Van Doren says. The implication is that he couldn't possibly do such a thing because he is a Van Doren, and Goodwin is a nobody. And a Jew.

Van Doren confesses at the congressional hearing. He has already told his shocked father, whose response—"Your name is mine!"—epitomizes the Van Doren mix of privilege and obligation. Several congressmen congratulate Charles for his frankness, but one says, "I don't think an adult of your intelligence ought to be commended simply for telling the truth at long last." The audience applauds.

Redford seems to take away a different moral from Charles Van Doren's experience than others of us would, something about the corruption of television. The film ends with a line from a slimy producer that is meant, apparently, to serve as an ironic kicker: In the fixed show, everybody benefits, the public is entertained, "So who gets hurt?" Or perhaps Redford has chosen to emphasize only one of several ideas that are implicit in the film. The perfidy of television and cynical executives is an easy target. However, having set up the anti-Semitism implicit in parts of the film, he makes nothing of it. And, having set up the idea of an American cultural aristocracy, represented by the Van Dorens, he lets that idea slide away, too.

In part, Redford has remained indifferent to what was happening to the Van Dorens' universe in 1957. I mentioned *Howl* and *On the Road* because they were significant weapons in a then-new war on high culture. So was television. Redford is content not to make that connection but to have a good guy and a somewhat bad guy, instead, and he is content not to see that the bad guy may have been "bad" partly because he was a man of his time and partly because he knew the cultural war was on. Nor should we be quite so persuaded of Goodwin's goodness, either: the film is based on his own book, after all.

The people who come off best in this film are Mark Van Doren and the Goodwin and Stempel wives (Mira Sorvino and Johann Carlo). *Quiz Show* is unusual in giving the wives penetrating insight into the moral conflict. When Stempel says that everybody is dishonest, and the people who believed in the show were "saps," his wife says, "I was one of those saps, Herbert." And when Goodwin wants to go easy on Van Doren because he has fallen for the Van Doren aura, his wife says, "You are ten times the man Charles Van Doren is. . . . You are bending over backwards for him. You are like the Uncle Tom of the Jews." Indeed, Mark Van Doren and the two wives are really the moral centers of the film, as well as its finest performances.

Quiz Show has a gloss that belies its seriousness. Beautifully produced, splendidly acted, it looks and often sounds so accessible as to preclude depth. Yet, the film is a moral one, and therefore one of uncommon historical interest. Although its final conclusion seems glib, buried in it are important questions about that decade in which America started the change from its modern to its postmodern self. In Charles Van Doren, Redford has found an illuminating exemplar—and, perhaps, victim—of that change.

IN THE 1990S, it is the films about the recent, not the distant past that are striking, and in a rather new way. The 1990s films about the modern period are less revisionist than postauthoritarian; all awe has gone out of them, except possibly for *Malcolm X* and, perhaps, *Apollo 13*, which shows awe for an official instituition, NASA, rather than an individual. *Nixon's* is a familiar subject, the presidency, but utterly denuded of respect, the more strikingly so because of the conventions that surrounded filmic presentations of presidents before the 1970s. In earlier times, too, some of the characters of *Quiz Show* would have been accorded the respect thought due an elite; now, significantly, they suffer some of the nakedness of the disempowered—indeed, disempowerment is what that film seems to be about.

Except for those three and *Ed Wood*, the rest of the films of the nineties seem hardly worth discussing. *Ed Wood* recovered a time and a figure who raise important questions about "art." The very asking of such questions is a postmodern concern, in that they undercut the foundations of ideas of high culture, authority, masterpieces, "art" itself—the world of the Van Dorens.

A large proportion of these films deal with a limited period of history—1950–74. Their disproportion and changed attack are significant, the more so because none of the films is about the most notorious event of those years, the Vietnam War. Rather, their subject seems to be an enormous transfer of power and change of attitude toward power, a perception that may be an effect of the Vietnam War but is not so recognized. Certainly, what is visible in these films is an almost total lack of confidence, even of interest, in traditional, patriarchal foci of history, including war and revered leaders. Vietnam may be a recent cause of this attitude, although I believe that *Quiz Show* is correct in adumbrating its beginnings in the 1950s. It is a remarkable change vis-à-vis history, one that would render a historical film of the 1990s unrecognizable as such to Griffith, perhaps even to Ford. It may also explain the contextual amnesia of a film like *Apollo 13*: historical memory has become not only short, but also selective.

CHAPTER 11

CONCLUSIONS _____

I have called the two parts of this book "Celebrating the Past" and "Democ-ratizing the Past," titles that I mean as processes, not monoliths. They are tendencies that cross in the 1950s: obviously, there is still some celebration of the past in the 1990s and there was some democratization of it in 1910, but what I intend are emphases and their changing balance. The X of this exchange in part mirrors the dominance of traditional historical or Western films as compared to films about the disempowered, and, again, the shift in balance seems to happen in the 1950s. However, the shift—or the metaphor, for perhaps that is all it is—is not carried out in the *numbers* of history films, which rise from 1920 through 1960 and then plummet and remain constant thereafter; nor does this rise and fall in the numbers parallel total film produc-tion, which has its biggest year in 1921 and slowly diminishes thereafter until it, too, has a fall in the early 1960s. I mention this only to suggest that history, judged by numbers of historical films, seems to have an increasing usefulness to film through 1960—that is, more films each decade—but that the pattern of this usefulness is different from the X of celebration–democratization.

This X reflects changing ideas of history but not anything so well-con-ceived as theories of history. Nonetheless, impervious as Hollywood probably has been to theory, the shift accords with what David Hackett Fischer has called "determinants" of American culture—until about 1960, Frederick Jackson Turner's frontier thesis; thereafter, an increasingly pluralistic one.[1] More inter-esting is Fischer's own idea of "folkways" and their role as cultural determinants. His long and elegantly reasoned argument cannot be summarized here; what seems relevant to film is his definition of the folkways of two eighteenth-cen-tury immigrant groups, the "Virgina cavalier" and the "backcountry borderers," whose different folkways seem to me quite visible as historical filmways at dif-ferent times. These times are roughly the same as those of the dominance of celebration and democratization—the hierarchical, ceremonious, and authoritar-ian ways of Virginia cavaliers dominant until the 1950s, the leveling, patriar-chal, and libertarian ones of the backcountry borderers increasingly so thereafter.[2] Griffith is recognizable in the first set of folkways, as are films like *Janice Meredith* and *Winners of the Wilderness*, and actors like Randolph Scott. The second set of filmways is visible early in a film like *Allegheny Uprising* and in the screen personae of John Wayne and Susan Hayward, both of whom reached superstardom in the 1950s; the country music films of the 1960s and after express these folkways, and arguably they are expressed in the patriarchy and symbolic incest of the old-male star/young actress casting of the 1950s; they inform a film like *Silkwood*, and they reach some sort of apotheosis in *The People v Larry Flynt*, the 1996 film about the Kentucky redneck who came to publish *Hustler* magazine. These two sets of determinants are also obvious in what I have called "awe" or the lack of it, deeply embedded in Griffith, utterly absent by the 1990s; but obviously they are not pure (e.g., the use of the back-country-borderer fringed buckskin on the cavalier–aristocratic Randolph Scott), nor are they exclusive, as shown by the presence of Jewish ethnicity in the musical biographies, beginning in the 1940s.

Much of what happens with democratization of historical film is more than a new set of folkways, of course, and some of it goes far beyond one set of folkways—the appearance of the first black characters in the 1950s, *The Jackie Robinson Story* and *St. Louis Blues*, the pro-Native American films in the same decade. The rise of the Italian–American gangster films is also different, but it suggests a common thread, the emergence of ethnic and cultural subgroups from cavalier, anglo, high-church dominance. Nonetheless, I think the backcountry-borderer folkways became the most important among these subgroups after 1960 in both film and American culture, visible in music (both country and rock), politics (the New South, the Southern strategy), and religion (the Christian right). The beginnings of this visibility coincided with the Dixiecrat withdrawal from the Democratic Party and realignment; they are repeated in Lyndon Johnson and Jimmy Carter and even Barry Goldwater. It is not that they caused democratization of culture, but that democratization found a model in them. And it is not that the concept of culture-determining folkways explains everything about historical film, or that political changes directly cause cultural changes, but that the X of shifting emphases in historical film is like the X of shifting cultural determinants and the X of national politics, all with a crossing-point in the 1940s through the 1960s.

THE CHANGES AND progressions within one kind of historical film are also worth tracing. What I have called the "traditional"—that dealing with war, politics, and great men, always assuming a white, Christian dominance—is the largest and, with the Westerns, the longest established and most consistent of historical film types. It began with short films, many of them actualities without plot or character; these were quickly replaced in the teens of the century by story films. The subjects came mostly from two periods, the Revolution and the Civil War. Simple visual signs communicated period; brought over from other visual arts, these signs were often loaded ones (e.g., the fringed buckskin suit) that also communicated "America." Especially early on, nonetheless, these films had an austere commitment to "actual reproduction," often including actual sites and even actual objects and people.

Films got longer and more complex (e.g., *Martyrs of the Alamo*), and fictional plots laid against or woven through historical narrative became common (Griffith's *America*). History in these films was decidedly nineteenth-century—"history according to Longfellow"—as was the concept of dramatic fiction (neoromantic melodrama). History was largely a matter of politics and war and was almost exclusively male; when women appeared, they did so as romantic objects outside the competing spheres of power (*The Beautiful Mrs. Reynolds*) or as victims (*Martyrs of the Alamo*). The reliance on Longfellow suggests the existence of a historical canon, the role of films a didactic or celebratory one.

Neither sound nor color appear to have changed this idea substantively, although sound enabled the consistent use of music that was mostly contra-historical—that is, music in the service of emotion and melodrama rather than thought. The big historical films of 1939–42, for example, were still mostly about men, still about war, politics, and such minor themes as technological innovation. Both sound and color gave them an appearance of greater realism, although their actual style was still neoromantic. At their most extreme (the films of DeMille, from *The Buccaneer*, 1938, through *Unconquered*, 1948), they were still rooted in the late nineteenth century and perpetuated an idea of history as moral melodrama. Such, certainly, was the idea called upon by Griffith and John Ford in the 1920s and DeMille and Zanuck in the 1930s and 1940s: America's struggles as moral battles between good and evil. These struggles were put on film as melodramas about heroes and villains, the former clothed in the now-conventionalized signs (buckskins, fur hat, movie-cowboy costume), the latter characterized in sometimes ludicrously improbable ways (Catherine Montour in *The Spirit of 76*, Walter Butler in *America*); this was moderated by the late 1930s, when the films reduced the roles of the villains and made them minor characters drawn in broad strokes (e.g., the evil gun-runner in DeMille's *The Plainsman*). Their frameworks of fact were shaky, at best; most were elaborate fictions laid against a historical background the way other neoromantic melodramas were laid against exotic places like the South Seas. Although such neoromanticism survived World War II, it was moribund by 1960, and the traditional films of the 1950s show movement in several directions (psychology, self-imitative neoromanticism, stylistic elaboration including greater realism).

It is unclear what the collapse of the nineteenth-century paradigm at this moment (from 1950 to around 1965) means. It is too easy to say that the war caused the change; however, some of the effects of the war may have been important—for example, the sudden education of a large number of men because of the GI Bill, which probably affected the national idea of history.

Education might help to explain a loss of belief in the false history retailed by the films—that is, educated people now knew better—but it would not explain the collapse of the underlying, and more important, idea of American history as moral drama. This essentially Manichaean view of American history persisted into the 1950s but was under direct attack in some films even then (e.g., *Broken Arrow*). By 1970, the conventionalized signs (except for anachronistic firearms) had pretty much disappeared, and the older subjects—the founding fathers, the Revolution, in fact all of pre–Civil War history—had disappeared with them.

What had happened? For one thing, the studio system had ended and the Production Code had been broken; the latter change may be as much symptom as cause, but it had the potential to allow what seemed like greater candor in sex, violence, nudity, language. Such candor looked like greater realism and in historical film may have seemed like greater "truth," but the complex effects of suddenly liberating previously forbidden subjects may have been to diminish historical figures, showing them performing the forbidden (*They* do *that?*).

As well, surely, the generational change within Hollywood that is symbolized by the studios' disappearance and the father–son, older–younger conflicts of the 1950s films explains both the remarkable drop in production figures after the 1950s and some of the change in content. DeMille, Ford, and many of the stars of the 1930s ended their careers in the 1950s and 1960s. But why did generational change bring a change in the idea of history as moral drama? I would again emphasize the importance of *The Beginning or the End?* Its title is significant: history cannot be a moral drama if it faces an unpredictable and catastrophic end. This idea, to be sure, cannot be the only cause; there cannot be a simple cause; but of the complex of causes that ended the traditionalist idea of filmed history, the Cold War and imminent annihilation were surely important. They make the 1950s a watershed: before them a fairly consistent idea of history as neoromantic melodrama, going back to at least 1915; after them, a troubled, multifaceted idea of history, with neoromanticism diminishing and ideas ranging from revisionism to outright nihilism ("history teaches us nothing") taking its place. Increasingly after 1960, history was recent history, and increasingly it was outsider history, as chapters 7–10 show. The shift suggests that earlier national experience was no longer a source of example and strength; it also implies that the traditionally empowered were being forced to share power, at least the power of popular attention.

Great men, war, and politics remained subjects of a diminished number of films, but history according to Longfellow died. A number of the post-1950 films had military support and encouragement; some were virtually recruiting films. Their subjects, however, tended to be nearly contemporary ones. In the 1970s, the traditional cluster dwindled to eight films, still concerned with male power but not with utter certainty (*Patton*); the cluster shrank to five in the 1980s and included two revisionist films, one celebration of an American Communist (*Reds*), and another look at the making of the atomic bomb; the cluster expanded in the 1990s but did so only because of revisionism and the insertion of subjects, figures, and approaches inimical to the old kind of history, e.g., *Nixon, Malcolm X.* As I suggested in Chapter 10, the changes were so great that categorization itself became meaningless. A number of films suggested that a corporate or collective idea was replacing individualism.

This shrinkage of the traditional cluster is only part of its story, however; equally important is what was filling the gaps it left. Most obviously, films about what I have called outsiders were ascendant, and if there is a single dominant thread since World War II, it is this expansion in films about people outside the traditional centers of power.

It cannot be said that theories of history as held by professional or academic historians were ever a cause of the nature or concept of American historical film. Scientific history, for example, cannot be shown to have exerted much effect on filmed history during its dominance of the first half of the century, except perhaps in the idea of "actual reproduction" and the interest shown in authentication, from 1910 to 1920. Arguably, theoretical positions have had more effect in the last couple of decades, especially feminist history and black history. However, such films as have emerged (e.g., *Mrs. Soffel, Glory*) would not have needed historical theory to urge their making; they have probably come out of stronger and nearer social forces in popular culture.

Overall, what the traditional films suggest is that the causes of American historical film did not lie in professional or academic history but in American society, although perhaps at some remove. That is, the immediate cause of the films' idea of history around 1915 would appear to have been the theater of the preceding generation; subsequent film until about 1960 would seem to have had the films and novels of its own immediate past as a cause, but only one of several. The films of 1915–25 are ideologically and stylistically much the same as those of the highwater years of 1939–42, except for sound and technological improvement (makeup, lights, film, color), suggesting that the early idea of history was institutionalized by the corporate system, most visible in the films and working methods of DeMille, but apparent also in the self-imitation that became genre, e.g., the Western, the musical biography. It is possible that such insitutionalization prolonged the life of a historical idea past its relevance outside of film, so that when outside changes demanded a change in film, the end was a crash rather than a slow transformation.

Nothing illustrates the differences at the two ends of the century better than the way historical films show the presidency. Washington and Lincoln are filmed with reverence by Griffith and Ford; there is even a reluctance to show the face of Washington in some films (even in the 1950s in *The Scarlet Coat*), as if he were a deity, masked; the convention is still working for FDR in the 1940s. By the 1990s, there are no films about Washington and Lincoln, and Richard Nixon is shown as a drunkard, a liar, a depressive; in an earlier film, he had been shown in a men's room. The differences are instructive: the idea of history in 1915–45 is heroic; the idea of history in 1980 and after is skeptical, even disillusioned.

OF THE OTHER types, the Westerns seem barely productive of evidence about historical film. They settled too early into genre (before 1920), and they have remained part of that genre, with a willful disregard of fact; they are historical, as it were, by accident. Their attempts after 1970 at revisionism were stylistic, as I have tried to show; they appear in the 1990s to be at a dead end, repeating old subjects without new ideas. Their most visible aspect is their violence; they are the principal venue of the firearms myth. They may represent an irreducible residue of an old idea of history, which has enough proponents among both filmmakers and filmgoers to give it the illusion of life.

The musicals and show-business biographies, on the other hand, have proven to be a cluster of surprising importance and vitality. They give evidence about women, business, and ethnicity, so much so that they are probably worth more study in their own right. Although in their original form they collapsed as quickly and as thoroughly in the 1960s as the traditional films, they found new life in different, democratized subjects.

The musical–show business biography, along with the outsider film, has been the particular venue of women. In the 1950s, it was about the only type in which women could be seen as active beings, doing something other than waiting or pouring coffee. However, their activity was bought at a high price—submission to gatekeepers ("Prince Ziegfeld"), drug addiction, physical and emotional punishment, humiliation. The stage mother was shown as a demonized woman, damned for having ambition and pushing another woman toward its realization; the apotheosis of this type was *Gypsy*, which brought the entire structure of traditional theater—Prince Ziegfeld's empire, Broadway, vaudeville, show biz—into question. Other women were shown quite specifically as victims of men and of a male world in which even helpers were victimizers (*I'll Cry Tomorrow, Too Much, Too Soon*).

Such victimization, it must be said, was apparently endemic to the show-business films of the 1950s but had certainly been shown in films of other clusters in many decades; scenes of overt punishment of women occurred from the 1923 *Little Old New York* through *Sweet Dreams*. Much of this punishment was specifically for imitating men, sometimes for excelling while attached men did not. The use of love as a plot driver in most of the musical biographies also put ambitious women in positions where they had to give up ambition in favor of subservience to a desired man.

This treatment of women in historical film did not spring from any interpretation of history, however; to the contrary, it appears always to have been contemporary with the making of the films. What it tells us, therefore, is not that American history shows widespread victimization of women but that Hollywood in several periods understood women in terms of victimization. The 1950s show it most markedly, but it appears in the 1920s; feminist films appear in the 1980s, but so do films in which women are battered. Many more prefer to dispense with women altogether. Sometimes, this erasure is not historically untrue so much as historically selective and historically atypical: many Westerns erase women, but only by fudging dates. That is, parts of the West were briefly male but quickly changed; too many films pretend to deal with that sliver of early maleness as if it were typical. More common, however, is the assumption that what women do is not history, true for virtually all but the outsider and musical bio–show biz clusters; the shift in emphases since 1960 shows that this assumption has been challenged, but not superseded.

The musical and show-business biographies also revealed a common interest in ethnicity, secularism, and the conflict of high and low culture. The three are in fact probably connected. Ethnicity in these films involves two groups, Jews and blacks. Many of the entertainers and composers shown are Jews, their ethnicity typically communicated by a parent with an accent, by the occasional Yiddish word, and by an establishing shot of New York's Lower East Side. Black ethnicity occurs in two mirror-image forms, blackface (on the white, often Jewish entertainer), and brief sequences of black musical entertainers who typically function to provide musical example to the white entertainer or composer. Blacks also appear fleetingly as servants in these films, a reminder of their white-perceived status, without reference to the diversity of black American life.

Secularism appears in these films as an absence. What is absent is the Judaism of the Jew who has been identified by parental accent. Except in the two Jolson films, religious practice has been erased; none of these Jews celebrates holidays, keeps kosher. The same can be said for the non-Jews in these films, but if they have ethnicity, it is merely cute or warm (usually Irish); such things as a crucifix or a holy picture on a wall are rare. The effect—and in fact this is true across all the historical films except those few that have professional religious in them—is to project an utterly secular America. This error is as grave as any committed by American film about history.

The conflict of high and low culture is overt in several films of the 1950s, but it is also implicit in the fairly large number of musical biographies that use a concert in a high-culture venue (e.g., Carnegie Hall) as their climaxes. Context makes it clear that these scenes are examples of success, yet often success has also been defined as a triumph (as, for example, in a love plot, e.g., *The Benny Goodman Story*) of popular over high culture. Most typically, popular culture is "jazz," a variable term used to cover everything from Jolson's mammy songs to Gershwin. Many of the films have minor characters with strong ties to European high culture who teach or mentor the protagonist; the rejection or death of the mentor, or his/her conversion to popular culture, is an important part of the films. The conflict of high and low culture is a conflict partly within the immigrant community, partly in America itself; it has resonances of both insecurity and self-assertion. It is not resolved in the films of the 1940s and 1950s, because it was not resolved in America or in an immigrant Jewish community at the time. Rather, it was resolved in the musical biographies of the 1970s and after, when country and rock music represented a democratizing force that swept both high culture and "the fabulous era" away. Significantly, these later films are not about Jews and not about blackface. There has been a changing of the guard.

These several lines briefly cross, however, in *Rhapsody in Blue* when the young Gershwin plays "Swanee" for the blackfaced Jolson. Two Jews, both now secularized, one in blackface, one trained in high culture, exchange a song that is neither Jewish, black, nor high-culture. I find inescapable the observations of Michael Rogin on this phenomenon: "Blackface as American national culture Americanized the son of the immigrant Jew. . . ." "Far from serving as an agent of Jewish assimilation, high culture set Jews apart," and East European Jews assimilated in America "by helping to create mass culture. . . ."[3] This view at least explains why the Jews in the musical and showbusiness biographies are secular and so often have connections with blackface: the films are myths of assimilation.

I am not satisfied that this view explains blackface itself. Rogin engages in a psychosocial, postmodern explanation that does not convince me; transformation, exchange value, gender-crossing—these are metaphors, not explanations. Nor do I accept Janet Brown's idea that blackface "expresses the projected self-hatred of the dominant group."[4] At the same time, there is no question that blackface is an ethnic insult; it cannot be "fun," as Eddie Cantor (a blackface performer) is supposed to have said. To the contrary, it is serious business—drearily serious business, something dredged from slavery's unconscious and paraded by white (and some black) men, women, and children for more than a century and a half. That a kind of historical film so casually showed it as an aspect of mostly Jewish assimilation is arresting.

So is the presentation in some of the same films of black musicians. These often brief scenes are an acknowledgement of indebtedness, sometimes quite literally so (e.g., biographies of Foster, Goodman). In *The Jolson Story*, it is the indebtedness of a blackface performer to black music that is shown. As he goes down on his knees and spreads his white-gloved hands and sings "Mammy," he would seem to be giving us the results of that indebtedness, but I believe he is also paying back in a cruel and vengeful way—not for the music, but for being indebted. I'd go a million miles for one of your smiles, but I wouldn't really be black for all the lights on Broadway—you *can* see that this is only makeup, can't you?

St. Louis Blues and *Leadbelly* write a revisionist history of this era and its music. They do not show something that is more true, however; they show something that is also true. The white musical biographies, for all their falsity of plot and their glitz, are not all wrong as history: at their core, they deal with very real historical matters of ethnicity, assimilation, and culture. The "fabulous era" is also the era of assimilation; the films are history as celebration of immigrant triumph.

The presentation of a business autocrat in these films—usually Ziegfeld— without ever presenting business suggests a number of things: Hollywood would not or could not deal historically with business; Hollywood believed unquestionably in the maleness of business heads (i.e., producers); Hollywood accepted, at least for public consumption, an idea of paternalism in business management; on the basis of what we see in the films, Hollywood understood business to be a matter of charming trickery. In that the men who ran things in Hollywood clearly knew that business was not charming trickery, one has to conclude that these figures, and Ziegfeld most of all, were wish fulfillments. The Ziegfeld of film was the idealized producer, including the film producer.

OTHER IDEAS RUN through the historical films, but they are not, by and large, historical ideas; they are emanations of the times when the films were made. The idea of women is one, already discussed; ideas of race and ethnicity are another, carried beyond the musical biographies as ideas of immigrants, ideas of Native Americans, and ideas of African Americans. The strong anti-immigrant content of some films (e.g., *The Iron Horse*) and the preference for Northern Europeans in others (*Knute Rockne, All-American*) provide context for the musical biographies' obsession with immigration and assimilation.

Native Americans were redefined in the 1950s (*Chief Crazy Horse, Broken Arrow*), but part of the redefinition was probably a more general plea for tolerance, with Native Americans as surrogates for blacks and Jews. Nonetheless, the demonization of Native Americans pretty well ended then; the moral melodrama of the winning of the West became a muddled search for values, without villains (*Cheyenne Autumn*). Too, an ambivalence toward Indians had always existed; after the 1950s, it tilted toward the positive. In that this was the same period in which the first black characters of importance appeared, it seems that a desire to ease racial barriers did exist, probably coming from the political left as in *Pride of the Marines*.

African Americans usually fared no better in these other films than in the musical biography and show-business cluster. They have been erased from history, except for the odd servant; even then, their slave status has not been acknowledged, and films about both North and South are careful not to say that the blacks who can be seen are probably slaves (e.g., *Janice Meredith*, *Northwest Passage*). The one film that deals with the slave trade never shows slavery; two films of 1939–41 even extoll it. Only in the 1950s do things begin to change: two sports films have black protagonists; black characters show up in war films. Still, it is only in the 1970s that large-budget films about African Americans are made, and only the 1980s before a major work of revision is made on a subject other than music (*Glory*), and only the 1990s before black self-assertion is given a voice (*Malcolm X*).

Other subjects are notable for their unimportance: business, in a nation supposedly founded on business; labor, at a time when labor organization was first peaking, then declining with much noise; art and literature. The general absence of labor may suggest a desire to avoid anything about "workers" (Hollywood having long had a hysteria about leftism); a capitalist system, nonetheless, is at least implicit in many of the films. It is the workings of capitalism that are missing, along with the heroes of capitalism. Perhaps filmmakers did not understand capitalism well enough to dramatize it; perhaps what they understood instead of business was salesmanship, a related but hardly identical thing. Certainly, the businessmen of the films are presented as if they were salesmen, in terms of flamboyance and persuasion (often as trickery). *Heaven's Gate* is atypical in relating business (as investment) to the West; it is more typical in showing business as oppressive, a seeming contradiction of film's acceptance of capitalism but one probably widely held among Americans. Overall, most film's view of both business and labor seems to have been a populist one—suspicious of both but willing to accept an unexamined capitalism, sympathetic toward victims of "the bosses" but likely to associate labor with antisocial and so unacceptable violence.

A corollary to this view of business is the recurring "bad white" in many films about Native Americans, whether in the eighteenth century or the nineteenth. The bad white is an easily constructed villain in a moral melodrama, but actually a type of businessman. His badness is defined by his market, not his methods or product. The badness, however, is ahistorical; governments had sold arms to Indians from the white arrival on the continent. What these characters accomplish is a transference of responsibility from the mass of whites to a scapegoat for the evils of expansion. That the villain is in business may represent subconscious recognition of unpalatable truth: what was happening was not a matter of manifest destiny but of business. As well, this muddle may be part of a view of "bosses" and banks common to nineteenth-century populism and progressivism, an inability to see the systemic nature of American capitalism; in film, it is expressed as the demonization of "the railroads" (*Jesse James*) and "the banks."

The view of labor was certainly from the point of view of capital, even as early as the first *Molly Maguires*; the second *Molly Maguires* (1970s) dramatized the dreadful conditions of labor but not the struggle of labor, nor, really, its justifications for taking action. *Matewan* did study those justifications, but largely in terms of company injustice—the use of detectives, violence, collusion with authorities. *Silkwood* came closest to making labor a real part of working life, showing negotiation, relations with a national, a local in operation. *Hoffa* pecked around the edges of the same matters but was really more interested in its protagonist's relations with organized crime and government.

For all that the dominant idea of history in films is elitist—male, white, "great," often affluent—historical films show conflicting feelings toward elites. The Ivy League colleges, for example, are accorded great respect in the mid-forties (*Wilson, Night and Day*), but in 1980's *Heaven's Gate*, Harvard is a sign for Eastern money, the source of evil in much of the film. Social elitism is democratized in early films (*America, Janice Meredith*), is ridiculed in mid-century Westerns (*Western Union*), and is one of the subjects of scrutiny in the 1990s (*Quiz Show*). Yet a connection between social elitism and political power goes unchallenged in films about the Roosevelts and Wilson, all made between 1944 and 1975. Again, a specific challenge to social elitism and political power is part of both *Hoffa* and *Nixon*, directed against the Kennedys in both films. Military elites in the war movies are accepted almost whole until the 1970s, then are mildly satirized for individual traits (Patton's and MacArthur's vanity), no real connection with social or other nonmilitary elites being made. Overall, the films suggest ambivalence toward elites—a very American attitude, and in part a conflict between "folkways."

A LIST OF THE areas of American history ignored by American historical film would be a long one—suffrage; education; religion; the press before c. 1900; virtually all of politics except for tepid forays in *Wilson* and *Sunrise at Campobello*, a presentation of the left in *Reds*, the dark fury of *Nixon*; international affairs, other than wars, with the exceptions of *The Barbarian and the Geisha*, *The Wind and the Lion*, and *Mission to Moscow*; other ethnic groups, e.g., Asian Americans; science and technology, except for the inventors' biographies of 1939–45 and the films about flight and space.

The gaps in chronology are as large as the gaps in subject. Little is touched on before the Seven Years War, which, contrarily, has had a remarkable attention. The Revolution received much attention before 1960. The War of 1812 has been touched on in films about Jean Lafitte, little else; Texas Independence has been a popular subject, although the years between 1812 and 1836 have been blank; ditto the years between 1847 and the Civil War. The West has been extensively covered, but mostly as the Indian Wars (really the 1870s and 1880s) and carefully selected sites of violence (Abilene, Dodge City, Deadwood, Tombstone) in the 1870s and 1880s. The fabulous era was popular, but only in a narrow stratum; the twentieth century has had much attention. American history according to film is markedly discontinuous.

HOW GOOD, THEN, are American historical films as history? If we mean as a history of America, it is clear that the films in toto will not write an American history; they are discontinuous in time and highly selective in subject.

How good are individual films as American history? To answer, let me pose some deliberately naive questions:

What would be the response if a person from the subject period of the film could be shown it?

The answer, in good part because of material error, would be that in most cases the person would be laughing too hard to give a response.

Could one teach a period of American history to, let us say, college undergraduates with American films?

Not unless the time of the films was so close to the making of the films that material culture and mode of perception were not an issue; probably not for films made before 1960 because the then-dominant idea of neoromanticism invalidates the films as history; probably not for any extended period before the twentieth century because the films are too discontinuous; probably not for social history involving African Americans and women; probably not for any area in which religion, science, education, politics, or technology was important.

However, it might be possible to teach selected periods and limited subjects with groups of film that, as it were, provided context for each other: *The Wind and the Lion, The Girl in the Red Velvet Swing, Leadbelly* for the first few years of the century; *Quiz Show, The Buddy Holly Story, I Was a Communist for the FBI, Battle Hymn, Bird, Lenny* for the 1950s. However, much context would still have to be provided.

Could one teach American history to high school students with the films? To elementary school students?

Probably not, unless you were willing that they learn untruths of material culture, society (e.g., erasure of blacks, falsification of the role of women), and fact. Individual films (e.g., *Glory*) might be used as correctives, but only if they could be put into a matrix that kept them from creating new misunderstanding.

Are there, then, no good American films about American history?

There are several, but they are thin in context and narrow in subject. Few embody questions; most are assertions. Few take account of alternatives. Most are distorted by their compromises with nonhistorical ends, e.g., melodramatic narrative, sensation for its own sake. Most celebrate or fictionalize; they do not analyze.

It must be said, however, that virtually all the films are useful historical evidence *for the time in which they were made.* Although *America* is not a useful history of the Revolution, it is an interesting artifact of the 1920s; *Plymouth Adventure* tells us nothing of any rigor about 1620, but much about 1952. This is not the sense in which we want such films to be historically useful, however.

It is perhaps cold comfort that recent films may seem less objectionable than early ones. The end of the Production Code enabled inclusion of some behaviors (sex, violence) that had the potential to make films more accurate, although they simply made most films more concerned with sensation; however, the end of the code also removed false awe and falsification of social fact (the ban on showing "miscegenation," for example). The visualization of material culture seems to have improved since about 1970, as well, but this may be a matter of our perception. It may be that the training of filmmakers (e.g., costume designers) improved; it may be that a generational change brought in a new awareness of visual authenticity; it may be that the greatly increased realism of American acting demanded greater authenticity. However, perception is important in all these matters: recent films are more accessible to recent eyes, and films are made to play to their contemporaries. Recent films may "seem less objectionable" without in fact being so; the intrusion of the observer is particularly problematic here.

At the same time, manipulation of authenticating signs has increased since 1970, markedly so since 1980, and films of the 1990s use film itself in ways amounting to deception, if not forgery. Computer manipulation of images now permits "authentic" film of people and things from different times (e.g., *Forrest Gump*), including the insertion of actors into quite old footage. Thus, while the standard of visual reliability may have risen vis-à-vis costumes and properties, it has fallen vis-à-vis manipulation of imagery.

WHAT IS THE RELATION of history to style? As we have seen, the dominant style until at least the 1960s was a putative realism, actually neoromanticism. A case could in fact be made that theoretically rigorous realism cannot deal with history, direct observation being essential to its nature, impossible to the treatment of the past ("the past" having variable limits, to be sure). Nonetheless, what film attempted to do, because it was what the theater had attempted to do, was apply neoromanticism to history and use much of the production style of realism to do so.

However, with neoromanticism came melodrama, hence perhaps the idea that history was a moral melodrama. The cart may be before the horse here; it is likely that early filmmakers, at least, had come to maturity in an age when history really was seen as a moral melodrama, with America as hero and its enemies as villains, and the events of history the melodramatic stories that illustrated America's moral standing.

Neoromantic melodrama and realism do not readily sympathize with each other; they can be merely made to seem to do so—Griffith's *America*, Zanuck's historical films of 1937–41. One reason is the neoromantic desire for beauty, especially in its heroes; rigorous realism is likely to see warts, scars, unpressed pants. Another is neoromanticism's willingness to throw over everything else for effect. We get a realism of landscape (what the camera sees) but an improbability of behavior (the villain rolls his eyes and breathes heavily while scantily clad foreign women dance for him, as in *Martyrs of the Alamo*). Another is melodrama's indebtedness to poetic justice and to a structure that requires greater and greater threats to heroism as the piece progresses. Another is neoromanticism's willingness to sacrifice accuracy to cultural sign, as with fringed buckskin and the cartridge revolver, nowhere more visible than in the Westerns: despite their dealing with the age of photography, they willingly, even enthusiastically, rejected the evidence of photography for the mythic "truth" of signs.

Parts of such films are sometimes pretty good history: some of the early sequences of *America*, some of *The Iron Horse*, some of *Wilson*. All these films, however, show the same difficulties, endemic to neoromanticism: a very early attack, in the name of establishing their credentials, that causes them to go forward in assertive, generalizing leaps until the action is reached; a concern with romantic love that is mostly irrelevant to history; an emphasis on public event as spectacle for its own sake (e.g., the conventions in *Wilson*) rather than as carefully argued history; an antirational use of music; a confusion of history and patriotism.

Neoromanticism, and its version of realism, were moribund by the 1950s. In the 1950s, several filmmakers tried to break loose, mostly through some kind of symbolism, typically related to a superficial Freudianism (*The Girl in the Red Velvet Swing, Gunfight at the O.K. Corral*). Others tried to go to a more rigorous realism: Newman's performances in *The Left-Handed Gun* and *Somebody Up There Likes Me*. Arthur Penn made a significant but isolated stylistic leap in *The Left-Handed Gun*. Otherwise, most of the films of the 1950s look like what they are, death throes. The films dealing with nearly contemporary events (e.g., *Too Much, Too Soon*) appear to contradict this; they look "real," but they do so mostly because their costumes and properties and backgrounds are contemporary.

The attempt to go deeper into realism rather than to find another style for history is what has doomed the Western since about 1970. *Doc* and *The Long Riders* are ludicrous because their attempts to make the West "real" (dirty, more or less correctly costumed, i.e., consonant with photographs) also made it without dignity or morality or religion or community, a distortion as foolish as the tight-pants costume of earlier Western heroes. The cynicism underlying the films also pushed them toward black comedy, an easy genre if mostly what you are doing is parodying the falsifications and pretentions of the earlier type (e.g., *Judge Roy Bean*). The films actually serve as anecdotal evidence of the antipathy of realism and history. (Note, for example, that the films did not become more accurate by trying to become more realistic; they simply became different—bad history in a different way.) They also serve to suggest that trying to make a style more internally redundant is the wrong way to go: a style for filmed history might very well fight redundancy, instead aim at a deliberate inconsistency of style (e.g., the use of music in *Butch Cassidy and the Sundance Kid*, although in that film the goal of the deliberate inconsistency was a mild self-mockery to get itself off the hook of good history).

Nonetheless, historical films have kept trying to reassert their realism. *Lenny* tried to do so with the look of *cinema verité*; *Raging Bull* tried to do so with a magnificent but boring performance and a lot of grainy black-and-white filming. The other films that seem to have written history somewhat successfully since 1970 have done so with a modified, nontheoretical realism that we accept because we accept the films' revisionism—e.g., *Leadbelly*, *Bound for Glory*, *Glory*. They are far less neoromantic than films of the 1940s; because they are revisionist, they cannot really see history as moral melodrama, which is all to the good for history.

Can no good historical film be made in the theoretically rigorous realistic style? Yes, but few: *Raging Bull* is pretty good history. It is extremely limited, however; it offers no context. It is an example, perhaps an extreme example, of Lukacs' "pathology." For it to be otherwise would entail its either moving away from rigorous realism (toward neoromanticism, probably) or its taking its realism into an application of that style (socialist realism) that would be uncongenial in America and that has been shown to be bankrupt, anyway. *Silkwood* is a splendid realistic film, but it is less than good history on at least two counts, its failure to provide context for the factory and the bosses, and its inability to cope with the open question of how Karen Silkwood died. It asserted—cautiously—but could neither argue nor offer alternatives.

To the question as to whether there is a relationship between historical film and style, the answer appears to be yes. The answer is not, however, that there is one style appropriate to history, but that there have been at least two that were inappropriate.

What, then, would be a style through which filmed history could work? For an answer, I would look at the thing (actually things) I most often saw lacking in the many films discussed here—accurate framework of fact and context. Framework of fact has most often been seen to have been bent or broken by neoromanticism; presumably, other styles exist that would allow it to survive intact.

By context I mean causes and consequences, as expressed in material culture, events, and people; these things, however, immediately raise the problem of argument, for they are the very stuff of historical dispute. Any style that is to enable or allow the writing of history in film must allow for argument, or at least for alternatives. It must, like a well-reasoned article, admit its opposite. It must prove, or at least persuasively present, its own idea. On the basis of the films discussed in this book, American historical film has been a failure at handling multifaceted historical issues—at engaging in argument. And no wonder; many of the films have been neoromantic moral melodramas, which are the opposite of argument.

Most of these films are assertions. They brook no argument. Assertion, except in the very simplest cases, is poor history. Most of even the simple events of American history are still surrounded by argument (motive, detail, meaning). A style that cannot embody argument cannot write good history.

I will borrow the Brechtian term "alienation," although I do not mean to imply that a Brechtian style is what is wanted. All I mean is that a filmic style that wants to present history other than assertively will alienate its viewers, not throughout the film, but at disputed points. It will do what the footnote or the rhetoric of argument (*however, perhaps, despite, it cannot be true that*) does. It will cause the audience to withdraw from emotional sympathy with the narrative. It will, for example, be the opposite of typical movie music; it will disengage, not engage.

How does one carry on argument in film? The traditional device has been to put counterargument into the mouth of a character and have it expressed and annihilated; this was the device of both stage and film drama. Neoromantic film usually put counterargument into the mouth of the unsympathetic or the patently villainous; in effect, there was no argument. Or the matter was resolved in a quite different way (e.g., Bowie's arguing for leaving the Alamo in the 1960 *The Alamo*, resolved by Crockett's getting him drunk). This incorporation of argument into narrative, however, does not alienate. It may cause the audience to hear some aspect of a historical argument, but it need not cause it to think (as the footnote or the reasoned non-narrative argument does).

A few films since the demise of neoromanticism have successfully distanced their narratives. *Patton* did so with its opening monologue and its remarkable production design; *Reds* did it with the Witnesses; *Walker* did it with its anachronisms, its excesses, and its deliberate incoherence. None of these defines a theory of a style for historical films, but all hint at what can work. In *Patton*, deliberate exaggeration of the visual environment for an actual speech served to alienate; in *Reds*, the frequent interruptions of the narrative, and the black backgrounds for the Witnesses, their aged faces and their mutual disagreement, pulled us back from utter commitment to the romantic narrative; *Walker* never really allowed us to commit ourselves emotionally and came the closest to a consistent embodiment of alienating style. However, *Walker* is also satire (as *Patton* to some extent is, as well), and satire, although alienating, is not so much argumentative as noisily persuasive. Yet, the three films offer examples of the direction that a more reasoned, more complex, more intellectually rigorous kind of historical film can take.

The films of Oliver Stone are a special case. Stone seems to me a polemicist, not a historian, although the difference between those may be shrinking. Stone seems mostly to manipulate cinematic devices to authenticate narrative rather than to alienate audience. Within those manipulations is a realistically conceived narrative, for all that, at least in *Nixon*, the narrative is not told chronologically, and the jagged sequence may itself have an alienating quality. *Nixon* may in fact be a special case, a historical film with verbatim historical dialogue for much of its text; it comes to us with a higher than usual degree of prior authentication. The downside of this authentication is the extra burden put on the invented parts, hence, perhaps, the manipulation of cinematography itself to compensate. One could imagine a *Nixon* with Witnesses to give it more stature as history.

As Stone's films suggest, polemic, or at least propaganda, cannot be utterly ruled out from historical film. *Mission to Moscow* and, perhaps, *Wilson* are persuasive films from the high point of studio-system neoromanticism; both deal with historical issues more successfully than other films of the time. If they are ultimately invalidated as good history, it is less for their propaganda than their neoromanticism, and a case can be made that *Mission to Moscow* is the more completely historical of the two because the less neoromantic—or, put the other way, because it is the more propagandistic. I do not mean to suggest that propaganda makes for good history. Rather, an overt propaganda that runs against the moral melodrama of neoromanticism seems at least a relief, probably a shock that itself alienates.

One can also imagine manipulations of narrative that alienate: alternative endings, alternative versions of scenes or speeches, changes in casting partway through, mutually contradictory information. Such notions assume, of course, that an American audience would put up with manipulation of narrative. Forms like MTV suggest it would. It should be obvious that multiplying the protagonist, although it will not alienate, will provide context, failure of context coming in most historical films from restricting focus and point of view to a single protagonist and blocking out other data as "noise."

Such ideas also assume, however, that narrative remain the basis of American historical film—an assumption I find inevitable. So long as we are talking about nondocumentary in America, I believe, we will talk about narrative, and probably about narrative with individual, rather than group protagonists. I am aware of the arguments about narrative and fictionalizing, and I would hardly deny that the shaping of narrative, especially to match a given running time, causes it to be different from the actual. But so are all kinds of history different from the actual; that is one way they are history. Re-enacting the Nixon tapes verbatim would obviously take years; it would be the ultimate realism, hardly imaginable as film, obviously not as commercial film, but it would still exist in the world of art rather than actuality because of the re-enactment. Practically speaking, compression would have to be made, hence more art. The least cut, the least emphasis, the least shaping, is art: that is to say, it is different from framework of fact, although not therefore mere fiction. Much history writing of necessity operates in the same ways.

However, fictionalizing has degrees. We can conceive of narratives that are different from the events in length and emphasis but not necessarily untrue to them. To the degree that such a thing is possible, then, narrative film and history are not deadly enemies; yet the problem of finding an appropriate style remains.

ROBERT ROSENSTONE HAS written that "even when [certain films] do not get the data exactly right, they show a way of looking at history that transcends their shortcomings."[5] This sounds like "lies like truth," or Picasso's "lie that reveals the truth"—essentially an idea of the cultural role of fiction, or at least of art. I do not believe it is the role of history. It has long been a defense offered by historical novelists that their fiction is "more true" than what historians do; would that it were so.

If we fall back on this defense for film, we shall be exactly where we started. If film is to write history, we must demand of it more than a lie that is like truth, and more than a fiction that provides a "way of looking at history." If we do not, we shall get what we have always got. We shall continue to get films that are sometimes compelling, sometimes beautiful, sometimes deeply moving, but historically unsound and, with few exceptions, intellectually empty. What we must demand are films that both "get the data exactly right" *and* give us ways to look at our history—and force us, through their style, to think about them.

ENDNOTES

When titles are cited here only by the author's last name and the short title of the work referred to, please see Bibliography for complete publishing information.

Chapter One
1900–1919: History according to Longfellow

1. Cameron, *Africa on Film*, 97, 181.
2. Vardac, *Stage to Screen*, xviii.
3. Perrett, *America in the Twenties*, 225.
4. Ibid., *xxv*.
5. Sorlin, *Film in History*, 20.
6. Glassberg, *Pageantry*, 16. Glassberg was talking specifically about tableaux vivants, but the statement applies equally well to the theater. He cites, for example, Benjamin West's *Penn's Treaty* and *Death of Wolfe*, Trumbull's Revolutionary War paintings, Leutze's *Washington Crossing the Delaware*, and others.
7. See, for example, such picture books as Butterfield's *The American Past* or *The American Heritage History of the American Revolution*, or the illustrations in the three-volume *Annals of America*.
8. Fischer, *Albion's Seed*, 687.
9. Hutton, *Curiosities of the American Stage*, 33.
10. In American Heritage, *American Revolution*, 74; Butterfield, 38; usually called "Daniel Boone Leading Settlers Through the Cumberland Gap," apparently from the collection of Washington University.
11. Fischer, *Albion's Seed*, 733.
12. Lattue, ed., *Motion Picture Pioneer*, 91.
13. James S. McQuade, *Motion Picture World*, 4 May 1912, 407.
14. The egg scene was "worthy of being ranked with a great painting." Ibid, 410.
15. Fischer, *Paul Revere's Ride*, 5.
16. Ibid., 331, 332.
17. De Grazia and Newman, *Banned Films*, 193–94.
18. "Copyright Description," 28 November 1916 and 25 January 1917, No. LU10068. In the Motion Picture Division of the Library of Congress, Washington, D.C.
19. Ibid. (all succeeding quotes from copyright descriptions cited).
20. *MPW*, quoted in Slide, *Selected Film Criticism*, 241.
21. *AFI Catalogue*, 1911-1920, 52.
22. *MPW*, 26 January 1918, 570.

23. Morrison, *Oxford,* vol. 2, 189.
24. Dippie, *Stand*, 97–98, 281
25. Welch, *Custer,* 73.
26. Lt. Alfred C. Sharpe, letter, 1876, in Greene, *Battles,* 130.
27. Dippie, *Stand,* 90–91.
28. AFI Catalogue, 1911–1920.
29. *MPW,* 12 December 1908.

Chapter Two
1920–1929: Making History Human
1. Izod, *Box Office,* 55.
2. Steinberg, *Reel Facts,* 42; but Izod, *Box Office* (52, 79) gives lower figures.
3. Hexter, *Historians,* 14.
4. Morrison, *Oxford* , vol. 1, 222.
5. Fischer, *Ride,* 194.
6. *Variety,* 22 November 1923.
7. *AFI Catalogue,* 1920–30, #F2,4710.
8. Rosenstone, *Visions,* 31.

Chapter Three
1930–1939: Movie Movies
1. Lukacs, "Sociology of Modern Drama" (first published in *Tulane Drama Review* 9), 941; see also his *Realism in Our Time,* 29ff.
2. This contradiction is seen clearly in D. H. Lawrence's essay on Cooper.
3. Jennings, *Empire.*
4. Usually called the Kentucky Rifle, the American long rifle derived from the German jaeger rifle of the eighteenth century. It was the subject of a number of influential books, starting in in the 1920s. It now has the agenda of the National Rifle Association attached to it; see, for example the ads for a privately minted set of medals, "A Nation of Riflemen," in *The American Rifleman* in 1970, ". . . dedicated to those American citizens who came before and won freedom. . . ."
5. Lorraine E. Williams, "Foreword," in O'Connor, *Hollywood Indian,* xv.
6. Ulrich, *Midwife's Tale,* 194.
7. Watt, *Burning of the Valleys,* 70, 71.
8. Gordon and Buble, "Sex and Class," in Carrol, *Liberating,* 284.
9. Ibid., 282–83.
10. *New York Times,*
11. Neely, Mark R., Jr., "*Young Mr. Lincoln,*" in Carnes, *Past Imperfect,* 126.
12. Grindon, *Shadows,* 22.
13. Schatz, *Genius,* 198.
14. Kaminsky, *Coop,* 83.

Chapter Four
1940–1949: Good War, New World

1. *Johnson Papers*, Johnson to Gage, 25 January 1766, vol.XII, 9.
2. Parkman, *France and England*, vol. 2, 1138; Jennings, *Empire*, 200.
3. MacLeod, *Canadian Iroquois*, 148.
4. See, for example, my *Africa on Film*, 181, 115, etc.
5. *New York Times*, 21 December 1940.
6. Aikman, *Wildcats*, 198.
7. Dippie, *Stand*, 97.
8. Ibid., 281–83.
9. However, see Rogin, *Black Face, White Noise*, for a detailed examination of some of the same ideas in *The Jazz Singer*.
10. Sarf, *God Bless You*, 13.

Chapter Five
The First 1950s: History from the Top Down

1. Shale, *Academy Awards Index*, 261.
2. Department of the Interior, *Lewis and Clark*, 95.
3. The real Sacajawea was left at the Mandan villages and "got nothing" for her services. Ambrose, *Courage*, 389.
4. Shale, *Academy Awards Index*, 219.
5. Wilentz, Sean, "*The Buccaneer*," in Carnes, *Past Imperfect*, 115.
6. See, for example, "McDougal and the Indian" in *Thrilling Stories*, 147–59; the play "Metamora" (Stone); the Squanto and Pocohontas stories, and so forth.
7. Cripps and Culbert, "*The Negro Soldier*" in Rollins, *Hollywood*, 132.
8. Mellen, *Wolves*, 15.
9. See Wellman, *Insanity*.

Chapter Six
1950–1959 II—History from the Bottom Up

1. Welch, *Custer*, 263–67.
2. Anderson, *Faces, Forms, Films*, 208–9.

Chapter Seven
1960–1969: Changing of the Guard

1. Robertson, *Guiness* 19–20, confirmed except for 1969 by Steinberg, *Reel Facts*, 43.
2. Reeves, Richard, "*PT 109*," in Carnes, *Past Imperfect*, 232.
3. King, *Southern Ladies and Gentlemen*.
4. Fischer, *Albion's Seed* , 605 ff.
5. Cott, Nancy F., "*Bonnie and Clyde*," in Carnes, *Past Imperfect*, 222.

6. See film, "Bonnie Parker and Clyde Barrow," Library of Congress coll., No. FEB 7777.

Chapter Eight
1970–1979: The Nineteenth Century Ends at Last
1. Tuchman, Barbara, "Perdicaris Alive or Raisuli Dead," in American Heritage, *Sense of History*, 548–60.
2. Ibid., 548
3. Ibid., 556.
4. Fussell, "*Patton*," in Carnes, *Past Imperfect*, 244–45.
5. Lukas, "*The Molly Maguires*," in Carnes, *Past Imperfect*, 142.
6. *New York Times*, 10 November 1974.
7. Leuchtenberg, "*All the President's Men*," in Carnes, *Past Imperfect*, 288.

Chapter Nine
1980–1989: Palimpsest
1. Rosenstone, *Visions*, 141.
2. Higginson, *Army Life*.

Chapter 10
World without Awe, Amen
1. See, for example, MacLeod, *People's Army*, 115 and elsewhere.
2. See, for example, Clayborne Carson, "*Malcolm X*," in Carnes, *Past Imperfect*, 280–82.
3. For an analogous print example, see Shama, *Certainties*, 3–8, 322.
4. Kissinger, Henry, "Stone's Nixon," *Washington Post*, 24 January 1996.

Chapter 11
Conclusions
1. Fischer, *Albion's Seed*, 5.
2. Ibid., 207–418 and 605–782.
3. Rogin, *Blackface*, 6, 65.
4. Brown, "'Coon-Singer'", 1.
5. Rosenstone, *Visions*, 242.

FILMOGRAPHY

The films are chosen according to the following criteria: they must be American-made; they must have one event from American history and a real person; they must, except before 1920, be feature films; they must not be documentaries.

The films are listed alphabetically by title; the date is the date of release where known, otherwise of copyright. To save space, the third column has data on the films, reduced to a code as follows:

First cell, cluster type:
A=arts; B=business; G=gangster; I=inventors; L=Labor; N=Native American; M=musical biography/show business; O=outsider; S=sports; T=traditional; W=Western.

Second cell, period:
R=Revolutionary War; C=Civil War; F=French and Indian War; T=Texas Independence; I=Indian Wars; K=Korean War; V=Vietnam War; 1=WW I; 2=WW II; 1812=War of 1812; E=western expansion; G=Western gun violence, c. 1865-1895; 17, 18, 19, 20=centuries.

Third cell, years between event and film:
1=0-25; 2=25-50; 3=50-75; 4=75-100; 5=100-125; 6=125-150; 7=150-175; 8=175-200; 9=200-225; 10=225-250; 11=250-275; 12=275-300;13=more than 300.

The fourth column lists where viewing copies can be found, if known: BFI=British Film Institute; LC=Library of Congress; MoMA=Museum of Modern Art, New York; NZFA=New Zealand Film Archive; UCLA=University of California at Los Angeles; WI=University of Wisconsin; V=video. NOTE: "V" means only that a video has been made of the film and is listed in *Leonard Maltin's Movie and Video Guide*. Older videos may not be found in stores. Maltin lists "Mail Order Sources for Videos" (pp. xii-xvii), and its eccentric alphabetizing must be kept in mind (e.g., *St. Louis Blues* is to be found near *The Sting* but far from *The Saint*). A list of video distributors of silents is located at http://www.cinemaweb.com/silentfilm/video.htm. Asterisked titles (*) are from a single source not confirmed elsewhere.

Title	Year	Misc	Availability
Abe Lincoln in Illinois	1940	T, 19, 4	LC, BFI, V
Above and Beyond	1952	T, 2, 1	LC, V
Abraham Lincoln	1930	T, 19, 4	MoMA, V
Abraham Lincoln's Clemency*	1910	T, C, 2	
Aces and Eights	1936	W, G, 3	
Act One	1963	M, 20, 2	
Across the Sierras	1941	W, G, 3	
Adventures of Mark Twain	1944	A, 19, 3	LC, V
Al Capone	1959	G, 20, 2	V
Al Jennings of Oklahoma	1951	W, G, 3	V
Alamo, The	1960	W, T, 5	LC, V
Alexander Hamilton	1931	T, 18, 6	
Alias Jesse James	1959	W, G, 4	
Alice's Restaurant	1969	O, 20, 1	V
All the President's Men	1976	O, 20, 1	LC,V
Allegheny Uprising	1939	T, F, 8	LC, V
America	1924	T, R, 6	LC, MoMA, V
Annie Get Your Gun	1950	M, 19, 3	LC
Annie Oakley	1935	M, 19, 2	LC, V
Apache Ambush	1955	T, I, 4	
Apollo 13	1995	T, 20, 1	LC, V
Attack on Fort Boonesboro	1906	T, R, 6	LC
Babe, The	1992	S, 20, 3	LC, V
Babe Ruth Story, The	1948	S, 20, 3	LC,V
Baby Face Nelson	1957	G, 20, 2	
Bad Men of Missouri	1941	W, G, 3	
Badlands of Dakota	1941	W, G, 3	
Badman's Country	1958	W, G, 3	
Badman's Territory	1946	W, G, 3	V
Barbara Freitchie	1915	T, C, 3	
Barbara Freitchie	1924	T, C, 3	
Barbarian and the Geisha, The	1958	T, 19, 5	LC, V
Barbary Pirate	1949	T, 19, 5	
Baron of Arizona, The	1950	W, 19, 4	
Battle at Apache Pass, The	1952	T, I, 4	
Battle Hymn	1957	T, K, 1	LC, V
Battle Hymn of the Republic, The	1911	T, C, 2	BFI
Battle of Bull Run, The*	1913	T, C, 2	
Battle of Gettysburg, The*	1913	T, C, 2	
Battle of Gettysburg	1914	T, C, 2	
Battle of Pottsburg Ridge, The*	1912	T, C, 2	
Battle of Shiloh, The*	1913	T, C, 2	
Battles of Chief Pontiac, The	1952	T, F, 8	
Beau James	1957	T, 20, 1	LC
Beautiful Mrs. Reynolds, The	1918	T, 18, 5	
Before Yorktown*	1911	T, R, 6	
Beginning or the End?, The	1947	T, 2, 1	LC
Belle Starr	1941	T, C, 4	LC
Belles on Their Toes	1952	O, 20, 2	LC
Beloved Infidel	1959	M, 20, 1	V
Benedict Arnold*	1909	T, R, 6	
Benny Goodman Story, The	1955	M, 20, 1	LC, V

Title	Year	Misc	Availability
Best of the Badmen	1951	W, G, 3	V
Best Things in Life Are Free, The	1956	M, 20, 1-2	
Betsy Ross*	1917	T, R, 6	
Beyond the Law	1918	G, 19, 1-2	
Billy the Kid	1930	W, G, 2	
Billy the Kid	1941	W, G, 3	V
Bird	1988	M, 20, 2	LC, V
Birdman of Alcatraz	1962	O, 20, 1	LC, V
Birth of the Star-Spangled Banner	1914	T, 1812, 5	
Black Hand, The	1906	G, 20, 1	MoMA
Black Hand, The	1950	G, 20, 2	V
Bloody Momma	1970	G, 20, 2	LC, V
Bob Mathias Story, The	1954	S, 20, 1	
Bonnie and Clyde	1967	G, 20, 2	LC, V
Bonnie Parker Story, The	1958	G, 20, 2	
Boston Strangler, The	1968	O, 20, 1	LC, V
Boston Tea Party, The	1908	T, R, 6	
Boston Tea Party, The	1915	T, R, 6	MoMA
Bound for Glory	1976	M, 20, 2	LC, V
Brigham Young, Frontiersman	1940	W, 19, 4	V
Broken Arrow	1950	N, 19, 4	LC, V
Buccaneer, The	1938	T, 1812, 6	LC (trailer)
Buccaneer, The	1958	T, 1812, 6	LC, V
Buddy Holly Story, The	1978	M, 20, 1	LC, V
Buffalo Bill	1944	W, 19, 3	LC, V
Buffalo Bill and the Indians	1976	W, 19, 4	LC, V
Buffalo Bill Rides Again	1947	W, 19, 3	
Bugler of Battery B, The*	1912	T, C, 3	
Bugsy	1991	G, 20, 2	V
Buster Keaton Story, The	1957	M, 20, 2	
Butch and Sundance: The Early Days	1979	W, G, 4	LC, V
Butch Cassidy and the Sundance Kid	1969	W, G, 4	LC, V
Calamity Jane	1953	W, 19, 3	LC, V
Calamity Jane and Sam Bass	1949	W, 19, 3	
California	1946	W, G, 4	
California	1963	W, G, 4	
California Conquest	1952	W, G, 5	
Capone	1975	G, 20, 2	LC
Captain Eddie	1945	T, 20, 1	LC
Captain John Smith and Pocohontas	1953	T, 17, 13	LC
Capture of Fort Ticonderoga*	1911	T, R, 6	
Cardigan	1922	T, R, 7	
Caught	1931	W, 19, 6	
Cell 2455, Death Row	1955	O, 20, 1	LC
Chaplin	1992	M, 20, 2, 3, 4	LC, V
Cheaper By the Dozen	1950	O, 20, 1-2	
Cheyenne Autumn	1964	N, 19, 4	LC, V
Chief Crazy Horse	1955	N, I, 3	LC
Christopher Columbus—The Discovery	1992	T, 15, 13	LC
Clark's Capture of Kaskaskia*	1911	T, R, 6	
Coal Miner's Daughter	1980	M, 20, 1-2	LC, V

Title	Year	Misc	Availability
Cobb	1994	S, 20, 3	V
Cole Younger, Gunfighter	1958	W, G, 4	V
Coming of Columbus, The	1912	T, 15, 13	LC
Commanche Territory	1950	W, I, 3	
Conquest of Cochise	1953	N, 19, 4	V
Conrack	1974	O, 20, 1	LC, V
Court-Martial of Billy Mitchell, The	1955	T, 20, 2	LC, V
Courtship of Miles Standish, The	1923	T, 17, 13	
Crazy Joe	1974	G, 20, 1	LC, V
Crazy Legs, All-American	1953	S, 20, 1	
Cross Creek	1983	A, 20, 2	V
Custer of the West	1968	W, I, 4	
Custer's Last Fight	1912	W, I, 2	LC
Custer's Last Fight	1925	W, I, 2	LC
Custer's Last Fight on the Little Big Horn	?	W, I	
Custer's Last Stand	1910	W, I, 2	MoMA
Dalton Boys, The	1912	W, G, 2	LC
Daniel Boone	1906	T, 18, 6	MoMA
Daniel Boone	1936	T, 18, 7	V
Daniel Boone Through the Wilderness	1926	T, 18, 6-7	
Daniel Boone, Trail Blazer	1957	T, 18, 8	V
Daughter of Rosie O'Grady, The	1950	M, 20, 2	
Davy Crockett and the River Pirates	1955	T, 19, 6	V
Davy Crockett at the Fall of the Alamo	1926	T, T, 4	LC, MoMA (part)
Davy Crockett, King of the Wild Frontier	1955	T, 19, 6	LC, V
Death of Nathan Hale, The*	1911	T, R, 6	
Declaration of Independence, The	1911	T, R, 6	
Deep in My Heart	1954	M, 20, 2	LC, V
Devil's Disciple, The	1959	T, R, 8	LC, V
Diamond Jim	1935	B, 19, 2	LC
Diamond Stud	1970	B, 19, 3	
Dillinger	1945	G, 20, 1	V
Dillinger	1973	G, 20, 2	LC, V
Dirty Little Billy	1972	W, G, 4	
Dixie	1942	M, 19, 3	
Doc	1971	W, 19, 4	LC
Dolly Sisters, The	1945	M, 20, 2	LC, V
Doolins of Oklahoma, The	1949	W, G, 3	LC, V
Dragon—The Bruce Lee Story	1993	M, 20, 1	V
Drum Beat	1954	W, I, 3	LC, V
Drums Along the Mohawk	1939	T, R, 7	LC, V
Eagle and the Hawk, The	1950	W, T, 5	
Ed Wood	1995	M, 20, 2	LC, V
Edgar Allen [sic] Poe	1909	A, 19, 4	LC
Eddie Cantor Story, The	1953	M, 20, 1-2	V
Eddie Duchin Story, The	1956	M, 20, 1-2	LC, V
Edison, the Man	1940	I, 19, 3-4	LC, V
Eight Men Out	1988	S, 20, 3	LC, V
84 Charing Cross Road	1987	O, 20, 2	V
Escape from Andersonville*	1909	T, C, 2	

Title	Year	Misc	Availability
Escape from Alcatraz	1979	O, 20, 1	LC, V
Evel Knievel	1972	O, 20, 1	V
Fabulous Dorseys, The	1947	M, 20, 1	LC, V
Falcon and the Snowman, The	1985	O, 20, 1	LC, V
Fall of Black Hawk, The	1912	T, I, 3	LC
Famous Dalton Raid on the Banks of			
Coffeyville, The	1909	W, G, 1	LC
Far Horizons, The	1955	T, 19, 6-7	LC
Fat Man and Little Boy	1989	T, 2, 2	LC, V
Fear Strikes Out	1957	S, 20, 1	V
Fighting Father Dunne	1948	O, 20, 2	LC, V
First Texan, The	1956	T, T, 5	LC
Five Pennies, The	1959	M, 20, 1-2	V
Flying Irishman, The	1939	T, 20, 1	
Follow the Sun	1951	S, 20, 1	
Fort Ti	1953	T, F, 8	LC
1492: Conquest of Paradise	1992	T, 15, 13	LC, V
Frances	1982	M, 20, 2	LC, V
Francis Marion, the Swamp Fox*	1914	T, R, 6	
Frontier Marshal	1939	W, G, 3	
Funny Girl	1968	M, 20, 2-3	LC, V
Funny Lady	1975	M, 20, 2	LC, V
Gable and Lombard	1976	M, 20, 2	LC
Gallant Hours, The	1959	T, 2, 1	LC, V
Gallant Journey	1946	I, 20, 2	
Gene Krupa Story, The	1959	M, 20, 1	LC, V
General, The	1927	T, C, 3	LC, V
General Custer at the Little Big Horn	1926	T, I, 3	LC
General Marion, the Swamp Fox*	1911	T, R, 6	
Gentleman Jim	1942	S, 19, 2	LC, V
George Raft Story, The	1961	M, 20, 1	LC
George Washington Under the American Flag	1909	T, R, 6	
George Washington Under the British Flag	1909	T, F, 6	LC
Geronimo	1962	N, I, 4	V
Geronimo	1991	N, I, 5	LC, V
Geronimo's Last Raid	1912	T, I, 2	
Girl in the Red Velvet Swing, The	1955	O, 20, 3	LC
Glenn Miller Story, The	1953	M, 20, 1	LC, V
Glory	1989	T, C, 6	LC, V
God Is My Co-Pilot	1945	T, 2, 1	LC
Good Morning, Vietnam	1987	O, V, 1	LC, V
Gorgeous Hussey, The	1936	T, 19, 5	V
Grant and Lincoln*	1911	T, C, 2	
Great Balls of Fire	1989	M, 20, 2	LC, V
Great Dan Patch, The	1949	S, 19, 3	V
Great Imposter, The	1960	O, 20, 1	LC, V
Great Jesse James Raid, The	1953	W, G, 3	
Great Jewel Robber, The	1950	O, 20, 1	
Great John L, The	1945	S, 19, 3	
Great Locomotive Chase, The	1956	T, C, 4	LC, V
Great Meadow, The	1931	T, 18, 7	EH

Title	Year	Misc	Availability
Great Missouri Raid, The	1950	W, G, 4	V
Great Moment, The	1944	I, 19, 3	V
Great Northfield, Minnesota Raid, The	1972	W, G, 4	LC, V
Great Sioux Massacre, The	1965	T, I, 4	LC
Great Victor Herbert, The	1939	M, 19-20,2	LC
Great Ziegfeld, The	1936	M, 19-20,1-2	LC, V
Guardian of the Wilderness	1977	O, 19, 4	LC
Gun That Won the West, The	1955	W, I, 4	LC
Gunfight at Dodge City	1959	W, G, 4	
Gunfight at the O.K. Corral, The	1957	W, G, 3	LC, V
Gypsy	1962	M, 20, 2	LC, V
Hands across the Sea*	1911	T, R, 6	
Harlow (C. Baker)	1965	M, 20, 2	LC, V
Harlow (C. Lynley)	1965	M, 20, 2	
Harmon of Michigan	1941	S, 20, 1	LC
Harmony Lane	1935	M, 19, 3	LC
Hawmps!	1976	W, 19, 5	LC
Heart of a Hero	1916	T, R, 6	
Heart of Lincoln, The*	191?	T, C, 3	
Hearts in Bondage	1936	T, C, 3	
Heaven's Gate	1980	W, G, 4	LC, V
Helen Morgan Story, The	1959	M, 20, 1-2	V
Hell to Eternity	1960	T, 20, 1	V
Henry and June	1990	A, 20, 3	V
Heroine of 76, A*	191?	T, R, 6	
Heroes of the Alamo	1938	T, T, 5	
Hiawatha	1913	N, ?, 13	LC
Hiawatha	1952	N, ?, 13	LC
Hoffa	1992	L, 20, 2	LC, V
Home, Sweet Home	1914	A, 19, 4	LC
Honeymoon Killers, The	1969	O, 20, 1	LC, V
Hoodlum Priest, The	1961	O, 20, 1	LC, V
Houdini	1953	M, 20, 2	V
Hour of the Gun	1967	W, G, 4	LC, V
House Is Not a Home, A	1964	O, 20, 1	LC
How Washington Crossed the Delaware*	1912	T, R, 6	
Howards of Virginia, The	1940	T, R, 7	LC, V
I Aim at the Stars	1960	T, 20, 1	
I Don't Care Girl, The	1952	M, 20, 2	
I Dream of Jeannie	1952	M, 19, 3	LC, V
I Killed Wild Bill Hickock	1956	W, G, 3	
I Killed Geronimo	1950	W, I, 3	
I Shot Andy Warhol	1996	O/A, 20, 2	
I Shot Jesse James	1949	W, G, 3	MoMA, V
I Want to Live	1958	O, 20, 1	V
I Was a Communist for the FBI	1951	T, 20, 1	LC
I Wonder Who's Kissing Her Now	1947	M, 20, 1-2	
I'll Cry Tomorrow	1955	M, 20, 1	LC, V
I'll See You in My Dreams	1951	M, 20, 1-2	V
I'm Dancing as Fast as I Can	1982	M, 20, 1	LC, V

Title	Year	Misc	Availability
Immortal Alamo, The	1912	T, T, 3	
In Cold Blood	1967	O, 20, 1	LC, V
In the Days of Daniel Boone	1923	T, 18, 6-7	
In the Mood	1987	O, 20, 2	LC
In the Shenandoah Valley	1908	T, C, 2	LC
Incendiary Blonde	1945	M, 20, 1-2	
Interrupted Melody	1955	M, 20, 1	V
Irish Eyes are Smiling	1944	M, 19-20, 2	LC
Irish Whiskey Rebellion, The	1973	O, 19, 4	
Iron Horse, The	1924	W, E, 3	LC, V
Iron Major, The	1943	S, 20, 2	V
Iron Mistress, The	1952	T, 19, 5	
Iroquois Trail, The	1950	T, F, 8	LC
Jack London	1943	A, 20, 2	V
Jackie Robinson Story, The	1950	S, 20, 1	LC, V
Janice Meredith	1924	T, R, 7	LC
Jeanne Eagels	1957	M, 20, 2	
Jefferson in Paris	1995	T, R, 8	V
Jesse James	1927	W, G, 2-3	
Jesse James	1939	W, G, 3	V
JFK	1991	T, 20, 2	LC, V
Jim Thorpe, All-American	1951	S, 20, 2	V
Joe Louis Story, The	1953	S, 20, 1	V
John Paul Jones	1959	T, R, 7-8	LC, V
Joker Is Wild, The	1957	M, 20, 1	
Jolson Sings Again	1949	M, 20, 1	LC, V
Jolson Story, The	1946	M, 20, 1-2	LC, V
Kansas Raiders	1950	W, G, 4	
Kentucky Feud, A	1905	O, 19, 1	
Kid From Texas, The	1950	W, G, 3	
Killing Fields, The	1984	O, V, 1	LC, V
King of Dodge City	1941	W, G, 2	LC
King of the Roaring 20s	1961	G, 20, 2	LC, V
Kit Carson	1903	T, 19, 3	LC
Kit Carson	1928	T, 19, 3-4	V
Kit Carson	1940	T, 19, 4	LC
Knickerbocker Holiday	1944	T, 17, 12	LC, V
Knute Rockne, All-American	1940	S, 20, 1-2	LC, V
La Bamba	1987	M, 20, 2	LC, V
Lady Sings the Blues	1972	M, 20, 2	LC, V
Lady With Red Hair	1940	M, 19, 2	
Lafayette Escadrille	1958	T, 1, 2	LC, V
Last Command, The	1955	T, T, 5	LC, V
Last of the Buccaneers	1950	T, 1812, 6	
Last of the Desperadoes	1956	W, G, 3	LC
Last of the Mohicans	1922	T, F, 7	V
Last of the Mohicans	1932	T, F, 7	V
Last of the Mohicans	1936	T, F, 8	LC, V
Last of the Mohicans	1992	T, F, 10	LC, V

Title	Year	Misc	Availability
Last of the Redmen	1947	T, F, 10	
Law and Order	1942	W, G, 4	
Law of the Golden West	1949	W, 19, 4	
Law versus Billy the Kid	1954	W, G, 4	
Lawless Breed, The	1952	W, G, 3-4	LC
Leadbelly	1976	M, 20, 2-3	LC
Leather Stocking	1909	T, F, 7	LC
Left-Handed Gun, The	1958	W, G, 3	LC, V
Lenny	1974	M, 20, 1	LC, V
Lepke	1975	G, 20, 2	LC , V
Life and Times of Judge Roy Bean, The	1972	W, G, 3-4	LC, V
Life of Buffalo Bill, The	1912	W, 19, 2	LC
Life of Daniel Boone, The	1912	T, 18, 6	
Life of Lincoln*	1908	T, 19, 2-3	
Lincoln Conspiracy, The	1977	T, C, 5	LC
Lincoln the Lover	1914	T, 19, 3	EH
Lincoln's Gettysburg Address*	1912	T, C, 3	
Little Big Horn	1951	T, I, 3	V
Little Big Man	1970	O, I, 4-5	LC, V
Little Egypt	1951	M, 19, 3	
Little Old New York	1923	T, 19, 5	LC
Little Old New York	1940	T, 19, 6	LC
Lone Star	1952	T, T, 5	LC
Long Gray Line, The	1954	O, 20, 1-2	V
Long Riders, The	1980	W, G, 5	LC, V
Look for the Silver Lining	1949	M, 20, 1	V
Lorenzo's Oil	1994	O, 20, 1	V
Louisiana	1947	T, 20, 1	
Love Me or Leave Me	1955	M, 20, 1	LC, V
Loves of Edgar Allan Poe	1942	A, 19, 5	
MacArthur	1977	T, 2+, 2	LC, V
Mad Dog Coll	1961	G, 20, 2	LC
Magnificent Doll	1946	T, 19, 6	
Magnificent Yankee, The	1950	T, 20, 2	LC, V
Maid of Salem	1937	T, 17, 12	LC
Malcolm X	1992	O, 20, 2	LC, V
Man Called Peter, A	1955	O, 20, 1	LC, V
Man of a Thousand Faces	1957	M, 20, 2	LC, V
Man of Conquest	1939	T, T, 5	
Martyrs of the Alamo	1915	T, T, 4	LC, MoMA
Masterson of Kansas	1954	W, G, 3	LC
Matewan	1987	L, 20, 3	LC, V
McConnell Story, The	1955	T, 20, 1	LC, V
Melvin and Howard	1980	O, 20, 1	LC, V
Messenger to Kearney, A	1912	W, 19, 3	
Midnight Express	1978	O, 20, 1	LC, V
Midnight Ride of Paul Revere, The	1914	T, R, 6	LC
Midway	1976	T, 20, 2	V
Mighty Barnum, The	1935	M, 19, 4	

Title	Year	Misc	Availability
Million Dollar Mermaid	1952	M, 20, 2	LC, V
Minute Man, The	1911	T, R, 6	MoMA
Miracle Worker, The	1962	O, 19, 3	LC, V
Missing	1982	O, 20, 1	V
Mission to Moscow	1943	T, 20, 1	LC
Mobsters	1991	G, 20, 3	LC, V
Molly Maguires, The	1908	L, 19, 2	
Molly Maguires, The	1970	L, 19, 4	V
Molly Pitcher (Kalem)	1911	T, R, 6	
Molly Pitcher (Champion)	1911	T, R, 6	
Mommie Dearest	1981	M, 20, 2	LC, V
Monkey On My Back	1957	S, 20, 1	LC
Montana Belle	1952	W, G, 3	V
Mrs. George Washington*	1909	R, 18, 7	
Mrs. Soffel	1984	O, 20, 4	LC, V
Murder, Inc.	1960	G, 20, 2	LC
My Darling Clementine	1946	W, G, 3	LC, V
My Gal Sal	1942	M, 20, 1-2	
My Wild Irish Rose	1947	M, 20, 2	
Naked in the Sun	1957	T, I, 5	V
Nathan Hale	1907	T, R, 6	
Nathan Hale*	1913	T, R, 6	
New Orleans	1947	M, 20, 2	
Newsies	1992	L, 19, 4	LC, V
Night and Day	1946	M, 20, 1-2	LC, V
Nixon	1995	T, 20, 1-2	LC, V
Northwest Passage	1940	T, F, 8	LC, V
Oh, You Beautiful Doll	1949	M, 20, 2	
Old Glory*	1910	T, 1812, 6	
Old Glory	1916?	T, 1812, 6	
On Secret Service*	1912	T, C, 2	
One Foot in Heaven	1941	O, 20, 1-2	LC
One Man's Way	1964	O, 20, 1-2	LC, V
Our Hearts Were Young and Gay	1944	O, 20, 1	LC
Our Hearts Were Growing Up	1946	O, 20, 1	
Outlaw, The	1943	W, G, 3	LC, V
Outlaws Is Coming, The	1961	O, G, 4	LC, V
Outsider, The	1961	O, 20, 1	LC
Overland Express, The	1938	W, E, 4	
PT 109	1963	T, 20, 1	LC, V
Papa's Delicate Condition	1963	O, 20, 2	LC, V
Parson and the Outlaw, The	1957	W, G, 4	
Pat Garrett and Billy the Kid	1973	W, G, 4	LC, V
Pathfinder, The	1952	T, F, 8	LC
Patton	1970	T, 20, 1-2	LC, V
Perils of Pauline, The	1947	M, 20, 2	V
Plainsman, The	1937	W, G, 3	V
Plainsman, The	1966	W, G, 4	LC

Title	Year	Misc	Availability
Plymouth Adventure	1952	T, 17, 13	LC
Pony Express	1907	W, E, 4	
Pony Express	1953	W, E, 4	V
Pony Express Days	1940	W, E, 4	
President's Lady, The	1953	T, 19, 5-6	LC, V
Pretty Boy Floyd	1959	G, 20, 2	LC
Pride of St. Louis	1952	S, 20, 1	LC
Pride of the Marines	1945	T, 2, 1	LC
Pride of the Yankees	1942	S, 20, 1	V
Prince of Players	1955	M, 19, 3	LC
Prisoner of Shark Island	1936	O, 19, 3	
Quantrill's Raiders	1958	T, C, 4	
Quiz Show	1993	O, 20, 2	LC, V
Raging Bull	1980	S, 20, 1-2	LC, V
Raid, The	1954	T, C, 4	LC
Railroad Raiders of 62, The	1911	T, C, 2	LC
Real Glory, The	1939	T, 19, 2	V
Red Runs the River	1963	T, C, 4	LC
Reds	1981	T, 20, 3	LC, V
Return of Frank James, The	1940	W, G, 4	MoMA, V
Return of the Badmen	1948	W, G, 3	V
Rhapsody in Blue	1945	M, 20, 1-2	LC, V
Right Stuff, The	1983	T, 20, 1-2	LC, V
Rise and Fall of Legs Diamond, The	1960	G, 20, 2	LC, V
Roger Touhey, Gangster	1944	G, 20, 1	
Rough Riders, The	1927	T, 19, 2	
Roughly Speaking	1945	O, 20, 1	WI
Ruby	1992	O, 20, 2	V
Saint Louis Blues	1958	M, 20, 2-3	LC
Saint Valentine's Day Massacre	1967	G, 20, 2	LC, V
San Francisco	1936	T, 20, 2	LC, V
Santa Fe Trail	1940	T, 19, 4	LC, V
Scarlet Coat, The	1955	T, R, 8	LC
Seminole	1953	N, I, 5	
Sergeant York	1941	T, 1, 1	LC, V
Serpico	1973	O, 20, 1	LC, V
Service Under Johnson and Lee*	1911	T, C, 3	
1776	1972	T, R, 8	LC, V
Seven Angry Men	1955	T, 19, 4	LC
Seven Cities of Gold	1955	T, 18, 8	LC, V
Seven Little Foys	1955	M, 20, 3	LC, V
Seventh Cavalry	1956	T, I, 4	V
Shenandoah*	1913	T, C, 2	
Sheridan's Ride (Vitagraph)	1908	T, C, 2	
Sheridan's Ride (Bison)	1912	T, C, 2	NZFA
Sheridan's Ride (Edison)	191?	T, C, 2	MoMA
Shine On, Harvest Moon	1944	M, 20, 2	LC
Silkwood	1983	L, 20, 1	LC, V
Sitting Bull	1954	N, I, 3	LC, V
Sitting Bull at the Spirit Lake Massacre	1927	T, I, 3	LC

Title	Year	Misc	Availability
So Goes My Love	1946	I, 19, 3	
So This Is Love	1953	M, 20, 1-2	LC
Somebody Loves Me	1952	M, 20, 1-2	LC
Somebody Up There Likes Me	1956	S, 20, 1	LC, V
Soul of the South, The	1915	T, C, 2-3	
Southerners, The*	1914	T, C, 2-3	
Spirit of Lafayette, The	1919	?	
Spirit of St. Louis, The	1957	T, 20, 2	LC, V
Spirit of 76, The	1905	T, R, 6	
Spirit of 76, The	1908	T, R, 6	
Spirit of 76, The	1917	T, R, 6	
Stanley and Livingston	1939	T, 19, 3	LC, V
Stars and Stripes, The*	1910	T, 1812, 8	
Stars and Stripes Forever, The*	1913	?	
Stars and Stripes Forever, The	1952	M, 19, 3	LC, V
Star-Spangled Banner, The*	1911	?	
Star-Spangled Banner, The	1914	?	
Story of Alexander Graham Bell, The	1939	I, 19, 3	LC (part), V
Story of Dr. Wassell, The	1944	T, 2, 1	V
Story of G.I. Joe, The	1945	T, 2, 1	
Story of Mankind, The	1957	T,——	LC
Story of Vernon and Irene Castle, The	1939	M, 20, 1-2	LC, V
Story of Will Rogers, The	1952	M, 20, 2	LC
Stratton Story, The	1949	S, 20, 1	V
Sullivans, The	1944	T, 2, 1	LC, V
Sunrise at Campobello	1960	T, 20, 2	LC, V
Sutter's Gold	1936	T, 19, 4	LC
Swanee River	1939	M, 19, 3	
Sweet Dreams	1985	M, 20, 1-2	LC, V
Swoon	1992	O, 20, 3	LC, V
Tall Target, The	1951	T, C, 4	LC
Ten Who Dared	1960	T, 19, 4	LC, V
Tennessee Johnson	1942	T, 19, 4	
They Died with Their Boots On	1942	T, C/I, 3-4	LC, V
Thirty Seconds Over Tokyo	1944	T, 2, 1	LC, V
This Boy's Life	1993	O, 20, 2	V
Three Faces of Eve	1957	O, 20, 1	V
Three Little Words	1950	M, 20, 1-2	LC, V
Till the Clouds Roll By	1946	M, 20, 1-2	LC, V
To Hell and Back	1955	T, 2, 1	LC, V
To the Aid of Stonewall Jackson*	1911	T, C, 2	
Toast of New York, The	1937	B, 19, 3	V
Tom Horn	1980	W, G, 4	LC, V
Tomahawk	1951	W, 19, 5	
Tombstone	1993	W, G. 5	V
Tombstone, the Town Too Tough to Die	1942	W, G, 3	
Tonight We Sing	1953	M, 20, 1	LC
Too Much, Too Soon	1958	M, 20, 1-2	LC
Tripoli	1950	T, 19, 6	LC
True Story of Jesse James, The	1957	W, G, 3	
Tucker	1988	B, 20, 2	LC, V

Title	Year	Misc	Availability
Unconquered	1948	T, F, 8	V
Union Pacific	1939	W, E, 3	LC, V
Untouchables, The	1987	G, 20, 3	V
Valentino	1951	M, 20, 1-2	
Verne Miller	1988	G, 20, ?	V
Viking, The	1929	contact	
W. C. Fields and Me	1976	M, 20, 2	LC
Walk the Proud Land	1956	O, I, 3	LC
Walker	1987	T, 19, 6	LC, V
Washington at Valley Forge	1908	T, R, 6	
Washington at Valley Forge	1914	T, R, 6	
Wells Fargo	1937	W, E, 2-3	
Western Union	1941	W, E, 3	MoMA, V
Westerner, The	1940	W, G, 3	V
When Lincoln Paid*	1912	T, C?, 3	
When Lincoln Was President*	1913	T, C, 3	
When Sherman Marched to the Sea*	1915	T, C, 3	
When the Daltons Rode	1940	W, G, 2	
When the Redskins Rode	1951	T, F, 8	
Where the Buffalo Roam	1980	O, 20, 1	LC, V
White Buffalo, The	1977	W, G, 4	LC, V
White Man's First Smoke, The	1907	T, 17, 13	
Wichita	1955	W, G, 4	V
Wild Bill	1995	W, G, 5	V
Wild Bill Hickok	1923	W, G, 2	MoMA
Wild Bill Hickok Rides	1941	W, G, 3	
Wilson	1944	T, 20, 1-2	V
Wind and the Lion, The	1975	T, 20, 3	LC, V
Wings of Eagles, The	1957	T, 20, 1-2	LC, V
Winners of the Wilderness	1927	T, F, 7	
Winning Team, The	1952	S, 20, 2	LC, V
Wired	1989	M, 20, 1	V
With a Song in My Heart	1952	M, 20, 1	LC
With Lee in Virginia	1913	T, C, 3	
With Longstreet at Seven Pines*	1911	T, C, 3	
With Sheridan at Murfreesboro*	1911	T, C, 3	
With Stonewall Jackson	1911	T, C, 3	
Wolfe or the Conquest of Quebec	1914	T, F, 7	
Woman of the Town, The	1943	W, G, 2-3	LC, V
Words and Music	1948	M, 20, 1-2	V
Wyatt Earp	1994	W, G, 5	V
Yankee Doodle Dandy	1942	M, 20, 1-2	LC, V
Yellowjack	1938	T, 20, 2	
Yellowstone Kelly	1959	W, 19, 4	LC
Young Jesse James	1960	W, G, 4	
Young Mr. Lincoln	1939	T, 19, 5	LC, V
Young Guns, The	1988	W, G, 5	V
Young Guns II, The	1990	W, G, 5	V

Title	Year	Misc	Availability
Younger Brothers, The	1949	W, G, 3	
Your Cheatin' Heart	1964	M, 20, 1	LC
Zoot Suit	1981	O, 20, 2	LC, V

Marginal

Actress, The, 1953
Advance to the Rear, 1964
All that Jazz, 1979
All the King's Men, 1949
Badge 373, 1973
Badlands, 1974
Boys Town, 1938
Call Me Madam, 1953
Cast a Giant Shadow, 1966
Chapter Two, 1979
Come See the Paradise, 1990
Compulsion, 1959
Confessions of a Nazi Spy, 1939
Darby's Rangers, 1958
Enforcer, The, 1951
Flight for Freedom, 1943
French Connection, The, 1971
Fury, 1936
Gaily, Gaily, 1969
Great White Hope, The, 1970
Good Dissonance Like a Man, A, 1977
Harvey Girls, The, 1946
Heartburn, 1986
Heller in Pink Tights, 1960
Horse Soldiers, The, 1959
I Am a Fugitive from a Chain Gang, 1932
I Never Promised You a Rose Garden, 1977
Inchon, 1982
Inherit the Wind, 1960
Jeremiah Johnson, 1972
Julia, 1977

King of the Hill, 1993
Last Hurrah, The, 1958
Lion Is in the Streets, A, 1953
Man on a String, 1960
Man Who Dared, The, 1933
Memphis Belle, The, 1990
Message to Garcia, A, 1936
Mississippi Burning, 1988
Moderns, The, 1988
Night They Raided Minski's, The, 1968
No Man Is an Island, 1962
Old Ironsides, 1926
Ox-Bow Incident, The, 1943
Pony Express, 1925
Public Opinion, 1915
Queen of the Mob, 1940
Ragtime, 1981
Rope, 1948
Rose of Washington Square, 1939
Silver Dollar, 1932
Souls at Sea, 1937
Star Maker, The, 1939
They Won't Forget, 1937
This Is My Affair, 1937
Titanic, The, 1953
Unsinkable Molly Brown, The, 1964
Waiting for the Moon, 1987
Walking Tall (and sequels), 1973–77
We Who Are about to Die, 1937
Where Do We Go from Here? 1945
Witches of Salem, The, 1959
You Can't Buy Everything, 1934
Young Tom Edison, 1940

PRODUCTION OF HISTORICAL FILMS BY TYPE, 1920–97

	20s	30s	40s	50s	60s	70s	80s	90s
Total film production	c. 7000	5009	4074	2949	1592	2687	c. 1500	?
Total historical films	21	41	93	150	41	39	37	36
Traditionals	15	17	24	42	8	8	5	12?
Westerns	5	11	24	35	8	8	4	5
Musical biography/ showbiz		8	20	38	8	7	9	3
Outsider		3	8	9	9	8	11	6?
Native American	1			10	2	1		2
Art			3				3	2
Gangster			2	6	6	6	2	3
Labor						1	1	1?
Sport			8	10			2	2
Technology/ Science		2	4					
Business	2					1	1	

*   Figures for the 1990s are extrapolated for the decade from totals through 1996; however, collapse of the categories is indicated by question marks for that decade.

BIBLIOGRAPHY

Aikman, Duncan. *Calamity Jane and the Female Wildcats*. New York: Holt, 1927

American Heritage, ed. *A Sense of History*. New York: American Heritage, 1985.

Ambrose, Stephen E. *Undaunted Courage: Merriwether Lewis, Thomas Jefferson, and the Opening of the West*. New York: Simon and Schuster, 1996.

American Film Institute. *Catalog of Motion Pictures Produced in the United States: Feature Films, 1921–1930*. New York: Bowker, 1971.

————. *Catalog . . . Feature Films, 1961–1970*. New York: Bowker, 1976

————. *Catalog . . . Feature Films, 1911–1920*. Berkeley: UCLA Press, 1988.

Anderson, Fred. *A People's Army: Massachusetts Soldiers and Society in the Seven Years' War*. New York: Norton, 1985 [1984].

Anderson, Gillian B. *Music for Silent Films, 1894–1929*. Washington: Library of Congress, 1988.

Anderson, Robert G. *Faces, Forms, Films: The Artistry of Lon Chaney*. New York: Barnes, 1971.

[anonymous] *Thrilling Stories of the Forest and Frontier*. Philidelphia, MA: Peck and Bliss 1857[1852].

Aros, Andrew A. *A Title Guide to the Talkies, 1975–1985*. Metuchen, NJ: Scarecrow, 1986.

Bataille, Gretchen M. and Charles L.P. Silet. *Images of American Indians on Film*. New York: Garland, 1985.

Blackey, Robert, ed. *History Anew: Innovations in the Teaching of History Today*. Long Beach, CA: California State Press, 1993.

Brodie, Fawn M. *Thomas Jefferson*. New York: Bantam, 1981 [1974].

Brown, Janet. "The 'Coon-Singer' and the 'Coon-Song': A Case Study of the Performer–Character Relationship," *Journal of American Culture*, Spring–Summer 1984, 1–8.

Campbell, Edward D.C., Jr. *The Celluloid South: Hollywood and the Southern Myth*. Knoxville: University of Tennesee Press, 1981.

Carman, W. Y. *British Military Uniforms from Contemporary Pictures*. Feltham, Middlesex: Hamlyn, 1968 [1957].

Carnes, Mark C., ed. *Past Imperfect: History according to the Movies*. New York: Holt, 1995.

Carrol, Berenice A., ed. *Liberating Women's History*. Urbana: University of Illinois Press, 1976.

Carroll, Noel. *Philosophical Problems of Classical Film Theory*. Princeton: Princeton University Press, 1988.

Clark, G. Kitson. *The Critical Historian*. New York: Basic Books, 1967.

Collier, Peter. *The Fondas*. New York: Putnam, 1991.

Cook, Don. *The Long Fuse: England and America, 1760–1785*. New York: Grove/Atlantic, 1995.

Cripps, Thomas, and David Culbert. "*The Negro Soldier* (1944): Film Propaganda in Black and White," in Rollins, *Hollywood*, 109–33.

De Grazia, Edward and Roger K. Newman. *Banned Films: Movies, Censors, and the First Amendment*. New York: Bowker, 1982.

Department of the Interior. *Lewis and Clark*. Washington, D.C.: Government Printing Office, 1975.

DeVoto, Bernard. *The Year of Decision.* New York: Book of the Month Club, Inc., 1984 [1942, 1943].

Dimmitt, Richard Bertrand. *A Title Guide to the Talkies.* 2 v. New York: Scarecrow, 1965.

Dippie, Brian W. *Custer's Last Stand: The Anatomy of an American Myth.* Missoula: University of Montana Press, 1976.

Drabelle, Dennis, "Jean Arthur." *Film Comment,* March–April 1996, 19–25.

Fisbein, Leslie, "*The Snake Pit* (1948): The Sexist Nature of Sanity," in Rollins, ed., *Hollywood,* 134–58.

Fischer, David Hackett. *Albion's Seed.* New York: Oxford University Press, 1989.

———— *Paul Revere's Ride.* New York: Oxford University Press, 1994.

Foster Harris, William. *The Look of the Old West.* New York: Bonanza, 1960.

French, Warren, ed. *The South and Film.* Jackson: University of Mississippi Press. 1981.

Funken, Liliane and Fred. *L'Uniforme et les Armes des Soldats de La Guerre en Dentelle.* 2 v.Tournai: Casterman, 1975, 1976.

Glassberg, David. *American Historical Pageantry: The Uses of Tradition in the Early Twentieth Century.* Chapel Hill: University of North Carolina Press, 1990.

Gordon, Ann D. and Mari Jo Buble, "Sex and Class in Colonial and Nineteenth-Century America," in Carrol, *Liberating,* 278–300.

Greene, Jerome A., ed. *Battles and Skirmishes of the Great Sioux War, 1876–77.* Norman: University of Oklahoma Press, 1993.

Grenville, J. A. S. *Film as History: The Nature of Film Evidence.* Birmingham: University of Birmingham Press, 1971.

Grindon, Leger. *Shadows on the Past: Studies in the Historical Fiction Film.* Philadelphia: Temple University Press, 1994.

Hamerow, Theodore S. *Reflections on History and Historians.* Madison: University of Wisconsin Press, 1987.

Hammon, Scott. *John Huston.* Boston: Twayne, 1985.

Haskell, Molly. *From Reverence to Rape: The Treatment of Women in Movies.* New York: Holt, Rinehart and Winston, 1973.

Hexter, J. H. *On Historians.* Cambridge: Harvard University Press, 1979.

Higginson, Thomas Wentworth. *Army Life in a Black Regiment.* Boston: Beacon, 1962.

Holger, Michael. *The American Indian on Film.* Metuchen: Scarecrow, 1986.

Himmelfarb, Gertrude. *The New History and the Old.* Cambridge: Harvard University Press, 1987.

Hutton, Laurence. *Curiosities of the American Stage.* New York: Harper, 1891.

Inglis, Ruth A. *Freedom of the Movies.* Chicago: University of Chicago Press, 1947.

Ireland, Joseph N. *Records of the New York Stage from 1750 to 1860,* 2 v. New York: Benjamin Blom, 1966 [1866].

Izod, John. *Hollywood and the Box Office, 1895–1986.* New York: Columbia University Press, 1988.

Jennings, Francis. *Empire of Fortune.* New York: Norton, 1988.

Johnson, William. *Johnson Papers.* 13 v. Albany: University of the State of New York, 1927–64.

Karsten, Eileen. *From Real Life to Reel Life: A Filmography of Biographical Films.* Metuchen, NJ: Scarecrow, 1993.

Kaminsky, Stuart M. *Coop.* New York: St. Martin's Press, 1980.

King, Florence. *Southern Ladies and Gentlemen.* New York: Stein and Day, 1975.

Knock, Thomas J., "History with Lightning: The Forgotten Film *Wilson*," in Rollins, ed. *Hollywood*, 88–108.

Lattue, Kalten C. *Motion Picture Pioneer: The Selig Polyscope Company*. New York: Barnes, 1973.

Leab, David. *From Sambo to Superspade: The Black Experience in Motion Pictures*. Boston: Houghton Mifflin, 1975.

Lerner, Gerda. "Placing Women in History: A 1975 Perspective," in Carrol, *Liberating*, 357–68.

Lucaks, Georg. *Realism in Our Time*. trans. John Mander and Necke Mander. New York: Harper and Row, 1964.

———— "The Sociology of Modern Drama," reprinted in Bernard Dukore, ed., *Dramatic Theory and Criticism, the Greeks to Grotowski*; first published in *Tulane Drama Review 9*, Summer 1965.

Lund, Karen C. *American Indians in Silent Film: Motion Pictures in the Library of Congress*. Washington, D.C.: Library of Congress, 1995 [1992].

Lyons, David, "Iron Mike," *Film Comment*, March–April 1996, 81–88.

MacLeod, D. Peter. *The Canadian Iroquois and the Seven Years' War*. Canadian War Museum Historical Publication No. 29. Toronto: Dundurn, 1996.

Maltin, Leonard. *Leonard Maltin's Movie and Video Guide*. NY: Plume (annual).

Mapp, Edward. *Blacks in American Films: Today and Yesterday*. Metuchen, NJ: Scarecrow, 1972.

Mellen, Joan. *Big Bad Wolves: Masculinity in the American Film*. New York: Pantheon, 1977.

Millett, Allan R., and Peter Maslowski. *For the Common Defence: A Military History of the United States of America*. New York: Free Press, 1984.

Moody, Richard. *Dramas from the American Theatre, 1762–1909*. Cleveland: World, 1966.

Morison, Samuel Eliot. *The Oxford History of the American People*. 3 v. New York: New American Library, 1972 [1965].

Motion Picture Almanac. Annual. New York: Quigley, various years.

Museum of Modern Art. *Circulating Film Catalog*. New York: Museum of Modern Art, 1984, 1990.

Nash, Jay Robert, and Stanley Ralph Ross, eds. *The Motion Picture Guide*, 1927–83 and annual volumes. Chicago: Cinebooks, 1985 and after.

Nevins, Allan. *Allan Nevins on History*, compiled by Ray Allen Billington. New York: Scribner's, 1975.

Newman, Peter C. *Company of Adventurers*. Vol. 1. Markham, Canada: Viking Penguin, 1985.

Niver, Kent. *Early Motion Pictures: The Paper Print Collection in the Library of Congress*. Washington: Library of Congress, 1985.

O'Connor, John E. *The Hollywood Indian: Stereotypes of Native Americans in Films*. Trenton: New Jersey State Museum, 1980.

———— and Martin A. Jackson, eds. *American History/American Film*. New York: Continuum, 1988 [1979].

Parkinson, Michael, and Clyde Jevons. *A Pictorial History of Westerns*. London: Hanlyn, 1972.

Parkman, Francis. *France and England in North America*. 2 v. New York: Library of America, 1983.

Perrett, Geoffrey. *America in the Twenties*. New York: Simon and Schuster, 1982.

Pitts, Michael R. *Hollywood and American History. A Filmography of Over 250 Motion Pictures Depicting U.S. History*. Jefferson, N.C.: McFarland, 1984.

Pollock, Thomas Clark. *The Philadelphia Theatre in the Eighteenth Century*. New York: Greenwood, 1968 [1933].

Quigley, Martin. *Decency in Motion Pictures*. New York: Macmillan, 1937.

Ringwood, Gene, and DeWitt Bodeen. *The Films of Cecil B. DeMille*. New York: Citadel, 1969.

Rogin, Michael. *Blackface, White Noise*. Berkeley: University of California Press, 1996.

Rollins, Peter C., ed. *Hollywood as Historian*. Lexington: University Press of Kentucky, 1983.

Robertson, Patrick. *Guiness Film Facts and Feats*.

Rosenstone, Robert A. *Visions of the Past: The Challenge of Film to Our Idea of History*. Cambridge: Harvard University Press, 1995.

Russo, Vito. *The Celluloid Closet*. New York: Harper and Row, 1981.

Sarf, Wayne Michael. *God Bless You, Buffalo Bill*. East Brunswick, NJ: Associated University Presses, Inc., 1983.

Schama, Simon. *Dead Certainties (Unwarranted Speculations)*. New York: Vintage, 1992.

Schatz, Thomas. *The Genius of the System*. New York: Pantheon, 1988.

Seydor, Paul. *Peckinpah: The Western Films*. Urbana: University of Illinois Press, 1980.

Shale, Richard. *The Academy Awards Index*. Westport: Greenwood, 1993.

Slide, Anthony. *The Encyclopedia of Vaudeville*. Westport, Conn.: Greenwood, 1994.

————, ed. *Selected Film Criticism*. Metuchen, NJ: Scarecrow, 1982–85.

Sorlin, Pierre. *The Film in History*. Totowa: Barnes and Noble, 1980.

Stannard, David E.: *American Holocaust: Columbus and the Conquest of the New World*. New York: Oxford University Press, 1992.

Steinberg, Cobbett S. *Reel Facts*. New York: Vintage, 1982 [1978].

Tuska, Jon. *The American West in Film*. Westport: Greenwood, 1985.

Tynan, Kenneth. *Curtains*. New York: Atheneum, 1961.

Ulrich, Laurel Thatcher, *A Midwife's Tale*. New York: Vintage, 1991.

Vardac, A. Nicholas. *Stage to Screen*. Cambridge: Harvard University Press, 1949.

Wakenknacht, Edward, and Anthony Slide. *The Films of D.W. Griffith*. New York: Crown, 1975.

Ward, James A. *Railroads and the Character of America, 1820–1887*. Knoxville: University of Kentucky Press, 1986.

Watt, Gavin K. *The Burning of the Valleys: Daring Raids from Canada against the New York Frontier in the Fall of 1780*. Toronto: Dundurn, 1997.

Wegelin, Oscar. *Early American Plays, 1714–1830*. New York: Literary Collector Press, Johnson Reprint Company, 1968 [1905].

Weisberger, Bernard A. *Cold War, Cold Peace*. New York: American Heritage, 1984.

Welch, James, with Paul Steckler. *Killing Custer*. New York: Norton, 1994.

Wellman, William. *A Short Time for Insanity*. New York: Hawthorn, 1974.

Winkler, Karen J., "Oliver Stone Wins Some Converts at a Meeting of Historians," *Chronicle of Higher Education*, January 17, 1997. A18.

PERIODICALS, VARIOUS DATES

Moving Picture World
New York Times
Variety
Washington Post

VISUAL REFERENCES

Adler, Mortimer A., ed. *Annals of America, The.* 3 v. Chicago: Encyclopedia Britannica, Inc., 1968.

Butterfield, Roger. *The American Past.* New York: Simon and Schuster, 1947.

McDowell, Bart. *The American Cowboy in Life and Legend.* Washington: National Geographic Society, 1972.

Neumann, George C. and Frank J. Kravic. *Collector's Illustrated Encyclopedia of the American Revolution.* Secaucus: Castle, 1977 [1975].

Time-Life Books. *The Old West.* 26 v. New York: Time–Life, Inc., 1973–79.

INDEX

NATIONAL UNIVERSITY
LIBRARY SACRAMENTO